An Introduction to Management Information Systems

A CUSTOM EDITION FOR SAN DIEGO STATE UNIVERSITY

GEORGE AND ANNETTE EASTON

Learning Solutions

New York Boston San Francisco
London Toronto Sydney Tokyo Singapore Madrid
Mexico City Munich Paris Cape Town Hong Kong Montreal

Pearson Learning Solutions, 501 Boylston Street, Suite 900, Boston, MA 02116
A Pearson Education Company
www.pearsoned.com

Printed in the United States of America

1 2 3 4 5 6 7 8 9 10 V3DZ 15 14 13 12 11 10

000200010270597244

RR

ISBN 10: 0-558-83490-6
ISBN 13: 978-0-558-83490-6

Table of Contents

Chapter 1
WHAT IS INFORMATION TECHNOLOGY ALL ABOUT?
Planning Ahead 1
Study Questions 1
Learning Preview 1
Opening Vignette 2
Visual Organization of Chapter 3

INFORMATION TECHNOLOGY IN BUSINESS & SOCIETY 3
Examples of Technology Products 4
Examples of Technology Used to Provide Services 7
Examples of Problems 9
Understanding IT 10
Learning Check 10

WHAT IS INFORMATION TECHNOLOGY 11
Information Technology Hardware 11
Information Technology Software 12
Putting Information Technology Together 12
Learning Check 13

WHY STUDY INFORMATION TECHNOLOGY 13
Information Technology and Your Career 14
Careers in Information Technology 15
Integrate IT 19
Learning Check 19

AN OVERVIEW OF THE BOOK 19

CHAPTER 1 WRAPPING IT UP 22
Study Questions Summary 22
Solutions to Chapter Activities 23
Key Terms 24
Multiple Choice Questions 24
Review Questions 26
Projects 26

Chapter 2
BUSINESS INFORMATION SYSTEMS
Planning Ahead 27
Study Questions 27
Learning Preview 27
Opening Vignette 27
Visual Organization of Chapter 29

INFORMATION SYSTEMS 29
What does an Information System do 29
What are the components of an information system 30
What are the functions an information system performs 31
Understanding IT 32
Learning Check 34

INFORMATION NEEDS OF BUSINESS EMPLOYEES 34
Characteristics of Information 34
Types of Employees 36
Organizational Structures 38
Understanding IT 39
Learning Check 39

TYPES OF INFORMATION SYSTEMS 39
Systems to Support Basic Operations 40
Systems to Support Decision Making 40
Integrate IT 43
Enterprise Wide Systems 45
Understanding IT 47
Learning Check 48

INFORMATION SYSTEMS IN THE FUNCTIONAL BUSINESS AREAS 48
Human Resources 49
Accounting 50
Finance 50
Engineering, Product Development and Manufacturing 50
Marketing and Sales 51
Learning Check 52

PRACTICAL APPLICATION 52

CHAPTER 2 WRAPPING IT UP 56
Study Questions Summary 56
Solutions to Chapter Activities 57
Key Terms 58
Multiple Choice Questions 58
Review Questions 60
Projects 60

BONUS PRACTICAL APPLICATION 61

Chapter 3

INFORMATION SYSTEMS DEVELOPMENT

Planning Ahead 71

Study Questions 71

Learning Preview 71

Opening Vignette 71

Visual Organization of Chapter 73

SYSTEMS DEVELOPMENT 73

Adding Value to an Organization 73

What is the Systems Development Life Cycle 74

The Project Team 76

Understanding IT 77

Increasing the Probability of Project Success 78

Learning Check 78

ACTIVITIES THAT CROSS PHASES OF THE LIFE CYCLE .78

How Can You Manage a Project 78

Is a Project Worth Doing 80

Integrate IT 84

Getting the Facts 85

Documenting the Process and the System 87

Learning Check 87

THE SYSTEMS DEVELOPMENT LIFE CYCLE 88

Planning 88

Analysis 88

Understanding IT 90

Understanding IT 93

Design 97

Integrate IT 99

Implementation 100

Support 102

Learning Check 103

OTHER APPROACHES TO SYSTEMS DEVELOPMENT 103

Prototyping 103

End-User Development 104

Rapid Application Development 105

Object-Oriented Software Development 105

Outsourcing 106

Learning Check 106

PRACTICAL APPLICATION 106

CHAPTER 3 WRAPPING IT UP 107

Study Questions Summary 108

Solutions to Chapter Activities 109

Key Terms 110

Multiple Choice Questions 110

Review Questions 112

Projects 112

Chapter 4

DATABASE MANAGEMENT

Planning Ahead 113

Study Questions 113

Learning Preview 113

Opening Vignette 113

Visual Organization of Chapter 116

DATABASE OVERVIEW 116

Data Concepts 116

File Management System Approach versus the Database Approach 118

Database Management Systems 121

Learning Check 123

DESIGNING A RELATIONAL DATABASE 123

The Relational Database Model 123

Creating an Entity Relationship Model 124

Understanding IT 130

Moving Forward – Transforming the ERD into Database Tables 131

Learning Check 133

DATABASE TRENDS 133

Data Warehouses 134

Data Mining 135

Knowledge Management 136

Learning Check 137

CHAPTER 4 WRAPPING IT UP 137

Study Questions Summary 137

Solutions to Chapter Activities 138

Key Terms 140

Multiple Choice Questions 140

Review Questions 142

Projects 143

Chapter 5

THE INTERNET – A NETWORK OF NETWORKS

Planning Ahead 144

Study Questions 144

Learning Preview 144

Opening Vignette 145

Visual Organization of Chapter 146

THE INTERNET 146

Background 146

Internet Architecture 147

Packet Switching and Protocols 148

Integrate IT 151

Learning Check 152

INTERNET DOMAIN NAMES 152
   THE DOMAIN NAME SYSTEM 152
   REGISTERING A DOMAIN NAME 153
   TOP-LEVEL DOMAINS 154
   INTEGRATE IT 155
   LEARNING CHECK 155

THE NETWORKS OF THE INTERNET 156
   TYPES OF NETWORKS 156
   NETWORKING MEDIA 157
   INTEGRATE IT 162
   LEARNING CHECK 162

INTERNET ACCESS 163
   BANDWIDTH AND BROADBAND 163
   INTERNET SERVICE 164
   LEARNING CHECK 166

CHAPTER 5 WRAPPING IT UP 166
   STUDY QUESTIONS SUMMARY 166
   KEY TERMS 167
   MULTIPLE CHOICE QUESTIONS 168
   REVIEW QUESTIONS 168
   PROJECTS 169

Chapter 6
THE WORLD WIDE WEB
   PLANNING AHEAD 170
   STUDY QUESTIONS 170
   LEARNING PREVIEW 170
   OPENING VIGNETTE 171
   VISUAL ORGANIZATION OF CHAPTER 172

WEB 1.0 172
   BACKGROUND 172
   WEB BROWSERS 173
   WEB ARCHITECTURE 175
   INTEGRATE IT 177
   LEARNING CHECK 177

MARKUP LANGUAGES 177
   SGML 177
   HTML 178
   XML 182
   XHTML 183
   CASCADING STYLE SHEETS 184
   LEARNING CHECK 184

WEB 2.0 184
   TWITTER 186
   BLOGGING 186
   RSS AND ATOM 187
   MASHUPS 191
   LEARNING CHECK 193

E-COMMERCE 193
   TYPES OF E-COMMERCE 194
   E-COMMERCE REVENUE MODELS 195
   SEARCH ENGINE OPTIMIZATION 196
   LEARNING CHECK 198

CHAPTER 6 WRAPPING IT UP 198
   STUDY QUESTIONS SUMMARY 199
   KEY TERMS 200
   MULTIPLE CHOICE QUESTIONS 200
   PROJECTS 201

Chapter 7
INFORMATION SECURITY AND CYBERCRIME
   PLANNING AHEAD 203
   STUDY QUESTIONS 203
   LEARNING PREVIEW 203
   OPENING VIGNETTE 204
   VISUAL ORGANIZATION OF CHAPTER 205

INFORMATION SECURITY 205
   INFORMATION SECURITY RISKS 206
   INFORMATION SECURITY REGULATIONS 208
   LEARNING CHECK 215

CYBER CRIME 215
   MALWARE 216
   SOCIAL ENGINEERING AND CYBER ATTACKS 221
   LEARNING CHECK 227

CYBER SECURITY 227
   1ST LEVEL OF DEFENSE 227
   ENCRYPTION 228
   ACCESS CONTROLS 229
   CYBER SECURITY SUGGESTIONS 233
   LEARNING CHECK 233

CHAPTER 7 WRAPPING IT UP 233
   STUDY QUESTIONS SUMMARY 234
   KEY TERMS 235
   MULTIPLE CHOICE QUESTIONS 235
   REVIEW QUESTIONS 236
   PROJECTS 236

Tutorial 1
SPREADSHEET BASICS
   PLANNING AHEAD 238
   STUDY QUESTIONS 238
   LEARNING PREVIEW 238
   VISUAL ORGANIZATION OF TUTORIAL 238

SPREADSHEET OVERVIEW **239**
WORKSHEETS AND WORKBOOKS.................. 240
TABS AND GROUPS.................................. 241
CELL DATA AND FORMULAS 243
ACCESSING HELP.................................. 243
LEARNING CHECK.................................. 244

WORKING WITH FORMULAS AND FUNCTIONS.......245
ENTERING AND VIEWING FORMULAS 245
ORDER OF OPERATIONS 246
UNDERSTANDING IT.............................. 247
ABSOLUTE AND RELATIVE CELL ADDRESSING 247
UNDERSTANDING IT.............................. 253
AN OVERVIEW OF FUNCTIONS 253
LEARNING CHECK.................................. 256

FORMATTING AND PRINTING A WORKSHEET 256
FORMATTING DATA................................ 256
PRINTING 257
LEARNING CHECK.................................. 259

PRACTICAL APPLICATION **259**

TUTORIAL 1 WRAPPING IT UP........................**261**
STUDY QUESTIONS SUMMARY 261
SOLUTIONS TO TUTORIAL ACTIVITIES.......... 262
KEY TERMS 262
MULTIPLE CHOICE QUESTIONS 263
REVIEW QUESTIONS 263

Tutorial 2
IMPROVING BUSINESS PRODUCTIVITY WITH SPREADSHEETS
PLANNING AHEAD.................................. 264
STUDY QUESTIONS 264
LEARNING PREVIEW................................ 264
VISUAL ORGANIZATION OF TUTORIAL........... 265

FUNCTIONS AND FEATURES **265**
LOGICAL FUNCTIONS.............................. 266
CONDITIONAL FORMATTING....................... 272
CREATING A COLUMN CHART 274
STATISTICAL FUNCTIONS 281
UNDERSTANDING IT 282
CREATING A PIE CHART 285
LEARNING CHECK.................................. 287

IMPROVING FUNCTIONALITY BY CONTROLLING DATA INPUT.......................................**287**
DATA VALIDATION 289
VLOOKUP FUNCTION 292
LEARNING CHECK.................................. 294

STEPS TO CREATING A SPREADSHEET **294**
ANALYZE THE BUSINESS PROBLEM 294
DEVELOP THE SPREADSHEET FRAMEWORK 295

ENTER THE FORMULAS 295
VERIFY FOR COMPLETENESS AND ACCURACY 295
DOCUMENT 296
GENERAL GUIDELINES 297
LEARNING CHECK.................................. 297

TUTORIAL 2 WRAPPING IT UP.......................**297**
STUDY QUESTIONS SUMMARY 297
SOLUTIONS TO TUTORIAL ACTIVITIES.......... 298
KEY TERMS 299
MULTIPLE CHOICE QUESTIONS 299
REVIEW QUESTIONS 300
PROJECTS 301

Tutorial 3
EXTENDING SPREADSHEET DEVELOPMENT
PLANNING AHEAD.................................. 303
STUDY QUESTIONS 303
LEARNING PREVIEW................................ 303
VISUAL ORGANIZATION OF TUTORIAL........... 304

DATA COMMANDS **304**
SORTING DATA 306
CALCULATING SUBTOTALS 308
INTEGRATE IT.................................... 310
WORKING WITH TABLES 311
LEARNING CHECK.................................. 314

MULTIPLE WORKSHEETS **314**
USING DIFFERENT WORKSHEETS 315
USING FUNCTIONS TO RECODE VALUES 316
UNDERSTANDING IT.............................. 317
REFERENCING CELLS ON SEPARATE WORKSHEETS 322
NAMED CELL REFERENCES 322
INTEGRATE IT.................................... 326
LEARNING CHECK.................................. 327

PIVOT TABLES..................................... **327**
CREATING A PIVOTTABLE 328
COMPLETING THE ROW, COLUMN AND VALUE AREAS 329
REFINING THE PIVOTTABLE 331
INTEGRATE IT.................................... 335
LEARNING CHECK.................................. 338

TUTORIAL 3 WRAPPING IT UP.......................**338**
STUDY QUESTIONS SUMMARY 338
SOLUTIONS TO TUTORIAL ACTIVITIES.......... 339
KEY TERMS 340
MULTIPLE CHOICE QUESTIONS 340
REVIEW QUESTIONS 343
PROJECTS 344

Tutorial 4

BUILDING A SIMPLE DATABASE

PLANNING AHEAD 346
STUDY QUESTIONS 346
LEARNING PREVIEW 346
VISUAL ORGANIZATION OF TUTORIAL 346

CREATING A SIMPLE DATABASE SYSTEM IN ACCESS 347

CREATE THE DATABASE 347
CREATE THE STUDENT TABLE 348
CREATE THE STUDENT FORM 355
CREATE A STUDENT QUERY 359
CREATE A REPORT 362
LEARNING CHECK 366

ENHANCING YOUR DATABASE SYSTEM IN ACCESS 367

ACCESS FIELD PROPERTIES 367
CUSTOMIZING A FORM 372
COMPOUND CRITERIA IN A QUERY 380
CUSTOMIZING A REPORT 382
LEARNING CHECK 386

TUTORIAL 4 WRAPPING IT UP 386

STUDY QUESTIONS SUMMARY 386
KEY TERMS 387
MULTIPLE CHOICE QUESTIONS 387
REVIEW QUESTIONS 388
PROJECTS 388

Tutorial 5

DEVELOPING ADVANCED BUSINESS SYSTEMS WITH DATABASES

PLANNING AHEAD 390
STUDY QUESTIONS 390
LEARNING PREVIEW 390
OPENING VIGNETTE 390
VISUAL ORGANIZATION OF TUTORIAL 392

CREATING THE PHYSICAL MODEL 392

CONVERT ENTITIES TO TABLES AND ASSIGN FIELDS 394
IDENTIFY PRIMARY KEYS 395
REPRESENT THE RELATIONSHIPS 395
STORE ADDITIONAL DATA VALUES 396
DECIDE ABOUT CALCULATED ATTRIBUTES...................... 396
BUILD THE PHYSICAL TABLES FOR THE HAIR TODAY
     DATABASE.. 397
LEARNING CHECK 399

CREATING RELATIONSHIPS IN ACCESS 399

REFERENTIAL INTEGRITY CHOICES 399
DEFINE THE CUSTOMER-ORDER RELATIONSHIP 401

DEFINE THE ORDER-LINE ITEM AND PRODUCT-LINE ITEM
     RELATIONSHIPS 405
LEARNING CHECK 406

CREATING A MORE COMPLEX DATABASE SYSTEM IN ACCESS.. 407

BUILD THE ONE-TABLE FORMS AND ENTER SAMPLE DATA . 407
CREATE A FORM USING A MAIN FORM – SUBFORM
     ASSOCIATION... 414
CREATE ADVANCED REPORTS 427
CUSTOMIZE THE NAVIGATION PANE............................... 439
LEARNING CHECK 443

TUTORIAL 5 WRAPPING IT UP 443

STUDY QUESTIONS SUMMARY 443
KEY TERMS 444
MULTIPLE CHOICE QUESTIONS 444
REVIEW QUESTIONS 446
PROJECTS 447

Tutorial 6

XHTML BASICS

PLANNING AHEAD 449
STUDY QUESTIONS 449
LEARNING PREVIEW 449
VISUAL ORGANIZATION OF TUTORIAL 450

HTML AND XHTML OVERVIEW 450

HTML OR XML?... 451
XHTML AND HTML 452
BASIC STRUCTURE OF XHTML.................................... 452
SAMPLE XHTML ELEMENTS 454
LEARNING CHECK 456

CREATING A WEB PAGE WITH XHTML 1.0............. 456

TEXT EDITORS VS. GRAPHICAL EDITORS 456
NOTEPAD VS. TEXTEDIT.. 457
CREATING A WEB PAGE IN XHTML............................... 460
INTEGRATE IT.. 460
VALIDATING YOUR XHTML CODE 462
INTEGRATE IT.. 463
INTEGRATE IT.. 466
LEARNING CHECK 466

TUTORIAL 6 WRAPPING IT UP 466

STUDY QUESTIONS SUMMARY 467
KEY TERMS 467
MULTIPLE CHOICE QUESTIONS 467

INDEX 469

CHAPTER 1

What is Information Technology All About?

PLANNING AHEAD
After reading Chapter 1, you should be able to answer these questions in your own words

STUDY QUESTIONS
How is information technology used in business and society?
What is information technology?
Why should you learn about information technology?
How will <u>What's IT All About</u> help you learn about information technology?

LEARNING PREVIEW

Information technology (IT) is all around you. Increasingly IT is transforming the way that we all work, play and live. But what exactly is Information Technology? Information technology refers to wide variety of computer-based tools used to manage information. This information could be business data, photos, movies, or voice conversation, among others. We are all living in an information society – where more jobs are involved in creating, using and applying information than in agriculture or manufacturing. As a result, there is no limit to how you can use information technology.

In Chapter 1 you will see how information technology is integral to conducting business for most organizations, large or small, public or private, for profit or non-profit. Through a variety of examples you will have a chance to see just how far information technology reaches. You will learn exactly what constitutes information technology. Most of you have grown up with this digital technology and as a result you already know quite a bit. So it might come as a shock to realize that there is so much more to learn about information technology. This chapter will help you leverage what you already know to jump-start your learning about how to successfully integrate information technology into an organization. You will also learn about technology skills needed in various jobs as well as career options within the information technology field. Let's get started in this exciting adventure!

OPENING VIGNETTE

It is hard to believe that Pacific Sunwear, more commonly known as PacSun, started as a small surf shop in Newport Beach, California in 1980. Today teens and young adults can buy trendy, casual apparel brands like Quicksilver, Billabong and Roxy at over 850 PacSun stores and 76 PacSun Outlet Stores, in the 50 states and Puerto Rico.

In 2005, as Pacific Sunwear continued with its rapid expansion, they realized that their approach to technology needed to change. Data needs to drive the retail business. With an increasing number of automated processes, warehouse systems and devices connected to the Internet, downtime can bring retail operations to a screeching halt. Ron Ehlers, Vice President of Information Services said, "Our aggressive growth has brought us to the point where we had too much at stake to rely on piecemeal approaches to network monitoring. With our scope of operations, our data center must operate 24x7 with an absolute minimum of downtime." Pacific Sunwear needed an easy-to-use solution that offered high-end functionality for datacenter management that could be implemented without adding employees to their current operations staff. Pacific Sunwear decided to purchase CITTIO's WatchTower 2.4 to address their problems. Within five weeks of purchasing WatchTower, they were able to better monitor their mission critical applications. This has allowed them to invest their time addressing industry trends rather than solving technology issues.

Building on these successes, Pacific Sunwear turned their focus towards improving their ability to make better business decisions by addressing industry trends and increasing productivity. Their goal was to increase their ability to make data-driven business decisions. To achieve this goal, in 2007 Pacific Sunwear implemented MicroStrategy's Business Intelligence Platform to provide enterprise-wide reporting and data analysis. This business intelligence (BI) software allows Pacific Sunwear managers to analyze merchandise sales, inventory data, store operations and customer loyalty.

The BI system converts the detailed transaction data captured by their point-of-sale system into personalized reports that can provide insights about sales trends and inventory levels. What is really helpful is the capability to slice-and-dice the data in many different ways. For example, merchandise planners, while looking at sales trends by product, can get data about a specific product by region, customer demographics and stores. This allows them to determine that their female clients in one store location prefer Roxy products while their female clients in another store prefer Volcom products. This should allow inventory to be better tailored to customer desires and increase sales. Store managers can get reports on sales volumes by time of day and day of the week. This results in the ability to have staffing ratios aligned with customer volume. Additionally, the system allows managers to track the effectiveness of their website as a generator of sales.

Through a combination of different information technology initiatives and solutions, Pacific Sunwear now has a set of stable systems that provides for maximum uptime for operations coupled with the ability to efficiently analyze volumes of sales and inventory data to gather the business intelligence needed to support effective company-wide decision making.

Note: All products or company names mentioned are used for identification purposes only, and may be trademarks of their respective owners.

(Sources: Compiled from MicroStrategy (March 19, 2007). "Pacific Sunwear Selects MicroStrategy as Enterprise Business Intelligence Standard," Press Release. Retrieved on September 30, 2008 from *http://www.microstrategy.com/news/pr_system/press_release.asp?ctry=167&id=1477*; and "Success Story: Pacific Sunwear of California, Inc.", Retrieved on September 30, 2008 from *http://www.microstrategy.com/Customers/Successes/detail.asp?ID=249*; and Cittio (September 7, 2005). "Pacific Sunwear Gets Maximum Network Monitoring Protection from WatchTower™; CITTIO Software Delivers Enterprise-Class Network Monitoring and Management," Press Release, Retrieved on September 30, 2008 from *http://www.cittio.com/pdf/Rel_CITTIO_Pacific_SunC8BA6.pdf*; and www.pacsun.com.)

In this chapter you will have a chance to explore the ideas introduced in this opening vignette. You will learn about the variety of information technology solutions that are available to individuals and businesses. You will also explore why it is important for you to increase your knowledge about information technology.

VISUAL ORGANIZATION OF CHAPTER

Study Question 1	Study Question 2	Study Question 3	Study Question 4
Information Technology in Business and Society	What is Information Technology?	Why Study Information Technology?	An Overview of the Book
• Examples of Technology Products • Examples of Technology Used to Provide Services • Examples of Problems	• Information Technology Hardware • Information Technology Software • Putting Information Technology Together	• Information Technology and Your Career • Careers in Information Technology	
Learning Check 1	Learning Check 2	Learning Check 3	Learning Check 4

INFORMATION TECHNOLOGY IN BUSINESS AND SOCIETY

You have grown up with computers and technology. You use them everyday – probably in more ways than you are even aware. You are known as a digital native. According to Wikipedia, "A **digital native** is a person who has grown up with digital technology such as computers, the Internet, mobile phones and MP3." Because you have grown up in a society where technology has always existed, you are familiar and comfortable with many aspects of technology. So why do you need to read a book about, or take a class in, "computers?" As you will learn in this book, there is much more to technology than you have most likely seen.

You probably are pretty comfortable with your cell phone, digital music player, writing papers in your word processor and using the ATM machine. But do you know how a business uses technology to keep their business running?

Some of you might think that you don't really need to learn about how businesses use technology. But we challenge you to change that line of thinking. No matter what your major is, you are going to need to learn how technology is used in *your* business. That's right -- you are all going into business. What? Some of you are going into what we think of as a traditional business major – finance, accounting, management, marketing and even management information systems. But for those of you who are economics majors, scientists, educators, criminologists, and artists, among others, you still need to learn about the business side of your field.

For example, all businesses have inventory that needs to be managed. Often that inventory is product-based – like WalMart keeping track of all the different items they have for sale. Other times the inventory might be people-based or service-based – like your university keeping track of the classes and sections that are offered in any given semester. Another example of inventory could be the evidence collected at a crime scene.

Most businesses today use many different technologies to help them develop products, manage inventory, process customer orders, track employee work hours, etc. Sometimes the technology is used to create an innovative product and sometimes it is used to help a business achieve its goals by solving problems or creating a competitive advantage. On the surface it may be hard to imagine what a child's doll, a neckband that translates thought into speech by picking up nerve signals, movies and television shows, a mobile internet device, and a self-check in kiosk at an airport all have in common. But once you start to look at them you will see that they are all examples of how computers, or information technology, are being used in a variety of innovative ways. In this section we will explore these examples a little bit more closely to help you broaden your understanding of what is possible. The examples will be grouped into products, services and problems.

Examples of Technology Products

Throughout this book we will cover many uses of technology that will indeed help solve business problems. But our first set of examples will explore how technology can be used to create innovative products. A **product** is something that has been made to be sold; commonly it is produced by an industrial process. The examples described can be classified into products that create a competitive advantage, provide increased opportunities, can entertain, provide mobility, and provide up-to-date information.

Technology products can create a competitive advantage

Playmates Toys developed a set of dolls integrating a tremendous amount of technology. Originally released in Fall 2005, Amazing Amanda integrates speech-recognition, memory chips, facial robotics, radio frequency tags and scanners. Figure 1.1 illustrates the internal components of Amanda. Since then, the "Amazing" doll line has expanded to include Allysen, McKayla and a dog named Lexie. While each doll has unique accessories and behaviors, the basic premise is the same. Each doll has an internal clock, which allows them to know the date and time, along with an internal computer programmed with different instructions. Amanda, as example, comes with a variety of different food items, each uniquely identified with a radio frequency identification (RFID) tag. If you try to feed a pizza piece to Amanda at breakfast time, her scanner will identify the item and her internal computer program will check the time of day. The logic in the computer program will result in a spoken response, coupled with a facial reaction showing surprise, of "Silly mommy, pizza is not for breakfast."

Figure 1.1   Amazing Amanda combines scanners, facial robotics and internal computers to create a doll that acts almost human.

Technology products can provide increased opportunities

Another technology that is being developed into an innovative product is the Audeo. Imagine a technological device that will give the ability to communicate orally back to a person unable to speak. The Audeo is being created to do just that. Developed as a device to assist people with disabilities, the Audeo is a neckband that picks up neurological signals and translates them into speech. Figure 1.2 details the process used to perform that translation.

Figure 1.2   The Audeo works by translating neurological signals into speech

In February 2008, Ambient Corporation (www.theaudeo.com) demonstrated the first voiceless phone call.

 You can see this first phone call on YouTube by clicking the following link: http://uk.youtube.com/watch?v=xyN4ViZ21N0

Technology products can entertain

In the entertainment industry we can explore examples of how technology usage is integrated into many films and television shows. Whether we look at how "Napster" broke into Los Angeles' traffic control department to override the traffic signals in *The Italian Job* or how *CSI* uses computer databases to search for DNA or fingerprint matches, technology is increasingly evident. But technology is also increasingly used in making the films themselves. Pixar Studios, for example, rely on technology to create the animation of their films such as *Toy Story* or *Monsters, Inc.* But it doesn't stop there. Video editing programs have brought the power of making movies to your desktop. In many elementary schools, kids are learning how to create IMovies to help present student reports. One "homemade" movie that made it to the big time is *My Date with Drew,* shown in Figure 1.3, the heart tugging story about Brian Herzlinger, a regular guy from

New Jersey, and his quest to get a date with Drew Barrymore. Aside from the fact that this movie was made using a low-cost video camera and PC-based video editing software and equipment, one of the hooks in the movie is the usage of the Internet to help spread the word about Brian and his efforts to get a date.

Figure 1.3   Increasingly movies are made using technology and have integrated technology usage into the storyline

Technology products provide mobile connectivity

A new category of pocketable communication products promises to make the Internet truly mobile and to keep us connected via email, instant messaging, chat or VOIP. These products, called Mobile Internet Devices, fall between small laptops and smart phones in size and capability. Mobile Internet Devices are designed to support Internet connectivity via various types of wireless networks and deliver an Internet experience similar that which people experience on standard PCs.

Nokia's N810 WiMax edition phone, shown in Figure 1.4, is one of the new Mobile Internet Devices that allow users to communicate via the new WiMAX networks that are extending the richness and the reach of the Internet. Nokia's N810 for example, includes Internet phone calling with an integrated webcam, email access, Global Position System, music and movie display capabilities, along with internet access. Intel predicts the market for Mobile Internet Devices will rival the PC business in five to ten years.

Figure 1.4   The Nokia N810 Mobile Internet Device allows communication via WiMAX networks

Technology products provide up-to-date information

Most of you are probably a participant in at least one social network like MySpace, Facebook or LinkedIn. New two-way Global Positioning Systems (GPS) are giving our cars the ability to be part of a new social network. Most GPS systems in use today are passive, that is, they receive location and time data transmitted from GPS satellites; they do not transmit any data. However, there are now GPS devices that are capable of transmitting the location and speed data of cars with these devices to a centralized computer system. The value of aggregating traffic data transmitted by these new GPS devices comes from the once-futuristic notion of the "hive-mind" - utilizing what everyone in a group senses individually. One example of this technology is the Dash Driver Network (www.dash.net). This network combines the real-time traffic data provided by two-way Dash Express GPS systems, shown in Figure 1.5, with historical and sensor-based traffic information yielding what the company considers to be the most complete and up-to-the-minute picture of traffic available.

Figure 1.5 Dash Express two-way, internet-connected GPS device provides drivers with up-to-the minute traffic information.

Examples of Technology Used to Provide Services

The examples we have just discussed involved integrating technology into the products offered by a company. Other businesses look to technology to address service needs. In contrast to a product, where you have something tangible, a **service** is the act of dealing with a customer to provide help or assistance, such as taking an order or providing transportation. Sometimes the service could be internal to the organization, such as providing information to employees to help them make better decisions. The examples introduced in this section will focus on how technology is used to provide a service, which often can help save money, create a competitive advantage, or make data more accessible.

Integrating technology into customer service can save money

Used wisely, technology can help a business save money in operating costs. British Airways thinks they have found a way to save in excess of $35 million dollars a year.   In 2003, British Airways hired IBM to begin a 5-year project that would develop self-service check-in kiosks. One of the big concerns was that the new kiosks, shown in Figure 1.6, had to integrate with the existing, industry-standard departure control and reservation systems still in use at the counters. After accounting for the cost of developing the system, British Airways estimated they could save $3.50 per customer transaction. With an annual passenger count of 27 million, coupled with a very conservative estimate that 38% of those customers would use the self-service check in terminals, they concluded that this would save over $35 million dollars a year. Not only does this save money for the airline, but it provides a faster check-in service to the passengers. Customers using the kiosks are meeting, or beating, a 10-minute target time to complete check-in, baggage drop off, and clearing security.

Figure 1.6 British Airways is hoping to save over $35 million dollars a year through self-service kiosks.

 You can see a video about British Airways integration of self-service kiosks by clicking on the following link:
http://www.tech2.com/biz/tv/sectionvideo.php?id=21471&secid=121&arrid=0]

Integrating technology into management information can create a competitive advantage

Dick's Sporting Goods integrated information technology to help them better manage their sales and inventory. In 2003 Dick's had a collection of many different systems spread out across the organization. They all worked to some extent, but there was no standardized way to access data and report results across the company. Dick's wanted to put in place a system that would allow managers to have one place, where anyone could go, to access any needed information. To solve this problem, they created a data warehouse, using an Oracle database, to store all of the company's sales and inventory data in one place. Next they integrated business intelligence software from MicroStrategy to mine their 800-gigabyte data warehouse. This dashboard software, illustrated in Figure 1.7, allows Dick's to know how products are selling across stores and regions. Managers can access data all the way from highly summarized results to being able to drill down to find how a specific product, broken down by style or color, is selling at different stores. These new systems have enabled Dick's to double earnings and produce annual operating margins better than their competitors – helping them realize a competitive advantage in their industry.

Figure 1.7 A Dashboard from Microstrategy's Business Intelligence Software can help managers track performance.

Integrating technology into data capture and distribution can make data more accessible

ShotLink is the data management system used by the PGA to record data at the vast majority of their golf tournaments. A representation of the system is shown in Figure 1.8. The system allows real-time delivery of information to fans at the tournament, as well as to television networks, newspaper reporters, the Internet and ultimately to the viewers at home. The heart of the system relies on a digital map of each hole, created using GPS technology prior to the golf tournament. This map allows measurements to be determined, such as the distance between the hole and the current location of a player's ball. During the actual golf match, hundreds of volunteers, carrying lasers and PDAs, follow each of the golfers. The volunteers record data about every shot by every player. This data includes the location of the ball, such as on the fairway or in a bunker, and the time the ball was stuck. Utilizing the mapping data already in the system, ShotLink can calculate the distance the shot travels as well as the speed. All of this data is allowing golf to become a sport much more driven by statistics. As a result, players and coaches can now use this data to help a player better analyze their strengths and areas of improvement. Ultimately, this can help a player understand how to improve their game.

Figure 1.8 The ShotLink scoring system links lasers and PDS devices to provide up-to-the minute data about golf.

You can learn more about ShotLink by watching the following video clip: http://www.pgatour.com/video/?/video/pga-tour/features/2008/06/20/feat_cdwgolfandtechnology_shotlink_liveatfeatures3.pgatour

Examples of Problems

But new technology doesn't always result in a success. The 2007 World Series ticket sales process frustrated Colorado Rockies baseball fans. Just as tickets went on sale the servers crashed. While the company says they were the victim of malicious hackers, others speculate that they just hadn't done all the right things to prepare for such heavy traffic cause by the thousands of fans trying to buy tickets. Ultimately the system was fixed and over 50,000 tickets were sold within three hours.

While we looked at British Airways' technology success story earlier, more recently they were in the news for a significant technology failure. On March 27, 2008 British Airways opened Terminal 5 at London's Heathrow Airport. Unfortunately the new computerized baggage system, as shown in Figure 1.9, didn't work as expected. Instead of automatically routing bags to the correct location, the baggage handlers couldn't even log into the system. Instead they had to manually unload and route the bags. British Airways cancelled 50 flights on April 1, 2008 so that they could spend the time returning an estimated 28,000 lost bags to their passengers during this five day period. This disruption to their service is estimated to have cost British Airways around $100 million dollars. The good news in this situation is that by September 2008 British Airways reported that all the kinks had been worked out and their new system is meeting all targets for baggage delivery, resulting in much happier customers and employees.

Figure 1.9 Technology problems at Heathrow Airport caused significant baggage problems.

As you can see, unless the development, testing and implementation of technology are properly managed, the impact can be disastrous. Many people are left wondering how an information technology problem with tracking baggage could have happened, *yet again*. Back on our side of the pond, many of you may remember the baggage handling problems at Denver International Airport in 1995. After millions of dollars had been spent to try and get that system working, United Airlines ultimately abandoned the system in 2005, while still having to pay the Denver Airport $60 million a year for the 25 years left on the lease of the system. Companies have to do a better job in analyzing and developing information technology, along with understanding the contractual obligations that accompany many business deals.

In this book we hope to help you understand the issues involved with integrating technology in an organization – from analyzing, developing, testing and implementing information technology – with the ultimate goal being to help you learn enough so you can avoid a mistake like those described.

Can you learn everything about technology in one book or one semester? Absolutely not! In fact, because technology is always changing it sometimes seems like you never know enough. But by learning the fundamentals about information technology, you can be prepared to adapt so that you can make good technology decisions on a personal and professional level. In the next section we will start learning some of the fundamentals about information technology.

Understanding IT?

Many information technology terms were used throughout the examples in this first section. Since the point of this first section wasn't to turn you into a technology expert, but rather to broaden your understanding of how technology can be used, most of these terms were not explicitly defined.

However, you need to realize that these terms are increasingly becoming part of society's normal vocabulary. As a result, newspapers and magazines are simply going to assume that you know what they mean.

While many of the terms will be explored in more detail later in the book, so that you can better understand their meaning and usage, in this exercise you are asked to define the following terms:

1) Define a computer program.

2) List three different programming languages.

3) Define database.

4) What is a byte?

5) How many bytes are in a gigabyte?

6) Can you find a common comparison to help someone understand how much information can be stored in a gigabyte?

7) Define hacker.

8) Briefly explain what VOIP stands for and what it is.

9) Briefly explain what RFID is.

Check your answers at the end of the chapter.

LEARNING CHECK
Be sure you can *describe one example of a technology product that can be used by individuals * describe one example of how technology can be integrated into a service * describe one situation when technology didn't work as planned

<u>WHAT IS INFORMATION TECHNOLOGY?</u>

Reflecting on the examples from the previous section, combined with your own experiences with technology, you should see a clear picture of how the way we live, work and play has been transformed by information technology. **Information technology**, in the broadest sense, refers to any computer-based tool used to create, manage and disperse information. Some people might say that IT is using computers, or hardware, and software to manage information. Let's introduce the hardware and software components of information technology. These will be covered in more detail in Chapter 12.

Information Technology Hardware

Did you know that you are living in what is known as the information age? This means that computers are no longer a luxury, but rather they are a commodity. Today over 60% of US households have a personal computer. Students in elementary schools learn how to use computers as part of the standard curriculum.

But what exactly is a computer? A **computer** is an electronic machine or device that can be programmed to perform different tasks. All of the equipment attached to it, including the computer itself, is called **hardware**. The hardware is usually classified into input devices, output devices, storage devices, communications devices and the system unit. Figure 1.10 illustrates examples of some common computer hardware.

Input devices are used to allow the user to enter data or instructions into the computer. Common examples are the mouse, keyboard, microphone and scanner. **Output devices** convert the information and data inside the computer into a format that is accessible to the user. Common output devices include a computer screen or monitor, printers and speakers. Some devices, like a touch screen, can be used for both input and output. **Storage devices** are used to hold data and instructions for future use. Hard disks, USB drives, CDs and DVDs are common examples of storage devices. **Communications devices** allow a computer to send data and information to other computers and to receive data and information from other computers. Modems, cables and network interface cards are examples of communications devices. The **system unit** is the case or container that holds the electronic components that make up the computer. The electronic components include the microprocessor and the memory.

To learn more about what's inside your computer, navigate to this website to watch this video: *http://videos.howstuffworks.com/howstuffworks/23-computer-tour-video.htm.*

	Input Devices
	Output Devices
	Storage Devices
	Communications Devices
	System Unit

Figure 1.10   Computer Hardware Devices

Information Technology Software

While a computer is an essential component in information technology, a computer, the basic hardware at least, can't do anything without software. The set of instructions, or programs, that tell the computer what to do are called **software**. There are two basic types of software. **System software** provides basic instructions so that the equipment knows how to operate and work together. This would include the operating system, and drivers that allow input or output devices to work with your computer. **Applications software** has been written to perform specific business tasks. Some applications software is general purpose (like a word processing program or a photo editing program) while others are designed for a specific purpose (to generate payroll at your business).

Putting Information Technology Together

How does the hardware and the software work together? At a very basic level all computers take in some kind of data and produce some kind of information. This is known as the **information processing cycle**, illustrated in Figure 1.11. Data comes into the processor through a variety of input devices. Following the instructions in the software program, the processor performs the required steps to produce the desire output. The results of the software program can be sent to a variety of output devices, as well as to a variety of storage devices.

Figure 1.11 In the Information Processing Cycle, the processor takes input, computes the results and sends the results to output and storage devices.

This brief overview hopefully gave you a better understanding about how computers work. Learning about computers is certainly important, especially because you use them all the time. But here is the kicker – this book isn't going to teach you all the nitty-gritty details about computers or computer literacy. The reality is that for most people, learning about the actual computer, and the technology by itself, isn't all that interesting, or necessary.

So, if this book isn't going to spend much time talking specifically about computers and how they work, what are you going to learn about? We are going to focus on putting computers, or information technology, to use – *to help solve problems*. This is where it gets interesting and exciting.

Organizations put information technology to work through information systems. An information system is used to help people gather and use information, communicate with other people both within and outside the organization, and make effective decisions. Information systems help businesses solve problems. Simply put, the purpose of an information system is to provide an organization with the information needed for decision making. An **information system** includes the hardware, software, and networks, along with the people, procedures and data necessary to accomplish the task. As you can see, computers are definitely a part of an information system, but they are only one part. If you look back at some of the examples introduced in the first section of this chapter, you should realize that many of them were describing information systems.

LEARNING CHECK
Be sure you can *explain what a computer is * describe the different types of hardware * explain the difference between system software and applications software * explain the IPO cycle * define an information system

WHY STUDY INFORMATION TECHNOLOGY?

If you haven't gotten the point yet, technology is everywhere! As a result, you need to learn more about how to use it, both personally and professionally. Think about your career choice. Perhaps you are considering becoming an accountant, a financial planner, a marketing director, an educator, a doctor, a journalist, or an engineer. Professionals in these careers, and many others like them, are known as knowledge workers. A **knowledge worker** is a person who is involved in the creation, distribution and application of information. Knowledge workers depend on information systems to get their job done. As such, no matter your profession, you need to learn about information systems. You need to learn different ways that they can be used to help a business be more productive and effective, what is involved in developing and implementing a successful information system, and how to manage the system. Some of you might be thinking that this stuff is only important if you are going into *business* or are a *business major*. Well, the reality is that all of you are going into business. Your business just might be medicine or education. Understanding how information systems will integrate with your career is critical.

Information Technology and Your Career

To help you better see some examples of technology usage in various jobs, a few different jobs will be described in this section.

Accountants and auditors are concerned with the fiscal accuracy of the business. As such they use information technology to a great extent. Ranging from spreadsheets used to make calculations more efficient and accurate to specialized accounting programs, technology is used to help with data management and record keeping.

Financial specialists are concerned with looking at how individuals and businesses use their monetary resources. They use a variety of technology tools and systems to compare the potential gain of various investments, determine optimal strategies to raise capital, manage portfolios and assets, and analyze the risks of various investments. Additionally, the electronic trading systems used by the major stock exchanges and brokers allows for stock trades to be conducted more efficiently.

Employees in the hospitality and tourism industries use information technology in automated reservation systems. Coupled with a variety of data analysis tools they can then easily determine occupancy rates, target promotions to customers, and effectively manage their inventories. Consumers also utilize many of these tools when they make reservations via e-commerce enabled websites.

Sales and marketing specialists will be involved with using technology to help develop promotional plans for products, track customers and sales, analyze the effectiveness of various pricing strategies and integrate web-based strategies to reach a larger market share.

Within the medical profession, technological advances have led to an increased use of electronic medical records, digital x-rays, and patient scheduling systems. Additionally many aspects of communication are shifting towards technology, such as email interactions with patients, online submission of prescription information to a pharmacy, and electronic submission of patient insurance claims.

Engineers and product development specialists use information technology to aid in the design of new products. Using tools that allow them to create a 3-D model, the design can be modified and tested before it ever goes into production. Automating the assembly line via robotics can increase efficiency and accuracy during manufacturing.

Employees in the management area often will focus in one of several specialties including human resources, sports, entrepreneurship or international management. Each of these specialties utilizes information technology. Human resources, for example, is heavily dependent on systems that manage employee records, attendance and sick leave, benefits, payroll, and retirement.

In Chapter 2 you will have a chance to explore in more detail the information systems that are specific to these different disciplines.

Careers in Information Technology

In addition to the careers introduced above, some of you may be interested in a career more directly involved with information technology. Are you creative? Do you like solving problems? Do you like an environment where you can learn about new advances and trends? Do you want a career that is interesting and challenging? If you like using information technology and the Internet to solve problems, or to create new and more efficient solutions for organizations, then a major or a minor in information systems might be for you.

But are there jobs in information technology? Absolutely! The Office of Occupational Statistics, in the United States Department of Labor, tracks data about the labor market. The 2008-2009 Occupational Outlook Handbook reports the fastest growing occupation between 2006 and 2016 is in *Networking Systems and Data Communications*. They are predicting an estimated increase of 54.4% growth in the number of positions. The 4th fastest growing occupation is in *Computer Software Engineers, Applications* with an estimated increase of 44.6% growth in the number of positions.

This predicted growth is fueled by everything we have already talked about. Look at all the new technologies. Somebody has to create them. What are some of the jobs available to a student pursuing a degree in information systems?

- **Systems Analysts** analyze and design information systems to solve business problems. A systems analyst, as shown in Figure 1.12, will work with groups of users and other information technology specialists to determine the business problem and then to devise the solution to that problem.

Figure 1.12 The Systems Analyst meets with a group of users to discuss the requirements of a new information system.

- **Software Developer/Application Programmers** take the specifications for an information system, which were prepared by the analyst, and develop the programming logic and code to build the actual system.

Figure 1.13 Programmers turn the specifications into a working system.

- **Web Developers** analyze, design and create Internet-based systems, including e-commerce systems.

- **Database Administrators** design, build and maintain corporate databases. This includes ensuring data security and privacy, along with integrity of all data.

- **Network Engineers**, as illustrated in Figure 1.14, design, build, and maintain the information technology networks used by a business. These networks range from small local area networks (LANS) to very large Wide Area Networks (WANS.) Increasingly networks are utilizing wireless capabilities.

Figure 1.14   Network Engineers ensure that users of the system are able to connect without problems.

- **End-user Liaisons** are IT specialists assigned to a particular business area, such as finance or marketing. As shown in Figure 1.15, the end-user liaison works to provide training, support, and assistance to users within that area. Often the end-user liaison will have specialized knowledge or training in the business area they support. This particular career can be very appealing to those who have a minor in Information Systems.

Figure 1.15   An End User Liaison works with an employee to help them learn how to better use new features in the system.

- **Technical Sales and Marketing Specialists** work to analyze client needs, sell and coordinate the integration of computer systems and technologies. These specialists must be able to translate the technological solutions into language the consumer understands.

- **Computer Center Operators** are responsible for scheduling and monitoring different computer program operations, performing system backups, as well as diagnosing and fixing hardware problems.

- **Quality Assurance Analysts/Testers** develop and implement software test plans to ensure that systems meet the desired specifications, perform as needed and are free of defects.

- **Technical Writers** write and edit user manuals and help systems, along with documenting the system specifications. The technical writer, as shown in Figure 1.16, must remember that they have to ensure that the user documentation meets the needs of the audience.

Figure 1.16 The Technical Writer must ensure that they understand the needs of the users.

- **Data Security Analysts** perform risk assessments and security audits. Based on these results they create security policies and procedures and make recommendations for enhancing security.

After gaining experience in the IT field, some professionals may decide to pursue management oriented positions. A few of these types of positions are described below.

- **Computer Center Managers** are responsible for ensuring that all the computer systems within an organization are functioning as needed.

- **Project Managers** are responsible for allocating resources (money, people, time and equipment) to various IT projects. Additionally they monitor the projects to ensure they stay on schedule, on budget and meet the needs of the client.

- **Vice President of Information Technology** is responsible for managing the day-to-day information technology operations within an organization. They serve as a liaison between the nontechnical departments and the IT department.

- **Chief Information Officers (CIO)** are responsible for planning and overseeing the overall information technology strategy. They provide leadership to all IT staff and make recommendations to other senior managers regarding technology initiatives.

Where do you find these jobs? All over! You can work in businesses of any size. Some organizations will have their own IT staff, while others will hire IT consultants on as-needed, project basis.   You can work directly for a computer or software manufacturer. Some people might work in government agencies, like a high school district, city planning department, or state department of motor vehicles. Banks or other financial institutions, medical offices, and retail organizations all need IT workers. Additionally, you might work for a consulting firm who will work on a contract-basis to help any of these types of business. The opportunities will only continue to grow as the uses and integration of technology expands.   To give you an idea of the salary range of these workers, Table 1.1 shows the 2008 average salary for the jobs described in this chapter.

Job Title	2008 U.S. National Average Salary Ranges
Systems Analysts	$66,000 - $90,250
Software Developer/Applications Programmers	$76,500 - $111,500
Web Developers	$57,250 - $86,250
Database Administrators	$74,250 - $106,750
Network Engineers	$67,250 - $93,500
End-user Liaisons	$47,500 - $68,500
Technical Sales and Marketing Specialists	$43,000 - $60,000
Computer Center Operators	$30,500 - $42,750
Quality Assurance Analysts/Testers	$54,500 - $79,250
Technical Writers	$48,250 - $72,000
Data Security Analysts	$76,250 - $104,000
Computer Center Managers	$55,000 - $74,250
Project Managers	$76,500 - $111,500
Vice President of Information Technology	$112,250 - $166,250
Chief Information Officers (CIO)	$126,750 - $210,000

Table 1.1 Salary Ranges for Various IT Careers

Throughout this book we will learn more specifics about the different careers in technology. Even if you don't choose to major in a "technology career", keep in mind that most of your careers will involve quite of bit of dependence and understanding about technology and the information systems that businesses utilize. Additionally, you will most likely interact with people in your organization who perform these functions. Having an understanding of how they contribute to the success of the corporation's information systems, will allow you to provide them with the information needed to help you solve your business problems.

Integrate IT

The integration of web-based systems into business and personal use is increasing at a very fast rate. One task that increasingly utilizes the web is the process of recruiting employees. There are many web-based job sites that can be used by an organization to post job openings and by individuals to find a job.

Visit one of the major job search websites (such as monster.com, careerbuilder.com, simplyhired.com, or dice.com).

Search for a job posting for one of the different information technology careers.

Create a document in your word processor where you record the following information:
- Job position title
- Salary range
- Company
- Job description
- Requirements

Now repeat this process at one of the other job search websites. Again record the information about the job posting you found.

Finally, add a brief write-up, after the job descriptions, describing your experiences at the two websites. Items you may want to consider are ease of use in searching for information, flexibility of using search criteria, amount of detail provided in results, and overall experience. Are you more likely to use one of the sites again instead of the other? If so, why?

LEARNING CHECK
Be sure you can * define a knowledge worker * explain the value of studying IT for all students * describe how information technology is used in various careers * describe the different types of information technology positions

AN OVERVIEW OF THE BOOK

This book has been designed and written to help you understand information technology, how it is utilized by organizations and how to be successful in working with information technology. Many of you will be involved in the process of implementing a new information system – whether you are the systems analyst, the end user, or the manager. As such, you will need to understand the potential roles you may play in an organization undergoing a systems development effort. Through this book you will learn more about those various roles.

Building an information system is similar to putting together a puzzle. You all know that a puzzle typically has many different pieces. You also know that depending on whether you are trying to put together a puzzle of the Eiffel Tower, Waikiki Beach, or a Ferrari F430, the number of pieces and the complexity level will vary from puzzle to puzzle, as will the exact shape, color, and image on each piece. Yet puzzles also have similarities, for example, all rectangular puzzles contain 4 corner pieces. Information systems can be thought of in the same way. One system might be a payroll system while another is built to process customer orders. Each of these systems is made up of different pieces, but they too have similarities. For example, all systems need to ensure security of their data. Figure 1.17 illustrates the major pieces involved in creating an information system.

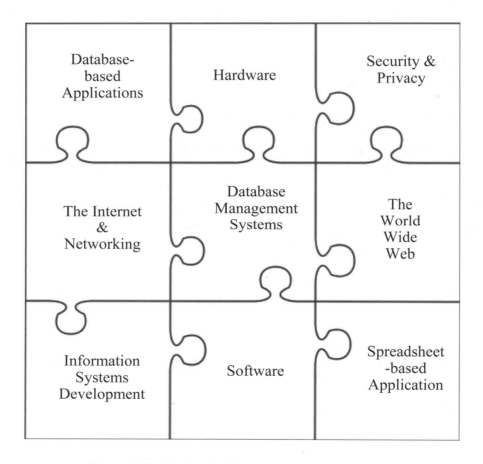

Figure 1.17   The Puzzle Pieces of an Information System

It is pretty obvious to state that books are divided into chapters to help manage the content, and courses are divided into separate class periods. However this inherent structure makes it easy to think that the chapters and material can be separated. Many students operate on the "I only need to know this material until the test happens" approach. Information systems material doesn't really work that way. This content truly is integrated. You will help yourself if you don't think about each chapter or unit separately. Instead, think of these chapters as helping you learn about the different puzzle pieces and how to put them together. Remember that a critical component to this puzzle analogy is that it requires people to bring together all of these different pieces.

In Chapter 2 you will learn about the different types of information systems used in organizations, along with exploring more about the exact components, or puzzle pieces, of an information system. With that foundation we next move into Chapter 3, where you learn how to analyze, design and develop information systems. You can think about this as learning the strategies for putting a puzzle together, quickly and successfully. At this point you are ready to start practicing developing different kinds of business applications.

Spreadsheets are one of the most common business software applications used in organizations. In Tutorial 1 through Tutorial 3 you will be introduced to spreadsheets. Tutorial 1 provides some basic review about spreadsheet usage, along with ensuring that you understand the importance of creating accurate formulas that will adjust correctly when copied from one cell to another.   Tutorial 2 describes how to develop business applications using spreadsheets. Incorporating your knowledge of analyzing, designing and developing information systems from Chapter 3, you will create several different business solutions that utilize a spreadsheet. In Tutorial 3 you will extend your knowledge of spreadsheets by looking at larger scale applications and some advanced spreadsheet functions and features.

Having worked with various data sets, and now having a better understanding of the importance of managing data correctly, you will next turn to Chapter 4, in which you will be introduced to databases. You will learn about the importance of these systems, and you will learn how to model organizational data. You will also be introduced to data warehouses, data mining and knowledge management. Once you know the basics about organizing data, you are ready to learn how to build an actual database using a database management system. In Tutorial 4 you will learn how to create a simple database, including building a table, form, query and report. In Tutorial 5, you will learn how to create a database that involves multiple tables. You will build more complex objects that take advantage of the relationships of these different tables.

Having now experienced how to create several different applications, the next set of chapters explores some of the cornerstone pieces of an information system. Chapter 5 will help you understand what the Internet really is and how the Internet, and networks in general, have become such a critical component of most organizations' IT infrastructure. In Chapter 6 you will learn about the World Wide Web and markup languages such as HTML and XML. Additionally, you will see how businesses have adopted many of the collaborative technologies of Web 2.0 and how the Web is facilitating the e-business activities within organizations. Some of you may be asked to develop a simple web page, once you have learned about the Web. Tutorial 6 introduces the basics about creating a web page using XHTML. This foundation will allow you to easily understand web page code generated from other web development programs. Ensuring that your computer systems are secure is of growing importance. Chapter 7 discusses issues organizations face in securing their systems, along with different threats and ways to increase security.

As you work through the textbook, our desire is for you to learn about creating and using a variety of information systems and applications, like spreadsheets and databases, throughout this book. The goal of this approach is so that you will realize that these applications, and the larger systems built using some of these applications in the infrastructure, are integrated into everything about information technology. We hope that as you are learning how to create a database, for example, that you are reinforcing the ideas introduced in other chapters – thinking about analyzing the business need of the database system, thinking about what security controls will be implemented in the database, addressing data communication needs and exploring issues related to making the system accessible via the web.

We hope you are excited to begin. The chapters that follow will help you explore the ideas introduced in Chapter 1. Technology is ever changing – continuing to offer new approaches to the ways we do just about everything. We hope you enjoy the journey as you learn What ITs all About.

Wrapping IT Up

In this chapter you learned about the far reach that information technology has in the world. The opening example of Pacific Sunwear illustrated several ways that PacSun utilizes information systems to improve their business. You also explored examples of technology products and services. In the chapter you learned about the hardware and software components of information technology. You gained a better understanding of how information technology is used in various careers and you also learned about careers in information technology. Finally, you explored how the organization of this book will help you become a better informed user and creator of information technology.

Study Questions Summary

1. How is information technology used in business and society?
   - Businesses use many different technologies to help them accomplish a variety of tasks including helping to develop products, manage inventory, process customer orders, and track employee work hours.
   - Individuals use information technology to aid in communication, find information, enjoy entertainment and make many daily tasks easier to accomplish.
   - Information technology can be used to create products that provide a competitive advantage, opportunities, entertainment, provide mobility, and provide up-to-date information.
   - Businesses use information technology to provide services to employees and customers.
   - If not properly managed during the development process, information technology can create problems for organizations

2. What is information technology?
   - Information technology refers to any computer-based tool used to create, manage and disperse information.
   - The two major components of information technology are the hardware and the software.
   - The most visible piece of information technology hardware is the computer.
   - Information technology hardware is classified into input devices, output devices, storage devices, communications devices and the system unit.
   - Information technology software is the set of instructions, or programs, that tell the computer what to do.

- The two basic types of software are systems software and applications software.
- Through the information processing cycle, input is transformed into outputs that are helpful to the computer users.
- One of the main ways that businesses put information technology to work is through information systems.

3. Why should you learn about information technology?
   - Information technology is used in almost every profession
   - Knowledge workers depend on information systems to assist them in the creation, distribution and application of information.
   - Office automation systems provide support for common tasks such as communications and presentations.
   - Across various jobs, employees use information technology to improve the accuracy of information, increase accessibility to data, increase productivity, provide better interactions with customers, and to increase the efficiency of different tasks
   - Job positions within information technology are among the fastest growing occupations
   - Specific jobs allow individuals to specialize in a variety of tasks from analysis, programming, networking, database management, web development and information security
   - Management careers in information technology include computer center managers, project manager, vice president of information technology and chief information officer.

4. How will <u>What's IT All About</u> help you learn about information technology?
   - Building information systems is similar to putting together a puzzle.
   - The different puzzle pieces for an information system include security & privacy, the Internet & networking, software, hardware, the world wide web, spreadsheet-based applications, and database-based applications
   - The process for putting an information system puzzle together is known as information systems development
   - It will be important to remember the interrelated nature of the different information technology material

Solutions to Chapter Activities

UNDERSTANDING IT?

Information Technology Terms pg. 10 (Your answers may vary.)

1) An organized list of instructions that tells the computer what actions to perform
2) Among others, your answer could include: Visual Basic, Java, C, C++, C#, Ruby, Fortran, Pascal, Cobol
3) An organized collection of data
4) A unit of data that is eight bits long. Each byte can store one character such as a digit (0-9), letter or symbol.
5) Approximately a billion bytes
6) Some common comparisons include: about 1000 novels or 18 hours of MP3 music
7) A person who tries to break, or hack, into computer systems

8) Voice over Internet Protocol. VOIP is a set of hardware and software facilities designed to allow for voice communication over the Internet. A major advantage is the reduction or elimination of phone charges

9) Radio Frequency Identification. RFID is a system of electromagnetic tags and scanners used to identify goods and products. Because RFID does not require a direct line-of-sight to scan the item, it is viewed as an improvement to standard bar codes.

Key Terms

Page number references are included in parentheses.

Application programmer (15)	Information processing cycle (12)	Software Developer (15)
Applications software (12)	Information system (13)	Storage devices (11)
Chief information officer (17)	Information technology (11)	Systems analyst (15)
Communications devices (11)	Input devices (11)	System software (12)
Computer (11)	Knowledge worker (13)	System unit (11)
Computer center manager (17)	Network engineer (16)	Technical sales & marketing specialist (16)
Computer center operator (16)	Output devices (11)	Technical writer (16)
Data security analyst (17)	Product (4)	Tester (16)
Database administrator (16)	Project manager (17)	Vice president of information technology (17)
Digital native (3)	Quality assurance analyst (16)	Web developer (15)
End-user liaison (16)	Service (7)	
Hardware (11)	Software (12)	

Multiple Choice Questions

1. Technology products can be classified into all of the following categories except _____.
   a. Products designed to create a competitive advantage
   b. Products designed to provide increased opportunities
   c. Products designed to provide up-to-date information
   d. Products designed to increase costs

2. Amazing Amanda used which of the following technologies?
   a. RFID
   b. scanners
   c. Facial robotics
   d. All of the above

3. Dick's Sporting Goods used _____ software to help create a competitive advantage.
   a. mobile Internet
   b. GPS
   c. business intelligence
   d. speech recognition

4. Which of the following is not an example of an Input Device?
   a. Mouse
   b. Printer
   c. Touch Screen
   d. Keyboard

5. _____ is the set of instructions that tells the computer what to do.
   a. Software
   b. An information system
   c. A communications device
   d. Information technology

6. The _____ describes how a computer takes input, computes the results and sends the results to output and storage devices.
   a. information processing cycle
   b. information technology cycle
   c. information system cycle
   d. problem solving cycle

7. Which of the following jobs uses information technology to help ensure the fiscal accuracy of a business?
   a. Health professionals
   b. Marketing specialists
   c. Engineers
   d. Accountants

8. Individuals who are likely to enjoy a career in information technology should have all of the following characteristics except _____.
   a. is creative
   b. likes to solve problems
   c. does not like to keep up on the latest trends
   d. likes challenges

9. Which of the following is a management oriented information technology profession?
   a. Systems analyst
   b. Data security analyst
   c. Computer center operator
   d. Chief information officer

10. E-Commerce systems would most likely be created by a(n) _____ ?
    a. Database administrator
    b. Web developer
    c. Network engineer
    d. End-user liaison

Answers:
1. d   2. d   3. c   4. b   5. a   6. a   7. d   8. c   9. d   10. b

Review Questions

1. What is a digital native?
2. Explain the differences between a product and a service.
3. Describe how technology products can provide mobile connectivity
4. Describe how the PGA uses information technology to make data more accessible.
5. What is information technology?
6. List and explain the five different types of computer hardware.
7. How do Systems Software and Applications Software differ?
8. Explain how the information processing cycle works.
9. Define an information system and explain its purpose.
10. What is a knowledge worker?
11. Explain the US Department of Labor's view about job growth in the information technology area.
12. Describe the puzzle analogy used in this book and how it will help you learn about information system.

Projects

1. Create a journal where you record all of the interactions that you have with information technology over a two day period. To the extent possible, classify the information technology as one that is a product or that provides a service.
2. Write a one-page report on how technology affects your daily life.
3. Research a technology product that is primarily designed to provide entertainment. Create a brief PowerPoint presentation that explains what the product is and why it is interesting. If possible, include a picture of the product
4. Interview an individual who works in a job related to your major. Find out how they use information technology in their job.
5. Interview a professor who teaches in your major to determine how your education will help you learn about the way information technology that will be used in your career.
6. Interview an individual working in the information technology profession (such as a programmer or systems analyst.) Ask them to describe their job and how they keep current with technological changes. Prepare a brief report of your results.
7. Investigate how the data provided by ShotLink are being used by professional golfers to improve their game. Create a brief PowerPoint presentation to convey the results.
8. Find an example, not discussed in the text, about an information system project that failed. Briefly describe the system and explain what caused the failure.

CHAPTER **2**

Business Information Systems

PLANNING AHEAD
After reading Chapter 2, you should be able to answer these questions in your own words

STUDY QUESTIONS
What is an information system?
What are the information needs of businesses?
What are the different types of information systems?
How are information systems used in the functional business areas?

LEARNING PREVIEW

As you learned in Chapter 1, organizations use information technology in a variety of ways. Not only is information technology used to support the day to day operations of an organization, but IT also supports managing, planning and strategy formulation. In this chapter you will learn more about what an information system is. You will also learn about the differences among the information that employees need to do their jobs effectively and efficiently. The chapter will also introduce you to the different types of information systems and how information systems are used across an organization to help the organization operate more effectively.

OPENING VIGNETTE

Global Business Excellence with Technology at Nestlé

When most of us hear the word Nestlé, our thoughts turn to Crunch bars or Toll House Cookies. But Nestlé produces much more than chocolates. As the world's largest food company Nestlé's product line includes Nescafe coffee, PowerBar performance bars, Stouffers' frozen foods and Buitoni pasta. Employing over 247,000 workers, Nestlé is a large, global organization with operations in virtually every country in the world.

But life at Nestlé wasn't always sweet – managing $70 billion in annual sales comes with lots of complexity. If producing over 127,000 different types and sizes of their products wasn't challenging enough, keeping track of thousands of supply chains, variations in customer billing processes and payment collections was becoming too large a problem to handle. Additionally, Nestlé was facing escalating spending on IT caused by uncoordinated planning and management of different information systems. As example, their IT spending grew 23% from about $575 million to $750 million from 1994 to 1999. The uncoordinated systems resulted in tens of thousands of customers listed multiple times in corporate databases along with vendors who were no longer in business. All of this was becoming too much for Nestlé to handle; their bottom line was being impacted.

To help address these problems, in July 2000 Nestlé set forth on their most ambitious business process reengineering project, designed to turn the company around, by using technology to create a strategic advantage. GLOBE (Global Business Excellence) was a worldwide initiative to create a single set of web-based information systems that would use a common set of factory and automation processes, along with a single way to format and store data. Through GLOBE, Nestlé was trying to operate as though they are in only one country, despite the fact that they actually are operating in hundreds of countries.

By choosing to think about using technology strategically, not only would GLOBE help control rising information technology costs, but also improve performance and operational efficiency. For example, Nestlé estimated that with GLOBE they could reduce the number of suppliers from 600,000 to 167,000, and save more than $750,000 million a year. More importantly, GLOBE would help Nestlé achieve a significant lead over their global competitors by operating more efficiently.

To achieve these benefits GLOBE had three main objectives:

- Develop Best Practices – create a set of common, best practices for purchasing, sales forecasting, production planning and customer service. Essentially, Nestlé wanted to create a standardized "back end" to doing business.

- Standardize Data – develop a common coding system for data items to allow for consolidated information. This would ensure that all systems across the company use the same coding number for a Cookies & Cream PowerBar. This would allow sales around the world to be easily consolidated.

- Build a Common Information System – construct four data centers with common hardware, software and networks to support all new GLOBE markets. This common platform would reduce development and maintenance costs for IT, in addition to promoting better sharing of data and information across Nestlé.

How would all of this happen? By replacing the 14 different enterprise planning systems with one new Internet-based enterprise program based on mySAP.com. Of course this wasn't going to be easy. But working with managers and employees around the world, resolving unexpected setbacks, and staying focused on the project goals has helped Nestle keep on track. Although the project took longer than originally anticipated, by the end of 2005, 23 markets had implemented all three elements of GLOBE. In September 2007, CEO Peter Brabeck reported that Nestle was now seeing significant improvements in efficiency and cost savings attributed to the Globe project.

(Sources: Compiled from Toom Steinert-Threlkeld, "Nestlé Pieces Together its Global Supply Chain," *Baseline Magazine*, January 20, 2006, www.baselinemag.com/print_article2/0,1217,a=169376,00.asp; and *www.ir.nestle.com/nestle_overview/operational_performance/globe/globe.htm*, *www.Nestle.com* accessed February 15, 2006; and Anita Greil, "Nestle CEO seeing first big improvement from efficiency drive," MarketWatch.com, September 21, 2007, *http://www.marketwatch.com/news/story/nestle-ceo-seeing-first-big/story.aspx?guid=%7BF61E88F8-9D45-4615-AF20-FFB348593B7B%7D&dist=TQP_Mod_mktwN*, retrieved October 6, 2008.)

In this chapter you will have a chance to explore the ideas introduced in this opening story. You will learn about how companies conduct business, and how they use technology, like supply chain management systems and enterprise resource planning systems, to help them with their business.

VISUAL ORGANIZATION OF CHAPTER

Study Question 1	Study Question 2	Study Question 3	Study Question 4
Information Systems	Information Needs of Business	Types of Information Systems	Information Systems in Functional Business Areas
• What does an information system do? • What are the components of an information system? • What are the functions an information system performs?	• Characteristics of Information • Types of Employees • Organizational structures	• Systems to support basic operations • Systems to support decision making • Enterprise wide systems	• What does an information system do?
Learning Check 1	Learning Check 2	Learning Check 3	Learning Check 4

INFORMATION SYSTEMS

As you saw in the opening vignette with Nestlé, companies today are using information technology to enable business strategy and to improve the way they do business. Nestlé, for example, was creating a system that would help them more efficiently gather and process information. Through the creation of information systems that support the goals of a business, organizations can use technology as a strategic advantage.

What does an information system do?

An **information system** collects, processes, stores and disseminates data or information needed for decision making. The exact methods used to collect, process, store and disseminate the data or information varies from system to system. At a simplistic level, the methods may all be paper-based and manual, such as the grade book used by a kindergarten teacher to keep track of student grades, attendance and behavior problems. The teacher collects, processes, stores and disseminates the data manually, without the aid of information technology.   In this information system, the teacher uses data in the grade book to make decisions about how to tailor instruction during the year, to provide feedback to the student and parents via report cards, and ultimately about whether to promote a student to the next grade level at the end of the year.

At a more complex level, the methods may include technology such as a high quality camera that takes a picture of your retina for a security system. A computer program analyzes that input data to determine your identity. Based on the results of the processing, the system determines whether to electronically open a door that will provide you access to a secure building. This system, using information technology, still collects, processes, stores and disseminates data related to identification and access control.

From these examples, you can see that an information system doesn't have to include computer technology. Because of this, some people differentiate *computer-based information systems* as information systems that include information technology to accomplish some of the tasks. Practically speaking though, most people don't distinguish between the two terms. In this book we will use the broader term of information system and will focus our discussion on information systems that incorporate information technology.

What are the components of an information system?

An information system, as illustrated in Figure 2.1, is made up of a number of different pieces. These pieces include hardware, software, data, people, procedures, and networks.

Hardware – The computer and peripheral equipment for input, output, storage
Software – The programs that tell the computer equipment what to do
Data – The inputs into the computer system. Many systems will store the data in a database, which is an organized collection of data.
People – The users and information systems professionals
Procedures – The policies within a company that form the basis for the logic in the programs
Networks – Specialized hardware and software that allows different computers to connect with each other to share data, software and other hardware resources

While most systems will contain all of these pieces, you will encounter systems that don't use all of the pieces. For example, a system that is designed to only be used on a single computer may not have a network component.

Figure 2.1 An information system usually contains hardware, software, data, people, procedures and networks.

On a daily basis you probably interact with many different information systems – the ATM system at your bank, the automated pumps at the gas station where you buy gas, and the email program you use to communicate. Some systems transform data into information while other systems, typically in the manufacturing area, transform raw materials into marketable, finished products. Recall from Chapter 1 that we introduced the analogy of building a puzzle to help you think about putting together an information system. What makes each system different is the selection of unique pieces combined to perform a task. While both an employee payroll system and a patient record management system need data and software, the exact specifications of those pieces will certainly be unique. Throughout this book you will learn more about the different types of puzzle pieces, or components in an information system, and how they are assembled into a variety of information systems.

What are the functions an information system performs?

No matter the exact pieces used, or the business task your information system performs, information systems perform five primary, fundamental functions.

1. **Capture Input. Inputs** are the data needed by the system. An information system must provide a mechanism to capture input. Input can come from many different types of devices including data entered via a keyboard, pushing a button, swiping a barcode or talking. Common input devices include keyboards, specialized keypads, a mouse, scanners and a microphone.

2. **Process.** The transformation of input into output is called **processing**. Performing calculations, validating information, updating records and transforming raw materials are all examples of processing.

3. **Convey Output. Outputs** are the result of processing the data. There are many different outputs that can be produced including a finished product, reports, documents, or even data to be used in another application. Printers and computer monitors are two of the more common output devices.

4. **Collect Feedback.** In order to see if the system is working as planned, **feedback** – data about the performance of the system – is collected. Feedback can come from users of the system, or be tracked automatically by the system itself. Often it involves tracking errors. The feedback signals travel from the input capture, processing or output.

5. **Control.** When feedback is monitored and analyzed, adjustments may need to be made to help ensure that the system is working correctly. **Control** involves monitoring, analyzing and making the necessary adjustments. As a result of the analysis, a control response may be returned to the input, processing or output, as warranted by the nature of the feedback.

Figure 2.2 shows the how these five functions interact in an information system. You should be able to identify these five functions in any information system. As we move ahead in the textbook and start building different systems, you will learn to define these functions relative to the system you are creating or using.

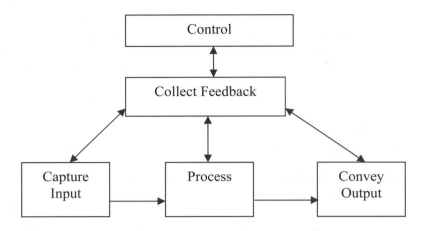

Figure 2.2   An information system performs five main functions.

Complete the exercise below to reinforce your understanding about how the pieces of an information system as shown in Figure 2.1 interact with the functions illustrated in Figure 2.2.

Understanding IT?

Automated Teller Machines (ATMs) are a type of information system in widespread use. By allowing customers to "serve themselves," banks are able to reduce the number of tellers needed inside the bank. Additionally, customers get improved service by having access to their bank accounts 24 hours a day.

Analyze an ATM system to help you complete the worksheet below. Identify the pieces used in the system and explain how those pieces are used to perform the five functions. You can check your answers at the end of the chapter.

ATM System Description

	Inputs Collected	Hardware Device Used
1	Account Number	Card Reader
2	PIN	Keypad
3		
4		

	Outputs Produced	Hardware Device Used
1	Money	Cash dispenser
2		
3		
4		

Processing is accomplished in software. List three examples of processing.

1 Check the PIN is correct
2
3

What kind of feedback do you think the system collects?

1
2
3

What kind of controls do you think are implemented?

1
2
3

Do you think the ATM system uses a Network? Why or why not?

1
2
3

What people interact with the ATM system?

1
2
3

Knowing the different pieces and functions of an information system is just the foundation. What really matters is how the resulting information system actually helps a business. No matter what business you are in – medicine, automobile sales, education, or accounting, to name a few – all businesses need information to survive and flourish. Information systems are designed to provide the information that employees in any organization need. Sometimes the needs, and the resulting systems, are very simple while other times the needs result in very complex systems. Figure 2.3 illustrates three examples, of varying complexity, of how information systems are used in industry.   In the next section you will look more specifically at how businesses are organized and the different types of information that a business needs.

Industry	Information System Example	System Output or Screen Sample
K-12 Education	Electronic Gradebook to record student attendance, assignment and project grades, exam grades, and discipline problems.	
Machine Tool Design	Computer Aided Design systems can be used to develop design models of various tool parts and components	
Hospitality and Tourism	Reservation System to track campground site reservations, including site specific needs, dates, and customer information	

Figure 2.3   Examples of information systems used in industry.

LEARNING CHECK
Be sure you can *explain what an information system does * describe the components of an information system * identify and explain the five functions performed by an information system

INFORMATION NEEDS OF BUSINESS

How many cashiers does Wal-Mart need to schedule each day? What is the most popular color chosen by Audi A4 customers? Does the number of dozens of eggs consumed at Denny's Restaurant vary by the day of the week? These are examples of the types of questions that businesses need answered. To be able to answer these questions, an organization needs information. Successful organizations know that information is a strategic asset, one that must be managed carefully. But organizations also know that they need different types of information depending on how it will be used. The way the information is used is influenced by the type of employee as well as the way the organization is structured. In this section you will explore these differences and how these differences influence the types of information needed within organizations.

Characteristics of Information

Organizations must ensure that they provide their employees with the information they need, when they need it. But what exactly is information and how does an organization get it? **Information** is data that has been organized, manipulated or processed to have meaning. Buried inside of this definition is the term data. **Data** are raw facts that are collected and stored – by themselves data don't mean anything. Data comes in a variety of formats including numbers, letters, images, videos, or audios.

Organizations can generate a tremendous amount of data. Consider just some of the pieces of data captured by Southwest Airlines when you purchase an airline ticket – first and last name, frequent flyer number, address, credit card number, credit card expiration date, departure date, departure time, departure city, flight number, arrival city, and arrival time. In February 2006 Southwest carried just under 6,000,000 revenue passengers. This translates into 6,000,000 names, credit card numbers, etc. in one month alone. When you look at any one airline ticket transaction, each piece of data, such as the departure city, doesn't provide much value to Southwest Airlines. However by processing the data from this one transaction, in conjunction with other transactions, information is produced that can add value. For example, Southwest can determine how many empty seats exist on departures from Las Vegas each day, helping them determine whether to make changes in the number and/or timing of flights.

Another dimension often used to describe information relates to the source. Much information used by organizations comes from internal sources. **Internal information** is produced by the company through the normal course of business operations. The passenger ticketing data described above is created inside of the business. But companies don't operate in a vacuum. They interact with the world, and as a result need to incorporate **external information** that comes from outside of the organization. Common types of external information include interest rates, economic indicators of projected growth, and employment projections. For Southwest, some of the external information they would utilize includes forecasts for oil prices, weather and insurance costs.

Understanding what information is, and the different sources of information, isn't enough because all information is not equally valued. Information technology provides an easy way for an organization to collect and process data, causing some companies to drown in too much information. To have value, information must be accurate, complete, economical, relevant, timely, verifiable and accessible. Figure 2.4 explains these characteristics of useful information.

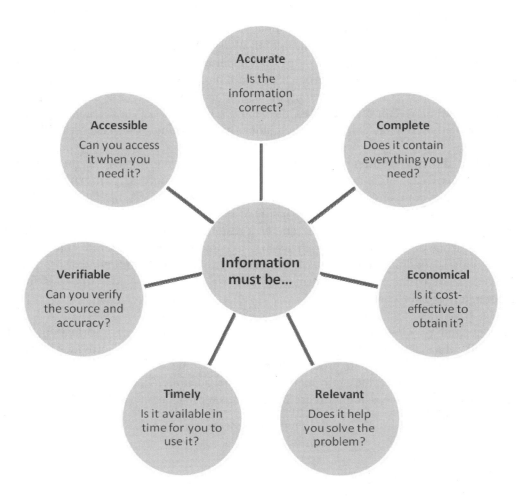

Figure 2.4   Characteristics of useful information.

Types of Employees

To create an information system that helps a business, you need to understand the work that employees perform.   There are many different types of employees in an organization, each performing different types of work.   The exact work and amount of responsibility assigned to each employee type may be influenced by the internal organizational structure.   However, independent of the internal structure, employees are typically categorized into one of four types of employees: *non-management employees*, *operational management*, *tactical management* and *strategic management*. Figure 2.5 highlights this categorization of employees as a pyramid, symbolizing not only the differences in the organizational hierarchy but also the number of employees found at each level.   Because employees perform different types of work, have different levels of responsibility and make different types of decisions, not all employees need the same type of information. It is helpful to realize that information flows up and down between these different levels.

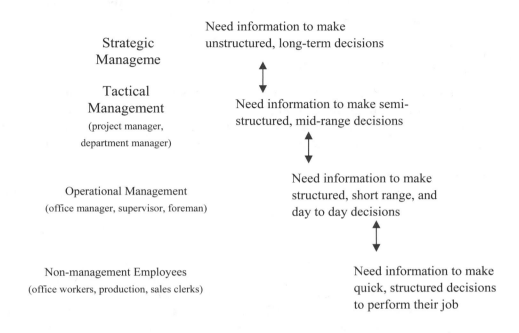

Figure 2.5 Types of Employees and their information needs

Non-management employees need information specific to performing their job. Jobs at this level include office workers, production, and sales clerks.   The tasks performed are highly structured usually requiring knowledge about the rules or procedures to complete the task at hand. For example, a sales clerk needs to know how to complete a sales transaction, which may involve checking various store locations for available inventory, or making a decision about which situations require supervisor assistance.

Operational management needs information to make short range and day to day decisions. Jobs within operational management include office manager, supervisor, and foreman. The tasks are still highly structured, routinely performed, and affect a short time frame. Operational managers often make decisions that affect the employees they supervise. For example, each week a supervisor needs to set the weekly work schedule for their employees. On a daily basis they may need to determine if more inventory needs to be ordered.

Tactical management   needs information to monitor and control activities within their department. Jobs at this "middle management" level include project manager and department manager. While still focusing on a functional area or department, the tasks are not as structured or routine as operational decisions, and affect a midrange time frame – several months up to a year. A middle manager may decide how the advertising budget should be allocated for the next quarter, departmental goals for the next year, or whether work areas should be moved to reduce bottlenecks in the production line.

Strategic management needs information to develop and monitor the overall strategy, goals and objectives for the organization. The work done at this level typically is unstructured, meaning that there is no set of rules to follow, and often involves creating plans with a timeline of several years. Example decisions include deciding to build a new factory or discontinue an existing product line. As you can see, these decisions are inherently more complex, and usually require incorporating external information.

Organizational Structures

Each organization has an internal **organizational structure** – the way their various parts are arranged to accomplish their work. Some common structures, illustrated in Figure 2.6, include functional, divisional and matrix structures. A **functional structure**, the most basic structure, groups together employees performing similar tasks. Typically, the organization would contain a central or main office which oversees various departments or major functions like marketing, engineering, human resources, or finance. In a **divisional structure**, employees are grouped together based on the product to which they are assigned. The organization is divided into various divisions, each producing or selling a specific product. Within each division, separate functional structures may exist. Finally, in a **matrix structure**, employees are assigned to a functional area, but then are also assigned into a cross-functional team or work group with people from other functional areas, and collectively these groups work on specific products or services. Due to increased competition from a global economy, organizational structures are evolving to allow companies to develop products more effectively and quickly, to provide increased customer service, and to become more efficient overall. Having evolved from a matrix structure, these newer **team-based structures** use cross-functional teams working on specific projects. This structure reduces the layers of hierarchy and breaks down functional barriers which limit information sharing. You will study more details about these structures, including tradeoffs, in a management class. For now you should understand that the organizational structure selected by a company can impact how information technology is used to support and enhance the needs of employees within the organization.

Figure 2.6 The way that the parts are arranged within an organization follows one of four different organizational structures

Properly designed information systems can help ensure that data is transformed into valuable information that moves seamlessly across the different levels in an organization. As organizations are able to provide information to lower level employees, enabling them to make quick, accurate decisions, higher level managers can spend more time on strategic issues. Ultimately this results in improved performance for the organization – which translates into increased profitability.

Understanding IT?

Recall that one goal of the GLOBE project at Nestlé was to develop best business practices. For example, what is the best way to process orders or to calculate demand for a product? To accomplish the goal Nestle first had to investigate the different ways they currently performed their business tasks or made decisions. Ultimately the most efficient and effective method would be identified and implemented into the new GLOBE system allowing employees and managers to perform their jobs via the new Web-based system.

Ensure your understanding by associating each of these job tasks at Nestle with the type of employee most likely to perform the task:

_____	Order supplies from a vendor
_____	Generate an invoice
_____	Close out financial reports for a quarter
_____	Establish schedule for roll out of a new manufacturing system

Check your answers at the end of the chapter.

You started this chapter by learning about the components and functions of an information system. Now that you have also learned about the different types of information that employees need, you are ready to explore the information systems that are available to help them perform their jobs.

LEARNING CHECK
Be sure you can * define the term organizational structure * describe the four types of employees and the types of information needed to perform their jobs * distinguish data from information * describe the qualities of valuable information

TYPES OF INFORMATION SYSTEMS

Within an organization you will generally find many different information systems. Sometimes the systems operate independently of each other while other times they are built to share data and information. Some systems are designed to support only one part of the business while others support the enterprise as a whole. Based on the type of function it provides, most information systems can be classified into one of the following types of information systems: *office automation systems, transaction processing systems*, *management information systems*, *decision support systems*, *expert systems* and *enterprise wide systems*. These systems can be grouped into those that support basic operations, decision making, or enterprise-wide functions.

Systems to Support Basic Operations

Every day, employees have many tasks they need to accomplish. Many of them are routine tasks that can be more easily accomplished with the aid of information technology. Office Automation Systems and Transaction Processing Systems provide support for these basic operations.

Office Automation Systems (OAS) improve productivity by supporting generic, daily work activities of employees. These activities include creating a presentation or document, sending an email, or coordinating employee calendars. Many of you are already familiar with personal office automation systems through your use of tools such as email and word processors. In addition to standard productivity software tools, other features often found in an OAS include software to create presentations along with electronic versions of calendars, appointment books, and contact lists. Because of their broad-based utility, they are used by a variety of non-management employees along with all levels of management.

Transaction Processing Systems (TPS) are designed to support the routine business transactions in a business. A **transaction** is a business interaction between two parties such as purchasing an airline ticket, requesting a repair-man to fix a product, or returning merchandise to a store. TPSs, the most widely used type of information system, allow organizations to record, process, and store transactions. Examples include order-entry, customer billing, and inventory control. While most of us think that transactions are between customers and organizations, sometimes the transactions are between employees and organizations. Examples of these transactions include stamping or recording employee timecards and enrolling employees in health benefit plans. Payroll and employee record management systems are two examples of TPSs to support these transactions. A TPS is primarily used by non-management employees and operational management. Because they process the basic business transactions, the data collected and processed is a critical input into organization databases that are used by some of the other types of information systems. Figure 2.7 illustrates a point-of-sale system used by many retail outlets to record customer purchases. In a point-of-sale system details about the products purchased include the quantity, product ID, and selling price while details about the customer include their name, customer reward number (if applicable) and payment information.

Figure 2.7 A Point-of-sale system is a very common type of transaction processing system

Systems to Support Decision Making

Managers make a variety of decisions every day – some are very structured and have an immediate impact while others may be very unstructured and will have a long term effect on the organization. As you learned earlier, the level of management influences the information needed to make the decision as well as the time frame and the scope of the decision. Information systems designed to support decision making can integrate data from transaction processing systems with external information. Management Information Systems, Decision Support Systems, and Expert Systems offer differing kinds of support for decision making.

Management Information Systems (MIS) support decision making activities through information and reporting capabilities. MIS were built as an enhancement to a TPS to provide managers with easier access to the data collected by the TPS. The input data into an MIS comes mainly from that captured by the transaction processing system, although sometimes an MIS will also get input data generated from external sources like government or industry projections. Primarily used by operational and tactical management, these systems are often built to produce three types of reports: *detailed*, *summary* and *exception*. A **detailed report** shows details of transactions such as a daily sales report, a **summary report** provides a consolidated view of the transaction data such as a monthly payroll by division report, and an **exception report** shows transactions that fall outside of normal bounds, such as a report of products where inventory is too low. Examples of these three reports are shown in Figure 2.8.

| Detailed Report Example | Summary Report Example | Exception Report Example |

Figure 2.8 Supervisors at Costco, a large warehouse retailer, get detailed reports about sales for each product, summary reports about the number of customers processed per hour by each cashier, and exception reports that show cashier's who have exceed the stores accuracy rate for scanning.

The three types of reports can be further classified by the regularity and flexibility with which you obtain the reports. An MIS can produce *standardized* reports (the same report design on a periodic basis) and *ad-hoc* reports (a unique report generated on demand). This is an important feature since reporting needs change over time. Because the reporting needs vary by department, Management Information Systems are typically designed to support a functional unit within the organization. For example, the reports needed in the accounting department are different than the reports needed in the production department. Sometimes an MIS will be built as a separate system from the TPS, while other times the MIS capabilities will be integrated into the TPS. The system access rights or privileges assigned to an account login, will determine whether the user is allowed to work in only the TPS portion, only the MIS portion, or both.

Decision Support Systems (DSS) help users analyze data to make decisions. For example a manager at Coca Cola may need to determine whether to introduce a new brand of soda. A DSS can vary from a simple spreadsheet-based system to a sophisticated, integrated system. Experian-Scorex, for example, is a DSS designed to help organizations improve their customer relationships. Figure 2.9 highlights some of the benefits offered by the Experian system.

The Experian-Scorex DSS can help you find and acquire the right customers

- **Maximize the power of prospecting** with precise targeting to increase response and conversion rates

- **Select the right customers and meet growth and quality** targets by accurately assessing applicants to identify and select the customers that meet your targets

- **Enrich data** with links to internal and external data sources, including more than 70 credit bureaus

- **Create customer intelligence** with powerful predictive analytics

- **Increase conversion rates, revenue and generate loyalty** with a relevant and personalized service by creating individual pricing, terms and offers for each applicant

Source: http://www.experian.com/products/pdf/eds_interim_102006.pdf

---

Figure 2.9 The Experian-Scorex DSS offers benefits to attract and retain customers

While many DSSs are created for tactical managers, you will find some use by operational managers and strategic management. The Agricultural and Resource Economics Department at the University of Arizona has developed a web-based DSS that helps ranchers decide which cows to cull, or remove, from their herd. Additionally decision support systems can be designed for use by customers. For example Smartmoney.com offers a variety of tools to aid in financial decisions, such as whether refinancing a loan makes sense. The American Medical Association offers a DSS to help find a physician at AMA.com.

A DSS contains different types of models that perform simulations, forecasting or optimization. Typically they incorporate external information, which wasn't used in the other systems, and also use data from the other systems. Figure 2.10 illustrates the components of a typical DSS.

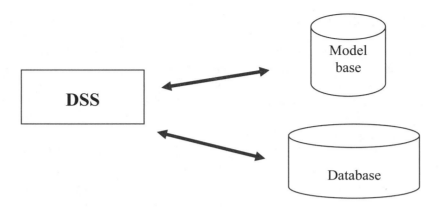

Figure 2.10   The architecture of a DSS

Complete the **<u>Integrate IT</u>** exercise below to expand your understanding about Decision Support Systems.

<u>Integrate IT</u>

As you just learned, a Decision Support System helps users analyze data to make a decision. In this exercise you are going to work with an online DSS designed to help you make a car buying decision.

Car dealers offer a variety of incentives when purchasing a new car. Two of the more common incentives are rebates and reduced interest rates. FinanceCalc.com is a website that offers a variety of free, online financial calculators.   Navigate to the http://www.financecalc.com/sub_auto.htm website. Click on the **Low Rate or Rebate** calculator.

Your screen should be similar to that shown below.

You are interested in purchasing a new Ford Mustang Shelby GT Coupe. The purchase price of the car at the dealer is $42,640. You can choose between a $4,500 rebate or a 0% interest rate for 48 months. You want to put $8,500 as a down payment. Your local credit union will offer you a 4.99% loan for up to 60 months.

1) Fill in the Low Rate or Rebate DSS calculator with the values specified above.

Integrate IT - continued

What option provides the lowest car payment? What is the difference in the dollar amount on the total payments of both options? Don't forget that you need to add the down payment cost onto the total payments to determine the total cost of the car. Which option should you select?

2) Since the Dealer option interest rate is 0%, you are considering reducing the amount of your down payment. Because of your excellent credit the dealer will allow you to put $0 down. However the credit union will require at least $4,000. In order to figure out the best result you will need to use the calculator twice. First change the down payment to $0 and get the total dealer cost. Next change the down payment to $4,000 to get the total Rebate cost.

What is the difference in the dollar amount on the total payments of both options? Don't forget that you need to add the down payment cost onto the total payments to determine the total cost of the car. Which option should you select?

Although this DSS is limited to this comparison, you also need to consider that because you don't need to put any money down with the dealer financing, you can choose to invest the $4,000. You should investigate what the interest earned on a $4,000 investment for 4 years would be worth.

In Tutorial 2 you will learn how to use a spreadsheet program to create a spreadsheet that will offer similar functionality.

Check your answers at the end of the chapter.

Two special types of decision support systems are group decision support systems and executive information systems.

Group Decision Support Systems (GDSS) are designed to provide tools that support groups or teams of people working together to accomplish business tasks. For example, a systems development team may need to solicit input from a group of users on features for a new system, while a marketing team may need to decide a promotion campaign for a new product. A GDSS can help a team generate a list of ideas, clarify and organize the ideas, prioritize the ideas, and build consensus. A GDSS includes the decision making elements of a DSS, but also includes groupware components to enhance communication. They are designed to support the sharing of information, reduce domination by a few people, and increase participation and commitment from the entire team. Because they can be used in a variety of problem settings, a GDSS may be used by a variety of non-management employees along with all levels of management.

Figure 2.11 illustrates how ThinkTank, a leading web-based GDSS, works.   Using the system, the team leader creates an electronic agenda designed to accomplish the meeting goals. The meeting wizard then alerts participants and sets up necessary URLs for everyone to log into. During the meeting, participants may generate, elaborate and organize ideas.   The participants might also use different tools to help analyze and prioritize the different ideas.   Finally, since all of the input is captured electronically, a variety of reports are available as soon as the meeting is over.

Figure 2.11   ThinkTank, a leading GDSS, supports group work through a variety of activities

Executive Information Systems (EIS)   or **Executive Support Systems (ESS)** provide information in support of strategic decisions.   An EIS is an interactive system that initially displays graphic, summarized information showing ratios or trends, or key performance indicators for the company.   Executives can *drill down* or view more detailed information about areas they select.   An EIS typically incorporates external information such as stock prices from Dow Jones or Interest Rates from major banks.   An EIS typically doesn't make a recommendation for what to do – rather it just provides the information.   While primarily built for strategic management, depending on the focus of the system, you may also see them designed for and used by lower management levels.

Expert Systems (ES)   provide expert advice for a variety of situations.   By capturing the knowledge and wisdom of experts and incorporating it into an information system, companies create a valuable resource that allows the knowledge to be accessed by a wider range of employees.   An added benefit is that the knowledge isn't lost when an employee leaves the organization.   Expert Systems can be used in many different areas.   Ohio State University Health System has been using a Computerized Physician Order Entry (CPOE) expert system.   When a doctor's orders are entered, the system checks the orders against the expert knowledge base looking for allergy alerts, drug interaction and duplication alerts, and radiology and laboratory data.   In a different example, Amerinet, a health-care purchasing group, has provided a disaster-management expert system to its 1,800 hospitals.   The system provides expert support for a range of situations from small-scale internal fires to large-scale bio-terrorism attacks. Compared to other types of systems, one distinguishing characteristic of an ES is that it contains a knowledge base – the rules, data, and procedures followed by an expert in analyzing a situation and making a recommendation.

Enterprise Wide Systems

Enterprise Wide Systems   are designed to integrate information across different functional business areas.   Many companies are moving towards creating these types of systems that support multiple departments, if not the entire enterprise, instead of having different systems for each department or function.   Logically this makes good business sense.   By improving data sharing and integration among the various departments, these systems help business better manage their resources.   Some of the more common enterprise wide systems include supply chain management systems, customer relationship management systems and enterprise resource planning systems.

Supply Chain Management Systems (SCM) track inventory and information related to creating products. A *supply chain* includes the location of facilities and goods, the production capabilities and patterns, the inventory of raw materials through completed products, and the costs and methods of transportation of raw materials through finished products. Simply put, a supply chain management system lets an organization deliver the right goods or services to the right place at the right time. It incorporates raw materials, suppliers, manufacturers, wholesalers, retailers, and consumers. By effectively managing the supply chain, an SCM helps identify what supplies are required, what level of production will meet customer demand, and how products will be shipped to customers.

Adidas America, partnered with United Parcel Service (UPS) to streamline their supply chain and increase their distribution capacity. Adidas ships millions of units of footwear, sportswear and sporting goods each year. The increased flexibility helps them adapt to changing customer demands. They have increased their order accuracy and improved on-time delivery. Figure 2.12 illustrates the benefits that UPS offers its supply chain customers. One of these benefits is leveraging UPS's IT network to provide full visibility into global shipments. This concept is key in supply chain systems. Essentially this means that companies along the supply chain "open their books" so that their partners know exactly what is going on with their part of the chain.

Figure 2.12 UPS offers supply chain management services to its customers

However, as you will learn more about in Chapter 3, getting a real payoff from an information system often involves changes to more than technology. For an SCM project, companies report that real savings will require a major investment in process improvement and a minor investment in the actual technology. But the payoff from these investments can be great. Deere & Company, manufacturers of tractors, lawn mowers and more, was able to dramatically increase on-time factory shipments, decrease aged inventory, and streamline planning tasks, through the implementation of a supply chain management system which ultimately translated into $107 million in increased shareholder value.

Customer Relationship Management Systems (CRM) help businesses build and maintain long-term, profitable relationships with their customers. Businesses know that it is much easier and more profitable to sell to an existing customer than to a new one. With this in mind, CRM systems help businesses integrate sales, marketing and customer support. Using a CRM, businesses can identify and track their best customers, develop targeted marketing campaigns to select customers and track customer contacts. The Las Vegas Hilton, a member of Resorts International Casinos, uses a CRM to enhance player tracking by analyzing both products and customers on the casino floor and develop multi-channel targeted marketing programs.

Figure 2.13 show a model of the customer life cycle, and how the NetSuite CRM system impacts stages of the life cycle. The customer life cycle includes different tasks or stages from a "suspect" all the way through "repurchase." The Oakland Athletics implemented NetSuite in

September 2004. By providing better access to customer data, including new ways of being able to analyze that data, the system has helped the Oakland Athletics better understand customer preferences and improve the effectiveness of their sales representatives by reducing errors and improving tracking of sales leads.

Figure 2.13   NetSuite CRM software illustrates how it impacts the customer life cycle.

Enterprise Resource Planning Systems (ERP) help manage business operations by integrating production processes into one centralized system. An ERP system usually contains a suite of software modules for manufacturing, distribution, finance, human resources. Companies can select which modules they want to implement to create an integrated, unified system to support *back-office* processes. Back-office processes are ones that involve fulfilling a customer order, after the sale has been completed. Replacing separate applications allows for easier access to consolidated information. TrailTech provides state-of-the-art trailer equipment to the agriculture, construction and transportation industries. Through their implementation of an ERP system, TrailTech has improved their Bill of Materials process to significantly reduce inventory inaccuracies, manufacturing backlogs and missed delivery dates. As we learned earlier, the GLOBE system at Nestle is another example of an ERP.

Understanding IT?

ERP systems are an increasingly important way that businesses are integrating technology. The benefits offered by having one centralized system, with data that then can be easily and effectively shared across divisions, can provide significant improvements for a business.

 Navigate to the following website to learn more about ERP systems by viewing the Online Product Tour of the Made2Manage ERP system.

http://www.made2manage.com/made2manage/default.aspx?pageid=12

Write a one to two paragraph summary about the features of the ERP system and the benefits it can provide to adopters of the system.

Were you aware of all of these different types of information systems? To help put these in perspective, Figure 2.14 summarizes where these different information systems are used across the four levels of employees.

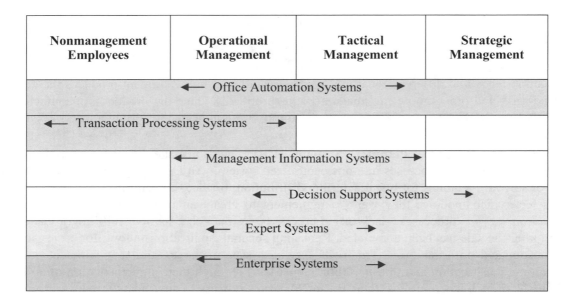

Nonmanagement Employees	Operational Management	Tactical Management	Strategic Management
← Office Automation Systems →			
← Transaction Processing Systems →			
	← Management Information Systems →		
	← Decision Support Systems →		
← Expert Systems →			
← Enterprise Systems →			

Figure 2.14 Usage of different types of information systems by employee level.

As you have seen, businesses have a lot to think about as they look for ways to integrate technology. When a company is looking to create or improve an information system, the starting point is to look at what the system needs to do – does it need to support day-to-day transactions or provide expert analysis and advice. With this in mind, the company will determine the exact components to create a system to meet that need. In Chapter 3 you will learn more about the process companies follow to create an information system. But for now, the last task you will accomplish in this chapter is to take a broad look at information systems that are used within the functional departments of a business to help them operate. This will help you understand some specific ways that companies use information systems to help them accomplish business tasks, support company goals and objectives, and develop a competitive advantage.

LEARNING CHECK
Be sure you can *explain how office automation systems and transaction processing systems support basic business tasks * differentiate among the information systems for decision making * identify three types of enterprise wide systems

INFORMATION SYSTEMS IN THE FUNCTIONAL BUSINESS AREAS

Now that you've learned about the different types of information systems you are ready to see how those systems are put to use in supporting the operations of a business. The internal organizational structure will influence how these systems are designed, the exact functions performed by each system, and how these system interact with each other.

As you learned earlier, businesses are often divided up into different functional areas. These areas typically include human resources, accounting, finance, engineering/product development/ manufacturing, marketing and sales. This section will explore a few of the more common uses of information systems found in these functional areas. Keep in mind that many of these systems are dependent on data initially collected or processed by another system. For example, Figure 2.15 illustrates how the information systems used in the different functional areas are interrelated. When a salesperson enters an order into a transaction processing system, data from this transaction feeds into different departments. The manufacturing department produces the goods, if necessary, and orders more raw materials as appropriate. Once the product is manufactured, the warehouse clerks needs the information to get the shipment ready for shipment. When the order has been shipped, the accounting department will either process the credit card payment or generate an invoice to send to the customer. Finally, the payroll department is able to produce a paycheck. To produce the paycheck, the payroll department needs data from the Order Processing System to know the dollar value of the sales, along with employee data from human resources such as the commission rate and required deductions.

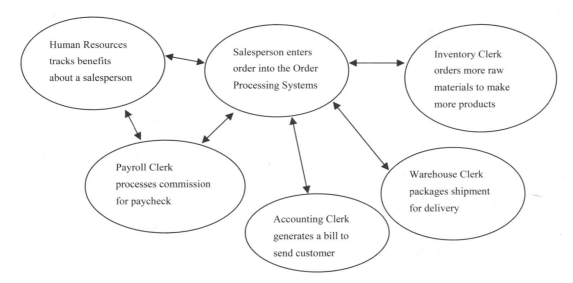

Figure 2.15 The interrelated nature of information systems.

Human Resources

The Human Resources area is responsible for supporting the needs of an organization's employees. Data collected and processed in human resources is used to track job applicants, to maintain personnel records related to salary, payroll, benefits and vacations, to track employee evaluations, promotions, and salary changes, and to produce government reports including W-2 tax information. Employee records management is the broad category for all of these records. In addition, human resources provides corporate training, often through computer-based training, and maintaining records about the training that employees have completed.

Accounting

Accounting departments focus on recording every financial transaction within an organization. They are responsible for ensuring that the financial transactions and data are collected and processed accurately. Information systems within accounting are used to represent the general ledger, which records every financial transaction. The general ledger records the transactions according to various categories. This allows the organization to track accounts receivable (details about money owed to the organization), accounts payable (details about money the organization owes to others), cash and inventory.

Organizations rely on the data within their accounting system to produce various financial reports including balance sheets, cash flow reports and profit-loss reports. The Sarbanes-Oxley Act of 2002 (SOX) had a profound impact on information technology in accounting. The SOX Act, passed in the wake of ethical scandals related to financial and accounting improprieties, requires Chief Executive Officers and Chief Financial Officers to certify the accuracy of all financial reports. Further, it specifies that companies must have adequate internal controls over financial reporting. This includes establishing, evaluating and monitoring the internal controls related to the information systems used to process financial data. IS auditors are utilized to ensure that the correct financial rules are built into the system and performs as needed. In addition to systems to track financial transactions, accounting departments also use asset management systems to track the assets of the organization and cost accounting systems track data about how much it costs to produce products.

Finance

The Finance department is tasked with managing an organizations' money as well as supporting the financial planning needs within an organization. Controllers and treasurers use financial information systems and cash management systems to accomplish these tasks. These systems support budget development, tracking investments, collecting money as soon as possible and making payments as late as possible. Increasingly, these systems use **Electronic Funds Transfer (EFT)** to electronically transfer cash from one bank account to another.

Engineering, Product Development and Manufacturing

Depending on the size and type of firm, engineering, product development and manufacturing may be distinct departments or may be grouped into one department. The work in this department involves determining if changes need to be made to existing products and whether it is profitable to bring a new product to market. Additionally, this area is responsible for deciding on the most economical way to manufacture products, while still ensuring quality. Many different types of information systems support this department. **Computer Aided Design (CAD)** systems decrease the time needed by engineers and designers to develop new products including cars, airplanes, buildings and bridges. CAD systems can be used for rapid prototyping - developing a model very quickly, which then can be more thoroughly analyzed and tested. Automobile manufacturers can print models of cars, which then can be placed in a wind tunnel to test aerodynamics. Bianchi has been a leading Italian manufacturer of bicycles for over 100 years. They produce about 60,000 bikes a year with different models targeted towards racing professionals and mountain riders along with recreational bikers. In 2007 Bianchi started using SolidWorks, a leading 3D-CAD product to aid in the bike and part design process. Through the successful integration of CAD technology, Bianchi has been able to shorten the time to market of new bicycle models while ensuring high quality and strength in the high-stress areas of a bike. Figure 2.16 illustrates a part design model created in SolidWorks for Bianchi.

Figure 2.16 Bicycle part model created using SolidWorks CAD system

The benefits of a CAD system can be broadened when they are linked with other new technologies like 3D printing systems. Strottman International produces promotional toys. Over the last few years, Strottman has migrated from clay models to CAD systems. Recently they purchased a 3D printing system to have greater control over their process. By being able to generate 3D models in a very short time, they have increased sales and paid for the system in just 3 months. Figure 2.17 shows the quality and detail available in a toy train model printed through a 3D printer. By having this model available to show to their customer, Strottman was able to make a sale of a promotional line.

Figure 2.17 Toy train model created with a 3D printer

Computer Aided Manufacturing (CAM) systems can support manufacturing by determining machine settings, production line layouts, and automating the manufacturing process through robotics. When a product is being manufactured, companies may use Inventory Control systems may be used to track and manage inventory. **Supply Chain Management Systems**, which integrate many of these stand-alone systems, may be used to more effectively manage the delivery of items from suppliers to the company.

Marketing and Sales

Establishing and maintaining relationships with customers is critical to any business. Central to this is the ability of a business to conduct market research, targeted marketing campaigns, and sales. Systems to support market research help analyze market demand for products and provide information related to the likely success of different marketing strategies. Increasingly companies are collecting market research data through online surveys. There are a variety of systems that can support the sales functions.

Initially a sales person may use a **Customer Relationship Management System** to help with identifying leads and building customer relationships. At the point that an order is taken, the transaction often is recorded through an order entry system. Order entry systems generally support either point-of-sale transactions (sales recorded at the point of purchase) or e-commerce transactions (sales recorded via the Internet). Once a transaction has been made, the sale then becomes part of the order processing system which ensures that the product is produced and/or delivered to the customer. This may include specific systems to identify the most efficient shipping methods and track the shipment.

As mentioned earlier, these tasks are increasingly being handled through integrated ERP systems which minimize duplicated data and time spent on reentering the same information. Additionally, many of these tasks may be handled through a supply chain management system. Sales Force Automation is another type of system used in this department to help determine the appropriate number of sales persons to assign to different product lines or geographic regions.

LEARNING CHECK
Be sure you can *explain how information systems support the various functional business areas
* illustrate how functional systems can be dependent on other functional systems

PRACTICAL APPLICATION

In this exercise you will have a chance to explore in a bit more depth the usage of an Inventory Management and Sales System. You will use a product called iMagic Inventory.

iMagic is an Australian company that has been developing software for over 15 years. iMagic has developed software solutions for large, multinational companies including Barclays Bank and IBM. They are now focusing on creating products to meet the business needs of small to medium businesses. They offer off-the-shelf solutions to support the reservation needs in a variety of industries including hotel, restaurant, marina and kennel businesses.

Working in groups, as assigned by your instructor, you are going to use their product to allow you to manage and sell inventory. Download a 10-use Trial Copy of iMagic Inventory by going to the following link:

http://www.imagicinventorysoftware.com/

You should see a screen similar to that shown below:

Practical Application Image 1

Take a few minutes to scroll through the screen reading about the features and benefits of the Inventory Control system.

Select the Try It for Free option in the upper right corner of the menu bar. Follow the instructions to download the software.

Once you have installed the software, launch the system. The opening screen should be similar to that shown below:

Practical Application Image 2

Imagine that you are the owner of a retail store. Determine what types of products you will offer.

One of your first tasks is to build the product listing of your inventory. Select the **Inventory** Icon located near the top of the screen. At the Inventory Screen, select the **New Item** button to start building your inventory.

Practical Application Image 3

Your screen should now be similar to the **Item Details** screen shown below. Notice that the only required field is the Item Name. If you truly wanted to use all of the integrated functionality, you would need to navigate to other parts of the system first. For example, notice the drop-down arrow for Vendor. You might want to track details about the different vendors from whom you purchase products. Doing this would allow you to know how many products you get from each vendor. This information might allow you to ask for a discount if you determine that you are purchasing a significant quantity and/or dollar amount from a particular vendor. Vendor information would be entered by selecting **Vendors** on the Menu Bar. Also notice the drop-down arrows for Warehouse and Storage Location. Details about these items would be entered through the **Configure** choice on the Menu Bar.

Given the exploratory nature of our usage, we will not use all of the possible features.

Practical Application Image 4

- Enter the name, long description, sales price, purchase price and the number in stock for at least 3 different products. Enter 0 for the number in stock for one of the items. If you wish to use the Category option, those choices should be entered on the Configure Menu.

Now you are ready to build your list of customers. Select the **Customers** Icon. At the Customer Screen, select the **Add Customer** button. Your screen should now be similar to the **Customer Details** screen shown below.

Practical Application Image 5

- Enter information for at least 3 different customers. All of the fields are not required. Enter different Shipping Information for at least one of the customers.

Congratulations! Now you are ready to create some sales. Select the **New Invoice** Icon. Your screen should now be similar to the **New Invoice** screen shown below. At the New Invoice Screen, you can either enter data for a brand new customer, or you can use the **Customer Search** button to select one of your existing customers. If you select an existing customer, the details will be completed automatically for you. Click on the **Add Order Item** button to select the products that are being ordered. Notice that based on the choices selected, only products are in stock are shown on the listing.

Practical Application Image 6

- Enter at least four different orders. Assign them to a variety of your customers. Have each order be for a subset of the products you have available for sales. Select **Complete Invoice** when you are done with each invoice. Do not print the invoice.

Finally, view some of the reports available to you. Initially select the **Reports** icon. You will see a graphical display of some summary statistics, as shown below.

Practical Application Image 7

- Now select the **Reports** option on the Menu Bar. Try creating a few of the different reports that are available.

Good Job. You have had a chance to explore in more detail how an inventory management and sales system works.

Now let's think about this product from an Information Systems perspective. Based on your exploration, look at the components of this particular system. For each of the components listed below, explain as much as you can from your usage and investigation. You may need to return to the company website for some additional information.

Hardware – explain what hardware is necessary to run the program

Software – this is the program you are using now

Data – explain the data files that are created/used and make more detailed related to the specific data fields they are manipulating in the exercise.

People – identify the different users of the systems

Procedures – explain the common procedures that are used in the system

Networks – explain what networking components are needed

Building on this, let's look in a little bit more detail into the functions of this system. Can you identify what inputs, processing, output, feedback and control are available in the system? You don't need to create an exhaustive list, but try and identify one or two answers for each item. Perhaps look at some of the options that you didn't have available to use (like barcode scanners.)

Input _____

Processing _____

Output _____

Feedback _____

Control _____

Through this exercise you should have gained a deeper understanding of the parts of an information system and how they are linked together. You also should have a better sense of the processes business must use in order to function. For example, you first need to have products available before you can generate sales. You also should have a sense of how the design of an interface can make a system easy, or not so easy, to use. In the iMagic System you hopefully were able to complete the tasks without too much difficulty. The ease of use of a system can greatly influence its ultimate usefulness to an organization.

As you have discovered, information systems can be very complex. As companies look for ways to integrate information technology into their operations they need to be aware of how an information system can help them achieve their objectives. You now have a solid foundation for continuing to explore the information systems puzzle. In the next chapter we will learn more about the process companies use to determine what the correct puzzle pieces, or information system components, are, and how to put them together.

Wrapping IT Up

In this chapter you learned about the different ways that companies use information technology to conduct business. The opening example of Nestle illustrated several ways that Nestle was planning on utilizing information technology. In the chapter you learned how to identify the different components in an information system, and gained a better understanding about the functions that an information system performs. You also learned about supporting the entire enterprise through integrated systems that can manage a supply chain and integrate it with other components in an enterprise resource planning system.

Study Questions Summary

1. What is an information system?
   - An information system is used by organization to collect, manipulate, store and disseminate data or information.
   - Information systems are made up of hardware, software, data, people, procedures, and networks.
   - The exact configuration of these components varies for each system
   - The functions of an information system include input, process, output, feedback and control.

2. What are the information needs of business employees?
   - Employees in an organization are typically classified as either non-management employees, operational management, tactical management or strategic management.
   - Job functions, and information needs, vary by type of employee

- As you move up the levels within an organization, decisions tend to become more unstructured and affect a longer time frame
- Organizational structures define the way work is done within a business
- The three common organizational structures are functional, divisional, and matrix
- Data are raw facts that are collected and stored. Information is data that has been transformed to have meaning.
- Organizations need both internal and external information.
- Information is valuable if it is accurate, complete, economical, relevant, timely, verifiable and accessible.

3. What are the different types of information systems?
    - Office automation systems provide support for common tasks such as communications and presentations.
    - Transaction processing systems, the most widely used type of information system, are used to conduct routine business transactions.
    - Management Information Systems support decision making by providing a wide variety or reporting options.
    - Decision Support Systems, including group decision support systems and executive information systems, help businesses solve decisions by integrating decision models and external information.
    - Expert Systems provide access to expert knowledge and advice to aid in recommending a solution.
    - Enterprise wide systems such as supply chain management, customer relationship management, and enterprise resource planning systems provide integrated support across functional areas.

4. How are information systems used in the functional business areas?
    - Organizations use a wide variety of systems to support the functional business areas.
    - Functional systems often will have a need to access data used in other systems
    - Human resource systems support basic employee records management
    - Accounting systems are responsible for recording every financial transaction in a business
    - The Sarbanes-Oxley Act has increased the scrutiny placed on the accuracy of accounting systems
    - Financial systems help businesses manage their cash assets and improve financial planning
    - CAD/CAM systems are increasingly used to automate engineering and product development.
    - CAM and SCM systems help manufacturing better control the production process
    - CRM systems and order entry systems are vital pieces to the Sales and Marketing Department

Solutions to Chapter Activities

UNDERSTANDING IT?

ATM Problem pgs. 32-33   Complete Answers will be provided

UNDERSTANDING IT?

Nestle pg. 39 - operational management, non management employees, tactical management, strategic management

INTEGRATE IT?

Loan Comparison DSS pgs. 43-44

Question 1: $34,140 ($711) Dealer Option vs $32,758 ($682) Rebate Option. Choose Rebate option based on total cost for a savings of $1,382. (Need to add $8,500 to each for cost of down payment)

Question 2: $42,640 ($888) Dealer Option vs $37,731 ($786) Rebate Option + 4,000. Choose Rebate option based on total cost for a savings of $909.

Key Terms

Page number references are included in parentheses.

Computer Aided Design (CAD) (50)	External information (35)	Organizational structure (38)
Computer Aided Manufacturing (CAM) (51)	Feedback (31)	Output (31)
Control (31)	Functional structure (38)	People (30)
Customer relationship management (CRM) (46)	Group decision support system (GDSS) (44)	Procedures (30)
Data (30, 34)	Hardware (30)	Processing (31)
Decision support system (DSS) (41)	Information (34)	Software (30)
Detailed report (41)	Information system (29)	Strategic management (37)
Divisional structure (38)	Input (31)	Summary report (41)
Electronic fund transfer (EFT) (50)	Internal information (35)	Supply chain management (SCM) (46)
Enterprise resource planning system (ERP) (47)	Management information system (MIS) (41)	Tactical management (37)
Enterprise wide system (45)	Matrix structure (38)	Team-based structure (38)
Exception report (41)	Networks (30)	Transaction (40)
Executive information system (EIS) (45)	Non-management employees (37)	Transaction processing system (TPS) (40)
Executive support systems (ESS) (45)	Office automation system (OAS) (40)	
Expert system (ES) (45)	Operational management (37)	

Multiple Choice Questions

1. Which of the following is not a component of an information system?
   a. Software
   b. Procedures
   c. Hardware
   d. Feedback

2. All of the following are functions performed by an information system except _____?
   a. Feedback
   b. Output
   c. Control
   d. Hardware

3. The most basic organizational structure is _____?
   a. Divisional
   b. Functional
   c. Matrix
   d. Tactical

4. Work at the strategic management level _____.
   a. focuses on functional or departmental areas
   b. is highly structured
   c. often involves creating plans for several years
   d. centers around day to day operations

5. Which of the following is not a characteristic of valuable information?
   a. Accurate
   b. Timely
   c. Complex
   d. Economical

6. A Customer Relationship Management System is an example of a(n) _____.
   a. Office Automation System
   b. Enterprise Wide System
   c. Executive Support System
   d. Expert System

7. Which of the following systems are not used to support decision making?
   a. MIS
   b. GDSS
   c. EIS
   d. OAS

8. An order entry system would be used in which functional area?
   a. Finance
   b. Accounting
   c. Marketing/Sales
   d. Human Resources

9. A report of students with more than 5 overdue library books would be classified as a _____?
   a. MIS report
   b. Detailed report
   c. Summary report
   d. Exception report

10. A(n) _____ is an integrated system that contains software modules for manufacturing, distribution, finance, human resources.
    a. CRM
    b. ERP
    c. EIS
    d. GDSS

11. CAD systems automate which of the following tasks?
    a. payroll
    b. shipping
    c. general ledger
    d. product development

Answers:
1. d   2. d   3. b   4. c   5. c   6. b   7. d   8. c   9. d   10. b   11. d

Review Questions

1. What does an information system do?
2. What are the basic components of an information system?
3. List and explain the functions of an information system.
4. Describe the four basic types of employees and the information needed to accomplish their work.
5. How do TPSs and MISs differ?
6. How can a DSS help make decisions?
7. What are the most common types of information systems used in business today? Give an example of each.
8. What is a supply chain? What are the benefits of a supply chain management system?
9. List the different characteristics of valuable information.
10. Explain how an Executive Information System supports decision making?
11. Provide some examples of the Accounting tasks supported by information technology.
12. What is the impact of Sarbanes-Oxley on information systems?
13. Describe the interrelated nature of information systems in the functional areas.

Projects

1. Starting tomorrow, create a new journal (don't use the one you created in Chapter 1) where you record all of the interactions that you have with information technology. To the extent that you can find information, describe the information systems in terms of components that are visible and functions that you can see being performed.
2. Write a one-page report on how technology affects your daily life.
3. Investigate how information systems are used in your major. Write a one-page report detailing your results.
4. Investigate the current status of the GLOBE project at Nestle. Prepare a one-page report summarizing the business benefits achieved to date.

5. Create a spreadsheet that you can use to record grades for different assignments and exams for a class over the semester. The class has 3 exams (100 points each), a final exam (125 points) and 7 assignments (15 points each). Assume that you earned the following scores to date: Exam 1 – 75 points, Exam 2 – 80 points, Assignment 1 – 10 points, Assignment 2 – 12 points, Assignment 3 – 8 points. Create a DSS component that will allow you to conduct a "what if" analysis to determine what grades you need on the remaining work to achieve a grade of 85% in the class. What grades do you need for a 90% in the class?

6. Search the Internet to find three different Customer Relationship Management systems available to purchase. Compare and contrast the features available. Develop an efficient way to organize and present the results. Include company name, price, location, hardware requirements, software requirements, and the target consumer for the software.

7. Identify an industry in which you are interested. Research an information system that is used in that industry. You need to find a specific information system that is available for purchase. Produce a brief write-up about that product that identifies the following information:

    a. Name of the product
    b. Company that makes the product
    c. Web address for the company & for the specific product (if available)
    d. What are the hardware requirements?
    e. Cost of the product – does it vary based on number of users, etc.?
    f. Target industry for the product
    g. Organization level the product is geared towards (e.g. senior mgt, middle management, etc.)
    h. Type of Information System (e.g. TPS, DSS, etc.)
    i. Brief summary of what the system does – how it works
    j. Benefits of the system (how does the system help an organization?)

BONUS PRACTICAL APPLICATION

In this exercise you will have a chance to expand your understanding about Transaction Processing and Management Information Systems. As you learned in this chapter, a Management Information System allows managers to view reports of the data collected in a Transaction Processing System. In this exercise you are going to work with a system that has both TPS and MIS functionality.

Database Management Systems, which allow companies to capture, process and store large amount of data, are an important information technology tool. In this exercise you are going to work with the Northwind 2007 system built in Microsoft Access. Access is a Database Management System. The Northwind 2007 system was created to help individuals learn about the capabilities of Access. In Chapter 4 you will learn more about using Access to build your own database systems. At this point don't worry that you don't much about databases or Microsoft Access. This exercise is designed to help you get your feet wet and to provide you with a frame of reference for many of the concepts we have introduced so far.

1) Start Microsoft Access 2007 by selecting the Microsoft Office Access 2007 program from the Start button. The opening screen for Access, shown below, will appear. Depending on whether the window is maximized, the exact position of the objects may vary.

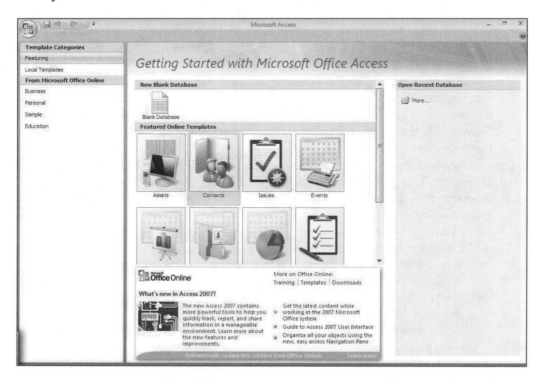

The right side of the opening screen shows a list of recent databases that have been used. Depending on who used Access previously on your computer, the files shown on this side will vary. In the screen shot above, no files are listed since this is the first time Access was used.

2) Locate the Northwind 2007 database system.

Depending on how Access was installed on your computer, the Northwind sample may not have automatically been loaded. The first task is to see if the database is already on your computer.

a. Look in the Open Recent database area.

If you see a listing for Northwind 2007.accdb, click on the Northwind 2007.accdb file to launch the database.
GO TO STEP 3.

If you do not see a listing for Northwind 2007.accdb, click on More… in the Open Recent Database area.

The Open dialog box will appear, similar to that shown below.

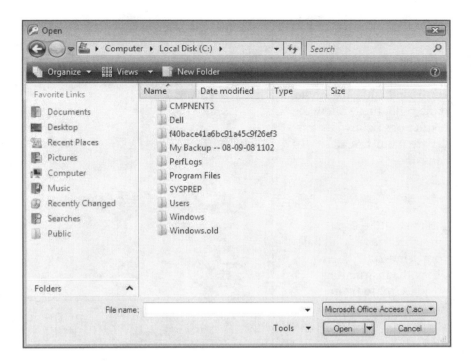

In the Search Box of the Open Dialog Box window, enter Northwind. If the file is on your computer, it will be displayed in the listing of folders and files.

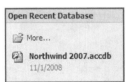

If the file is found, select the file and click on the Open button. **GO TO STEP 3.**

If the file is not found, perform the tasks below, described in step "b".

b. Load the Northwind 2007 database onto your computer.

Click on Local Templates. ⟶

(*Located in the Template Categories pane of the Opening Screen.*)

The middle portion of the main screen, shown below, will change to display the list of templates that are available locally on your computer.

If the list of the local templates includes Northwind 2007, as shown to the right, then follow the instructions below labeled **Create from Local Template**.

If the list of the local templates does not include Northwind 2007, then follow the instructions labeled **Create from Sample.**

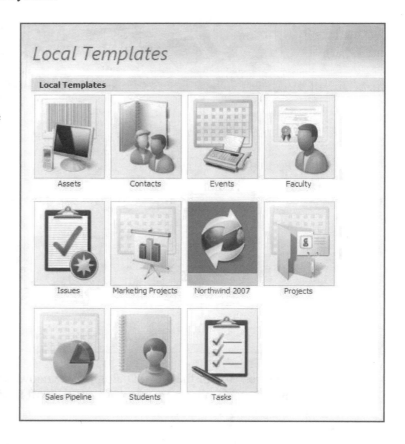

Create From Local Template

Click on the Northwind 2007 icon in the local templates pane.

The right pane of the main opening screen will change as shown to the right.

Make any necessary changes to the path of the file by clicking on the file folder icon.

Select the Create button to create the sample database. <u>**GO TO STEP 3.**</u>

Create From Sample

If the Local Templates did not include Northwind 2007 you will download the file from Microsoft Office Online. Make sure that you are connected to the Internet before you continue.

In the From Microsoft Office Online, click on Sample.

(*Located in the Template Categories pane of the Opening Screen.*)

The middle portion of the main screen, shown to the right, will change to display the list of sample templates that are available.

Click on the Northwind 2007 icon in the Sample pane.

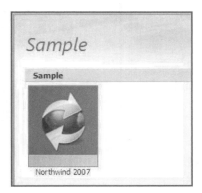

The right pane of the screen will change as shown to the right.

Make any necessary changes to the path of the file by clicking on the file folder icon.

Select the Create button to create the sample database. **CONTINUE ON TO STEP 3.**

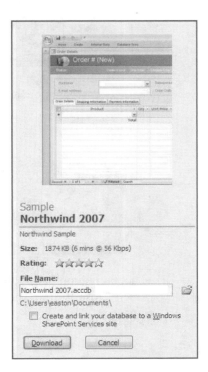

3) Using the Northwind 2007 database system.

Once you have opened the Northwind 2007.accdb file, the opening screen for the Northwind Traders system will appear. The screen will either have the Access navigation pane open (top figure) or closed (bottom figure.)

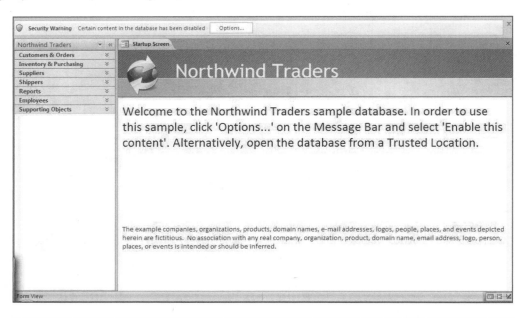

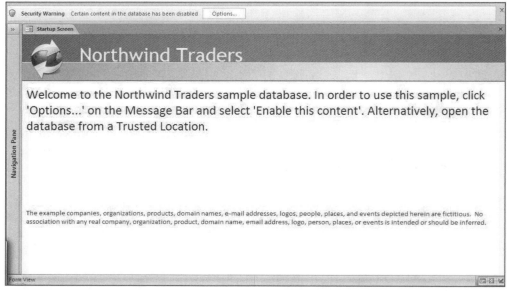

The navigation pane can be opened and closed by pressing on the Shutter Bar Open/Close Button, shown to the right. For this exercise leave the navigation pane closed.

In the main screen, click on the Options button in the Message Bar.

The security alert message box, shown below, appears. The security alert, standard with all Microsoft Access databases, warns you about the possibility of unsafe code (VBA Macro code) residing inside of an application program. If you trust the source of your program then you can enable the content.

Select the Enable this content radio button and click OK. You are now ready to start using the system. The Login Dialog box will be the first screen that displays.

You will begin your exploration in the role of Nancy Freehafer, a sales representative. Use the drop-down arrow to select Nancy Freehafer. Click on the Login button.

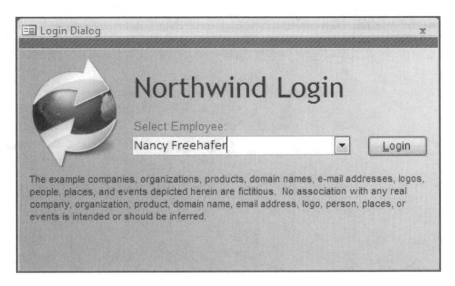

The main screen of the system will appear, as shown below.

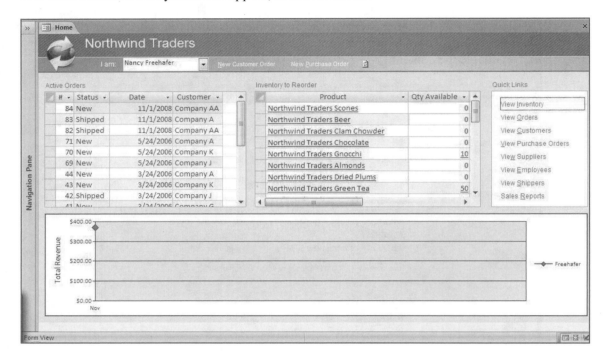

The sample database has been designed to simulate a fictional company, Northwind Traders, which sells specialty food products to different customers. For demonstration purposes, the company names of their customers are simply entered as Company A through Company CC.

Explore the Transaction Processing System Side of Northwind Traders

Task One: You have noticed that the quantity available for many of your products, visible in the Inventory to Reorder window, is running low. Click on View Inventory in the Quick Links to view the details of your inventory list. Click on the purchase button for several of the products that have a number greater than 0 in the Qty to Reorder column. Click on Home in the Menu Bar to return to the Home tab. Now that your inventory has been replenished you can return to the job of processing orders for your customers.

Task Two: One of your customers, Anna Hellung-Larsen from Company AA, has called to place an order. Click on New Customer Order in the menu bar of the Home Tab. Company AA has requested 10 units of Northwind Traders Ravioli. This week the Ravioli is on special with a 10% discount. On the shipping tab, indicate the order should be shipped using Shipping Company A. The order should be shipped 5 days from now. The shipping fee is $10.00.

Your completed order will be similar to that shown in the following screen:

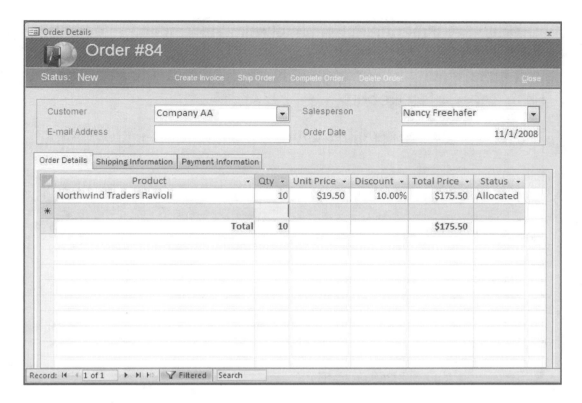

When you have completed the order, click on Close in the menu bar. Access automatically saves an order when you "leave" or close the record.

Evaluate some of the system features.

Did you notice how the order form provided you with drop down lists to select customers, salepersons, and products? Did you notice that the company address was automatically completed for you on the Shipping Information tab?
> These features help ensure accuracy of the information and save time entering information that the systems already knows.

Explore the Management Information System Side of Northwind Traders

Assume that you are now Steven Thorpe, a sales manager. In the menu bar, in the drop down arrow next to menu bar choice of "**I am**" select Steven Thorpe. Notice that the information in the Active Orders portion of the screen was updated. In this case, you don't have any active orders that you created.

One of your tasks is to analyze the sales trends of different products. Click on the Sales Report choice in the Quick Links area. Make the following selections: *Sales by Category* report, select Yearly Sales as the sales period, and enter 2006 for the Year.

If you get a message box indicating that the text (2006) isn't in the list, select the choice edit the items in the list. Update the default value if desired and click OK.

On the Sales Report Dialog box, select Preview to see the report. Your report should look similar to the following screen: (if prompted to save your changes select yes.)

Yeary Sales Report

Saturday, November 01, 2008   4:07:14 PM

2006

Product	Q1	Q2	Q3	Q4	Total
Northwind Traders Coffee	$14,720.00	$230.00	$0.00	$0.00	$14,950.00
Northwind Traders Beer	$1,400.00	$5,418.00	$0.00	$0.00	$6,818.00
Northwind Traders Marmalade	$0.00	$3,240.00	$0.00	$0.00	$3,240.00
Northwind Traders Mozzarella	$0.00	$3,132.00	$0.00	$0.00	$3,132.00
Northwind Traders Clam Chowder	$1,930.00	$868.50	$0.00	$0.00	$2,798.50
Northwind Traders Curry Sauce	$680.00	$1,920.00	$0.00	$0.00	$2,600.00
Northwind Traders Chocolate	$1,402.50	$1,147.50	$0.00	$0.00	$2,550.00
Northwind Traders Boysenberry Spread	$250.00	$2,250.00	$0.00	$0.00	$2,500.00
Northwind Traders Crab Meat	$0.00	$2,208.00	$0.00	$0.00	$2,208.00
Northwind Traders Dried Apples	$530.00	$1,590.00	$0.00	$0.00	$2,120.00
Northwind Traders Ravioli	$0.00	$1,950.00	$0.00	$0.00	$1,950.00
Northwind Traders Fruit Cocktail	$0.00	$1,560.00	$0.00	$0.00	$1,560.00
Northwind Traders Dried Pears	$300.00	$900.00	$0.00	$0.00	$1,200.00
Northwind Traders Cajun Seasoning	$220.00	$660.00	$0.00	$0.00	$880.00
Northwind Traders Chocolate Biscuits M	$552.00	$230.00	$0.00	$0.00	$782.00
Northwind Traders Green Tea	$598.00	$0.00	$0.00	$0.00	$598.00
Northwind Traders Olive Oil	$0.00	$533.75	$0.00	$0.00	$533.75
Northwind Traders Syrup	$0.00	$500.00	$0.00	$0.00	$500.00

Evaluate some of the system features.

Was your report standardized or ad-hoc?
> Even though you were given the chance to select a specific category, this is still a standardized report. If you had been able to change the fields you want to display on the report, then it would be an ad-hoc report.

Did you create a detailed, summary or exception report?
> Since you are only showing totals for the products across all of the orders, this is a summary report.

Can you think of a way to make the reporting from the system better?
> You might consider allowing the supervisor to select multiple categories or products – right now you can either see totals for everything or only one category or product. You might also consider allowing more flexibility in the date range, instead of limiting it to one month, quarter or year.

Exit Microsoft Access when you are done. This exercise gave you a brief, hands-on introduction into seeing both the transaction processing and management information reporting sides of a system built using Microsoft Access.

CHAPTER **3**

Information Systems Development

PLANNING AHEAD
After reading Chapter 3, you should be able to answer these questions in your own words

STUDY QUESTIONS
Why study systems development?
What activities cross the different life cycle stages?
What happens during each stage of the systems development life cycle?
What are some other approaches to developing information systems?

LEARNING PREVIEW

In Chapter 2 you had a chance to look at different types of information systems and how organizations use them for a competitive advantage. In this chapter you will look at how organizations actually create these systems. Whether you are working on a transaction processing system (TPS) designed to track checked-out books at a library or a decision support system (DSS) to help create a balanced investment portfolio, information systems are created by following a process. Your involvement in that process may vary. While some of you may participate as the IT specialist who actually builds a system, many of you will participate as an end-user. But no matter your role, all business students need to understand the process of developing information systems.

OPENING VIGNETTE

Will Miami-Dade County cast a vote for E-voting?

In the aftermath of the hanging-chad controversy from the 2000 presidential election, Miami-Dade County invested in an e-voting system. They selected a new system using touch-screen technology from Election Systems & Software Inc, an Omaha-based software developer. The new system, installed in 2002, replaced the old punch-card machines responsible for the hanging-chads. But the voting problems have not gone away. Instead there are ongoing technical glitches with the new system.

Coding errors were made by county personnel. These errors resulted in the iVotronic system undercounting votes in five local elections. The problem escalated in a countywide election on March 8, 2005. Hundreds of votes were uncounted. ES&S, the developers of the system, stand behind the integrity of the iVotronic system. Ultimately the problems were determined to be the result of human error and the responsibility for the coding errors was that of Miami-Dade County.

The situation has gotten so bad that Constance Kaplan, the county elections supervisor resigned and county election officials are considering scrapping their $25 million investment in the e-voting system and possibly switching to optical scanning equipment. But because the state has mandated a very strict deadline for counties to switch to automated voting systems, some argue that optical scanners really are not an option. The list of possible vendors and technologies has also been limited by the state. One solution that some argue will help the current situation is to have the system provide a printed receipt of the vote. Since touch screens don't produce an actual, physical ballot that each user can inspect before casting their vote, some critics argue that the systems are susceptible to fraud and errors. State regulations in Florida don't allow printers to be used with the electronic voting systems.

Is it worth it in the long run to switch to optical technology? The old punch-card system cost between $1 million and $2 million dollars per election. Keeping the old systems wasn't an option due to new state requirements. But costs to run elections have dramatically increased using the new system. Aside from the initial $25 million investment in the iVotronic system, the cost to now conduct an election rose to $6.6 million in the November 2004 election. Some of that was attributed to increased transportation costs in moving the equipment back and forth to polling locations.

Lester Sola, the new elections supervisor, was not involved in the initial decision to purchase the touch screen systems. Across the state, about half of the state's voters are currently using touch screen systems to cast their votes with the rest of the voters using optical scanning technology. Although other election's chiefs using the same iVotronic system see no reason to move away from their systems, Sola is recommending that the county switch to optical scanning to save money and increase voter confidence. Previous estimates about the cost of optical scanning are between $3 million to $10 million. Why didn't Miami-Dade select optical scanning instead of touch screens? Sola indicates that officials thought optical scanning would still allow for the same types of problems found in punch-card technology.

(Sources: Compiled from Marc L. Songini, "E-voting may face recall in Florida County," *ComputerWorld*, April 18, 2005,   http://www.computerworld.com/databasetopics/data/story/0,10801,101146,00.html accessed 8/8/05; and   Marc L. Songini, "Fate of $25M e-voting system in Miami-Dade dangling," *ComputerWorld*, April 14, 2005, http://www.computerworld.com/governmenttopics/government/policy/story/0,10801,101105,00.html - accessed 5/30/06; and George Bennett, "Miami-Dade's elections chief wants to boot touch-screen system," Palm Beach Post, June 6, 2005, http://www.verifiedvotingfoundation.org/article.php?id=5821, accessed 5/30/06)

In this chapter you will have a chance to explore the ideas introduced in this vignette. You will learn about how companies develop information systems, and how they can avoid some of the problems introduced in the case. By the end of this chapter you will be able to answer the following questions about this story:

- What was the reason why the new system was implemented?
- What kind of installation approach do you think Miami-Dade used? Could they have used other approaches?
- Discuss how a system like this can be tested.
- What factors would you include in a recommendation on whether to switch to the optical scanning system?
- What would you recommend that the County should have done differently?

VISUAL ORGANIZATION OF CHAPTER

Study Question 1	Study Question 2	Study Question 3	Study Question 4
Systems Development	Activities that Cross Phases of the Life Cycle	The Systems Development Life Cycle	Approaches to Systems Development
• Adding value to an organization • What is the Systems Development Life Cycle? • The Project Team • Increasing the Probability of Project Success	• How can you manage a project? • Is a project worth doing? • Getting the facts • Documenting the process and the system	• Planning • Analysis • Design • Implementation • Support	• Prototyping • End user development • Rapid application development • Object-oriented software development • Outsourcing
Learning Check 1	Learning Check 2	Learning Check 3	Learning Check 4

SYSTEMS DEVELOPMENT

Organizations spend a tremendous amount of money on Information Systems, and increasingly rely on them for the basic operations of their business. In 2005 the median Information Systems budget for U.S. and Canadian IS organizations was $10.8 million, approximately 1.7% of annual revenues (Source: Computer Economics 2005/2006 Information Systems Spending and Technology Trends). It is important for an organization to be certain that they are spending their money wisely. The Standish Group International in their 2003 report found that only 34% of major IT projects were completed on time, 51% finished with some problems (such as over budget, over schedule and/or lacking significant functionality), and 15% of the projects were considered failures (Source: Chaos Report by The Standish Group International.)

Systems Development is a set of activities designed to produce an information system that solves a business problems or meets a business need. These activities help a business investigate a business situation, designing a solution to improve that situation, and ultimately build and implement that solution.

Adding Value to an Organization

Why is it important for all students to have an understanding about information systems development? To help avoid problems like we saw in the e-voting vignette, you need to become aware of what it takes to successfully develop an information system. You also need to be aware of the fact that developing and implementing information systems is much broader than just building the technology piece. Even if you develop the best system, users may be reluctant to use the system if the tasks associated with introducing this new system have not been handled correctly. For example, new systems often will require changes in business processes and organizational structures in order for users to switch to the new system. These changes can be very large and complex and require the involvement of many people across the organization. In some cases these changes may involve updates to job descriptions and classifications which may require contract negotiations with employee unions.

Your knowledge about systems development can help ensure that your organization spends its IT money wisely, that they get a system that meets their needs, and that users have a smooth transition.

Before looking at the process organizations follow to create new systems, it is helpful to first look at four of the reasons why organizations decide to create new systems or to change existing systems. Some of these reasons include

- Problems in existing systems need to be corrected – the current system (manual or computerized) doesn't work properly. This may be caused by errors or defects from the original design, or may be as a result of changes made to other systems in the organization.
- Existing systems need additional features – the current system may not provide all of the functionality needed.
- Outside groups may mandate a change – the government may enact new laws that require you to capture different data or provide certain security controls on the data you collect.
- Competition may lead to change – changes in common business practices may provide a compelling reason to create a new system. For example, if the majority of your competitors provide fully-functional online shopping, you may need to create this capability to remain competitive.

Sometimes you may uncover multiple reasons to work on a system. But keep in mind that the main reason why an organization embarks on a systems development project is to add value to the organization. An organization shouldn't be building a new system "just because" there is a new technology. You need to clearly define the business case – what are the business benefits from this project. Keep in mind that just about every IT project is really just a business project that has an IT component. By following the guidelines in a standardized process, like the Systems Development Life Cycle (SDLC), organizations have the best chance of achieving the business benefits by minimizing their chances of failure and increasing their likelihood of getting systems that meet their needs.

What is the Systems Development Life Cycle?

Recall that the components found in an Information System are hardware, software, people, procedures, data and networks. So how do you discover which of these components will be needed in a new system and the exact specifications for each of these components? Most organizations follow a standardized process like the Systems Development Life Cycle to help them answer these questions.

The **Systems Development Life Cycle** is a structured approach used to build information systems. The SDLC involves 5 phases that a developer will follow when creating a system. The phases of the SDLC, including their main purpose, are:

1. Planning – Determine the problem and whether it is feasible to solve
2. Analysis – Identify what the new system will do
3. Design – Establish how the new system will work
4. Implementation – Build and install the new system
5. Support – Maintain the system

Figure 3.1 identifies the main activities of each phase. Notice that the arrows connecting each phase provide for opportunities to return to a previous phase. Additionally, at the end of each phase the company makes a decision about whether to continue. You may encounter organizations that use an SDLC with more or fewer than 5 phases. What is important to remember is that the same activities are there – they are just packaged differently.

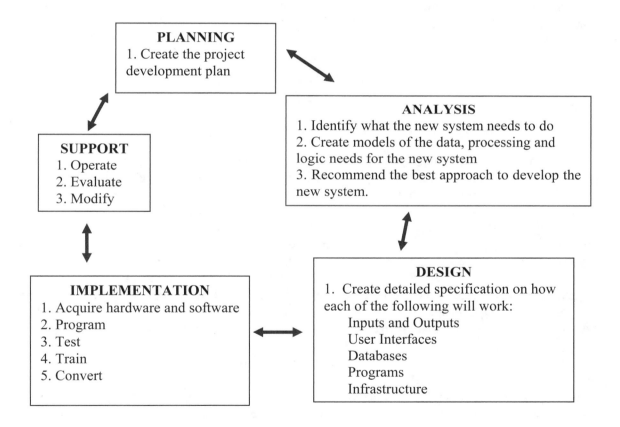

Figure 3.1 An overview of the Systems Development Life Cycle

The starting point for a new system is a project request or proposal. Organizations typically will have many more requests for information systems projects than they have resources to complete. A proposed project is usually submitted as a *project request* that will briefly explain the purpose of the project and the expected value to the business. Often project requests will identify the *project sponsor*, usually a high-level manager who will provide leadership and support for the project. Project requests may be created by users or systems analysts. In many organizations a **steering committee** performs an initial screening of the project requests to determine whether to begin an investigation of the project. The steering committee is typically made up of senior executives and managers from the different division in the organization. Often you will also find non-management user representatives and IT personnel on the committee.

The Project Team

Many different people are involved in the development of an information system. Collectively this group is known as the **project team**. As illustrated in Figure 3.2, the project team usually consists of user representatives from departments that will use the system, the project leader, the systems analyst, and other IT technical specialists. Recall from our analogy in Chapter 1 that an information system is similar to putting together a puzzle. From the project team perspective, the participants then may be considered experts on the different puzzle pieces or on the process of putting together a project. The **project leader** is in charge of the entire project. They manage the schedule and control the budget to ensure that the project meets the original goals, is finished on time and within budget.

Figure 3.2 The Project Team works together to develop an information system

The **systems analyst** is responsible for analyzing, designing and developing the information system. This includes identifying ways to improve the current process, developing solutions, and training and motivating users to work with the new system. The analyst serves as a critical link in bridging the communication between the users (who may have limited experience with technology) and the IT technical specialists. They help users identify the requirements of the new system and transform those requirements into technical specifications. To be successful a systems analyst must have excellent communication skills, technical skills, and interpersonal skills. They need to be creative and to be able to work with people at all levels of the organization. The systems analyst is sometimes called the *systems developer* or *systems designer*. Depending on the size and complexity of the project you may have more than one analyst. Additionally, the systems analyst may or may not serve as the project leader.

The other *IT technical specialists* involved with the project typically specialize in one area of IT. For example, a network engineer may be given the task of designing, installing and maintaining the computer network necessary for the system. The number and type of technical specialists will vary with the specific requirements of each project. Some of these specialists include database administrators, programmers, and web developers. In the later chapters where we talk more about these specialties you will learn more about their unique jobs. For example, we will learn more about network engineers and the computer network in Chapter 5.

Finally, we have the **user representatives**. Users, as a general term, encompass all employees and managers who will be interacting with and using the system. Since it is not practical to include all of the system users in the development effort, on the project team you typically will find a few user representatives. These team members are not specialists about any one puzzle piece, but they serve a very important role to ensure that the final puzzle is correct. This is accomplished by clearly explaining the needs of the users who will actually use the system and staying involved through design, development and testing – ensuring that those needs are ultimately met in the finished product. They should represent a good cross-section of employees across different departments, experience levels, needs from the system, etc. Keep in mind that sometimes your users will include customers or other people external to your organization. Depending on the reach of the system, it could be important to include their input in the development process to help ensure success of the project.

Complete the **Understanding IT** exercise below to reinforce your understanding about the systems development life cycle and the people involved with it.

Understanding IT?

Many different tasks are done during the development of an information system.

For each task identified in the table below, fill in the correct choice for the phase of the SDLC where this task will most likely occur and fill in the correct choice for the project team member most likely to complete the task.

Task	Occurs in which SDLC phase?	Performed by which project team member?
1. Install the computer network		
2. Build additional reporting capability to interface with a newly acquired system		
3. Fill in a questionnaire about what their department needs the new system to do		
4. Plan out the necessary tasks for the project		
5. Create sketches of the user interface screens for the new system		
6. Train new employees on how to use the system		

SDLC choices: Planning, Analysis, Design, Implementation, Support
Project Team Member choices: User, Project leader, Network engineer, System Analyst/Developer, Programmer, Help Desk

When you are finished, check your answers at the end of the chapter.

Increasing the probability of project success

As you begin to study the issues involved with developing an information system, it will be helpful for you to be aware of some of the most common factors that influence the success of an information systems project. These success factors include:

- Involve users throughout the development of the system. This needs to be broader than just the users who are on the project team. Look for ongoing ways to keep users involved.
- Identify reasons that users are resistant to change and develop a plan to mitigate the impact of the change.
- Ensure that the project development schedule is realistic.
- Ensure that the project expectations are realistic. There must be a clearly defined understanding of what the system will do as well as clearly identified methods to measure project success.
- Ensure that the project has visible management support.
- Choose a manageable level of project complexity and risk. The project team should have proven experience with projects of comparable size and with projects developed with similar technology.
- Develop complete and clear programming specifications. The IT specialists who will create the system must have a clear understanding of the system requirements.
- Ensure that a thorough testing plan has been created and followed.
- Ensure that the system implementation has been well planned and is appropriate.

Keep these in mind as you continue to read, and look for ways to make sure they are done well by using the tools and techniques explained in this chapter.

LEARNING CHECK
Be sure you can *explain how information systems add value to an organization *explain what the systems development life cycle is *describe the makeup of the project team including the tasks of the project leader and systems analyst * discuss the factors that influence the success of a project

ACTIVITIES THAT CROSS PHASES OF THE LIFE CYCLE

As you learned earlier, the SDLC contains 5 phases. Later you will learn more specifics about those phases. But some project activities will occur across more than one of the phases of the life cycle. These activities include project management, feasibility assessment, data/information gathering, and documentation.

How can you manage a project?

Project management involves planning, scheduling and controlling the activities involved in developing a system. The larger a system, the more tasks and people involved – resulting in a more difficult project to manage. However, all projects, even small ones, need some project management. Remember that the project leader works to ensure that the project meets the original goals, is finished on time and within budget. To accomplish this, the project leader must create a **project plan**, a document that explains what the new system will do, what tasks are needed, how long it will take and how much it will cost to build the new system. Specifically, the project plan will contain the following:

- The project scope – a clear understanding of the exactly what the new system will do (system objectives) and how it will be evaluated (system success measures). The **project scope** sets the boundaries on what will be done.
- The tasks that need to be done to accomplish the project goals
- Time estimates for each task
- Cost estimates for each task
- A work breakdown structure – identifies the order in which tasks must be completed and which tasks can be completed at the same time

The project plan sets the *project deadline* – the date the project will be completed. Sometimes there may be penalties associated with not meeting a deadline. As a result, it is important that accurate estimates be used in developing the schedule so that the project deadline can be met. There are many tools available to help the project leader create the project plan and to ensure that the project is on schedule.

One tool used to create and manage the project schedule is a **Gantt chart**. A Gantt chart, as illustrated in Figure 3.3, is a bar chart that identifies tasks and deadlines. It provides a quick way to see how long different tasks will take. Sometimes the bars will be color-coded to indicate similar tasks or to compare the initial schedule to actual progress.

Figure 3.3   Gantt charts show project tasks and deadlines

Another tool the project leader can use to estimate times for each task is called a **Program Evaluation and Review Technique (PERT) Chart.** With PERT you identify the shortest possible time, most likely time, and the longest possible time for each activity. A formula is then used to arrive at a single time estimate. PERT is often used to identify the *critical path*, the tasks in a project that depend on each other, and collectively determine the length of the whole project. Any change in the time it takes to accomplish a task on the critical path will affect the overall length of the project. Even without being an expert in PERT, notice how easily you can determine the critical path of the project shown in Figure 3.4.

Figure 3.4 A PERT Chart highlights the critical path of a project

Project management software can be used to help automate the tasks associated with managing the project. Popular project management software packages include Microsoft Office Project Professional 2007, Super Project by Computer Associates and Project Planner by Primavera. By using these tools, the team can update the schedule as tasks are completed. The project leader can view an up-to-date schedule and identify possible problem areas when tasks are behind schedule. Project management software can help a business schedule their resources more effectively, stay on track and within budget, and more effectively manage multiple projects. Many of you will study more about project management software, including how to create and use PERT and Gantt charts in a project management or operations management course.

Having a well defined project plan will help avoid **scope creep**. Scope creep is when new requirements are added to an already approved project. Scope creep can cause many problems including delaying the completion date and causing the project to cost more than anticipated.

Finally it is important for the project leader to have a realistic understanding of the complexities of the specific project and the amount of work that the project team can be expected to accomplish by certain deadlines. While organizational managers and users may try to push to have a project completed earlier, if the project leader develops an unrealistic schedule it will only start the project off on the wrong foot. Hopefully you won't be involved in a project that uses an unrealistic schedule such as the one illustrated in the Dilbert cartoon shown in Figure 3.5.

Figure 3.5 Project managers must develop realistic schedules for a project to succeed

Although the project leader is the person responsible for determining the schedule, the user representatives and the steering committee should critically analyze whether the proposed schedule is realistic. Some of the questions they should ask include: what is the project manager's experience on similar projects (similar size, complexity, staff), what percentage of their projects finish on-time and on-budget, and what tools did they use to help them in creating the estimates.

Is a project worth doing?

Early in the project it is important to determine the **business case** for completing a project. The business case identifies what the organization will gain from the project along with the expected costs and limitations. It is important to ensure that the business case includes information on how this project is aligned with the overall goals and mission of the organization. Additionally, the business case will contain the results of the **feasibility analysis** conducted by the project team. The feasibility analysis helps the organization determine if the project is worth doing. Some common measures of feasibility are described below:

- **Technical feasibility** – Do we have the technical skills to be able to build this system? Does the technology exist, or is it stable enough, to enable the system to be built?
- **Economic feasibility** – Will the benefits gained from the system outweigh the costs to build and operate the system?
- **Organizational feasibility** – How easily will the users adapt to the new system? Will the system be disruptive to existing organizational processes?
- **Schedule feasibility** – Can we build the system within an acceptable time frame?

While each of these feasibility measures serves an important role, the bottom line in many projects is the economic feasibility. Economic feasibility is often calculated through a *cost-benefit analysis*. At the early stages of a project this can be very difficult to calculate. As a project progresses, the analyst should be able to provide more accurate estimates of the costs and benefits. The costs of the new system are often broken down into two categories:

- *one-time development costs* (non-recurring)
- *operational costs* (on-going).

Examples of one-time development costs include hardware for the new system and the development of the system. Operational costs can include maintenance agreements, software licenses and operating costs of the new system. Likewise, benefits are often classified as either:

- *tangible benefits* (easily measured with a dollar value)
- *intangible benefits* (difficult to measure with a dollar value).

Some examples of tangible benefits are reducing processing costs, reducing errors, and increasing sales. Some examples of intangible benefits are improving employee morale and increasing customer goodwill.

The following scenario provides an excerpt of some benefits that may be obtained from an information system for child welfare.

The United States Department of Health and Human Services states that a comprehensive child welfare information system "will result in more efficient and effective practices in administering child welfare programs which in turn will ultimately result in improved service delivery. *The emphasis is not solely on cost reduction but on program improvement.*" The Department provides some general benefits that may be realized by these systems including:

- *Controls costs* by supporting children in their homes, where possible - and where not, by placing them as soon as possible in permanent care,
- *Reduces administrative casework*, allowing caseworkers more time for contact with clients, analysis, and decision-making, and
- *Reduces cases in the long-term by identifying solutions that work.*

They also illustrate that as departments work to clarify these general objectives they may end up with more specific benefits including:

- Reduce Aid to Families with Dependent Children (AFDC) overpayments to families with children in foster care
- Reduce response time for initiating the investigation of child abuse/neglect (CA/N) reports
- Reduce pre-printed forms costs.
- Increase amount of child support collected.
- Increase worker satisfaction.
- Increase the pool of foster care homes.

Source: Feasibility, Alternatives, and Cost/Benefit Analysis Guide and the Companion Guide: Cost/Benefit Analysis Illustrated (for generic public benefit systems) published by the U.S. Department of Health and Human Services, Office of State Systems (OSS) of the Administration for Children and Families (ACF). http://www.acf.hhs.gov/programs/cb/systems/sacwis/cbaguide/chapterone.htm accessed 11/18/08

It is important to remember that the system users are the experts related to the business processes, users play an important role in helping the systems analyst estimate costs and benefits of the proposed system. For example, users can help to estimate the dollar value of "reducing data input errors by 15%" or "reducing customer service requests by 12%". Once the costs and benefits have been determined, the systems analyst will typically calculate several different measures of economic feasibility including Net Present Value (NPV), Internal Rate of Return (IRR), Payback, and Return on Investment (ROI).

To help you better understand these measures of feasibility, we will briefly discuss an example using the Payback measure of feasibility. Payback is used to calculate the length of time required to recover the costs of an investment. Assume that you are considering purchasing a new information system for $25,000. This new system is expected to provide better inventory management which will increase the speed at which you can process sales as well as reduce the number of errors. These benefits are expected to result in an increase in revenue of $7,000 per year. How long will it take you to recoup the cost of the system? To determine the answer you take the cost of the system divided by the savings. In this case $25,000/$7,000 = 3.57. This means that if you are planning on using the system for at least 3 ½ years you will realize a financial benefit.

Figure 3.6 shows an example of an Excel spreadsheet used for a feasibility assessment. At this point it is not important that you understand the complete details about these calculations. Many of you will be learning more about how to use these financial techniques in a finance or managerial accounting course. The analysis shows details about the benefits that the proposed system will offer, along with both the one-time development costs as well as the ongoing operational costs. The summary analysis shows that the business will have a 16.6% overall return on their investment. Additionally, when factoring in the time value of money to obtain the discounted costs and benefits, the overall net present value for the project is $48,108. From an economic standpoint it looks like this project would be worth pursuing. Of course, the other measures of feasibility still will need to be evaluated, and the overall feasibility of this project must be compared with the overall feasibility of any other potential projects.

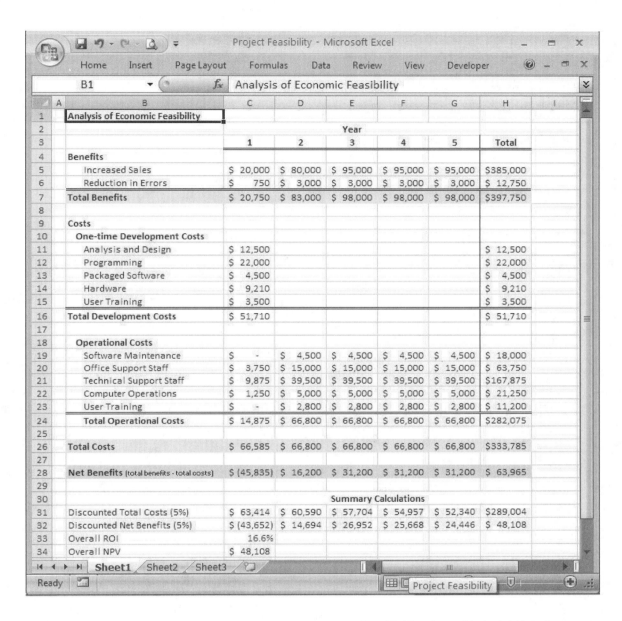

Figure 3.6 Economic feasibility analyses, such as this one developed in Excel, provide insight into the economic costs and benefits of an information system

Complete the **Integrate IT** exercise below to expand your understanding of economic feasibility and to gain additional knowledge about working with spreadsheets.

Integrate IT

Spreadsheets, such as the one shown in Figure 3.6, are useful tools for performing calculations. As you begin to learn how spreadsheets can be used to help you solve business problems it is useful to explore issues related to spreadsheet design. Open the Excel Workbook "Project Feasibility.XLSX" that you have downloaded from Blackboard. It contains the Economic Feasibility spreadsheet shown in Figure 3.6. Analyze the Economic Feasibility spreadsheet by addressing the questions raised below. Once complete, check your answers at the end of the chapter.

A formula is used in cell C31 to calculate the Discounted Total Costs. This formula is: =C26/(1+0.05)^C3

Click in cell C31. Notice how the 5% Discount Rate (the interest rate) is "hard coded" into the formula. One benefit of using a spreadsheet model is to easily perform "what if" calculations. For example, what if the business thought they could only get a Discount Rate of 4%? Or if the Discount Rate was increased to 7%?

❖ Discuss the impact of hard coding values, like the 5% rate, into formulas. What could be done to the design of the spreadsheet to make it easier to perform these "what if" calculations?

❖ To help address this problem you have decided to create an area in your worksheet where you can enter these "assumption values." This area will be located below row 35. In cell B36 enter Economic Feasibility Assumptions. This will serve as a label for this area. Enter the discount rate in cell C38. Enter an appropriate label in cell B38. Change the formula in cell C31 to remove the hard coded 5% and instead reference the discount rate in C38.

Did you enter =C26/(1+$C$38)^C3 as your formula? The dollar signs indicate that C38 is an *absolute cell reference*. This means that when the formula is copied into a different cell, the C38 cell will not change. This makes sense because the Discount Rate is always in cell C38. The other cells are called *relative cell references*. This means that they will change to reference a different cell when the formula is copied. Tutorial 1 discusses absolute and relative cell references in more detail.

❖ You have decided that your economic feasibility spreadsheet will look better if you place the assumptions area on a separate worksheet. Cut the assumptions area (B36 through C38) and paste into cell A1 on Sheet2. Rename Sheet2 to Assumptions by right-clicking on the worksheet tab. Select *Rename* and enter Assumptions as the new name. Go back to Sheet1 and look at the formula in cell C31. The formula was updated to reference the discount rate stored in cell B3 on the Assumptions sheet. You will learn more about using different worksheets in Tutorial 3.

❖ Discuss the use of fonts, colors, alignment, line spacing and borders and how they support or detract from the readability of the spreadsheet

Once each individual feasibility measure has been determined, the project team will look at the overall project feasibility. This is determined by combining the different feasibility measures. Some organizations may place different weights on each feasibility category, and those weights may change from project to project. Initially feasibility will be assessed during the planning phase of the SDLC. However it will be important to regularly revisit the project's feasibility during the later phases as additional detail becomes available. Changes at just about any phase of a project can make it no longer feasible. Project feasibility is especially susceptible to changes in the work environment or project requirements. For example, if the senior manager backing or sponsoring your project leaves the organization, there may be a high likelihood that the person filling that position may have different business priorities.

Getting the facts

To create a successful system, the project team needs to gather many facts related to the hardware, software, people, procedures, data and networks that will be needed in the proposed system. During the early stages of the SDLC the analyst will be gathering information related to the current system, improvements needed in the system, constraints that must be accommodated and specific requirements for the new system. Specific examples of the types of information that will be gathered include:

- What tasks are done in each department (including when, by whom, where, and how often?)
- Details of all inputs to the system and outputs from the system
- Formats and locations of all information that is stored
- Details about the amount of data that is processed and stored
- Existing costs for processing tasks in each department

During later phases the analyst may gather information related more to the specific hardware or off-the-shelf application packages that may be needed.

There are several different **fact-finding techniques** that the systems analyst will use to help gather the needed data and information. The techniques vary in how long they take to gather the information, how involved individual users are, how much breadth of information is reviewed, and how much depth of information is reviewed. The systems analyst will carefully look at the current project and choose the appropriate mix of the techniques to use. The following paragraphs briefly introduce each of the techniques you may see used on a project. The first four techniques allow for a higher degree of user participation. Recall that involving users throughout the design process is a key factor in helping to have a smooth implementation of a new system.

- Interviewing – The interview is the most important and common technique used to gather information. Usually the interview is done in a one-on-one format. While it is time consuming, it does allow the analyst to adjust the questions asked based on user responses and also allow the analyst to gauge body language. Since you typically can't interview all users, this technique is frequently done in combination with other techniques.
- Joint application design (JAD) – In a JAD session the analyst will meet with a small group of users. Collectively they will provide input to the analyst. A key benefit of this approach is that users will better understand how their needs and wants may be in conflict with the needs of other users, or priorities of the business as a whole. A JAD session can be used early in the SDLC to gather requirements, or later in the SDLC to help determine design options.

- Questionnaires – Questionnaires allow the analyst to gather information from a wide variety of users. While some analysts may distribute paper-based questionnaires, increasingly you will find analysts using electronic questionnaires. Figure 3.7 shows an example of an online survey created using SurveyMonkey (www.surveymonkey.com).

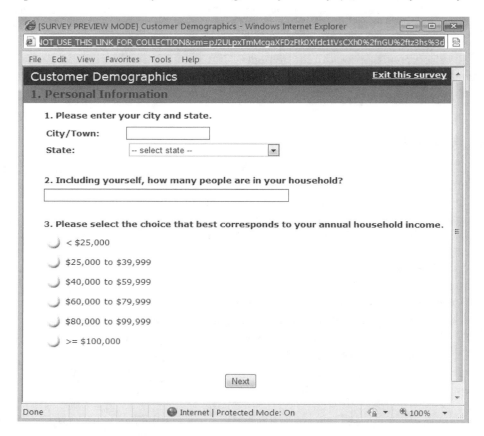

Figure 3.7 Online surveys provide a convenient way for analysts to gather user information

- Observation – Observation involves the analyst either watching users perform their jobs, or in some cases actually doing the task themselves. Observation can help an analyst verify details of a task, especially when tasks are complicated and it is difficult for users to explain all of the steps involved. This will also help gather facts that users might not provide because they don't consider them important or they take them for granted.
- Reviewing existing documentation – An analyst often begins gathering information about a new system by looking at documentation (forms, reports, screen shots, files, policies, procedures) about the current system. Additionally, the analyst should also review documents that provide information about the organization such as organization charts, memos and meeting minutes that have discussed either problems with the current system or requirements for the new system.
- Research – Reviewing trade publications and computer magazines, reference books, websites, and newspapers can help the analyst learn more about trends in the industry and how other companies may have solved similar problems. Additionally, these resources can provide details and comparisons about available hardware and software solutions.

While the analyst is the person responsible for gathering all of the facts, it is the job of the user representatives on the project team to help ensure that the analyst has all of the necessary information. If you know that a project is controversial, it is likely that some users have intentionally given wrong or misleading information to the analyst in hopes of sabotaging the project. In cases like this it will be very important that the analyst gets input from a wide variety of users and that the analyst uses a variety of the fact-finding techniques.

Documenting the process and the system

Throughout the SDLC the project team will be creating a variety of project deliverables. Initially these may include samples of existing system reports, notes from interviews and questionnaire results. As the project continues the deliverables will begin to take the form of more formal reports including diagrams and programming specifications, just to name a few. The project leader should develop a plan for organizing and accessing documents related to the project. Often this is done in something called a *project notebook* or *project binder*. Ultimately this project notebook should contain all of the details about the project.

As you saw above, a tremendous amount of data will be gathered by using the different fact-finding techniques during the development of an information system. Even more information will be created as developers begin to design the new system. As a result, the amount of documentation created for a system development project can become overwhelming. Consider for example just tracking the details (what data needs to show on the report, where does the data come from, what calculations are used, how many people get the report, etc.) about all of the reports that a system will create. Exploring further, consider just one of these reports and how many different versions or samples of that report may be created to respond to "change requests" by different users. The project team needs to be able to keep track of which report version is the final one that needs to be built. In order to avoid have piles of paper that are not manageable, and to be able to answer the question of "why does this summary report look this way?" the project team must update the project notebook regularly. Keeping the documentation up-to-date will help the project team avoid the situation where *"We don't have time to do it right the first time, but we must find the time to do it over."* Remember that project documentation needs to be done in all of the phases of the SDLC.

Now that you have an understanding of some of the activities that will cross multiple phases, the next section will begin to look in more detail at each of the individual SDLC phases. It is important to keep in mind that these activities that we just discussed will be integrated into the SDLC phases. For example, ensuring that a project is worth doing has a primary focus early in the SDLC, but needs to be a continual question that is asked throughout each stage of the project.

LEARNING CHECK
Be sure you can *how to manage an IT project including describing the tools used in project management *describe how a company determines the feasibility of a project * explain the different fact-finding techniques *discuss approaches to documentation

THE SYSTEMS DEVELOPMENT LIFE CYCLE

As you learned earlier, the SDLC is an approach to developing an information system. Ultimately you may be involved in a project that uses a different version of the SDLC, or uses a different approach to developing systems. No problem – our coverage of the SDLC is designed to introduce you to the tasks that must be completed when an information system is being created. No matter what development approach is used, understanding these basic tasks will help you be more effective as part of a project team. This section explains what happens in each of the five SDLC phases. To allow you to focus on the specifics of each phase, during our discussion in this section we are operating under the assumption that the project is moving smoothly and continues to meet the needs of the organization. However it is important for you to remember that problems may arise during the development of a system. In those cases the project team will need to meet to determine the appropriate solutions.

Planning

Remember that organizations typically have more requests for systems development projects than they have resources to complete. When a steering committee approves a project request, the project will be given to a systems analyst and the **planning phase** begins. The planning phase answers the general questions of what problem is being solved, is the solution feasible, and how long will it take? The output of the planning phase is a **project development plan** that includes:
- A statement of work (SOW) which identifies the problem to be solved along with project scope, including goals and objectives of the project
- Estimates of project feasibility
- Identification of the project team and resources required
- Project Schedule

From reading this list, it is safe to expect that the project development plan should include the project management and feasibility assessment techniques discussed earlier.

The completed project development plan will be presented to the project sponsor and the steering committee. The steering committee will evaluate the project development plan from an organization-wide perspective. In addition to looking at the broad question of the overall benefit of the project for the organization, the steering committee should determine if the schedule and project expectations are realistic. Some of the questions they should ask include: what is the project manager's experience on similar projects (similar size, complexity, staff), what percentage of their projects finish on-time and on-budget, and what tools did they use to help them in creating the estimates. If they determine that the project is worth continuing, the analysis phase of the life cycle begins.

Analysis

The activities in the **analysis phase** are structured to accomplish three main tasks:
- identify what the new system needs to do
- create models of the data, processing and logic needs for the new system
- recommend the best approach to develop the new system.

The primary output of this phase is a **system proposal** that will detail the concept of "what" the new system will do, along with possible approaches to developing the new system. In most cases the project team will include their recommendation of the best approach.

Identify what the new system needs to do

To identify what the new system needs to do the analyst will need to gather answers to the following questions: (1) how does the current system work? and (2) what improvements and changes need to be made? Answers to these questions will help the analyst identify the specific **system requirements** of the new system. System requirements are the detailed set of features that must be included in the new system. Requirements can either be functional or nonfunctional. Functional requirements refer to a specific activity that the system must do such as "calculate quarterly taxes." Nonfunctional requirements refer to any characteristics about the system other than "basic functional activities." These might involve security, reliability and performance-based issues such as "perform 25 transactions per minute" or "access to confidential data must be regulated." Based on the specifics on the project, the first activity the analyst will do is to select the appropriate mix of fact-finding techniques that will help uncover the answers to these questions. It is helpful for the analyst to begin with looking at how the current system works, even if the current system is not automated. While studying the current system, the analyst can begin to identify any resistance that users may have to the new system and can explain to the users how they will be involved throughout the development to ensure that their needs are met.

What if the users are having a hard time explaining what they want the system to do? **Prototyping** is a process where the analyst and users create an initial version of the system. Although we will talk later on in the chapter about using prototyping as a complete development approach, sometimes analysts will recommend creating a simple prototype to help illustrate how parts of a system could look or function. This often helps users to better describe what they require in the new system. Figure 3.8 shows a prototype of a screen used for a system that will be used by a Quality Assurance department to track system defect reports. When creating prototypes during analysis, functionality is not built into the buttons, etc.

Figure 3.8 A prototype of an input screen helps users determine necessary system inputs

What does the analyst do with all of the answers to these questions? Earlier you were introduced to the concept of the project notebook. The project development plan created in the planning phase should already be in the project notebook, but during the analysis stage we really start to see an increase in the quantity of information stored in the notebook. For example, notes from interviews and answers to questionnaires will be included, along with examples of inputs and outputs from the current system, and prioritized lists of the requirements of the new system. The analyst will use this information to help identify the *business rules*, the allowable conditions or scenarios, for this business. For example if a library only allows you to have a maximum of 10 books checked out at a time, this would be a business rule. Other business rules might be that a part number must contain 4 digits, the re-order point for a product is 100 units, or a customer only has one sales representative. Because these rules sometimes limit what can occur they are also referred to as *business constraints*.

Complete the exercise below to reinforce your understanding about how to identify the requirements for a new system.

Understanding IT?

Windy Knoll Tennis Club is a small tennis club with 10 courts, a pro shop and a small restaurant. Over the last two years their memberships have increased and they now have over 200 members. As a result they are finding that they are processing more reservations for court times. The base membership fee allows for six hours of court time per week. If members exceed that time they are billed for the additional hours. Courts are reserved in one-hour increments, for either singles or doubles play. The courts are open from 7:00 am to 8:00 pm six days a week. The location, seating accommodations, and court surface (hard, clay or grass) of each court varies. If members are making a reservation for special activities they will often request to have a court that meets specific criteria. On average, each member plays at the club two times per week for two hours each time.

The staff at Windy Knoll have been keeping the reservations in a central reservations book (CRB). When a member calls to reserve a court time, an employee is supposed to check the CRB to see if a court is available at the requested time. If the reservation can be made, they write the member's name and phone number in the day/time slot for the assigned court. They are also supposed to write down the name of the employee who made the reservation. Sometimes if the book can't be found, employees will write the reservation request down on a notepad. Often these requests never make it into the CRB. Increasingly the tennis staff have been noticing more errors in having multiple members showing up at the same court. Additionally, some of these "unrecorded reservations" are beyond the member's six-hour allotment and should be billed for additional court usage. But since they are not recorded, the billing never is processed.

Windy Knoll's club manager, Jim Kettle, is aware of the need to make improvements. The club has never had the need for a formal steering committee, but the manager has done some preliminary investigation into the problem. He believes that if the club does not solve this problem, members will become increasingly dissatisfied and may cancel their memberships. While he hasn't done a formal feasibility study, his business instinct is that he should proceed. He has hired an IT consultant, Martha Johnson, to analyze their current system and make a recommendation on how they should best solve this problem.

Activity One – Fact-Finding at Windy Knoll

Martha Johnson started off by talking to Jim about his concerns. She gathered the basic information provided in the case study statement. With that as a starting point she began her more detailed analysis by looking at the central reservations book, samples of membership forms, and monthly billing statements. Next she talked to the employees and asked questions about how they did their jobs and the types of problems they were experiencing. Finally she created a list of questions to mail to the members to find out their opinions about the reservation process.

What three fact-finding techniques did the consultant use? _____, _____, _____
Would you suggest any other fact-finding techniques?

Next, Martha has begun to list the different business rules discovered through the analysis process that will need to be reflected in the new system. The rules she has identified so far include:

1) There are only 10 tennis courts.
2) Each member can play for up to 6 hours per week at no additional charge.
   (*Follow-up question: Ask if a week runs Sunday through Saturday.*)
3) Reservations require a member's name and phone number.

Notice that for the second rule the consultant has created a note about a follow-up question she needs to have answered to understand how billing will work.

Identify two more business rules that are described in the case write-up.

4) _____

5) _____

Martha has continued to gather data about this project. The data she has gathered has helped her understand how the current system works, what improvements and changes should be implemented, and what the specific requirements are for the new system. She is ready now to begin to create models based on what she has learned.

Check your answers at the end of the chapter.

Create models

Once the project team knows the requirements of the new system the analyst is ready to begin creating models that will detail the data, processing and logic required in the system. These models provide a standardized approach to representing requirements. An important step for the analyst is to review the models with the users to make certain that the analyst correctly understood the user. The systems analyst uses these modeling tools to provide a common understanding among all of the IT specialists about the system requirements. Later in the design phase, for example, the models will be used to develop concrete programming specifications so that the programmers know exactly what to build.

Data Models For an information system to produce the desired results, it is important that the correct data be captured, processed, and stored in the system. In this sense, data are simply the raw facts that we need to capture. Your university, for example, probably captures the following data about you: first and last name, identification number, street address, and cumulative GPA. Many systems developers think that building a correct data model for the system is the most critical modeling activity because it sets the foundation for the entire system. **Data modeling** is a technique for representing the structure of the data in the system.

The modeling of data is usually done with an **entity-relationship diagram (ERD)**. An entity-relationship diagram is a tool that is used to graphically represent the structure of the data. An *entity* is a person, place, or thing that has data we need to store in the system. The rectangles on an ERD represent entities. An ERD shows the different entities and how they are related to one another – this is the *relationship*. Relationships can be either one-to-one, one-to-many, or many-to-many. When reading an ERD you will be able to identify many, but not all, of the business rules relative to the system under development. In the university example above, you, the student, are the entity. So what do we call your identification number or street address? They are *attributes* – a characteristic of an entity. Sometimes analysts will choose to show some, or all, of the attributes on the ERD.

An example of a simple entity-relationship diagram for a dentist office is shown in Figure 3.9. The diagram shows two entities: Patient and Appointment. This ERD example does include some of the attributes that will be captured for each entity. The relationship "makes" shows a one-to-many association. A patient can make many appointments, but an appointment is for only one patient. Determining the relationship comes after analyzing the business rules. In this example, the Dentist's office requires that each appointment be for only 1 patient (no appointment sharing.) This is a typical rule in the medical profession.

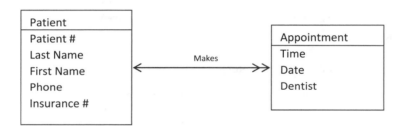

Note: The relationship line indicates a one-to-many relationship. A single-side arrow indicates "one" while a double-side arrow indicated "many."

Figure 3.9 An Entity-Relationship model graphically displays the data needs of a system

Complete the following exercise to reinforce your learning about data modeling.

Understanding IT?   **Activity Two – Data Modeling at Windy Knoll**

Based on the facts Martha gathered earlier, she has created an Entity-Relationship diagram, shown in Figure 3.10 to represent the data needs for the reservation system. Martha also learned that each member is allowed to designate one secondary member. Usually this is a spouse, but it could be any other person. The secondary member is allowed to also make and use court reservations. The time used comes from the member's 6-hour monthly allotment, or gets billed at the member rate for additional hours used.

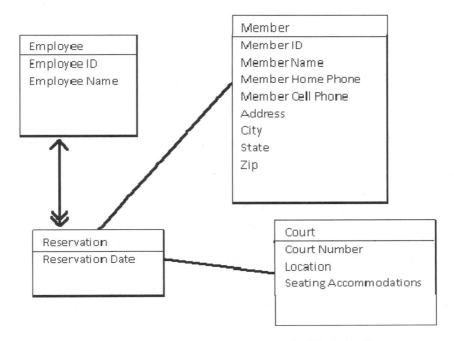

Figure 3.10 The Entity-Relationship model for Windy Knoll

The analyst still has a few attributes that need to be added to the ERD. Assign each of the following attributes to the appropriate entity.

Court Surface _____   Reservation Time _____

Date Hired _____   Secondary Member Name _____

The relationship between employee and reservation is one-to-many. Add the symbols below onto the 2 other relationships to indicate the correct relationship.

One: $\longrightarrow$ Many: $\longrightarrow\!\!\!\!\!\rightarrow$

Check your answers at the end of the chapter.

The next step would be for Martha to work on the process models. As you are beginning to see, it is important that the analyst and project team do a thorough job of gathering the facts so they can build complete and accurate models. We will revisit data modeling in greater detail in Chapter 4 when you will learn more about using database management.

Using Process Models In addition to knowing about the structure of the data for the system, we also need to understand about the process used to convert the inputs to the system into outputs. **Process modeling** is a technique for representing how the business operates. The modeling of processes, or activities, is often done with a **Data Flow Diagram (DFD)**. A data flow diagram is a tool that is used to graphically show the inputs, process, outputs, and data storage of a system on one diagram. DFDs vary in the amount of detail shown. Figure 3.11 represents a sample of a data flow diagram showing a high level view for part of the data and processing flow for a customer order. From this we can visually see the processing of an order will involve interaction with customers, orders, and invoices.

Figure 3.11 This DFD shows how data flows from a customer in an order processing system.

Using Logic Models While analyzing the data and processes, the analyst will also perform **logic modeling** to capture specific details about the decision logic that is used in different business tasks. Decision trees and decision tables are two common tools used to model complex logic. A **decision tree** graphically shows conditions and the resulting actions while a **decision table** represents the conditions and actions in a tabular format. Both tools help the project team realize if all of the possible conditions and actions have been identified. Building correct logic models is an important step in creating an information system that works. Many of the errors found in information systems are a result of errors in logic that was not correctly modeled. Figure 3.12 shows a decision tree used to represent the logic to determine whether to approve a request to increase a customer's credit limit. That same logic is represented in a decision table in Figure 3.13.

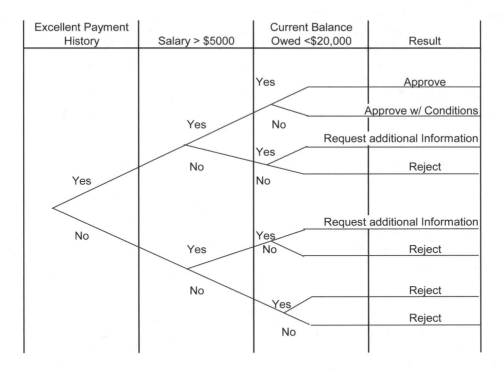

Figure 3.12 The decision tree shows the logic used to determine whether to increase a customer's credit limit

Increase Credit Limit Decision		Rules							
		1	2	3	4	5	6	7	8
Conditions	Excellent Payment History	Y	Y	Y	Y	N	N	N	N
	Salary > $5000 month	Y	Y	N	N	N	Y	Y	N
	Current Balance Owed < $20,000	Y	N	Y	N	Y	N	Y	N
Actions	Approve	X							
	Approve with conditions		X						
	Reject				X	X	X		X
	Request Additional Information			X				X	

Figure 3.13 Decision tables provide a more compact way to show the decision logic

Recommend best approach

By now the analyst and the project team should have a good grasp on what the new system needs to do. They should have a complete description of the system requirements supported by a comprehensive set of data, processing and logic models. The last task to complete is to recommend the best approach for developing a system that will meet the needs of the company. To be able to recommend the best approach, the project team needs to first consider the range of options. The options are usually thought of on two dimensions: (1) what the system will have and do, and (2) how we will acquire the system.

To address the first dimension, what the system will have and do, many project teams will often develop three different alternatives – a low-end option, a mid-range option, and a high-end option. All of the alternatives will meet the system requirements; the difference is in how they do it. For example a low-end option usually does not offer anything beyond the minimum requirements. As a result this alternative is usually the least expensive. At the other end, a high-end option will go beyond minimum requirements, perhaps offering extra features or solving additional problems. As you might expect, the high-end alternative is typically the most expensive. In the middle you will find the mid-range option – offering features beyond the minimum requirements, but not as sophisticated as the high-end, for a middle-of-the-road price.

The second dimension deals with how we will acquire the system. Acquisition can simplistically be thought of in terms of a **"make or buy" decision**. At the extreme ends of these choices, making software involves writing the software code – creating a custom piece of software, whereas buying software involves purchasing a software system that has already been built. But the reality is that there are many subtle variations along the make or buy dimension. There are advantages and disadvantages to each of the variations. The ultimate decision should weigh the advantages and disadvantages relative to the specifics of the information system under development.

Packaged software systems have already been written and are available for purchase. Packaged software ranges from stand-alone word processing software purchased at your local computer store, to web-based shopping carts you can use to process online orders, to construction management systems for a home builder, to enterprise resource planning systems used to support the operations of a business. You can probably find a packaged software product for all of the different types of information systems we covered in Chapter 2. Because the software has already been created and tested, advantages include fast implementation of a product that you know works. Many companies use this option when the system they are developing solves a common business need, such as payroll or accounting. A disadvantage to packaged software is that it may not fit your needs exactly. When an organization is unable to find a *commercial-off-the-shelf (COTS)* software package that meets its needs, they will need to write the program. This results in a program that completely meets the needs of the organization, but usually takes longer and is more expensive. The middle ground in the make or buy decision could include options to customize packaged software so that it fits your needs, but this will usually increase costs and delivery time. In cases where significant modification will need to be made, this may not be your most effective option. Another option is to plan to assemble your information system through different software components that you integrate together. A related consideration is who is going to write the software. If an organization has experienced staff they may choose to write the program themselves using **in-house development**, while some organizations may choose to **outsource** -- to contract with another company to develop an information system.

The choice of whether to make or buy is not simple. The variables of time (how quickly do you need the system completed), skill competencies (does the project involve a technical skill that is important for the organization to acquire) and corporate resources (do we have the money, people, etc. available for this project) all need to be considered. Certainly the costs and benefits of each option need to be analyzed.

The completed system proposal will contain a discussion of the alternatives, including feasibility assessments for each alternative, to developing the system. Additionally it will contain the project team's recommendation along with their rationale. Remember that by now the analyst and project team have uncovered many more details about the proposed system. As a result as they discuss the feasibility of the different approaches, the values should be much more accurate. The completed system proposal will be given to the steering committee. Often a formal presentation is given by the project team.   The steering committee will evaluate the recommendation and decide which alternative, if any, to pursue. If the decision is made to continue, then the project team will begin the design phase.

Design

The purpose of the **design phase** is to establish *how* the new system will work by translating the requirements into detailed design specifications. The components that must be designed include:
- Inputs and Outputs
- User Interfaces
- Databases
- Programs
- Infrastructure

While the analysis phase answered the question of "What is the new system going to do?" the tasks of the design phase supply the answers to the question of "How is it going to be done?" During design each component of the system is methodically detailed. Because of the interrelated nature of these different components (an input form requires data fields and appears as a result of an interface choice), it is not easy to separate design into a set of sequential activities. The resulting output of this phase is a set of detailed design specification. At the end of this phase the users should have a very clear understanding of how the new system will work. Additionally, the programmers and technical specialists will know what to start building and assembling to create a functional system.

Inputs and Outputs   Many systems analysts will start the design process at the end, by defining what the outputs of the system will look like. By starting with looking at the outputs needed, the analyst can focus on identifying the input data that will be needed to produce the required outputs. This can help reduce unnecessary and costly data collection.

To ensure that the outputs meet the needs of the users, an example or *mock-up*, of each printed reports or display screens is often created. A mock-up shows a sample of what the report will look like. Figure 3.14 shows an example of a mock-up for a report that will be generated from a Dental Office System. This particular report is one related to an insurance claim for services provided by the dentist. Often another version of the mock-up, called a *layout chart*, is created, that will link each data item on the report to the specific source of data in the system or to the calculation that produces the piece of data. In addition to the basic layout, the analyst should also document answers to the following questions: Who gets the report? How often is it generated? Are there any security issues about who sees the report? For inputs forms, the analyst should also note whether specific data items will be provided by the system (e.g. once a customer number is provided the system could look up and fill in the customer name and address), what kinds of data validation will be used (e.g. part numbers must be 4 digits ranging from 1000 – 4999), and what fields will be the result of calculations.

Figure 3.14   A mock-up of an output screen (with sample data) helps users visualize the system

Sometimes screens are used for both input and output as shown below in Figure 3.15.   This screen is used in a dental office to both collect inputs about what is currently being recorded andto display the dental history for the patient.

Figure 3.15   Some mock-ups represent screen used for both input and output

User Interfaces   While most people think of the user interface as only the set of screens in the system, it really encompasses much more including the dialogue as well as what happens when you select a choice on a screen. You may have noticed that the screen shown in Figure 3.15 has user interface components such as menu buttons and icons, as well as input and output elements. When designing the user interface a few of the issues to think about are whether the menu choices are intuitive, whether the interface provides all required functionality, and whether the flow from screen to screen makes sense.   In terms of the dialogue, it is important to consider word choice and tone when choosing phrasing for menu choices and writing help instructions and error messages.

Data Design   Each piece of data that is going to be used in the system needs to be identified in terms of the type of data item, length, location, range of values, etc. For example, an address is an alphanumeric field, with a maximum of 30 characters, while a part number is a numeric field, with 4 characters, and a valid range of 1000 - 4999. This information is documented in a **data dictionary**, a tool used to record the name, description and characteristics about the data used in an information system. During the design phase, the analyst will work with database specialists to determine the best structure for the data. Most information systems today include a database component. In Chapter 4 you will learn more about creating and managing database systems. Some systems have a need to store data in other file formats.   During data design the specifications for these file storage formats will also be defined.

Programs   Using the decision tables and decision trees created during analysis, the analyst transforms that logic into a detailed set of program specifications. These program specifications will allow a programmer to understand the logic necessary to build the program. The program specifications will be tightly integrated with the other design specifications because of their interrelated nature.

Infrastructure and Controls   The infrastructure of the information system includes computer equipment as well as the network platform. Sometimes the new system will be able to work on existing hardware, while other times the infrastructure may need to be completely redesigned. In addition to the infrastructure, the project team must also decide on how the necessary controls will be built into the system. For example, security controls may be handled through hardware infrastructure or through the software programs, or a combination of both. Another control that needs to be addressed relates to ensuring that any necessary laws or regulations are followed. Recall from Chapter 2 that the Sarbanes-Oxley Act of 2002 requires companies to establish, evaluate and monitor the internal controls related to the information systems used to process financial data. Sometimes there are industry controls that must be incorporated. For example, if your system will utilize credit card payment processing, the Payment Card Industry (PCI) Data Security Standard required by Visa and Master Card must be followed.

It is worth noting at this point that prototyping can be a very useful tool throughout the design phase. In the analysis phase you learned that prototyping can be used to help gather requirements. During design, the prototype models that you have created for the inputs, outputs and interface help the user visualize the system. This allows for additional verification that requirements have been understood and modeled correctly, and that the proposed design will meet the needs of the users. Additionally, prototypes of the user interface and the inputs/outputs can be tested to look at characteristics of ease of use, minimizing operator errors, and reducing training times. Keep in mind that it is much easier and less expensive to make corrections and changes in the requirements at this stage than after the system has been built.

However, as users get a better handle on the design of the new system it is very easy for them to start suggesting additional features. While some of these features may prove beneficial, if they were not planned for originally, adding them at this stage may cause the program development to take longer or to cost more than planned. This problem is known as *scope creep*. It is critical that any modifications to the system requirements be done formally, including appropriate adjustments to costs and schedules.

Complete the exercise below to expand your understanding about interface design and prototyping.

Integrate IT

Axure RP Pro 5 is an interface design and prototyping tool. Users of development tools such as this often benefit by having decreased development time along with being able to create a product more closely aligned with customer needs.

Open your Web Browser and Navigate to http://www.axure.com/demo.aspx.   Click ***Play All*** to view the video tour overview about the RP Pro 5 design and development tool.

Hopefully you have a better appreciation for how an interface design and prototyping tool can help systems developers. In the Practical Application activity at the end of the chapter you will have a chance to work with the Axure RP Pro tool.

Implementation

At the end of the design phase, the project team has a clear understanding of what the system is going to do and how it will be done. During the **implementation phase** the project team will turn these specifications into a working system by accomplishing the following activities:

- Acquire any needed hardware and software components
- Write software programs
- Test the system
- Train users
- Convert to the new system

Acquire hardware and software
During this activity the project team will purchase any hardware and pre-packaged software components needed for the new system.

Write software programs
Computer programmers perform the task of turning the program specifications into a working set of computer programs. When an organization has chosen to write the programs themselves using in-source development, this activity is very critical to the overall success of the project. On projects where the development has been outsourced, the project team's task is to ensure that the contract programmers meet the project specifications. If the development is somewhere between "make" or "buy", the programmers will work to modify and integrate purchased components as appropriate. Program development follows its own set of structured steps to ensure that programs are built correctly to meet user needs. The programmer, using the program specification as a road map, will create the user interface, write the code to perform the processing, test the code, and document the programs.

Test the system
While testing is most visible during this implementation phase, parts of the testing activity occur throughout the SDLC. In the analysis phase when the project team identifies what needs to be tested and creates an overall test plan. During design the plan will be further refined and additional details will be added to the test plan as the project team decides on how the system will function. In implementation the programmers will test different pieces of the program to ensure they work correctly. Once the hardware has been installed and the entire system has been written, the project team will follow the pieces of the test plan to test all of the components of the system – this includes testing hardware and software.

There are a variety of tests that will be conducted along the way. Each test has a specific function and is used to help ensure that the overall system meets the needs of the organization. A **unit test** ensures that each individual program operates reliably and correctly by itself. At the next level a **system test** ensures that the different programs work correctly together. For example, does the data about an order that is processed in one program get passed correctly to the inventory management program? **Acceptance tests** ensure that the system as a whole meets the needs of the business, and works correctly with the actual data from the business. While unit testing and system testing are performed by the project team, acceptance testing is performed by users in the organization.

Train users

Preparing users to adopt and adapt to the new system is critical to the overall success of a systems development project. A key component to this preparation is **training** – teaching the users how to use the hardware and software in the new system. The project team must develop and implement a training plan. The training should cover not only how to complete day-to-day tasks, but also procedures related to back-ups and how to use the system help manuals to find additional information. Training can be delivered through a variety of methods. Many times it is conducted in a group setting, as shown in Figure 3.16, which allows for users to interact with each other. Sometimes it will be delivered as one-on-one sessions allowing more customized teaching, and sometimes it will be delivered as computer-based training modules, allowing users to work at their own speed.

Figure 3.16 Training is critical to preparing users to successfully begin using the new system

Convert to the new system

System conversion is the process of switching from an old information system to the newly developed information system. There are four main strategies a project team may use to convert to a new system. These are illustrated in Figure 3.17.

- Parallel – With parallel conversion the organization puts in the new system while continuing to run the old system. This results in both systems running for a period of time. This approach can be expensive since both systems are running and users have to do their jobs twice – once on the old system and once on the new. However it does allow for thorough testing to make sure the system is working correctly, and provides a built-in backup in case problems are experienced on the new system.
- Direct – In a direct conversion, the organization installs the new system and then turns off the old system. While this approach is certainly the quickest, it is also the most risky. If problems arise with the new system the organization doesn't have a backup in place.
- Pilot – A pilot implementation involves implementing the complete system in a small part of the organization such as one department or one division. This allows the company to try out the system and minimizes the impact in case of problems. However, the processing from this "pilot group" may not be able to be easily assimilated with the data and results produced by the old system still be used in the rest of the organization. As such, this approach works best when the different departments or divisions have fairly independent operations.
- Phased – In a phased installation, the new system is installed in phases across the organization. For example, the inventory modules may be installed first and the payroll module installed later. While this approach also helps minimize the impact of potential problems, it is only feasible when the new system has modules than work independently of each other.

Figure 3.17 The selection of a conversion strategy is an important choice

Most people only see the visible task of actually installing and starting to use the new system. However, the project team must also ensure that data from the current system is effectively migrated to the new system. The activity of data conversion will take place prior to, or as the first task in, converting the system. Data conversion can be a large, complicated task. Consider a business converting from a manual system to a computer-based system. If their current customer records and associated business data need to be entered into the system, someone must actually enter all of this data. When converting from one computer-based system to another, programmers often will write a program to convert the data. Additionally, the project team must be mindful of overall quality control during this process. After the installation, the new system must be tested to ensure that everything was installed correctly and operates as specified.

Support

The final phase in the SDLC is that of Support. Once a system has been built and is installed in the organization, it moves into the **support phase**. At this point the project team will no longer be responsible for the system. Instead the responsibility will be assigned to a support team. This phase is where systems spend the majority of their time – many systems will be in operation for years.

The support team provides **system maintenance** to ensure that the entire system, including all hardware and software components, is operating correctly. Maintenance may include fixing errors in the system that were not uncovered during testing and installing new hardware and software as required. Maintenance also includes making changes or improvements to the system. During the life of the system business conditions may change that require changes to the way the system works or requires new features to be added. When enhancements like these are required, a new iteration of the SDLC is often started to ensure that the enhancement will be effectively integrated into the system. At some point, the organization will make a decision that it is no longer cost effective to continue adapting the current system and will instead retire it. By formally analyzing requests for enhancements through the SDLC, organizations will be able to make the retirement decision at the correct time.

In addition to conducting ongoing maintenance, two additional activities performed at this time are system monitoring and system support. *System monitoring* involves tracking system activity, maintaining security, and performing system backups and recovery. *System support* involves providing assistance to users through help-desk and on-going training to ensure that the users are able to resolve any problems they may encounter.

LEARNING CHECK
Be sure you can *describe the components of a project development plan *explain the three main tasks of the analysis phase * describe the different components that need to be designed * explain the difference between the goals of the analysis phase and the design phase * compare the approaches to converting to a new system * explain the activities of the support phase

OTHER APPROACHES TO DEVELOPING INFORMATION SYSTEMS

The SDLC is good for providing a structured set of steps for a project team to follow. By having set milestones and deliverables, there are many opportunities to uncover errors made along the way. This helps produce systems that meet requirements by uncovering errors earlier, rather than later. However the SDLC can be a lengthy, expensive process. Depending on the type of system being developed, the expertise within an organization, and the time frame for development, some organizations may look to alternative approaches to developing systems. The alternative approaches can be used independently, but sometimes a project team may mix and match to help meet the needs of the business. For example, you already have learned about integrating prototyping into the SDLC to help elicit requirements. The alternative approaches include prototyping, end user development, rapid application development, object oriented development and outsourcing.

Prototyping

As you learned earlier, prototypes can be used to help an analyst uncover requirements during the analysis phase, and to validate and refine requirements during the design phase. Prototyping sometimes is used as a complete approach to develop a system. In prototyping, the systems analyst/developers will start by developing a small system, called a prototype. This prototype is based on an initial list of user requirements. Instead of being considered a "throw-away" model, used only in an earlier phase, the prototype continues to be worked on, and more functionality is added. During this iterative process, users stay involved throughout the development by clarifying user requirements, trying out new versions of the system and providing feedback. Eventually all of the functionality is built into the prototype and it becomes the completed system. Figure 3.18 illustrates the prototyping approach.

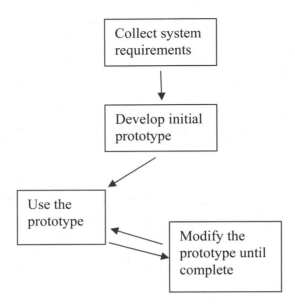

Figure 3.18 Prototyping provides an iterative approach to developing systems.

As you can see, in prototyping the analysis and design work is done together. Prototyping can be a very effective approach when users have a difficult time defining requirements and for systems that are not too complex. But there are several considerations you should be aware of. One concern is that sometimes the prototype is never completed. Users may continue to request changes or modifications never signing off on the completed system. Additionally, because the development is based on iteration, documentation related to the system design often tends to be less completed. Managing user expectations is another important task for the analyst. Some users adopt the misguided reasoning that if a prototype can be built so quickly that the rest of the system should be able to be built much sooner than anticipated. Finally another caution is that the system must be thoroughly tested. If the systems analyst is mindful of these cautions, prototyping can be beneficial by giving employees a better understanding of the new system, and this familiarity may decrease resistance to change.

End-user development

End-user development is an approach to building system by and for the users. In contrast to the other approaches discussed, the user is primarily responsible for the project. Users often use a prototyping approach to performing their work. End-user development is easiest with smaller scale systems. End users often select this approach because of the increasing availability of easy-to-use software tools or because the MIS staff is backlogged with project requests.

Concerns with this approach revolve around effective integration and compatibility with other systems, providing adequate security measures and maintaining required privacy regulations. Additionally, organizations need to be aware of the fact that time will be taken away from the user's "real job" if they are spending time developing systems. Even with these cautions, this approach may be appropriate in some situations. Benefits from this end user developing include completely meeting user needs, faster development times, and reducing demands on the MIS staff. However it should be noted that sometimes the demands only shift to another technology support area – if users get stuck in developing their own systems they often rely on a help desk to provide assistance.

Rapid Applications Development

The **Rapid Application Development (RAD)** approach was designed to determine systems requirements and convert those requirements in to a working system as fast as possible. RAD combines prototyping, computer-based software development tools, special management practices and close user involvement (McConnell, 1996.) The key to success of RAD is the tight integration and usage of tools to create user interfaces, prototyping to iterate on key components, automated code generators, and close teamwork among the users and developers. The development steps don't have to occur sequentially and often you will see different parts of the system being developed at the same time.

The RAD approach encourages the use of JAD sessions, as a fact-finding technique, to elicit and gain consensus on systems requirements. Recall that JAD brings users from different areas together with developers to work on the analysis and design of a system. Once the requirements have been collected, *computer aided software engineering* (CASE) tools are used to structure the requirements and develop prototypes. The prototypes are reviewed and refined in an iterative fashion. The fast time frame requires the users and developers to work closely together. Additionally, other CASE tools are used to support tasks such as automatic code generation, component integration and version tracking and control. Figure 3.19 shows a screen shot from Omnis Studio's suite of RAD development tools. RAD can be very effective in creating high-quality systems. The primary concerns raised about RAD are that systems may not be very scalable – able to be upgraded and enhanced easily – because they evolve from a prototype instead of having scalability built in from the beginning and that they may not have as many features since some features are pushed to later versions in order to meet strict development timelines.

Figure 3.19   The Component Store window in Omnis Studio provides an easy way to drag and drop different system components into your application

Object-oriented software development

The traditional structured analysis approach involves separating the analysis of the processes from the analysis of the data. **Object-oriented (OO) software development**, on the other hand, is an approach where the system is model as a collection of interacting objects. Objects represent real-world entities such as customers, products and employees. What's different is that when defining an object the analyst identifies the data or properties (such as customer name, address, and phone) of the object along with the processes (methods). Methods are the actions an object can do (such as place order), similar to the procedures you may have identified in a more traditional sense. By describing both the properties and methods together in one unified model, the analyst works to create components that are re-usable across different systems in the organization.

Object-oriented software development is increasing in popularity as a development approach. By creating modular, re-usable code, organizations are able to reduce development time and decrease system development costs. However since this approach requires retraining of analysts and developers, organizations need to balance expected gains against the challenges and costs of retraining staff.

Outsourcing

As you learned earlier, organizations must decide on whether they are going to make or buy a new system. In many small and medium sized firms, outsourcing has become a common approach to systems development. While some organizations may only choose to outsource the actual coding of the system, other organizations may choose to outsource the entire development and operation of a system. Outsourcing allows organizations to reduce development costs, gain access to expertise in both software development and the processes and functions that are being automated, reduce or eliminate staffing problems, and have easier access to newer technologies. Potential concerns with outsourcing include losing expertise within the organization, increased risk for security concerns in the system, and potential for loss of control in ensuring the new system works correctly.

As you study all of the approaches to developing information systems, it is important to keep in mind that analysts have a toolkit from which they can select their development approach. Analysts should become knowledgeable with several different approaches, learn where they can be most applicable, and then select the best approach for each project.

LEARNING CHECK
Be sure you can *describe how prototyping can be used as a development approach *discuss the concerns about end user development compared to the benefits * explain the key to success in RAD * explain the fundamental different between object-oriented software development and traditional structured analysis

PRACTICAL APPLICATION

You will learn more about systems development by completing a tutorial using Axure RP Pro 5.

Open your Web Browser and navigate to: http://www.axure.com/downloads.aspx

Download the 30-day free trial edition of Axure RP Pro 5. Once you have completed the download and installation, the program will automatically launch and the Welcome Screen will be displayed.

Practical Application Image 1

Select **Getting Started**, located in the Installed Resources section. The window shown below will appear.

Practical Application Image 2

Work your way through the **Getting Started Tutorial**. During this Tutorial you will be guided through building an interactive prototype. The completed prototype should match that shown below.

Practical Application Image 3

Congratulations! You have just built a prototype. While this is only a small part of an overall system, you have had a chance to experience a few of the tasks involved in the analysis and design activities needed to create a new information system.

Complete this activity by navigating to the **Why Choose** tab of the Axure website. Click on the **Case Studies** link. Select one of the Case Studies to read. After reading the Case, briefly summarize how the Axure RP Pro tools were used in that organization.

Wrapping IT Up

In this chapter you learned about the Systems Development Life Cycle, the process organizations use to develop information systems. You have seen the complexities involved with ensuring that new systems are well designed and have a better understanding of how you will be involved in the process. In the next few chapters we will see how these systems development concepts can be applied to creating some prototype systems using spreadsheets, programming languages, web tools and databases.

Study Questions Summary

1. Why study systems development?
   - Information systems require significant organizational resources to develop
   - Organizations create information systems for different reasons
   - Non-IT specialists must understand what occurs during systems development so that they can be effective participants
   - The Systems Development Life Cycle is a structured approach to building information systems
   - The project team works together to across the different SDLC phases to create an information system
   - Monitoring success factors during systems development can help ensure that your information systems project will be successful

2. What activities cross the different life cycle stages?
   - Project management involves planning, scheduling and controlling the activities involved in developing an information system
   - Gantt and PERT charts can help keep a project on schedule
   - The feasibility of a project should be assessed according to technical, economic, organizational and schedule feasibility measures
   - Users are an important factor in determining costs and benefits of a new system
   - Analysts should use a variety of fact-finding techniques to gather system requirements
   - Keeping thorough and accurate project documentation is important throughout the SDLC

3. What happens during each stage of the systems development life cycle?
   - The Planning phase defines the project scope, assesses project feasibility and establishes the project schedule
   - The Analysis phase answers the question of "what the system will do" by identifying and clarifying the system requirements and providing alternative approaches to meeting those requirements
   - The Design phase answers the question of "how the system will work" by translating the requirements into detailed design specifications.
   - The output of the Implementation phase is a functional system that has been tested and installed.
   - After the system has been implemented it moves into the Support phase, where a support team ensures the ongoing operations and maintenance of the system.

4. What are some other approaches to developing information systems?
   - There are many different approaches that can be used to develop an information system
   - Prototyping is an iterative process involving ongoing evaluation and modification of the system
   - End users may elect to develop systems themselves when the backlog for project requests is too long or when they have skills in the application tool
   - Rapid Application Development can be an effective way to develop systems quickly
   - Object-oriented software development combines the analysis of data and processes into objects
   - Outsourcing can be effective when organizations don't have in-house staffing resources or expertise to create an information system

Solutions to Chapter Activities

UNDERSTANDING IT?

SDLC tasks pg. 77

1. *Implementation, Network engineer*
2. *Support, programmer*
3. *Analysis, user*
4. *Planning, project leader*
5. *Design, analyst/developer*
6. *Support, help desk   *note that these are new employees*

INTEGRATE IT

Excel Feasibility Analysis pg. 84 – answers will be provided

UNDERSTANDING IT?

Fact-finding pg. 90-91

Review existing documentation, interviewing, questionnaires
Consider using observation
Additional rules: 1) courts are open from 7am to 8pm; 2) reservations are for 1-hour increments

UNDERSTANDING IT?

Data modeling pg. 93
<u>Assigning Attributes to Entities</u>

Court Surface – Court; Reservation Time – Reservation; Date Hired - Employee; Secondary Member Name – Member

<u>Completing the Relationships</u>
The Relationship between Member and Reservation is One-to-Many. A member can have many reservations, but a reservation is made (and linked back to) only one member.

The Relationship between Court and Reservation is One-to-Many. A court can be on many different reservations, but a reservation is made (and linked back to) only one court.

Key Terms

Page number references are included in parentheses.

Acceptance Test (100)	Logic modeling (94)	Rapid application development (105)
Analysis phase (88)	Make or buy decision (96)	Schedule feasibility (80)
Business case (80)	Object-oriented software development (105)	Scope creep (80)
Data dictionary (98)	Organizational feasibility (80)	Steering committee (76)
Data flow diagram (DFD) (94)	Outsource (96, 106)	Support phase (102)
Data modeling (91)	Packaged software (96)	System conversion (101)
Decision table (94)	PERT chart (79)	System maintenance (102)
Decision tree (94)	Planning phase (88)	System proposal (89)
Design phase (97)	Process modeling (94)	System requirements (89)
Economic feasibility (80)	Project development plan (88)	System test (100)
End user development (104)	Project leader (76)	Systems analyst (76)
Entity-relationship diagram (ERD) (92)	Project management (78)	Systems development (73)
Fact-finding techniques (85)	Project management software (79)	Systems development life cycle (SDLC) (75)
Feasibility analysis (80)	Project plan (78)	Technical feasibility (80)
Gantt chart (79)	Project scope (79)	Training (101)
Implementation phase (100)	Project team (76)	User representatives (76)
In-house development (98)	Prototyping (89, 103)	Unit Test (100)

Multiple Choice Questions

1. Which of the following is not a reason that organizations decide to create a new information system or modify an existing information system?
   a. New laws require a change in the way data is maintained
   b. The current system no longer does everything needed
   c. New technology has been created
   d. The existing system has problems that need to be fixed

2. Which phase of the SDLC determines "what" the new system will do?
   a. Planning
   b. Analysis
   c. Design
   d. Implementation

3. Who is primarily responsible for analyzing, designing and developing the information system?
   a. Steering committee
   b. Systems analyst
   c. Programmer
   d. User representatives

4. Which of the following feasibility measures is concerned with whether an organization has the skills to be able to build a system?
   a. Technical feasibility
   b. Economic feasibility
   c. Organization feasibility
   d. Schedule feasibility

5. Which of the following is the most common fact-finding technique?
   a. JAD
   b. Questionnaires
   c. Interviews
   d. Observation

6. Which of the following models is used to show the processes of an information system?
   a. Entity-relationship diagram
   b. Data flow diagram
   c. Gantt chart
   d. Business rule chart

7. Mock-ups of the user interface will be created during which phase?
   a. Analysis
   b. Design
   c. Implementation
   d. Support

8. A unit test _____
   a. Ensures that different programs work correctly together
   b. Ensures that the system as a whole meets the needs of the business
   c. Ensures that an individual program works correctly
   d. Ensures that a business unit is using the new system correctly

9. In general, which of the following conversion strategies is the riskiest?
   a. Parallel
   b. Pilot
   c. Phased
   d. Direct

10. Which development approach is characterized by iteration?
    a. Outsourcing
    b. SDLC
    c. RAD
    d. Prototyping

Answers:
1. c   2. b   3. b   4. a   5. c   6. b   7. b   8. c   9. d   10. d

Review Questions

1. List the phases of the SDLC and briefly explain their main purpose.
2. Briefly explain how the members of the project team work together to develop an information system.
3. List four factors that will increase your chances for success on an information systems project.
4. Define project scope. What is scope creep and why is it a problem?
5. Explain the four common measures of project feasibility.
6. Describe three of the techniques used for fact finding.
7. Explain the importance of keeping accurate and complete system documentation.
8. Briefly explain the five different components that must be designed for an information system.
9. What are the conversion strategies that a project team may use?
10. What are three activities that occur during the support phase?
11. Discuss the benefits and considerations of prototyping as a development approach.
12. List and briefly describe the alternative approaches to developing information systems.

Projects

1. Classify the benefits identified for the child welfare information system example (page 82) as either tangible or intangible.
2. Working with a team from your class, create an online survey using Survey Monkey.
3. Investigate a company that provides outsourcing services. Write a one-page summary about the services they offer.
4. Write a one-page report that summarizes an example of a system failure. Provide your own assessment as to why the system failed.
5. Find an example of a company that has successfully used one of the alternative systems development approaches. Explain which approach they used and why it was successful.

CHAPTER 4

Database Management

PLANNING AHEAD
After reading Chapter 4, you should be able to answer these questions in your own words

STUDY QUESTIONS
What is a database?
How is a relational database designed?
What are the emerging trends and uses of databases?

LEARNING PREVIEW

In Tutorial 3 you saw how spreadsheets can be used to help manage large quantities of data. But spreadsheets were designed primarily as a tool to crunch numbers. So while they work well for analyzing and reporting data, they do have limitations and typically are not the best choice to capture the transaction data generated by an organization.   Instead, another tool, a database is often used to process large sets of data into meaningful information. In this chapter you will learn about the advantages databases offer to organizations and how to design a well structured database. Additionally you will explore some emerging uses of databases.

OPENING VIGNETTE

Controlling Health Care Costs with Technology – The Dossia Project

Would you want to have access to your health records via the Internet? Five major companies are betting that their employees do and are prepared to spend millions of dollars on a new project that will do just that.

Intel, Wal-Mart, Applied Materials, British Petroleum and Pitney Bowes have joined forces in a consortium to develop a Web-based system that will allow their employees and retirees online access to their personal heath records as well as the records of their dependents. Together the consortium has invested millions of dollars in this project to create an online personal health record system named Dossia.

What is motivating these companies to make such a major investment?

The bottom line is that these companies believe that the new system will help reign in what seems like continually increasing health care costs paid for by the companies. The hope is that this can be achieved by having information available that will promote improved employee health through information and prevention. Additionally, by allowing employees quick and complete access to their health records, any errors in the records can be detected and corrected more quickly.

How will Dossia work?

Dossia is being designed as a personal health information network. Dossia will consist of up to seven databases located around the country. Each database will contain data pertaining to a different role such as claims, lab results, prescription information, etc. Once an employee joins the system and enters their personal information, Dossia will automatically gather records from outside systems such as medical practices, insurance companies and hospitals. This will allow an employee to have online access to their health record which would include immunization records, medical test results, etc. Initially the databases will store health data for the 2.5 million employees, retirees, and their dependents of the sponsoring companies. Employees will have the choice to opt in to the system and can control the amount of data they want to share, along with whom they want to share data. Employers and insurance companies will not have access to the health records.

Dossia is being designed and operated by Omnimedix Institute, a two-year old nonprofit research and development organization. According to the Omnimedix Institute, health care is the most information-intensive and information-sensitive activity in our world. Unfortunately health care is also one of the most under-computerized activities. In an attempt to design a system to provide quick, complete and secure access to health records, Dossia is being built according to a set of design principles and standards called Connecting for Health Common Framework. The framework was developed by a collaborative group of stakeholders and has support from consumer advocacy organizations, physicians, and the government.

Are employees ready for this change?

According to Zoë Baird, president of the Markle Foundation who funded the development of the Connecting for Health Framework, Americans realize the potential cost savings and improvements to care if their health information is available to them over the Internet and they are ready to do their part to improve the health care system. But others aren't as eager. Patients still have lingering concerns about privacy and the potential for misuse of their medical information, insurance companies may not have much motivation to share their data, and medical practices that don't use e-records will have additional work to scan in data results. The system was planned to be available in mid-2007. While few will deny that there is great room for improvement in patient health records and the health care system, as database technology starts to play an even bigger role in the health care industry, expect that there will be a few hiccups, bumps and bruises along the way. Let's hope that the cure to the problem won't be too bitter a pill to swallow.

(Sources: Compiled from Heather Havenstein, "Firms Invest Millions in E-health Records Plan," *Computerworld*, December 11, 2006, http://www.computerworld.com/action/article.do?command=viewArticleBasic&articleId=9005722; J. Nicholas Hoover, "Companies Unveil Data Pool to Assault Health Care Costs" InformationWeek, December 11, 2006, http://www.informationweek.com/showArticle.jhtml?articleID=196602778; http://www.intel.com/pressroom/archive/releases/20061206corp.htm, accessed on January 10, 2007; and http://www.markle.org/downloadable_assets/news_release_120706.pdf, accessed on January 10, 2007.)

In this chapter you will learn more about the ideas introduced in this case. You will learn about the importance of creating databases to provide organizations with access to their data. In addition to learning how to develop sound data models, you will extend your knowledge by learning about how to build databases. By the end of this chapter you will be able to answer the following questions about this story:

- What are some of the difficulties to managing this large set of data that you anticipate the member companies will face?
- What are some of the entities and attributes that should be contained in the Dossia system?
- What are some of the business rules identified in the case? Identify several other business rules you think will need to be implemented.
- How much do you think that the success of the project will be affected by defining and implementing business rules related to privacy?
- What does it mean that the Dossia system will have multiple databases?

VISUAL ORGANIZATION OF CHAPTER

Study Question 1	Study Question 2	Study Question 3
Database Overview	Designing a Relational Database	Database Trends
• Data Concepts • File Management vs. Databases • Database Management Systems	• The Relational Model • The Entity-Relationship Data Model	• Data Warehouses • Data Mining • Knowledge Management
Learning Check 1	Learning Check 2	Learning Check 3

DATABASE OVERVIEW

As you have seen in many of the earlier examples, organizations can generate a tremendous amount of data.   Consider just some of the pieces of data captured by UPS when you send a package – sender first and last name, sender street address, sender city, sender state, sender zip, recipient first and last name, recipient street address, recipient city, recipient state, recipient zip, date sent, package weight, and type of service (such as next day air, ground service, etc.).   In 2005, UPS delivered 14.8 million packages and documents on average each day. This translates into 14.8 million sender names, addresses, etc. and 14.8 million recipient names, address, etc. that are captured in one day alone. That's a lot of data! This doesn't even include storing any data about the 407,200 employees worldwide, or the 91,700 delivery vehicles used to transport the packages. Finding an efficient and effective way to capture, process, and store this data is critical for UPS to ensure that they are able to deliver your package on time and to the right location.   As the amount of data the organizations generate continues to increase exponentially, and as that data increasingly comes from a variety of sources, often with different storage formats, it becomes increasingly important for organizations to develop workable strategies to manage their data resources.

Data Concepts

Recall from Chapter 2 that **data** are just the raw facts that are collected and stored. Data comes in a variety of formats including numbers, letters, images, videos, or audios. You also have learned that an **information system** is used to collect, manipulate, store and disseminate data or information. Over the course of the last few chapters you have explored different types of information systems and some of the issues that go into creating them. Some of the systems have been very small and involved only a little bit of data while some have been very large. No matter the size or specific type of information system, what all of these systems have in common is data. Each information system does some kind of manipulation, or processing, of the data to create information. **Information** is data that has been organized, manipulated or processed to have meaning and value. Recall that in Chapter 2 we also discussed that for information to be useful and have value for an organization it must be accurate, complete, economical, relevant, timely, verifiable and accessible. But how does an organization make sense out of all of their data so that they can create information that has value?

To answer that question it is important to understand how data is organized and stored within an information system. The smallest unit of data in a computer is referred to as a **Bit**, short for binary digit. A bit has a value of either 0 or 1, representing a circuit that is either on or off. A **Byte** is a group of 8 bits and represents a single character. For example, the letter "A" would be represented as 01000001. Understanding bits and bytes is at the heart of the internal workings of a computer, the actual storage of the data, but for most users bits and bytes are not very exciting or useful. Instead users can benefit by understanding the *hierarchy of data* that begins with a field. A **Field** is a collection of characters, or bytes, that describe one aspect of a business object or activity – a single unit of data.   A **Record** is a collection of related data fields. A **File** is a collection of related records. A **Database** is a collection of related files. Table 4.1 shows an example of how this hierarchy works.

Unit	Description	Examples
Field	A single unit of data	Date enrolled, Student Name
Record	A collection of related fields	All of the fields for one student will be stored in a student record
File	A collection of related records	All of the students at your university are stored in the student file
Database	A collection of integrated and related files	The collection of the student file, faculty file and course file make a university database.

Table 4.1   The Hierarchy of Data

Now that you have the perspective of how data are organized, we can shift our focus to look at how organizations make sense out of all of their data. At the heart of many information systems is a **database**, an organized collection of integrated and related data files. Databases are used across all industries and have become a fundamental component of many organizations comprehensive information technology solution. A **database management system (DBMS)** is software that allows you to create a database, manage the data in the database by adding, deleting and updating records, sort and retrieve data, and creates queries and reports of that data. By using a database management system, database application programs can be built to allow shipping and receiving departments to keep track of orders and deliveries, airlines can track ticket sales on flights, human resources can maintain records regarding employee benefits, retail stores can record sales and better manage inventory, medical offices can update patient records, and universities can manage student records. How did databases become so fundamental to many organizations? The next section answers this question by briefly discussing the evolution of databases and their advantages.

File Management System Approach versus the Database Approach

File Management System Approach

When companies first started to build software applications to process their business data they built software applications using programming languages. Each software application had its own set of programming instructions and used its own set of data files. As more users in the organization saw the power of computers, more users wanted software applications built to help them. This meant that each new application needed its own set of programs and consequently its own set of data files. Figure 4.1 illustrates a subset of the software applications that an organization may have ended up with. This traditional environment is often referred to as a **File Management System.** As the organization continued to grow, more and more application programs and files were added into the organization. Each department ended up with its own set of program and files to store, manipulate, and retrieve large data sets.

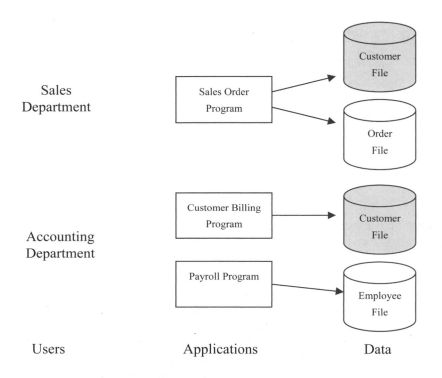

Figure 4.1 The File Management System Approach

File management systems can create several problems. The main two are data redundancy and data isolation. **Data redundancy** is when different systems/programs have separate copies of similar, if not identical, data. In the figure shown above you can see that customer information is stored in two separate files. Not only does this *waste storage space*, but it increases the chances for *inconsistencies* and *errors* in the data. It is very likely that both files will store the customer's address. Consider the situation when a customer calls the Sales Department to inform them of a new address. Since the change will only be made in the customer file in the Sales Department, the billing technician in the Accounting Department will not have the correct information. This could result in bills not getting sent to the correct address, and delays in the company receiving payment. **Data isolation**, the second problem, is when an application program can't access the data associated with other application programs. Data isolation occurs because the data files set up for each program each have their own formats. Let's assume that customer numbers are 7-digit fields, such as 1003245. What if the Sales Order Program Customer File stores the customer number as a text field while the Customer Billing Program Customer File stores it as a numeric field? This data won't be able to easily be compared. In some cases there may not even be agreement about the length of the customer number – one department may store a 7-digit field and another stores a 9-digit field. Not having any consistency in fields and formats stored in the data files is a result of a *lack of any centralized control of the data.* This limits the ability to share data. Data isolation also results in *more time required in programming* since each program will need its own data file. Table 4.2 summarizes the problems with file management systems.

Data Redundancy (Duplication of data)
- Different systems/programs have separate copies of the same data
- Wastes storage space
- Increases chances for data inconsistencies and errors

Isolated Data
- Limited data sharing
- No centralized control of data
- Requires more time spent on programming to accomplish tasks

---

Table 4.2 Problems with File Management Systems

As more file management systems were created, these problems became more obvious. Building new applications consumed more and more time and money, and the inability to get at common data became more problematic. As a result, a new approach to storing data, the database approach, evolved as a way to minimize these problems. While little new development is done using a file management approach, it still is important to understand that organizations have legacy systems built using a file management approaches and file management systems are still widely used for backing up database systems.

The Database Approach
In the database approach the focus begins by understanding the data used in an organization. The data that is needed is identified, and the formats agreed upon, separate from the different processing needs that individual departments have. This way all departments can agree that the customer number, for example, will be a 7-digit numeric field. Descriptions about what the different data values represent and their formats are known as **metadata**. The data is structured and organized into a database. The database stores not only the actual data values, but also the metadata. The database is created using a database management system. In addition to creating the actual database, the DBMS allows application programs to access the database. This allows the Sales Department to access the data and functions they need, while the Accounting Department can access the data and functions unique to them. Since the data is stored in one database, when the customer calls the Sales Department to update their address, there is only one address to update. The next time the billing technician pulls up that customer's record, they will have the new address. Figure 4.2 illustrates the database approach.

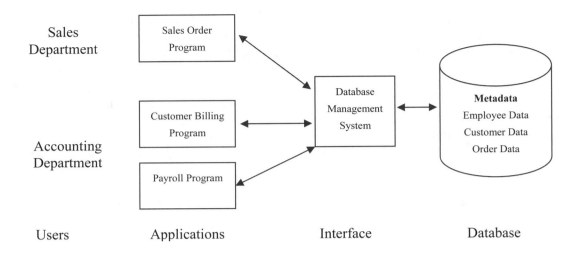

Figure 4.2 The Database Approach

The database approach offers many advantages. These are listed in Table 4.3.

- Minimize data redundancy – The data is stored in one location. This minimizes wasted storage space and increases consistency of the data.
- Minimize data isolation – Since the data is stored in one location the data can be more easily accessed and shared by different applications, departments and users.
- Increase data security – The DBMS offers features to automatically control user access to different parts of the database. This helps ensure more uniform enforcement of security procedures.
- Increase data integrity – In addition to increased integrity due to redundant data being reduced, the DBMS is able to consistently enforce data integrity constraints such as allowing only numbers in certain fields or checking that values fall within certain ranges.
- Increase data independence – Since the data is stored separately from the application programs, the application program isn't affected if changes are made to the data. This results in less maintenance required on application programs.

Table 4.3 Advantages to the Database Approach

Switching to the database approach is not a panacea. There are some considerations or potential disadvantages that an organization must keep in mind before implementing a database. These include increased costs to hire trained database specialists to ensure that the database is properly built and maintained, costs to acquire the DBMS, and increased impact of a failure since the data for all or most of the corporation are now stored in the database instead of being stored in multiple files.

It is also important to recognize that the problems inherent in the file management system approach can be found even in systems built using databases. Consider for example a business where users in different departments start building their own database applications. If each department creates its own database, each with unique fields and formats, the problems of data redundancy and data isolation will still exist. As a result it is important for an organization to have an overall information processing strategy that integrates end-user development into the organizational information systems plan but still maintains the advantages that should be obtained by utilizing the database approach. The next section explains in a little bit more detail the components and features of a database management system.

Database Management Systems

A DBMS is a set of programs, the software, that provides users with tools to create the database, manage the records in the database, and access and analyze data stored in the database. The DBMS takes care of managing the requests to perform a task so that the users (and the application programs) don't have to worry about where the data is stored and who else might be trying to access the data. Essentially the DBMS takes care of managing the data resources (finding, accessing, and returning data to an application program) much like an operating system takes care of managing the hardware resources of a computer system (finding the correct file you want to open in your word processor.) Three of the primary tasks performed by a DBMS are database creation, data manipulation, and data security.

The first task performed with a DBMS involves creating the database. When the database is built each field needs to be described. These descriptions about the data fields create the metadata that was introduced earlier. Figure 4.3 shows an example of metadata entered into a Microsoft Access database.

One of the most common tasks asked of the DBMS will be data manipulation, sometimes called file maintenance. **Data manipulation** keeps the data current and involves adding, updating, and deleting data. It is important that when these tasks are being performed, the integrity of the data is maintained. By having integrity in the data we will be able to create information that has value. You may hear people talk about *garbage in – garbage out (GIGO)*. This refers to the fact that if you accept bad data (garbage) into your system, you will get garbage out of the system (instead of information that has value.)

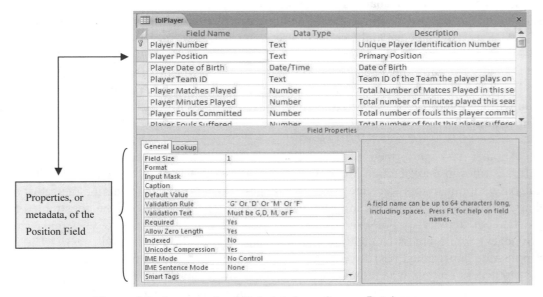

Figure 4.3 An example of Metadata in an Access Database

Integrated into the data manipulation task, the DBMS also enforces data validation. This helps maintain the integrity of the data which can minimize the "*garbage in*" part of the problem. **Data validation** compares data against a set of rules to make sure it is correct. In Chapter 3 you were introduced to the concept of a *business rule* – a rule or constraint about what is allowed or not allowed in the business. Examples of business rules include "you can't have more than 10 library books checked out at one time" or "an employee must be enrolled in a health insurance plan."   Some business rules may be specific to one organization, like those described above, while others are applicable across organizations and situations, like January has 31 days. Depending on the specific nature of the constraint, a business rule may apply to a field, record, file or database.

One of the key advantages to a database is that you define all of the metadata when building the database and the DBMS then automatically performs a variety of validity checks which enforce the business rules you have established. Some of the more common validity checks are described in Table 4.4.

Check	Description
Data Type	ensures that a value entered into a field matches the data type established for that field
Range	ensures that the a value entered into a field falls within the range of acceptable values that have been established for that field
Consistency	ensures that a value entered into a field is consistent with a value in another field
Completeness	ensures that a field contains a value if it is required

Table 4.4 Validity checks performed by the DBMS

Look back at the metadata in Figure 4.3 for the player position field. Based on the choices shown, the database will enforce the following business rules for the *player position* field:
- The field can only contain a 1 character text entry (the *data type* and *field size* properties.)
- The entry must be a G, D, M or F (the *validation rule* property.)
- The user must enter a value into this field (the *required* property.)

You will learn more about how to implement business rules in Access later in this chapter, as well as in Tutorial 4.

Another task performed by the DBMS involves ensuring security. **Database security** enforces rules to make certain that only authorized users can access the data. The DBMS allows database administrators to create access privileges. **Access privileges** define the set of activities that different users, or groups of users, can perform. The activities can be constrained based on the type of activity.   For example, some users may only be able to view data (read only privileges), while others can add, delete or change data (full update privileges).   The activities can also be constrained based on the content of the data. For example, some users may only be able to access records which they created, or have ownership over, while other users can access all of the records. Taken together the access privileges specify what records you can access and what you can do to them. Consider the online grade system at your university. As a student you are only allowed the ability to view grades; further you are only allowed to view your own grades. An instructor, however, is allowed to view grades, but can also add, delete or change grades. But that instructor can only view or update grades for students who are in their class.

Finally, you should also be aware that there are a number of different ways to represent or model the database structure. These database models include relational, network, hierarchical, and object. Database Management Systems are usually classified according to the data model on which they are based. The relational model is the most common model in use today. In the next section you will learn more about the relational model.

You started this chapter by reviewing the basic concepts about data and how data are organized. Now that you have also learned about the differences between file processing and data base management systems, you are ready to learn how to design an application using a database management system.

LEARNING CHECK
Be sure you can *explain the differences between data and information *identify the hierarchy of data *explain the problems with file managements systems *explain the advantages of the database approach *describe the primary tasks of a database management system

DESIGNING A RELATIONAL DATABASE

When you create a database system you must determine how the data is going to be organized and stored. Most database designers will begin by creating a conceptual or logical data model. This **conceptual data model** focuses on representing the data from a business perspective. The focus is on describing the different pieces of data and how they are related. In this section you will learn how to create an entity-relationship model to perform this task. After the conceptual model is built, then database specialists will create a **physical database model** which shows exactly how the database will be implemented within the specific database management system. The physical model describes how the different pieces of data will be stored. In theory it is good practice to create the conceptual model independently of the physical model. This allows you to ultimately pick a physical model that works best for your situation. Practically speaking, most companies have already settled on a particular physical model and don't have the luxury of choosing a different model. For that reason, we will focus first on learning about the relational model, and then will turn to creating a conceptual model that we will ultimately build.

The Relational Database Model

As you just learned, database management systems are built according to a particular physical model. The **relational database model**, the most common DBMS model, represents data as a collection of related tables. Each table stores data about one part of the system. For example, a database for a medical office would likely include a table with information about the different doctors, a table with information about the patients, and a table with information about appointments. The different tables would be associated with each other through common fields.

To be considered relational, a database must follow certain specifications. First, you already learned that the data must be stored in tables. The columns of a table are the different fields while the rows represent the different records. No two rows in a table can be identical. This is accomplished by requiring that each table has a primary key. The **primary key** is a field (or set of fields) that uniquely identifies one row from the next. In order to link the different tables together, there must be a field in common across the different tables. This field in common is called a **foreign key**. Relational databases are built using **normalization**, a design process which helps limit redundancy by dividing data into different tables. While learning all of the specifics about normalization is beyond the focus of this introductory chapter, the modeling techniques we will cover will be based on helping you develop a database that is normalized.

There are several different relational DBMS systems from which you can choose to create your database applications. Popular DBMS products include IBM's DB2, Oracle, and Sybase. Some open source DBMSs include MySQL and PostgreSQL. Popular DBMSs for personal computers include Microsoft Access and FileMaker Pro. Access works well for single user or small-group user databases. Microsoft's SQL server is an example of a client-server database. This means that the DBMS can handle requests from multiple client users. Each of these systems has features that may be unique, but they all provide the basic features described in this section.

Creating an Entity Relationship Model

In the first section of this chapter you learned that a database offers many advantages. However, a database will only produce these advantages if it has been designed to capture, process and store the *correct* data. In Chapter 3 you had a brief introduction to conceptual data modeling – a technique for representing the structure of data in a system. Learning how to model data correctly is a critical task. If a database is not designed correctly it can result in a system that has inconsistent data, is not able to provide information, and performs poorly. A common approach to data modeling is to create an **entity-relationship diagram (ERD).** Recall that an ERD is a tool used to graphically show the structure of the data. An **entity** is a person, place, thing or event. The ERD shows not only the entities, but also the **relationships** – how the entities are related to each other. How do you determine the entities and relationships? Remember that during the analysis phase you review different documents, forms, business rules, etc. By analyzing these you will uncover the entities and relationships. Sometimes they are quite ovbious, while other times you will need to do a bit of exploring to find the correct answer. Keep in mind that data modeling is often an iterative process – you may start with only a few entities and through the process of clarifying relationships you may decide that you need to add or subtract some entities.

During the data modeling process it is helpful to also identify the **attributes**, the characteristics that describe an entity. Listing the attributes helps to ensure that you have a clear understanding about an entity. When you draw the ERD you can choose to include none, some, or all of the attributes in the ERD. Generally you won't include any attributes if you create a high-level, or summarized, entity relationship diagrams to provide a summarized view. These may be paired with more detailed ERDs that show not only the entities, but also the attributes. Collectively, the set of diagrams shows the complete data model.

When you build an ERD it is helpful to distinguish between an entity and an instance of an entity. An **instance** is a specific representation of an entity. For example, if you were building a student database that contained a student entity, each student would be an instance of that entity. When you start building the ERD it can be helpful to think about instances of an entity to help you clearly understand each entity and the relationships. Another piece of data modeling is determining how to uniquely identify one instance of an entity from another instance. An **identifier** is an attribute that uniquely identifies one instance of an entity from another instance. How can you uniquely identify you from another student? Your name won't work since more than one student can have the same name. You probably have a StudentID Number which was assigned to you by your university. Since each student only has one StudentID Number and that number is assigned to only one student, it would be a great identifier. If you are able to indicate your identifiers during the ER modeling stage, it will save you a step later in the database design process.

In Tutorial 2 you built an Excel spreadsheet to help automate the ordering process for Hair Today. Figure 4.4 shows an example of the order form you built previously. While the spreadsheet allowed the users to more accurately enter data about a single order, it didn't provide any mechanism for storing the orders electronically. A database will provide a more comprehensive solution to the information processing needs for Hair Today.

Hair Today
Customer Order Form

| Customer ID | 12922 | | | | Order Date | | July 10, 2007 |
| Customer Name | Angela Escobar | | | | | | |

Product ID	Description	Quantity Ordered	Unit Cost		Extended Price	
1003	Barrette - Gold Filigree Crystal Flower - Ruby	2	$	17.00	$	34.00
1007	Pin - Austrian Crystal Mini Flower - Green	1	$	6.95	$	6.95
1008	Pin - Guppy Bobby Pins - Tortoise	5	$	4.00	$	20.00
1010	Pin - Tiger Eye Bobby Pins (set of 2) - Blue	3	$	6.35	$	19.05
				Subtotal	$	80.00
				Discount	$	4.00
				Tax	$	5.70
				Total	$	81.70

We appreciate your business! Please call if you have any concerns about your order.

Figure 4.4 Hair Today Order Form

Let's review data modeling concepts by creating an ERD for the Hair Today order process.

Step 1: The first step in creating an ERD is to analyze the business situation to determine the entities. The starting point for Hair Today will be the order form shown above. Based on that, what are the things, the entities, that Hair Today needs to capture data about?

Orders, Customers and Products

Although it may seem obvious, it is helpful to be certain that you understand what each entity represents. The Order entity will store data about each order placed by a customer. The Customer entity will store data about the customers. The Product entity will store data about all of the products that Hair Today sells, essentially the inventory listing.

Step 2: To help clarify your understanding about the entities, assign the attributes you see on the Order Form to the appropriate entity. Does your list match that shown in Table 4.5?

Customer	Order	Product
Customer ID	Order Date	Product ID
Customer Name	Subtotal	Description
	Tax	Unit Cost
	Discount	
	Total	

Table 4.5 Attributes for the Order form

Where do the attributes of extended price and quantity ordered belong? They might belong in the order entity, but it is possible for an order to have more than one extended price? Yes, since you can order more than one product. Do the attributes belong with product entity? Probably not. It is not uncommon to realize that you may not have enough information to make a decision. In cases like that it may be helpful to create a list of unresolved issues that need to be further investigated. These issues may include clarification on entities, attributes or business rules. For now, let's put the attributes of extended price and quantity ordered on an unresolved issues list. You may want to include a short note about why an item is on the list. For example, "need to decide where to store these attributes."

Step 3: Indicate identifiers for the entities. Look at the attributes assigned to each entity. Is there an attribute that can serve as an identifier? In the Customer entity, since each customer will receive their own Customer ID this could serve as the identifier. In the Product entity, each product will have a unique Product ID. At this point there doesn't appear to be a unique identifier for the Order table. Eventually we will need to find an identifier, but for now we can simply add a note to the unresolved issues list that this needs to be done. Figure 4.5 shows a sample of the unresolved issues list.

Figure 4.5 Unresolved Issues List

Step 4: Determine how the three entities are related to each other. Some of the questions you might ask are:
- How many orders can a customer have? A customer can place *many* different orders.
- Does an order belong to only one customer?   Yes, each order is only associated with *one* customer.
- How many products can be ordered on one order?   An order can be for *many* products. The order shown in Figure 4.4 is for 4 different products.

- Can the same product be ordered by many different customers? Yes, a product can be ordered by *many* customers. For example, many different customers can order an Austrian Crystal Pin.

Do you see that many of the questions are related to understanding the business rules of the situation? The answers to these questions show you the nature of the relationships.

Recall that relationships can be either one-to-one, one-to-many, or many-to-many. Relationships can also show whether the entities have to be associated with each other (mandatory or optional). For now we will skip showing the mandatory or optional piece. An ERD will show many, but not all, of the business rules relative to the system under development

Step 5: Now that we have identified the entities and the relationships we can create the first draft of the ERD shown in Figure 4.6.

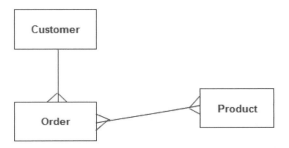

Figure 4.6 A summarized view of the Hair Today ERD

Depending on the complexity of the situation, along with the number of attributes, sometimes it is helpful to create a version of the ERD that includes the attributes. This can help ensure that everyone clearly understands each entity the same way. Figure 4.7 shows a more detailed view of the ERD with attributes assigned.

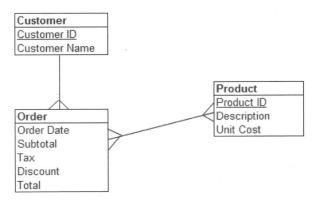

Figure 4.7 A Detailed Representation of the Hair Today ERD

Let's look a little more closely at the ERD in Figure 4.7. The relationship between Customer and Order is one-to-many. If you look only at the attributes in Customer you don't see anything about their orders. If you look only at the attributes in Order, you don't see who the customer is.

The way you know which customers have placed which orders is through the relationship line. Eventually when we convert the ERD into a set of tables to build in the database, we will add an additional attribute to represent the relationship.

In the ERD the relationship between Product and Order is many-to-many. Because a relational database cannot directly support a many-to-many relationship, you must convert this relationship into two one-to-many relationships. You perform this conversion by adding a new entity between the two other entities. In this situation, the new entity is the intersection of a product on a particular order. When you look at the order form in Figure 4.4 notice that the middle section lists each of the individual products ordered, including the quantity ordered and extended price. Conceptually this represents a line item, or order line or detail line – the listing of each product ordered. When you add this new entity to the ERD, as shown in Figure 4.8, it is connected to each of the original entities via a one-to-many relationship.

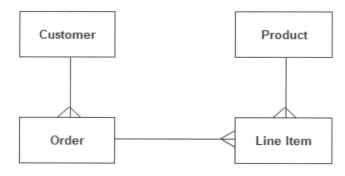

Note: When an intersection entity is inserted between two entities to resolve a Many-to-Many relationship, each of the original entities will be connected to the intersection entity via a One-to-Many relationship.

Figure 4.8 The Hair Today ERD with the Line Item entity added.

To help understand this new entity, let's revisit the attributes. Table 4.6 shows a revised attribute listing. The Line Item entity includes the specifics about how much of each product was ordered. This entity contains a new attribute called Unit Price, and also the two attributes we put on our unresolved issues list earlier – the Quantity Ordered and Extended Price. Where did Unit Price come from and what is the difference between Product and Line Item? Think of the Product entity as storing basic information about each product that you sell—in other words, your inventory listing. When a customer wants to place an order, your information system will look in the Product entity to see what products you have. Once you select a specific product to order, some of that information (like the Unit Cost) is copied into the Unit Price Line Item entity. The Unit Price represents what the cost of the item was on a particular order. This is important since the Unit Cost of an item in inventory is likely to change over time, but the price you sold it for on any particular order will not change. Additionally, in the line item entity you will record the quantity ordered for each product.

More About IT

A note about calculated fields: The Extended Price attribute in the Line Item entity, along with the Subtotal, Tax, Discount and Total in the Order entity are examples of calculated fields or calculated attributes. A **calculated attribute** is one whose value can be determined by completing a calculation using values from other attributes. Some data modelers recommend not including calculated attributes on an ERD. Others differ in this viewpoint and recommend including them on the ERD and then deciding when you build the actual tables whether they will be stored or calculated in the database.

For our purposes we will including calculated attributes on the ERD so that you have a true sense of what each entity represents. When you get to building the database tables, in Tutorial 4, you can decide then whether you will store the attribute in the table or simply calculate it for display when needed in a form or report. It would be good practice to include a comment on the unresolved issues list about still needing to decide whether to store the calculated attributes. In the attribute listing in Table 4.6, calculated attributes will be noted with an * and a comment will be attached to the table.

Most likely there are additional attributes that you would want to store about these entities that were not included on the sample order form, such as Customer Address and Order Number. But to keep our example manageable, for now let's just stay with the attributes included on the original order form.

Customer	**Order**	**Line Item**	**Product**
Customer ID	Order Date	Unit Price	Product ID
Customer Name	Subtotal*	Quantity Ordered	Item Description
	Tax*	Extended Price*	Unit Cost
	Discount*		
	Total*		

Note: * = calculated attribute; still need to decide whether to store as a field when the tables are built

Table 4.6 Updated Attributes for the Order form

Hopefully as we have worked through this example you have a better grasp of the data modeling concepts. Data modeling is a complex activity. To really learn the techniques it is important for you to work through different practice exercises on your own. One problem that beginning data modelers often encounter is differentiating between entities and attributes. How can you tell an entity from an attribute? Entities have many different characteristics that describe them. Those characteristics are the attributes. So if you identify something you think is an entity, but can't think of any attributes to describe that entity, most likely you have really identified an attribute. As you work through different scenarios, keep in mind that an ERD does not show all of the details about the information system. For example it doesn't show information about processing such as who enters a transaction (such as a teller or clerk), how it gets entered (scanned, touch screen, or keypad), or what validation is performed (the part number needs to be between 1000 and 5000.)

An important step for the analyst is to review the data models with the users to make certain that the analyst correctly understood the business situation. Remember that if the data model is not correct, the resulting system will not be correct.

Complete the **Understanding IT?** exercise below to reinforce your understanding about creating data models.

Understanding IT?

Develop an ERD for a student registration system at your university. To help provide some structure you will be asked to develop the diagram in stages.

Part 1: Begin the data modeling process by using the entities of Student, Professor, Course and ClassRoom. Identify some of the attributes that you store about each entity. Identify one or two instances of each entity. Create an ERD that includes a few attributes for each entity. Include footnotes, as needed, to explain your reasoning behind the relationships. You can leave many-to-many relationships in the ERD if needed.

Check your answer to part 1 at the end of the chapter.

Did your ERD match the one shown at the end of the chapter? If it is different, it may be because you used different assumptions about what the entities meant and/or the nature of the business rules that determine the relationships.

Discussion: To help ensure that you are clear on all of the relationships, let's work through this example. Since the system is designed to support registration for courses, it seems natural that the course entity is where you should start. Perhaps you have taken a "Principles of Economics" course for your major. Let's assume that it was numbered ECON 101. Obviously, many different students take that course. Typically each student will take additional courses as well. This indicates a many-to-many relationship between Student and Course.

The Economics course usually will be offered in different sections, each taught by a different professor. In our example let's say that Professor Smith and Professor Wilson each teach the different sections. But Professor Smith also teaches the "Advanced Seminar in Macroeconomic Theory". From this you should be able to see that there is a many-to-many relationship between Faculty and Course – a professor can teach many courses and a course can be taught by many professors.

Likewise, the different sections of Economics will most likely be taught in different rooms. Over the course of a day, a variety of different courses are taught in each room. Take for example the room you are taught in for this course. What is the class that comes in after you leave? In my case, an Art History class comes in when I leave. What does this tell you about the relationship between Room and Course? Did you conclude that it is a many-to-many relationship?

Critical thinking questions: 1) How many majors can a student have? 2) How many offices does a faculty member have? 3) How many faculty share an office?

Check your answers to the Critical Thinking questions at the end of the chapter.

Part 2: Since a many-to-many relationship can't be implemented directly, revise the ERD to convert the many-to-many relationships into one-to-many relationships. How do you decide what the new entity will be? In this case, as you read through the discussion you may have noticed that the term "section" was used a couple of times. While the concept of a course still is needed, a student doesn't actually enroll in Econ 101, but instead they enroll in a specific section of Econ 101. Keeping the existing entities, add a Section entity into your ERD, adjusting all relationships as needed. Reassign attributes as needed, and identify any new attributes needed in the Section entity.

Check your answer to part 2 at the end of the chapter.

Discussion: Do you agree with the one-to-many relationships between Section and Course? As drawn, this means that a Course (such as Econ 101) can have many different sections and a particular section of a course (like the one you are enrolled in) relates back to only a course. For example, your section at 11:00 is only for Econ 101 it can't also be for Math 119. What about the relationship between Room and Section? The same logic applies. A room has many different sections scheduled in it (but obviously at different times), but any particular section is only scheduled into one room. Look at the relationship between Faculty and Section. Based on the relationship as drawn, is team teaching allowed? No. As a one-to-many, this means that each section only has one faculty member assigned. If the business rule is different at your university you would need to change this to a many-to-many relationship.

Part 3: The addition of Section did resolve most of the many-to-many relationships, but a many-to-many relationship still exists between Student and Section. Students enroll in many different sections, and a section still has many different students enrolled. Revise your ERD to convert the many-to-many relationship into two one-to-many relationships.

Can you think of what the new entity will be? Recall in the Order Form exercise for Hair Today, the intersection between Product and Order was the Line-Item. This is where you stored how many of a particular item were on a particular order. Is there an equivalent "intersection" based on a student enrolling in a section? When a student enrolls in a section the university keeps track of the grade earned. Keeping the existing entities, add an Enroll entity into your ERD, adjusting all relationships as needed.

Check your answer to part 3 at the end of the chapter.

Hopefully your ERD for part 3 matched the solution provided. After completing the **Understanding IT?** exercise, you should have a better sense of the process involved in conceptual database design.

Moving Forward – Transforming the ERD into Database Tables

One of the confusing parts of data modeling for many students is seeing how all of the entities listed on the ERD will work together in the actual database – the physical design of the relational database. Generally the conversion of the conceptual ERD into the physical tables begins by taking each entity and making it a table. Figure 4.9 shows a sample of how part of the University Registration ERD would be converted into tables in a database.

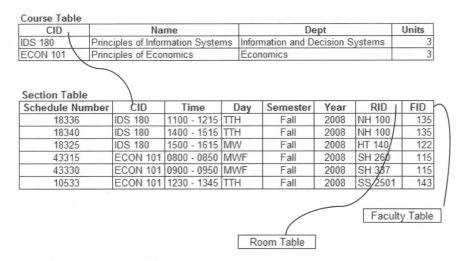

The lines show the relationships between the tables.
Relationships are made via the foreign keys.

Figure 4.9 Database Table Structure based on ERD

Look at the Course and Section tables. The CID field is included in both tables. But when you refer back to the ERD solution, notice that CID is only listed in the Course entity. Why? The answer requires us to expand on a concept introduced earlier, a foreign key. In the ERD, relationships between entities are shown via the lines that are drawn. But when you convert the ERD into database tables, the relationships must be converted as well. To do that you must identify the "field(s) in common" between the entities. It is those fields that actually form the relationship as the tables are created.

How do you implement a foreign key? First you need to look at the type of relationship that exists between the entities. Between Course and Section there is a one-to-many relationship – a course can have many sections, but a section is associated with only one course. The rule that you follow to convert a one-to-many relationship is:

> Take the primary key from the entity on the "one" side and add it as a new field into the entity on the "many" side. This added field is known as a foreign key.

Using the final ERD created in Part 3 of the Understanding IT exercise, can you see how the one-to-many conversion was implemented in the tables shown in Figure 4.9? The CID field in the Section table is a foreign key. Since the section entity is on the "many" side of two other relationships, do you see two additional foreign keys? Notice RID provides the link to the Room table and FID provides the link to the Faculty Table.

Table 4.7 summarizes the implementation process for a one-to-one and one-to-many relationship. Since any many-to-many relationships on an ERD must be resolved to one-to-many relationships before building as a database, the foreign key conversion is handled using the one-to-many process.

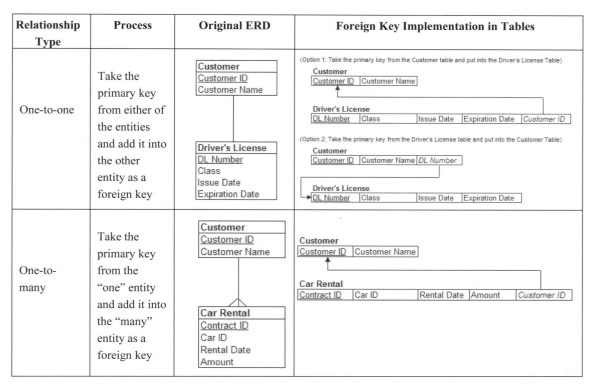

Table 4.7 Converting Relationships from an ERD

In this section you learned about designing a relational database system. You learned about what it means to have a relational database and the process used to create an entity relationship model. You will build on this foundation in Tutorial 4 when you learn how to create a database using a DBMS.   Before we get to that, in the next section you will have a chance to explore more about database trends and how organizations use databases to help them manage their business.

LEARNING CHECK
Be sure you can *explain the requirements of a relational database *differentiate between a primary key and a foreign key *understand the meaning of an entity relationship model *explain the three different types of relationships

DATABASE TRENDS

Now that you have a better understanding about how to design a relational database, it is important to revisit the bigger picture about why you are studying databases. Data, and the associated databases used to store that data, are one component of an information system, and these systems are only important to an organization if they produce information to help that organization succeed. If the Hair Today data model is built into a database application it would be an example of an **online transaction processing system (OLTP).** The objective of an OLTP is to quickly process the business transactions, such as selling hair accessories to a customer. In addition to processing the transaction, the OLTP does allow managers to get answers to different business questions. For example, through a query or report an operational level manager at Hair

Today could find out which products are their best sellers over the last quarter, or they could find out which customers have bought the most over the last six months.

However the OLTP is not practical to use in the long run to support the decision making needs of senior level managers for several reasons. First, over time the number of transactions accumulated in the database becomes too large to allow for efficient decision making. But the data associated with these historical transactions are still needed to be able to analyze trends. To keep the necessary performance in the OLTP, the organization must find a different place to store the historical data. Second, the OLTP is designed to maximize processing performance, not querying performance. Simple queries, like those illustrated earlier, will perform fine in the OLTP. However, to ask a more complicated query such as "over the last 7 years what products have been purchased the most by our top 10 customers" would require more sophisticated processing. Running that query could take a long time and could negatively affect the performance of processing transactions. A third reason is that the data needed to answer more complicated queries may be spread out over several different systems within an organization. This would make it impossible to get the answer to some questions. To address these concerns, companies may decide to store historical data in a data warehouse. This section will discuss data warehouses, tools like data mining used to analyze that data, and the knowledge management process used by organizations to more effectively utilize the knowledge resulting from their information systems.

Data Warehouses

A **data warehouse** is a repository of the historical data from an organization. Data warehouses came into existence in the late 1980's and early 1990's as the number of information systems grew and the quantity of data being stored by corporations exploded. The data in a data warehouse may come from a variety of different internal systems as well as from external sources. The data are organized in a way that will support management's ability to have a multi-dimensional view of the data through a user-friendly reporting interface. This allows executives and managers to better analyze data and make business decisions. A data warehouse should have the following characteristics:

- *Organized by subject* - data elements that relate to the same subject (e.g., vendor, customer, employee) are all linked together
- *Nonvolatile* - data are not changed or updated after having been entered into the data warehouse
- *Integrated* - contains data from all of the organizations operational information systems
- *Time-variant* - stores historical data so that trends can be tracked over time
- *Consistent* - storage formats/coding of the data that may vary across different systems are made consistent
- *Online analytical processing* - uses a multidimensional data model such as a star or data cube to support **online analytical processing** – rapid processing of complex, analytical and ad-hoc queries.

Data warehouses are the foundation of an organization's Business Intelligence system. **Business Intelligence Systems** help organizations better understand their business situation, analyze the impact of changes in the marketplace, and forecast future trends. Ultimately these systems help organizations make better decisions about their business. They are the evolution of Decision Support Systems and Management Information Systems. Continental Airlines, for example, uses a data warehouse that gets data from more than 25 different enterprise systems including reservations, customer information, schedules, airline maintenance and employee data. The data warehouse enables Continental to get a comprehensive view of each of their 31 million frequent flier customers. Continental uses this data to identify the value of each customer and then target individual offerings to their most valued customers.

The key advantage offered by data warehouses is that users have access to vast amounts of data, including historical data, that have been integrated in a way that provides answers to complex queries. They often support the Customer Relationship Management needs of an organization. Unfortunately they do take a considerable amount of time and effort to build. It is not uncommon for a data warehouse to contain hundreds of gigabytes of data. Additionally, the costs to build and implement often run in the millions of dollars. This is compounded with added expenses associated with the need to continuously clean and organize data before loading it as well as ensuring security of all the data.

In contrast to a data warehouse that integrates data from across the organization, a **data mart** is a subset, or scaled-down version, of a data warehouse. Data marts usually contain data related to a specific unit or function within an organization. A *dependent data mart* gets its data from the larger data warehouse in an organization, while an *independent data mart* gets data directly from the organization's application programs. Because data marts are smaller they can minimize some of the concerns such as expense and complexity associated with data warehouses. Data marts are often used in small to medium-sized organizations, or in departments within a larger organization. The departments, such as finance or marketing, typically have control over the design of the data mart, whereas with a data warehouse the control is centralized with the organization. This can provide for a more customized design which may result in better decision support for an individual department.

Data Mining

Data mining is a tool that managers or business analysts can use to help them make better decisions. One of the primary uses of a data warehouse, or a data mart, is data mining. **Data mining** is a process used to analyze and sort through data to find patterns and relationships among data – to produce the needed business intelligence. Because of the substantial contributions that data mining can make, you can find it used across a broad range of industries. Insurance companies use data mining to identify and reduce fraud, retailers can better manage the customer life cycle by profiling customers, and the medical community can predict the success of different treatments. While most organizations have always analyzed the data generated by their information systems, data mining goes beyond simple reporting. Through the use of advanced algorithms, data mining helps companies predict trends and behaviors and discover new patterns in the data.

One of the most common prediction applications is in target marketing. The Washington Post newspaper uses data mining to improve the targeting of their direct mail program. Other prediction examples include identifying customers who are likely to go bankrupt based on credit card usage or consumers who are a good risk for a loan.

Applications involving discovery of new patterns include fraud detection and purchasing patterns. Stuart Maue, a St. Louis based legal auditing firm, uses data mining to review and audit legal bills to identify potential fraud. For one case alone they loaded 200 boxes of litigation invoice data into their data warehouse. The audit team ultimately analyzed more than 1 million billing entries from 322 partners, 849 associates and 1,023 paralegals, billing more than 1.2 million hours of services plus associated costs and expenses. The IRS uses data mining to analyze tax returns and the associated financial data looking for potential fraudulent tax refund requests. WalMart allows their supplies to access their data warehouse. This allows suppliers to analyze customer buying patterns and better manage store inventory levels.

What all of these examples have in common is that organizations are able to use the vast amount of data they have captured to better focus their attention and efforts on improving their business. But data mining is not without concerns related to privacy. Because the data warehouse brings together data from many disparate sources, data mining allows information to be produced that would not otherwise be available. There is a great potential for abuse. Concern must be taken to ensure that privacy laws are followed in the design and usage of these systems.

Before we leave the topic of data mining it is important to come back to the issue of data integrity. The results you obtain from data mining are limited by the quality of the data that you capture and store in your information systems. In Tutorial 4 you will learn several different features inside of Access to help ensure that the data captured in your systems is valid. During the analysis stage of developing your system you must identify what types of validation need to be performed on the different pieces of data. When designing and building the system ensure that the features are implemented, and finally test, test, test to verify that the system works as intended.

Knowledge Management

Knowledge management (KM) is the process of identifying, capturing, organizing, and sharing the knowledge, or **intellectual assets**, within an organization. Simply put, this means taking what your employees, business partners and customers know, and sharing that with your employees, departments, and perhaps even other companies, to develop best practices. **Best practices** are the most effective and efficient way of accomplishing a task.

Generally knowledge is classified into two types: explicit or tacit. **Explicit knowledge** consists of anything that can be documented, archived, and codified. Examples of explicit knowledge include procedures and policies, marketing research, reports, and business plans. **Tacit knowledge**, on the other hand, is what people know. Often it is hard to capture. Ultimately it is up to the organization to decide what knowledge they need to capture.

Most organizations have always been doing some type of knowledge management. For example, they may conduct exit interview of an employee to solicit feedback on the company, develop mentoring programs for new hires, or cross-train employees. But with the increase in the amount of data generated by organizations, the need to integrate explicit and tacit knowledge, and the retirement of the baby-boom generation, effectively managing knowledge has taken on a new spotlight. To that end, knowledge management systems are being developed. A **Knowledge Management System (KMS)** is not a single tool; rather it is the collection of information resources used to manage knowledge. These information resources may include groupware, email, intranets, extranets, databases, and data warehouses. To gain a benefit from a KMS an organization must realize that knowledge management requires a cultural shift within the organization to encourage employees and decision makers to share their knowledge through collaboration. For example, if sales employees compete with each other for bonuses will a salesperson be motivated to share their "secrets to success?" The Los Angeles Joint Regional Intelligence Center (JRIC) recognizes the need to address the cultural shift. Started in July 2005, the JRIC is a cooperative effort involving the Los Angeles County Sherriff's Department, the Los Angeles Police Department, the FBI and the Department of Homeland Security. They are implementing an intelligence management and analysis system that will allow analysts to gather and track leads and information from the various law enforcement agencies. The project manager realizes that whether the JRIC succeeds or not isn't dependent on the technology. Rather success will depend on whether the different agencies can work out disagreements on what information to share and even how to share it.

If a cultural shift towards encouraging a free flow of ideas, fostering creativity and valuing employee knowledge occurs, organizations should see a variety of benefits from a KMS including:

- Increased innovation
- Decreased response times
- Improved customer service
- Streamlined operations
- Cost savings
- Enhanced employee retention rates

In this section you learned how data warehouses are used to organize and store historical data. You learned about predictive and discovery applications of data mining used to generate business intelligence. Finally you learned about the knowledge management process used to help organizations manage their intellectual capital.

LEARNING CHECK
Be sure you can *describe the characteristics of a data warehouse *explain how data mining is used in an organization *describe knowledge management, including the differences between explicit and tacit knowledge *identify the benefits of a knowledge management system

WRAPPING IT UP

In this chapter you learned about database systems and how they are used by organizations to manage large quantities of data. You learned how to create an entity-relationship data model. Finally you explored data warehouses, data mining and knowledge management. In the next chapter you will learn how to create a database using Access.

Study Questions Summary

1. What is a database?
    - A database in an organized collection of integrated and related files
    - Database Management Systems are software that allow you to create and use a database
    - Compared to a File Management System, a database system can help solve the problems of data redundancy and data isolation

- The three primary tasks performed by a DBMS are database creation, data manipulation, and data security.

2. How is a relational database designed?
    - A conceptual data model represents the data from a business perspective while a physical data model shows how the data will be built in a specific database system.
    - The relational database model represents data as a collection of related tables
    - An entity relationship model is a common tool for building the conceptual data model
    - The ERD is converted to a physical database model by converting entities into tables and relationships into foreign keys

3. What are the emerging trends and uses of databases?
    - Data warehouses integrate and store data from a variety of internal and external sources
    - Business intelligence systems help organizations better analyze and understand their business situation
    - Data marts are scaled-down data warehouses offering a more customized data analysis solution
    - Organizations use data mining to predict trends and behaviors and to discover new patterns
    - Knowledge management is used to help organizations identify, capture, organize, and share the knowledge assets within an organization.

Solutions to Chapter Activities

UNDERSTANDING IT?
Student Registration Problem (pages 130 – 131)
Part 1 ERD:

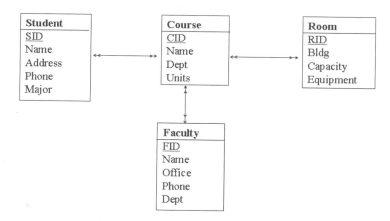

Part 1 Critical Thinking Questions:

1. **How many majors can a student have?** An attribute can only have one value placed inside of it. This means that since major is an attribute of the student entity, each instance of the student entity (each individual student) can only have one major. If your

university allowed students to have more than one major, then we would need to represent major differently. (We will revisit this situation in the next chapter.)

2. **How many offices does a faculty member have?** Following the same logic just explained, since office is an attribute of the faculty entity, a faculty member can only have one office.

3. **How many faculty share an office?** However, the ERD is unable to tell us the answer to this question. Remember that an ERD is unable to show all of the business rules. If there was a limitation on sharing, that requirement would need to be noted and implemented through programming or validation checks when the system is created.

Part 2 Revised ERD with Section Entity Added:

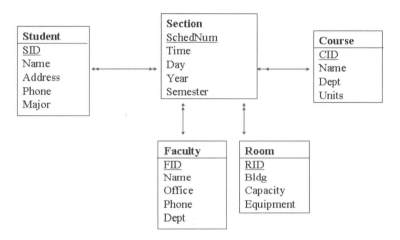

Part 3 Revised ERD with Section Entity Added:

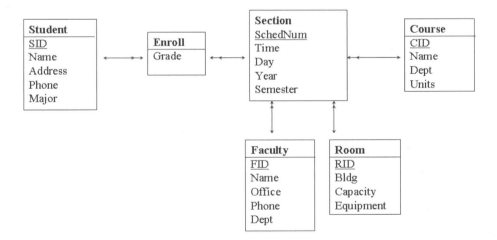

Key Terms

Page Number references are included in parentheses

Access privileges (122)	Data validation (122)	Instance (124)
Attribute (124)	Data warehouse (134)	Intellectual assets (136)
Best practices (136)	Database (117)	Knowledge management (136)
Bit (117)	Database security (122)	Knowledge Management System (136)
Business Intelligence Systems (134)	Database Management System (DBMS) (117, 121)	Metadata (119)
Byte (117)	Entity (124)	Normalization (124)
Calculated attribute (129)	Entity-Relationship Diagram (ERD) (124)	Online analytical processing (134)
Conceptual data model (123)	Explicit knowledge (136)	Online transaction processing system (OLTP) (133)
Data (116)	Field (117)	Physical database model (123)
Data isolation (118)	File (117)	Primary key (124)
Data manipulation (121)	File Management System (118)	Record (117)
Data mart (135)	Foreign key (124)	Relational database model (123)
Data mining (135)	Identifier (125)	Relationship (124)
Data redundancy (118)	Information (116)	Tacit knowledge (136)

Multiple Choice Questions

1. The relational database model represents data as a collection of related _____.
   a. fields
   b. records
   c. tables
   d. databases

2. Based on the information shown in the Student Entity, how many majors can a student have?

Student
SID
Name
Address
Phone
Major

a. One
b. Two
c. Many
d. Impossible to tell from the information provided

3. Which of the following would be the best relationship between the entities of Author and Book?
a. One-to-one
b. One-to-many
c. Many-to-many
d. Impossible to determine

4. Validity checks include all of the following except _____.
a. Range checks
b. consistency checks
c. data type checks
d. completeness checks
e. relationship checks

5. Which of the following is a correct table, based on transforming the ERD into database tables?

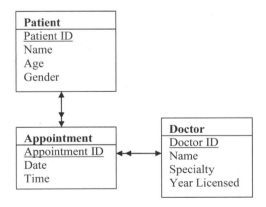

a. Doctor(DoctorID, Name, Specialty, YearLicensed, AppointmentID)
b. Patient(PatientID, Name, Age, Gender, AppointmentID)
c. Appointment(AppointmentID, Date, Time, PatientID, DoctorID)
d. Appointment(AppointmentID, Date, Time)
e. A, B, and C are all correct

6. Data mining _____.
    a. helps companies predict trends and behaviors.
    b. helps companies discover new patterns in their data.
    c. is a primary use of data warehouses
    d. All of the above

7. Which of the following is not a characteristic of a data warehouse?
    a. Nonvolatile
    b. Organized by subject
    c. Uses OLTP
    d. Consistent

8. A _____ typically includes groupware, email, intranets, extranets, databases, and data warehouses.
    a. Tacit knowledge system
    b. Data mining system
    c. Networked information exchange system
    d. Knowledge management system

Answers:
1. c   2. a   3. c   4. e   5. c   6. d   7. c   8. d

Review Questions

1. Explain the hierarchy of data.
2. Describe the two main problems with file management systems and how a database can help overcome these problems.
3. Explain the difference between a database and a database management system.
4. Describe the three primary tasks performed by a DBMS.
5. Define primary key and foreign key and give an example of each.
6. What is the purpose of an Entity Relationship Model?
7. Define each of the following terms and provide an example of each:
    a. Entity
    b. Attribute
    c. Relationship
8. List and briefly explain the characteristics of a data warehouse.
9. Describe two examples of Data Mining.
10. Explain the differences between Knowledge Management and a Knowledge Management System.

Projects

1. **Pets for the Heart** is a non-profit business that rescues unwanted animals and helps to find them homes. Up until now they have kept paper records on all of the animals and families that adopt the animals. They are interested in exploring how a database might be able to help them better manage their records. An example of their Animal Registration Form is shown below. Unfortunately, data for several of the fields (e.g., date of birth and previous owner) are not always available.

    As a first step in the process, create an ERD for Pets for the Heart.

Animal Registration Form

Pet ID: _____   Date of Admittance: _____

Pet Name: _____   Date of Birth: _____

Pet Type: _____   Pet Breed: _____   Color: _____

Previous Owner: _____

List of Shots *(if more space needed list additional shots on back of card)*
          Shot Name   Date

    _____

    _____

    _____

Date of Adoption: _____

Adoptive Owner Information

Last Name: _____   First Name: _____

Address: _____

City: _____   State: _____   Zip: _____

Phone: _____

CHAPTER **5**

The Internet – A Network of Networks

PLANNING AHEAD

After reading Chapter 5, you should be able to answer these questions in your own words

STUDY QUESTIONS

What is the Internet and how does it work?
What is an Internet Domain Name?
What types of networks and media make up the Internet?
What are the typical ways that people access the Internet?

LEARNING PREVIEW

The Internet and networking technologies have extended the reach of business and propelled the concept of a global economy. Today, businesses are not constrained by geographic and temporal boundaries. Whether we are at work, at home, or on the road, we increasingly rely on the Internet and a variety of wired and wireless technologies for communication and for sharing and leveraging resources. The convergence of data, voice and video technologies via the fast, wired and wireless channels has significantly extended business capabilities and has equipped the global economy with efficient worldwide communication capabilities. The Internet and networking technologies have also altered personal communication, allowing us to use a variety of devices to communicate anywhere in the world, at any time, with colleagues, family and friends for fraction of the cost of a few years ago. Today, individuals and organizations all over the world rely on the Internet and its cast of networking technologies as a primary means of communication.

Besides business and personal communication, the Internet and its networks have changed computing. Today, it seems that there are as many new software applications that are developed to run in our web browsers as there are applications that require installation on our computers. *Hosted software*, *Software-on-Demand*, and *Software as a Service* are all terms that suggest that the future of computing is evolving as Sun Microsystems predicted in 1984 in its company slogan, "the network is the computer." Today, many people truly view the computer as just a network appliance.

OPENING VIGNETTE

Agathon AG

Figure 5.1 Agathon Headquarters, Solothurn, Switzerland

Agathon AG is an innovative Swiss manufacturer of machine tools and press-tool standards. Founded in 1918 as a tool maker for the clock and watch industry, this third generation business is headquartered in Solothurn, Switzerland and run by Dr. Walter Pfluger, Agathon's President and CEO. Dr. Pfluger helped Agathon secure its successful position in the global machine tool market by developing high performance, precision grinding machines for the automobile, medical, hydraulics and electronics industries. He also had the vision to implement a global, customer-oriented information and communication infrastructure that allows Agathon to optimize its supply chain and enhance its dialogue with customers and distributors. Agathon's information technology infrastructure relies on SAP/R3, the leading software for Enterprise Resource Planning (ERP), for supply chain support, and the Internet and modern networking technologies for communication with Agathon customers and distributors. These technologies make it possible, for example, for an engineer in Switzerland to remotely monitor, adjust, and control Agathon grinding machines anywhere in the world using the Internet. This gives Agathon customers immediate access to technical expertise, minimizing the idle time of expensive equipment and mitigating the need for slower, costly, on-site customer service. Agathon engineers, in fact, have remotely diagnosed and corrected customer equipment issues well before the customer was even aware of a problem.

Agathon relies on Swisscom Mobile, a national cellular service provider of Switzerland, to help key employees who travel keep in touch with the office and with customers. Swisscom Mobile's Unlimited service provides Agathon employees with a secure, high-speed connection to the corporate network via a virtual private network (VPN) over the Internet. This leading-edge broadband cellular service also senses the availability and speed of up to five different data communication technologies and seamlessly and instantly switches Agathon employees' laptops to the wireless technology that provides the best Internet connection at the time. The data communication technologies supported by Swisscom Mobile's Unlimited service include four Wireless WAN technologies: GPRS a 53.6Kbps GSM data standard, as well as the third-generation (3G) cellular technologies EDGE (256Kbps), UMTS (384Kbps), and 3.5G HSDPA (up to 1.8Mbps). The Swisscom Mobile Unlimited PCMCIA cards can also sense Wireless LAN ("WiFi" 802.11b/g) technologies that are common to most WLAN "hot-spots" today.

Figure 5.2 Swisscom Mobile 3G notebook card

Agathon's implementation of broadband service for its mobile devices and its use of the Internet provides a good example of how the convergence of networking technologies has extended an organization's global reach and given competitive advantage to companies that know how to leverage these technologies. For Agathon, the Internet and its network of networks provides the capabilities to provide outstanding customer service and up-to-the- minute information as it is needed in the organization and in its supply chain. In this chapter, we focus on the Internet and these networking technologies.

VISUAL ORGANIZATION OF CHAPTER

Study Question 1	Study Question 2	Study Question 3	Study Question 4
The Internet	Internet Domain Names	The Networks of the Internet	Internet Access
• Background • Internet Architecture • Packet Switching and Protocols	• The Domain Name System • Registering a Domain Name • Top-Level Domains	• Types of Networks • Network Media	• Bandwidth and Broadband • Internet Service
Learning Check 1	Learning Check 2	Learning Check 3	Learning Check 4

THE INTERNET

The **Internet** is literally a network of many discrete networks that are united by a set of evolving communication standards and ostensibly, a universal desire for a non-proprietary, politically-neutral, global communications network. To better understand the Internet, we feel it is important to have a basic understanding of its architecture and of the technologies associated with the Internet's networks. Generally, understanding these technologies can help individuals and organizations leverage their investment in their networking infrastructure. Additionally, the more we know about the Internet and the networking technologies that allow us to share information resources, the better prepared we will be to protect these resources from loss, unauthorized use, and other data disasters that we discuss in Chapter 7. We begin this section by with a brief history of the Internet followed by a discussion of the fundamental architecture of the largest network in the world, the Internet.

Background

The Internet grew out of a Department of Defense initiative undertaken by the Advanced Research Projects Agency (ARPA) in 1969 to link ARPA-funded university computer networks at UCLA, UCSB, Stanford and the University of Utah to its network. Over the next decade, as more networks were added to the ARPANET, the benefits of a high-speed communications network were pretty clear. By 1984, the ARPANET had grown to about one thousand computer hosts. In 1985, the ARPANET was essentially adopted by the National Science Foundation (NSF) when the NSFnet, a network of supercomputer centers, joined the ARPANET. The NSF managed the network until it became privatized in the early 1990s.

Today, no single organization, or country, controls the Internet. Instead, the Internet is governed by a number of independent boards and groups who manage various aspects and activities of the Internet (see Table 5.1). The global appeal of the Internet is furthered by its open architecture which gives participating networks the freedom to choose their individual network technologies and resolves the internetwork communication issues at a meta-level that many refer to as the "Internet Architecture."

The major governing bodies of the Internet include:
- Internet Architecture Board (IAB) → Helps define Internet structure
- Internet Corporation for Assigned Names and Numbers (ICANN)→ Oversees IP addresses and Domain Names
- Internet Engineering Steering Group (IESG) → Helps set Internet standards
- Internet Engineering Task Force (IETF) → Oversees Internet operations and growth
- Internet Society (ISOC) → Monitors Internet practices and policies
- World Wide Web Consortium (W3C) → Sets Internet programming standards

---

Table 5.1 The Internet's Governing Organizations

Internet Architecture

Since clouds are frequently used to represent communications networks, the large cloud in Figure 5.3 is used to depict a simplified, high-level view of the Internet. Inside the Internet cloud are numerous other clouds, or networks, that have the ability to communicate with each other. The *inter*network communication capabilities of these networks explain why the term **Internet** is literally, a network of networks. By drilling down into one of the network clouds, we get a glimpse of the hardware, software and communications channels that typically make up networks all over the world.

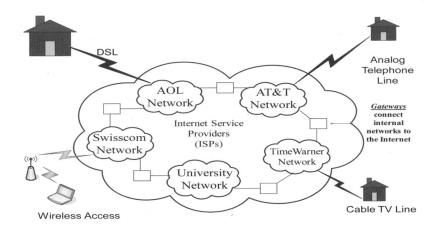

Figure 5.3 Internet Architecture – A Simple View

While organizations sometimes have compelling reasons to use proprietary and non-standardized technologies in their communications networks, our discussion generally focuses on the common, standardized networking technologies. Essentially, the technology standards are designed to ensure *inter*network operability and to help maintain *intra*network security and reliability.

Packet Switching and Protocols

In this section, we discuss the fundamental Internet technologies and concepts, such as packet switching and protocols that allow the Internet's internetwork communication.

Packet Switching
The ARPANET successfully demonstrated that a survivable, decentralized, wide-area communication network could be developed using a communications technology known as **packet switching**. Packet switching essentially made it possible for data to traverse networks without using dedicated, circuit-switched connections that were typical of the public telephone system at that time. Packet switching allows multiple computers and communications devices to simultaneously share a communication link by splitting the communication into small **packets**. Figure 5.4 shows the packet-switching process for sending a file (called File) between Point A and Point B. Besides carrying part of the original message, each packet is numbered and labeled with a destination address. Essentially, this allows the individual packets to travel independently to their network destination via any available communications link. When the packets reach their destination, they are organized and reassembled. Today, packet switching is a fundamental networking technology for both voice and data communication worldwide.

Figure 5.4 Packet Switching
(Photo Source: http://www.pbs.org/opb/nerds2.0.1/geek_glossary/packet_switching_flash.html

TCP/IP

Computer networks, including those that made up the ARPANET, rely on rules, or **protocols**, to facilitate communication with computers and other devices on that network. Not surprisingly, the protocols of one network are often incompatible with those used on other networks. In order to achieve internetwork communication, as was the goal of the ARPANET, network designers had to create a new set of protocols. Robert Kahn and Vinton Cerf are credited with the original design of the set of protocols now known as **Transmission Control Protocol/Internet Protocol (TCP/IP)** that were used to unite the individual networks on the ARPANET and that are still used today to facilitate Internet communication. TCP and IP were the first two, and arguably the most important, of the communications protocols in the Internet protocol suite.

The Internet protocol suite is an evolving set of protocols that individually define discrete aspects of Internet communication. Often the Internet protocol suite is shown as a 4-layer model (Figure 5.5) that is analogous to the networking industry's standard, OSI 7-layer reference model. Both models were conceived to allow interoperability across various types of computers and networking devices and to keep the protocol design issues relatively simple. Conceptually, each protocol layer is only concerned with communicating with the protocol layers above and below that particular layer. Collectively, a stack of protocol layers, or **protocol stack**, describes the flow of data from the physical media are that used to connect devices to the network up to the particular application run by the user, such as web browsing (e.g., HTTP).

The Internet 4-Layer Model

The Internet 4-Layer model gives you a general idea of the relationship between the Internet protocols. Essentially, each layer of the model is designed to handle a specific aspect of Internet communication. We will be discussing a few of the application layer protocols, such as HTTP, FTP, and SMTP in Chapter 6, The World Wide Web. TCP handles the sequencing of packets and helps to ensure the in-order delivery of data from sender to receiver.   In the next section we discuss Internet Protocol (IP) and the IP addressing system used to facilitate communication over this global, packet-switched network.   The Network Access layer of the 4-Layer Model is primarily concerned with the network-level functionality such as **Ethernet**, the most common protocol for connecting devices on a Local Area Network.

Internet 4-Layer Model

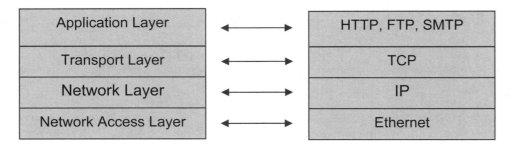

Figure 5.5 Internet 4-Layer Model

IP Address

The **Internet Protocol (IP)** is dependent on each computer and network device having its own unique Internet address, known as an **IP address**. Figure 5.6 shows how an IP address is similar to a mailing address with fields for an individual name, street address, city, and state.

Postal Address (bottom to top)	Internet Address
• State → California • City →San Diego • Street→111 Main Street • Individual→The Eastons The Eastons 111 Main Street San Diego, California	• Region → 146 • Organization →191 • Network →1 • Computer →1 146.191.1.1 eastonandeaston.com

Figure 5.6 IP Addressing

Typically, we don't pay too much attention to the numeric Internet addresses because IP addresses can also be expressed as Domain Names (which will be discussed in the next section). In IPv4, the current version of the Internet Protocol, numeric Internet addresses are shown in **dotted decimal** format, or four decimal numbers separated by periods. For example, 66.102.7.99 is an IP address in dotted decimal format assigned to one of Google's computers. Try typing a valid, dotted decimal IP address into your web browser. Does it return a web page? It is certainly possible to use an IP address to access a web page. Most of us, however, are better at remembering a name, such as Google.com, rather than trying to remember a set of numbers. For now, it is useful to remember that regardless of the format, IPv4 addresses inevitably resolve to four 8-bit numbers (four binary numbers each containing eight bits) between 0 and 255. Figure 5.7 shows how the binary equivalent of Google's dotted decimal IP address can easily be determined.

Google's IP Address in Decimal Form	Decimal Number System				Binary Number System							
	1000s	**100s**	**10s**	**1s**	**128**	**64**	**32**	**16**	**8**	**4**	**2**	**1**
66			6	6	0	1	0	0	0	0	1	0
102		1	0	2	0	1	1	0	0	1	1	0
7												
99												

Figure 5.7 Binary Number System

Each eight-bit string has 2^8 or 256 different combinations that can be used in an IP address. Theoretically, the IPv4 addressing scheme supports nearly 4.3 billion IP addresses. The IP address for Google given above (66.102.7.99) is actually 01000010 01100110 00000111 01100011 in the 32-bit format.

The IPv4 specification was published in 1981 and it has not been substantially changed since. At that time, the IP addressing scheme gave the Internet community ample capacity to assign unique Internet addresses well into the future. However, the growth in Internet usage, propelled by new network-aware devices such as mobile phones and new IP-based services such as VoIP, is depleting the IPv4 address space. In 1994, IPv6 was adopted by the Internet Engineering Task Force. **IPv6** is a 128-bit addressing scheme that has been slow to implement but it should be in widespread use by the 2009 to 2011 timeframe when the IPv4 address pool is expected to be depleted. IPv6 addresses are 128 bits long and appear in the hexadecimal (base-16) number system where IPv4 addresses appear in dotted-decimal (base-10) format. Additionally, IPv6 uses colons to separate its 16-bit fields instead of the decimal point used to separate the 8-bit fields in IPv4. As example, the fully uncompressed IPv6 equivalent of Google's IPv4 address above would appear as: 0000:0000:0000:0000:0000:0000:4266:0763.

Complete the following **Integrate IT** exercise to learn more about Internet addresses.

Integrate IT

1. Find the dotted decimal IP address of the current computer that hosts Google's website using "Ping." (e.g, Start→Run→ping google.com should return the current IP address used by the Google site). Note: Ping is a network tool that is typically used by network administrators to check the network connections.

2. After acquiring a valid dotted decimal IP address, determine its 32-bit equivalent or complete the partially filled table below.

Google's IP Address in Decimal Form	Decimal Number System				Binary Number System							
	1000s	**100s**	**10s**	**1s**	**128**	**64**	**32**	**16**	**8**	**4**	**2**	**1**
66			6	6	0	1	0	0	0	0	1	0
102		1	0	2	0	1	1	0	0	1	1	0
7												
99												

Integrate IT (continued)

3. Use the Excel function =DEC2BIN to convert a dotted decimal IP address to its binary equivalent or =BIN2DEC to convert an IP address in binary format to its decimal equivalent. (Note: in pre-2007 versions of Excel, this function is available with the Add-In *Analysis ToolPak*).

In this section, we learned that about two of the fundamental technologies of the Internet: packet switching and the TCP/IP protocols. Additionally, we learned that each device on the Internet must have a unique IP address and that the current version of that addressing system, IPv4, is running out of addresses. We also learned that IP addresses can actually be represented in a number of different formats including dotted-decimal, binary and as a Domain Name. In the next section we take a closer look at Internet Domain Names.

LEARNING CHECK
Be sure you can * explain an IP address * describe IPv4 and why it is being replaced * explain packet switching *

INTERNET DOMAIN NAMES

As we discussed in the previous section, IP addresses are the numeric addresses of computers on the Internet that host email accounts and web pages. A dotted decimal number is typically not as easy to remember as a company name or a descriptive term. This is one of the reasons that the Internet's **Domain Name System** was developed. Registering a Domain Name is one of the first things a business will do in order to establish a presence on the Internet.

The Domain Name System

A **Domain Name** is essentially the text version of a numeric IP address. Businesses register a Domain Name for their website so customers can access the site using words, such as the company name, rather than the numeric IP address. Internet Domain Names are organized by their extension, the letters or word that follows the "dot" in the Domain Name (for example, .com, .org, .net). This extension is referred to as a **Top-Level Domain (TLD)**. Currently, ICANN accredits domain-name registrars for the TLDs shown in Table 5.2 below. We will discuss Top-Level Domains later in this section.

.aero - used by the aviation community
.asia - used for the Pan-Asia and Asia Pacific region
.biz - restricted to businesses
.cat - reserved for the Catalan linguistic and cultural community
.com – reserved for businesses
.coop – reserved for cooperatives
.info – unrestricted, stands for "information"
.jobs - reserved for the human resource management community
.mobi – used by consumers and providers of mobile products and services
.museum - restricted to museums
.name – reserved for use by individuals
.net – designed for network-related
.org – intended for non-profit organizations
.pro – restricted to "licensed" professional
.tel – used by individuals and businesses for contact information in the DNS (check out the simulator for a .tel TLD at http://www.telnic.org/individual-simulator.html)
.travel – reserved for the travel industry

Table 5.2 Current generic Top-Level Domains

Internet websites and email accounts, reside, or are "hosted," on computers that typically have lots of disk storage and fast, enduring, or static, connections to the Internet. As we discussed in the previous section, each host also has a unique Internet address, or IP address, that functions like a mailing address but is formatted, or appears, in dotted decimal format, such as 66.102.7.99. It would be difficult for many of us to remember a number like this every time we want to visit a particular website. Furthermore, even with razor sharp memory, there is a strong possibility we would not be able to access the website because maintenance issues and security policies require many companies to periodically change hosts and/or IP addresses.

These situations make a strong case for using a domain name rather than an IP address for public websites and email addresses. An Internet domain name is typically a word, acronym, phrase or other mnemonic device that makes websites and email addresses easy to remember – www.google.com, for example, is the domain name for Google's website. Domain names also provide a persistent address for websites and email accounts that periodically move to different Internet hosts and different Internet addresses.

Registering a Domain Name

Domain Names can be easily registered with agents, or registrars, of the Internet's Domain Name System (DNS). Registering, or leasing, a domain name is often the first step many businesses undertake after the decision to develop a website has been made and a domain name has been selected. This is a relatively easy process and there are hundreds of *registrars*, such as GoDaddy.com and InterNIC.com, that will handle the registration process for you. A complete listing of domain name registrars can be found at http://www.icann.org/en/registrars/accredited-list.html

Before actually registering a domain name, one typically uses the registrar's site to check an Internet database of domain names, called the *whois* database, to verify that the desired domain name is available. What makes a good Domain Name? While there are no universal rules for Domain Names, many experts believe you should keep three points in mind when you register a business (.com) Domain Name:

- keep the name simple and under ten characters, if possible; currently you can register a name with up to 63 characters.
- Domain names can only use letters, numbers, and hyphens. Spaces and symbols are not allowed.
- Domain names are not case sensitive.

It should not be a surprise if the name you first select is unavailable considering more than 70 million domain names have been registered since the Internet's **Domain Name System (DNS)** began in the early 1980s. Not all of these registered domain names are active. Many of these names were leased by *cybersquatters* who routinely registered numerous domain names with the intent of re-leasing the names for a profit. Some cybersquatters have been very successful. For example, Domain Names such as Autos.com and Seniors.com reportedly sold for more than $1 million each. Recently, the practice has been limited by court rulings and by the domain name registrars. If a desired domain name is unavailable, many registrars will automatically generate a list of alternative names that are available.

There is new twist to cybersquatting that is being referred to as 'domain kiting.' This practice involves 'pre-registration' of a large number of domain names. A generic website is then associated with that name for the purpose of testing the click-through and/or affiliate revenue potential of the domain name. If the domain name generates any revenue during the pre-registration period, the name will usually be formally registered. If not, the registration will be cancelled.

More About IT
According to the Language Monitor, there are approximately 850,000 words in English and there are over 30 million domain names under .COM top-level domain. That means that there are approximately thirty-five .COM domain names for every word in the English language. http://www.abramex.com/

Top-Level Domains

Registering a domain name takes only a few minutes after you have chosen the name and verified that it is available. Currently, domain names can be registered in one-year increments, up to ten years, for an annual fee. The annual fee to register a particular name can vary by registrar but the fee is highly correlated to the generic **Top Level Domain (TLD)**, e.g., .com, .net, .org, etc, that is appended to the domain name. TLDs help organize the websites found on the Internet by type and by country. For example, businesses often use the .com TLD and educational institutions use .edu as a TLD. TLDs may also include a country code, such as .mx for Mexico, .ch for China and .jp for Japan. The country code TLDs were designed to give countries control of the management of domain names issues within the country. Today, domain names with traditional TLDs such as .com and .net typically cost less to register than domain names using newer TLDs such as .us and .pro.

The Internet Corporation for Assigned Names and Numbers (ICANN) is currently the organization that oversees the Internet's Domain Name System (DNS). ICANN authorizes companies, called domain name registrars, to register Internet domain names. Today there are hundreds of ICANN-accredited registrars.

For practical purposes there are two types of Top Level Domains: generic TLDs (gTLD) that were originally intended for particular types of organizations, e.g., .com and .biz for business or .edu for educational institutions, and country code TLD (ccTLD), that are used by countries and dependent territories, e.g. .it for Italy or .jp for Japan. Currently, there are 18 generic TLDs and 240 country code TLDs. For a complete listing of all valid, top-level domains see http://www.icann.org/registries/top-level-domains.htm.

Top Level Domains provide the mechanism to resolve domain names and IP addresses. Each Top Level Domain has a designated organization that maintains an online database of all domain names and current IP addresses in that TLD. To find the current IP address of Google.com, for example, your request for Google's web site is first directed to the .com database.

More About IT

There is a direct relationship between disasters and domain name registrations. As hurricane Ernesto approached the US in 2006, nineteen new "Ernesto" domains were registered on a single day. All but one of these names was hurricane related. Be careful when donating to any disaster relief, especially online.

Complete the following **Integrate IT** exercise to learn more about Top Level Domains.

Integrate IT

1. You are beginning the process of creating a new business. Write a brief description of what that business will do.

2. Select a domain name that you would like to use for this business. Using an accredited registrar's web site, find out if your desired domain name is available. If the name is not available, pick another domain name that is available.

3. A number of domain names have cleverly used the ".us" TLD as part of a word in their domain name (e.g., del.icio.us). Can you think of other words that could incorporate a ccTLD or generic TLD in the same way? Check to see if the names domain names you identify are already registered.

LEARNING CHECK
Be sure you can * explain the purpose of a Domain Name * describe how to acquire a Domain Name * identify the major Top-Level Domains

THE NETWORKS OF THE INTERNET

As we mentioned at the beginning of the chapter, the Internet is essentially a network of networks. The networks that appear as clouds in Figure 5.3 represent a small sample of the many individual networks that make up the Internet. The networks of the Internet and the devices that constitute these networks are very diverse. Some of the networks include many devices that extend over a wide geographic range and rely solely on high-speed wireless communications media. There are other networks that consist of only a few, relatively low-speed devices that extend over a very short range and rely on both wired and wireless media. This diversity somewhat limits the way networks are categorized. However, there are a couple of simple ways to distinguish networks, even those not connected to the Internet. One of the most common ways to classify networks is by the geographic size of the network. In this section, we discuss networks of various sizes.

Types of Networks

There are various ways to categorize communication and data networks, One of the most common ways to classify networks is by size, that is, by the geographic area that is covered by the network. The four major types of networks, by geographic area, are WANs, MANs, LANs, and PANs.

Wide Area Networks (WANs)
Communication networks that operate over long distances and large geographic areas are called **Wide Area Networks (WANs)**. For example, the AT&T and Swisscom networks shown in Figure 5.3 could both be considered WANs because of the nationwide service offered by each company. The Internet is essentially the world's largest WAN whose backbone consists of the individual WANs of the telecommunications companies that provide the actual media for high-speed global communication. WANs are important to the telecommunications companies and to organizations like the military, brokerage firms, banks, and airline reservation systems that require long distance communication capabilities in real time.

Metropolitan Area Networks (MANs)
Communications networks that service regional and metropolitan areas, such as the networks associated of a geographically-dispersed university and those of a multi-site business, are examples of **Metropolitan Area Networks (MANs),** the next largest network by size. MANs often connect businesses and other individual networks within a city or a region to a WAN over a high-speed medium such as optical fiber.

Local Area Networks (LANs)
The individual communications networks that operate in relatively small geographic areas, such as within a building or within a home, are called **Local Area Networks (LANs)**. LANs are useful for sharing computer resources, such as printers, databases, and high-speed Internet connections. While Figure 5.3 does not specifically depict LANs, a LAN would be the type of network we would find if we looked inside the clouds in Figure 5.3. An understanding of LAN technology is important as the typical business network is a LAN.

Personal Area Networks (PANs)

Short-range **Personal Area Networks (PANs)** are created whenever we connect a USB or Firewire device to our computer. Wireless PANs are increasingly prevalent because of the personal communication gadgets that most of us carry. For example, devices equipped with **Bluetooth** technology can communicate with other similarly equipped devices when the devices are within a few meters of each other. Another increasingly important wireless technology associated with PANs is **Radio Frequency IDentification (RFID)**. This short-range wireless technology is being used in "contactless" payment applications such FasTrak ® and Speedpass™ and in an increasing number of inventory control applications.

Today, the geographic area of a network generally does not tell much about media used to connect the devices on the network. Today, networks increasingly rely on a combination of both wired and wireless media to communicate among the devices on the network. In the next section, we discuss the different types of wired and wireless networks and the important characteristics of the various media types.

Networking Media

Network devices require some type of conductor, or media, to link the various devices and to carry communication signals among the network devices. Historically, copper wire has been one of the most popular media used to link network devices because of its efficient electrical properties and it's relatively low cost. Copper wire is still a very common communication medium but it has ceded some of its networking popularity to **optical fiber**, the cabling typically made from glass or plastic that can carry communication signals over long distances at very high speeds using pulses of light.

Wireless technology, particularly *radio technology*, is also an important medium for network communications. Today, radio technology is the medium for wireless communication within and between all types of networks (WANs, MANs, LANs and PANs). In this section we discuss the wired and the wireless networking media and identify the relevant properties and characteristics of the media to help us make informed networking decisions.

Wired Communication

There are various types of wired media that are used to connect devices within and between today's networks. Often, the communications capacity of fiber-optic cabling is used as a backbone for, or extended to, other wired media such as phone lines, the cableTV infrastructure and, in some places, the electrical power grid, to provide the 'last mile' of service to homes and businesses. The LANs inside office buildings and homes today have historically been configured using **twisted pair** wires and **coaxial cable**.

There are a number of characteristics of wired media that are particularly important to ensure reliable, cost-effective communications. For example, it is useful to understand the data transmission speeds that each medium can support. The basic measurement of transmission speed is **bits per second (bps)**, however most data communications devices today are capable of transmission speeds that are more aptly denominated in *kilobits per second (Kbps), megabits per second (Mbps)* or *gigabits per second (Gbps)*. It is also useful to know how the media is typically used and some of the advantages and disadvantages of each type of media. Table 5.3 below provides a quick guide to the most common types of wired media found in networking today.

Wired Media	Maximum Data Rate	Typical Implementation	Advantages	Disadvantages
Twisted Pair (Category 1,3) (Category 5-6)	<1Mbps 100-1000Mbps	Telephone LAN	Inexpensive, multipurpose	Noise, Security
Coaxial Cable (Thin-baseband) (Thick-broadband)	10 Mbps 10-100Mbps	LAN LAN, MAN, CableTV	Low noise	Security
Fiber-Optic Cable (LEDs) (Laser)	100-1000Mbps 100 Gbps	LAN LAN, MAN, WAN	Fast, Secure, High capacity, little noise	Expensive

Table 5.3   Wired Media Characteristics

Wireless Communication

The worldwide demand for anytime/anywhere computing and communications has accelerated the development of **wireless** technologies and media. Collectively, the wireless media are the most viable technology for extending the reach of the Internet over the next few years. Wireless technology is viewed as the primary networking media for connecting the next billion people to the Internet. Wireless technologies are being implemented in networks of all sizes, from PANs to WANs and increasingly wireless networking technologies converge or overlap in the same network space. Converging and overlapping wireless technologies are the reason many new of the new wireless devices are multi-functional, networked devices. It is very common in some countries, for example, to use a cell phone on a WiFi network. In the opening case, the Swisscom Mobile network interface card used by Agathon employees could simultaneously sense both WiFi and 3G networks and seamlessly select the network with best Internet connection. In this section we discuss some of the wireless media that are currently being used for business purposes.

WiFi (IEEE 802.11a/b/g/n) is a family of wireless technologies that conform to the 802.11 specification developed by the Institute of Electrical and Electronics Engineers (IEEE, often pronounced "I, triple E"). The specification acquired the name, WiFi, from the WiFi Alliance, an organization independent of the IEEE, that certifies 802.11 products. There are a number of variations of the specification. The a/b/g/n variations are those that currently have achieved WiFi certification.

The features of particular interest for these WiFi variations, at least for most of us, are the **throughput**, or data rate, and the size of the **hot spot**, or range, that we can expect from the **wireless access point** (Figure 5.8), the device that connects us to the Local Area Network. Table 5.4 lists the data rates and estimated range for each of the 802.11 variations.

Figure 5.8 Wireless Access Point

802.11	Data Rate	Estimated Range
A	54 Mbps	30 meters
B	11 Mbps	30 meters
G	54 Mbps	40 meters
N	200+ Mbps	70 meters

Table 5.4 Data Rates and Range for 802.11

Today, wired LANs can be easily configured to support wireless devices. By adding a wireless access points LANs become wireless LANs (WLANs). WiFi "hot spots" are everywhere today; in our homes, on college campuses, in airports, hotels and in coffee shops. Hot spots can essentially extend the reach of the Internet, but only within the limited range of the access point.

Many WiFi networks are "open," or unsecured. Generally, this means that those using a notebook computer or other compatible, WiFi-enabled device, within range of the network access point, can join the network. Other WiFi networks are "secure" which means that the communication on these networks is encrypted and you must be authorized to use these networks. In Chapter71, the Information Security chapter, we will discuss some of the methods network administrators use to secure WiFi networks. This is an important topic because many information security breaches today are related to wireless networks, including the TJX, Inc breach that allowed criminals access to the credit card information of over 45 million people. A basic understanding of the WiFi technologies is important today considering the many wireless options that are available.

Like WiFi, **WiMax (IEEE 802.16d/e)** is not a specific technology but a certification of interoperability with an IEEE standard. WiMax provides bandwidth that is comparable with cable and DSL connections and it could be an option for residential and business customers with these types of connections. WiMax's wireless range (1 to 6 miles) enables considerable mobility within this "canopy" of wireless service. WiMax is increasingly being used in environments where wired media is unavailable or too expensive to deploy over moderate distances. There are actually two versions of the WiMax technology. 802.16d is designed for communication with subscribers at a fixed location. 802.16e is being designed for roaming within a service area, allowing mobile users more persistent Internet connections.

As we discussed earlier in the chapter, the **3rd Generation of mobile broadband (3G)** cellular technology is becoming an increasingly popular wireless medium for Internet access for both handheld devices, such as cell phones and PDAs, and for notebook computers. Notebooks with embedded 3G modems will soon be as ubiquitous as those with embedded WiFi cards. It should not be too long before most of us have mobile broadband service similar to the service offered by Swisscom Mobile and used by Agathon that senses the availability and speed of different wireless communication technologies and seamlessly and instantly switches our laptops to the wireless technology that provides the best Internet connection.

Figure 5.9 shows the relative operating ranges of WiFi, WiMax and 3G technologies and how these wireless technologies may be simultaneously deployed.

Figure 5.9 Relative Range of WiFi, WiMax and 3G Networks

Bluetooth (Figure 5.10) is one of the wireless networking technologies that popularized Personal Area Networks (PANs). Recall that PANs are the short range networks that are created when personal gadgets, such as your cell phone and car's audio system communicate with each other. Bluetooth devices communicate through short-range, ad hoc networks known as *piconets*. Each device can simultaneously communicate with up to seven other devices within a single piconet. Each device can also belong to several piconets simultaneously.

Figure 5.10 Bluetooth icon

Radio Frequency Identification (RFID) is short-range, wireless networking technology that is being deployed in a variety of business applications. The retail giant, Wal-Mart, for example, uses RFID technology to track its inventory. There are many other applications for this short-range wireless technology. One of the most prevalent today are the "contactless" or "touchless" payment systems that can accept your payment information from a variety of objects embedded with RFID technology. Figure 5.11 shows some of the objects that are used for contactless payment including key fobs, payment cards and cell phones.

Figure 5.11 Contactless Payment Options

Near Field Communications (NFC) is an evolving short-range wireless communication technology that also facilitates peer-to-peer communication. Communication can be established between two NFC-enabled devices by touching the devices together or by holding the devices close to one another. NFC is based on RFID technology which gives it the functionality of RFID plus it is designed to compliment other wireless technologies such as Bluetooth and WiFi which are also discussed in this section. Two friends with NFC-enabled cell phones could, for example, buy and store movie tickets using one of their cell phones and then distribute the tickets to the other's cell phones simply by touching the phones together. They could also use the phones to collect from their friend for the ticket using a person-to-person payments system that is being developed for NFC devices. Cell phones with NFC capabilities are generally more secure than traditional smart cards because phones can be turned off, require a password or be protected from access by a biometric security device.

 Watch NFC animation at:
http://www.nfc-forum.org/resources/multimedia/6-00147_NFC_Forum_v07.swf

Ultra-Wideband (UWB). This wireless technology is being developed for short-range consumer applications such as connecting high-speed peripherals to PCs and providing wireless capabilities for in-home entertainment devices such as HD TV. The range of this technology (<30 feet) is less than that of the WiFi technologies but the speed (up to 400Mbps) make it attractive for consumer applications with high bandwidth requirements.

Table 5.5 below provides a quick guide to the maximum data rates, the typical implementation, the advantages and the disadvantages of the most common types of wireless media found in networking today.

Wireless Media	Estimated Maximum Data Rate	Typical Implementation	Advantages	Disadvantages
Near Field Communication	454kbps	Payment and Storage	One-touch connectivity; Wireless compatibility	Requires cell phone with NFC capabilities
Bluetooth	1-3 Mbps	WPAN	Inexpensive, Low power	Short distance < 10 meters
RFID		WPAN, WLAN	Does not require line of sight	Security and Cost questions
UltraWideband	<400Mbps	WPAN, WLAN	Very High Speed	Short distance < 10 meters
WiFi (802.11a) (802.11b) (802.11g) (802.11n)	54Mbps 11Mbps 54Mbps 200Mbps	WLAN	Ubiquity,	Short distance, Security, noise, Crowding on 802.11g/b
WiMax (802.16d) (802.16e)	70Mbps	WLAN, WMAN	Long distance	Availability, Relatively Expensive
3G Cellular (3G:UMTS,EDGE, EV-DO) (3.5G: HSDPA)	384kbps <2Mbps?	WMAN, WWAN	Digital, Mobile,	Expensive, Speed, Availability, Competing standards

Table 5.5 Wireless Media Characteristics

Complete the following **Integrate IT** activity to reinforce your understanding of WiFi.

Integrate IT

Assume the graphic below is displayed on your WLAN utility on your notebook computer. Use this graphic to answer the questions below.

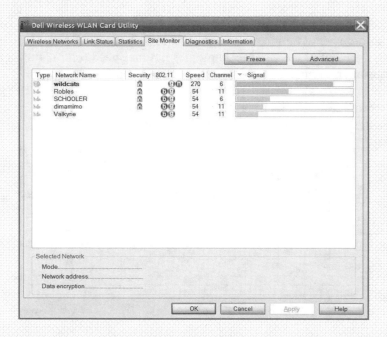

1. How many "hot spots" are in the area?

2. What is the speed and the 802.11 technology of the fastest "hot spot?"

3. What is a problem with investing in equipment that can operate at 802.11n speeds?

4. How many of these "hot spots" are easily available to anyone with a WiFi card?

LEARNING CHECK

Be sure you can * identify the various types of networks by geographic size * describe the types of networking media used in networks today * define a network 'hot spot'

INTERNET ACCESS

Bandwidth and Broadband

The richness of the media that is available on the Internet today, particularly on the World Wide Web, has increased the demand for bandwidth. Internet audio, video, gaming, and collaboration are all Internet experiences that seem to improve with an increase in bandwidth. Internet video, for example, need not be constrained to a 2 x 2 inch window on our computers if there is sufficient bandwidth to deliver that video in full screen.

Bandwidth, for most digital devices, refers to the data transfer rate, i.e., the amount of data a device can transfer in a fixed amount of time. Bandwidth is usually expressed in bits per second. For example, if you use a traditional phone line (dial-up service) for Internet access, the bandwidth of this dial-up session will usually between 28.8kbps and 56kbps. Table 5.6 shows the data transfer rates and typical range of costs for Internet access today.

Type of Service	Data Transfer Speed	Approximate Monthly Cost
Dial-up	Up to 56kbps	Local phone rates
DSL	128kbps to 10Mbps	$15-$75
Cable Service	128kbps to 10Mbps	$30 - $70
Powerline Service		
Satellite Service		
Cellular (EV-DO; EDGE)	200-400kbps	$60-80

Table 5.6 Internet Access options

Generally, network devices that can sustain data transfer rates greater than 256kbps are considered **broadband** devices. Many **Internet Service Providers (ISPs)** that offer Internet access at speeds greater than 256kbps claim their service is high speed or broadband service. For some Internet applications, such as reading and sending email, connection speeds at the lower end of the broadband range will probably not be too frustrating. However, there are an increasing number of things to do on the Internet, particularly on the web, that will be unavailable or frustrating at the lower broadband speeds.

Most individuals, households and small businesses acquire access to the Internet and a requisite IP address for Internet-enabled devices from an Internet Service Provider. Usually, ISPs are companies, such as AT&T and Time Warner, who lease IP addresses individually on a monthly basis. Large organizations, such as universities and many businesses, typically acquire a license for a class, or range, of IP addresses that they can assign to the devices of students and employees. In the following section we discuss the role of Internet Service Providers and their source of Internet access, the Network Service Providers.

Internet Service

Network Service Providers
Many large communications companies lease portions of their communications infrastructure and capacity to smaller companies. Those that provide direct backbone access to the Internet are often called **Network Service Providers (NSPs)**. NSPs have very high speed connections to the Internet and they typically have access to regional Network Access Points (NAPs) where Internet traffic between the national and international communications networks is exchanged. Table 5.7 shows a list of some of the major global Network Service Providers.

Provider	Country
AT&T	USA
Verizon	USA
Spring	USA
BT	UK
NTT DoCoMo	Japan
VSNL	India
MIRZA	India
Singtel	Singapore

Table 5.7 Major Global Network Service Providers

A regional equivalent of a Network Service Provider is an Internet Service Provider (ISP) which is described in the next section. Internet Service Providers typically get their Internet access from one of the NSPs.

Internet Service Providers
Today, approximately one billion people access the Internet worldwide. Generally, most of us have Internet access because we belong to, subscribe to, or are in the proximity of, organizations that have a computer network already attached to the Internet. Our membership, subscription, or proximity usually provides us with an account on these networks.

Regardless of whether we pay a subscription fee for Internet service, or whether we take advantage of seemingly 'free' access through our employer, through our college or university, through the public library, through the hotel where we are staying, or through the city that provides wireless Internet service to its residents and guests, we must still obtain a unique IP address for every device that we want to connect to the Internet. Generally, the source of that address is, or is affiliated with, one of the many commercial **Internet Service Providers (ISPs)** that has a permanent connection to the Internet and leases temporary and long-term connections to subscribers, members and guests.

Internet Access Methods
Dial-up service. Many people still use a **dial-up** service and the public telephone system to connect to the Internet. ISPs such as Earthlink® Dialup and AT&T Worldnet® both offer subscribers the ability to access the Internet from anywhere in the US using a conventional telephone line. This type of service is particularly useful for people who do not need a high speed connection and for those who live or travel in areas where high speed connections are expensive

or unavailable. For years, frequent international travelers maintained accounts with ISPs that had local access numbers in foreign countries because it provided an inexpensive way to access the Internet while abroad.

Digital Subscriber Line (DSL) service. Increasingly, individuals and organizations have upgraded their existing phone lines to **DSL**, a faster, always-on, telephone service that supports simultaneous voice and data communication.   Normal DSL service gives subscribers two communication channels over the single phone line.   Generally, a voice communication is assigned to the lower frequencies of the copper wire and data communication assigned to the higher frequencies. Some DSL providers offer faster downstream communication (e.g., receiving e-mail, downloading a song from iTunes, etc) than for upstream communication (sending email, uploading a file, etc). This is known as **Asymmetric Digital Subscriber Line (ADSL).**

Cable Internet Access (Cable modem) service. The cable TV infrastructure is also used to provide high speed Internet access to homes and businesses in North America, Australia and Europe.   Cable modem service is similar to DSL in that the cable (wire) is divided into multiple frequency ranges, or communication channels, that can support various forms of communication such as TV, voice, and data.

Powerline Communication and Broadband over Powerline service. There are still some areas in the US, particularly in rural areas, that do not have the infrastructure for DSL or cable modem service. A few companies are testing the viability of using the electrical power grid as a means of delivering electricity and high speed Internet access to homes and businesses in some of these areas.

Satellite Internet service. Satellite Internet service is also an option for those who are not able to receive DSL or Cable service. Satellite Internet service is typically slower and more expensive than both DSL and Cable, but it can provide a high-speed Internet connection to almost any location.

3G Wireless Broadband service. The cellular phone system provides an increasingly popular option for Internet access. 3G (3rd generation) cellular technologies such as EDGE (Enhanced Data GSM Environment), UMTS (Universal Mobile Telephone System) and EV-DO (Evolution-Data Optimized) are giving mobile users high-speed Internet access on laptops and on handheld devices similar to the service used by the Swiss firm, Agathon, in the chapter's opening case. In the US today, Verizon Wireless and Sprint both offer high-speed EV-DO Internet access via their cellular networks for about $60 per month (Figure 5.12). Cingular offers the EDGE high-speed Internet service for its GSM network customers.

Figure 5.12 3G Wireless Broadband from Sprint and Verizon

The demand for Wireless Wide Area Network (WWAN) service is expected to increase dramatically in the next few years considering the forecast that most new notebooks will soon be assembled with *embedded* 3G modems (see the More About IT) similar to the WiFi cards that are embedded in most notebooks today. If true, the PCMCIA cards shown in Figure T5.5 will soon be relics.

More About IT

Forecasts for the deployment of 3G technologies are very optimistic. Strategy Analytics estimates that by 2010, about 1.3 billion people worldwide, or about 50% of all mobile user, will be subscribers to 3G technologies. Furthermore, the number of notebook computers assembled with *embedded* 3G modems is expected to account for more than 50% of all cellular modems sold in 2009.

LEARNING CHECK
Be sure you can * define broadband * identify the various Internet access methods * explain 3G technology

Wrapping IT Up

In this chapter you were introduced to the architecture of the Internet. You learned about packet switching and about the Internet addressing method used by the Internet Protocol. You were also given a glimpse of the various types of networks by size, including PANs, LANs, MANs and WANs. You were also able to review the characteristics of both wired and wireless media and ideally you got a sense of the enormous potential the wireless media has on Internet growth. Finally, you learned about the types of networking technologies that are used to access the Internet today, such as dial-up, DSL, and cable service and you became familiar with the role of the Internet Service Providers.

Study Questions Summary

1. What is the Internet and how does it work?
    *   A global wide-area network that is not controlled by a single company or country.
    *   A network of networks connected by common, non-proprietary protocols.
    *   The largest communications network in the world
    *   The Internet uses packet switching technology and a set of protocols called TCP/IP for communication among Internet devices.

2. What is an Internet Domain Name?
    *   Every device on the Internet requires a unique numeric IP address, similar to a postal address.
    *   A Domain Name is the text version of a numeric IP address.
    *   A Domain Name makes it unnecessary to remember an IP address. A Domain Name gives organizations, and individuals, a permanent Internet address as IP addresses will change periodically.
    *   Internet Domain Names can be leased for up to ten years at a time through Domain Name registrars.

- The Internet's Domain Name System serves as a directory for all of the IP addresses and Domain Names.
- Top-Level Domains represent the major categories of Domain Names.
- IPv4, the current numbering system for IP addresses, is running out of numbers. It's replacement is called IPv6.

3. What types of networks and media make up the Internet?
   - The Internet is a network of other networks that range in geographic size. The size, or reach, of a network generally determines whether the network is a Wide Area Network (WAN); a Metropolitan Area Networks (MAN); a Local Area Network (LAN); or a Personal Area Networks (PAN).
   - Devices, such as computers, connect to networks using both wired and wireless media.

4. How do people access the Internet?
   - Internet access is usually provided by an Internet Service Provider.
   - Today, most Internet Service Providers offer high-speed connections to the Internet.
   - High speed connections are typically called "broadband."
   - Broadband speeds can be achieved over wired and wireless networks

Key Terms

Page Number references are included in parentheses

Bandwidth (163)	Internet service provider (164)	Radio Frequency Identification (RFID) (157, 160)
Bluetooth (160)	IP address (150)	Third Generation (3G) (159)
Binary number system (151)	IPv6 (151)	Top Level Domain (152, 154)
Bits per second (157)	Local Area Network (LAN) (156)	Transmission Control Protocol/Internet Protocol (TCP/IP) (149)
Broadband service (163)	Metropolitan Area Network (MAN) (156)	Twisted pair (157)
Coaxial cable (157)	Near field communications (160)	Ultra-Wideband (161)
Domain name (152)	Network service provider (164)	Wide Area Network (WAN) (156)
Dotted decimal (150)	Optical Fiber (1157)	WiFi (158)
802.11 a/b/g/n (158)	Packet switching (148)	WiMax (159)
802.16 (159)	Packets (148)	Wireless (158)
Ethernet (149)	Personal Area Network (PAN) (157)	Wireless access point (158)
Hot spot (158)	Protocols (149)	
Internet (146)	Protocol stack (149)	

Multiple Choice Questions

1. What protocol is associated with the Internet's addressing scheme?
    a. packet switching
    b. IP
    c. Ethernet
    d. RFID

2. IPv4 uses a _____-bit scheme for IP addresses.
    a. dotted decimal
    b. 64
    c. 128
    d. 32

3. What is the minimum data transfer rate for broadband?
    a. 56kbps
    b. 64kpbs
    c. 128kbps
    d. 1.5Mbps

4. What is the term for the technology that divides communication into small pieces, numbers and addresses each piece, and then sends the individual pieces to their destination?
    a. TCP/IP
    b. DSL
    c. dotted decimal
    d. packet switching

5. How is bandwidth measured?
    a. in dotted decimal
    b. in binary
    c. in bits per second
    d. in pixels

6. Which wireless networking technology is also known as WiFi?
    a. 802.16
    b. 802.11
    c. WiMax
    d. Bluetooth

Answers:
1. b   2. d   3. c   4. d   5. c   6. b

Review Questions

1. What is packet switching?
2. What was original name of the network we now call the Internet?
3. What is a network protocol?

4. IPv4 addresses are how long in binary form?
5. IPv6 addresses are how long in binary form?
6. What is causing the shortage of IPv4 addresses?
7. What are three popular Top Level Domains?
8. WiFi refers to what type of network?
9. What wireless technology is associated with 'contactless' payment systems?
10. What are the primary differences between WiFi and WiMax?
11. What is one advantage of a 3G network over WiFi?

Projects

1. List some of the software applications that you regularly use that are *installed* on your computer. See if you can find at least one *web-based* equivalent application for each item on your list. For example, do you use Microsoft's Outlook, or do you use Google's gmail? If possible, compare the applications and note the things you like and dislike about each.

2. Create a small application in Excel that will automatically convert an IP address in dotted decimal format into its 32-bit equivalent.

3. Create a list of the various Internet Service Providers in your area that are available for home/personal use. Include in this list as much information as you think is necessary to help someone make a decision when choosing an ISP. Create this list in Excel.

4. In the opening case, the Swisscom Mobile service used by Agathon was described as having the capability of moving between cellular and WiFi networks seamlessly and instantly, depending on the best service available. Discuss the implications of this capability in terms of IP addressing.

5. Use a drawing tool (Visio, PowerPoint, or similar) to create a logical diagram of a small computer network (it could be your dorm or home network). Include in your diagram, the hardware devices (modems, routers, switches and access points) in your network and show how these devices are connected.

6. Make an international phone call using VoIP technology. Assess the quality of a "packet-switched" phone call.

CHAPTER **6**

The World Wide Web and E-Commerce

PLANNING AHEAD
After reading Chapter 6, you should be able to answer these questions in your own words

STUDY QUESTIONS
What are the key components of the Web?
What are markup languages such as HTML?
What is Web 2.0?
What is Search Engine Optimization?

LEARNING PREVIEW

Many people consider the Internet and the World Wide Web to be synonymous. We learned in Chapter 5, however, that the Internet originated in 1960s with ARPANET, the U.S. Department of Defense initiative that effectively established the wide-area communications capabilities of computers. Before ARPANET computers were generally viewed as arithmetic engines, not communication devices.

ARPANET introduced two important communications technologies, packet-switching and TCP/IP, that made it relatively easy for other computer networks to append to this increasingly popular "network of networks." As this aggregation of *inter*-networks grew, a global communications infrastructure was created that supported a variety of communications services such as telnet, file transfer, and e-mail, the Internet's original killer application. Over the years, numerous other Internet communication services and applications have been introduced that leverage the technologies and the autonomy of this global communications infrastructure. No Internet service to date, however, has been as comprehensive, or as revolutionary, as the **World Wide Web** (the **Web**). The Web has effectively become the universal interface of the Internet and has surpassed email as the Internet's killer application.

Today, the Internet has over a billion users worldwide. Many of these people have never used anything but the Web, or specifically, a web browser, to access the Internet's vast resources and services. The Web has become the medium many of us rely on to find information, to read and send email, to get directions, to make a phone call, to watch a video, to socialize with friends and to shop for goods and services. The Web has not only facilitated the convergence of existing Internet services and resources, it has also created a new generation of collaborative applications that has been dubbed *Web 2.0*.

The objective of this chapter is to help you better understand this revolutionary medium and to consider the various ways business is employing this technology. We begin by looking at the Web's early years, the period sometimes referred to as *Web 1.0*. This background will give you the opportunity to become familiar with some of the fundamental technologies and practices that created the World Wide Web and influenced its growth. Later in the chapter, we provide a survey of the era and the technologies that have been christened Web 2.0, the highly collaborative Web services and Internet technologies that promote community-driven Web content.

OPENING VIGNETTE

"Today, at any Net terminal, you can get: an amazing variety of music and video, an evolving encyclopedia, weather forecasts, help wanted ads, satellite images of anyplace on Earth, up-to-the-minute news from around the globe, tax forms, TV guides, road maps with driving directions, real-time stock quotes, telephone numbers, real estate listings with virtual walk-through, pictures of just about anything, records of political contributions, library catalogs, appliance manuals, live traffic reports, archives to major newspapers – all wrapped up in an interactive index that really works." (Source: "We Are the Web," Kevin Kelly, *Wired*, August 2005, pp. 96)

This was *Wired* magazine's view of the World Wide Web in 2005. This view was similar for people around the globe who were privileged enough to have access to the Internet at broadband speeds. Millions of Internet users were astonished at the information facility of the World Wide Web, often to the point that it changed how some people worked and played. Information of almost any kind was available immediately, usually only a mouse-click, or hyperlink, away. Since 2005, the World Wide Web has astonished us yet again. The new Web, Web 2.0 as it has been called, has not only changed the way people work and play, but according to *Time* magazine, it has also changed the way people think!

"The new Web is a very different thing. It's a tool for bringing together the small contributions of millions of people and making them matter. Silicon Valley consultants call it Web 2.0, as if it were a new version of some old software. But it's really a revolution." "Web 2.0 is a massive social experiment," "... an opportunity to build a new kind of international understanding, not politician to politician, great man to great man, but citizen to citizen, person to person. It's a chance for people to look at a computer screen and really, genuinely wonder who's out there looking back at them." (Source, "Time Person of the Year – You," *Time*, December 25, 2006-January 1, 2007, pp.40-41).

Whether you prefer emailing to "tweeting," (the term for communicating with Twitter®, a popular Web 2.0 application which we discuss later in the chapter), it is hard to disagree that the Web has significantly increased the sources and the availability of information worldwide. The World Wide Web has also undeniably become an important medium for personal and business communication as well as a global medium of commerce. In this chapter we trace the metamorphosis of the World Wide Web and provide a description of the fundamental technologies associated with this revolutionary communications, commerce and information medium.

VISUAL ORGANIZATION OF CHAPTER

Study Question 1	Study Question 2	Study Question 3	Study Question 4
Web 1.0	Markup Languages	Web 2.0	E-Commerce
• Background • Web Browsers • Web Architecture	• SGML • HTML • XML • XHTML • Cascading Style Sheets	• Twitter® • Blogging • RSS and Atom • Mashups	• Types of E-Commerce • E-Commerce Revenue Models • Search Engine Optimization
Learning Check 1	Learning Check 2	Learning Check 3	Learning Check 4

WEB 1.0

Background

The World Wide Web was conceived in the 1980s with the objective of leveraging the Internet to enhance collaboration among a community of scientists and researchers. Tim Berners-Lee, a researcher at the European Particle Physics Laboratory (CERN) in Geneva, Switzerland, is the person who is credited with accomplishing this objective by combining a *markup language*, computer code used for describing how computer documents are displayed, with *hypertext*, a method of linking documents so they are available on demand. The result was the **Hypertext Markup Language (HTML)**, the primary code behind the more than 600 billion web pages that are available today on the Internet.

In order for the HTML documents to be shared and displayed, Berners-Lee also developed the first web server, the software that manages and services requests for HTML documents, as well as the first web browser, the client software that is used to request and to render the documents encoded in HTML. These technologies, first made available to the public in 1991, were fundamental components of a new generation of Internet services and resources that became known as the World Wide Web.

Surprisingly, the World Wide Web was publicly available for almost three years before most people, including many who were familiar with the Internet, even realized it existed. Popular awareness of the Web is generally attributable to the 1993 release of *Mosaic*, the first web browser that ran on both PCs and Macs. As you will see, web browsers have played an important role in the evolution of both HTML and the World Wide Web.

Web Browsers

To request, send, interpret and display Web documents and other resources, Berners-Lee developed the client and server software needed to handle these tasks. The client software he developed was initially called *WorldWideWeb* and later renamed Nexus. This software was actually the first graphical web browser and HTML editor. Berners-Lee's browser was designed to run on the NeXT computer, a high-end computer/workstation that Steve Jobs designed after he was ousted from Apple Computer in 1985. Figure 6.1 shows the graphical interface of Berners-Lee's *WorldWideWeb* browser.

Figure 6.1 Berners-Lee's web browser, *WorldWideWeb*

(Source: http://www.w3.org/History/1994/WWW/Journals/CACM/screensnap2_24c.gif)

Today, the most popular web browsers are Firefox, Safari, Internet Explorer and Opera (Figure 6.2). Google's browser, Chrome, released in September 2008, will undoubtedly join the list of popular browsers soon because it has already attracted attention due to its speed and that it was built using *open-source technology*. Chrome is considered by some to be the equivalent of a *browser-based operating system* that was specifically designed to help integrate the web browser with the growing list of web-based applications, such as Google Docs, that are gaining credibility in the workplace. Today, Chrome, like the traditional browsers, is free, generally compatible with the popular microcomputer operating systems, and arguably, similar in functionality. Chrome however, is threatening the relatively recent harmony in the browser market and is positioned to re-ignite the "browser wars," which introduced many idiosyncrasies and irregularities into the Web environment.

		Windows	Mac OS X	Linux
	Firefox www.mozilla.com	X	X	X
	Safari apple.com	X	X	
	Internet Explorer microsoft.com	X	discontinued	
	Opera www.opera.com	X	X	X
	Chrome www.google.com/chrome	X	Forthcoming	forthcoming

Figure 6.2 Popular web browsers for desktop and notebook computers

As previously mentioned, *Mosaic* was the web browser that generated popular interest in this new, exciting Internet service that acquired the name of Berners-Lee's original web browser, the **World Wide Web**. Mosaic was created in 1993 by Marc Andreeson and other graduate students from the National Center for Supercomputing Applications (NCSA) at the University of Illinois. Mosaic was a relatively robust web browser with a graphical user interface that supported features such as icons and bookmarks. More importantly, Mosaic could run on both PCs and Macs. Not long after Andreesen created Mosaic, he left the university and teamed with Jim Clark, the founder of Silicon Graphics, to start Netscape Communications. Their web browser, which later became known as Netscape Navigator, was the first *commercial* web browser.

More About IT

Much fun has been poked at Al Gore, the former Vice-President of the United States, for his gaff about creating the Internet. While we know he did not create the Internet, he does deserve recognition for initiating the High Performance Computing and Communications Act of 1991 (the Gore Bill) which funded the development of Mosaic.

Until late 1995, Netscape and Mosaic were essentially the only web browsers with graphical user interfaces that could run on both PCs and Macs. Netscape reportedly held about 80% of the browser market until Microsoft offered *Internet Explorer* as an add-on to its operating system *du jour*, Windows 95. The ensuing "browser wars" resulted in significant changes to HTML as both Netscape and Microsoft eagerly introduced browser "plug-ins" and "extensions" to HTML for such things as tables, frames and support for JavaScript.

It should not be a surprise that many of these HTML extensions were proprietary, at least initially, and required the most recent version of Netscape Navigator or Internet Explorer in order to function as desired. This was the essence of the browser wars; develop innovative HTML extensions that required a particular browser and you will gain market share. Generally, Netscape browsers were considered more innovative, and secure, but Microsoft had one major advantage, Internet Explorer was free. Netscape did not start offering a free web browser until early 1998, the same time it announced that the development of the Netscape browser would move to an open-source process that is coordinated by the Mozilla Foundation (see Figure 6.3). By then, Microsoft's share of the browser market had increased, making Internet Explorer the apparent winner of the browser war.

Figure 6.3 Mozilla Organization

More About IT
Mozilla, the term associated with a number of open-source technologies today, including the organization responsible for the popular Firefox browser, was the original codename and mascot for Netscape Navigator. The term, said to be a contraction of the terms *Mosaic killer* and *Godzilla,* refers to Netscape's effort to force Mosaic from its early position as the web's most popular browser.

Web Architecture

Tim Berners-Lee is better known for creating the HTML markup language than he is for creating the first graphical web browser. HTML, the underlying code of the billions of Web pages that exist today, is a key component in the architecture of the World Wide Web. Berners-Lee combined HTML with two other key Internet technologies, the **HyperText Transfer Protocol (HTTP)** and **Universal Resource Locators (URLs),** to create the basic architecture of the World Wide Web. Before we discuss HTML, it is useful to review these other Web technologies.

HTTP
As we learned in Chapter 5, TCP/IP is the acronym for the suite of Internet protocols, or rules, that facilitate Internet communication. **HTTP, or the HyperText Transfer Protocol,** is one of the protocols in the TCP/IP suite. HTTP is the set of rules for requesting and receiving web resources, such as web pages, that are hosted on a variety of Internet and *intranet* devices.

Requests for web resources are typically initiated using a web browser, the most common type of HTTP client. A web browser, or other HTTP client, sends an HTTP request for web page to a web server, or host, that stores the resource. If the web page is available, the web server responds by sending the resource, typically the HTML code, to the web browser. The browser then interprets the HTML and displays the page. Figure 6.4 depicts the request-response dialogue that is typical of the Web and characteristic of a networking architecture referred to as the *client/server model*.

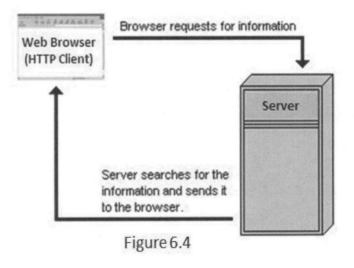

Figure 6.4

The **hypertext** attribute of the HTTP protocol is the technology that gives us the ability to access Web resources *on demand*, simply by clicking on a link, or **hyperlink**, to the resource. When we click on a hyperlink to a web resource, our web browser builds the request and sends it to the web server that is associated with the location, or URL, of that specific resource.

More About IT
The terms hypertext and hypermedia were coined by Ted Nelson in 1965 but the concept for a non-linear information retrieval system originated with Memex, a device described by Vannevar Bush in 1945 [Source: "As We May Think," *The Atlantic Monthly,* July, 1945]. Sixty years later, *Wired* magazine described the significance of the hypertext link as "the most powerful invention of the decade" [Source: "We Are the Web," Kevin Kelly, Wired, August 2005, pp. 99).

URLs and URIs

Another key component of the Web architecture is the uniform syntax that is used to identify network-retrievable resources, such as a web page. This syntax is often referred to as a **URL (Uniform Resource Locator)** or **URI (Uniform Resource Identifier).** The "U" formerly stood for universal. Today, these terms are generally considered synonymous but URLs are technically derived from URI schemes, the official and unofficial syntax for locating and accessing network resources. In simple terms, URLs and URI schemes are what reduce the process of accessing a Web resource to a single mouse-click.

Many, but not all, URLs and URI schemes are associated with Internet protocols such as *http, ftp, and mailto* because the Internet is logically where many of the desirable network resources reside. The *file:* scheme, for example, is not an Internet protocol but provides the required syntax to locate and access a resource on a *local file system,* such as on your local computer. URI scheme names are delimited by a colon (":") and followed by a hierarchical identifier, such as a domain name and directory path, i.e., folders separated by the forward slash ("/"), that lead to the Internet resource. For example, an email address is the hierarchical identifier of the *mailto:* URI scheme. Table 6.1 illustrates the variations in syntax of a few official URI schemes.

- *http://somecompany.com/textbook/chapter9/eastonandeaston.txt*
- *ftp://somecompany/~user/eastonandeaston.txt*
- *mailto:JohnDoe@somecompany.com*
- *file:///C:\Users\ Documents\textbook\eastonandeaston.docx*

Table 6.1   Examples of URI Schemes

As you can see by Figure 6.5, there are both official and unofficial URI schemes. Official URI schemes are those that have been approved by the IANA (the Internet Assigned Numbers Authority). You may also be familiar with some of the common, yet unofficial URI schemes such as *skype:<username|phonenumber>*. This particular URI scheme displays the appropriate syntax required of Skype®, the popular Internet calling (VoIP) application.

Figure 6.5 Official and Unofficial URI Schemes

Complete the following **Integrate IT** activity to learn more about URI schemes.

Integrate IT

If you have Skype® installed on your computer, you can launch an Internet phone call directly from your browser using the *skype:* URI scheme. For example, try making a free Skype test call by inputting *skype:echo123* into your browser's address bar.

Internet Explorer users can use the *about:home* internal URI scheme to access their browser's default start page.

Firefox users try using the *about:mozilla* internal URI scheme to access a Mozilla "Easter egg."

LEARNING CHECK
Be sure you can * discuss how the 'browser wars' influenced the Web * describe the architecture of the Web * describe a URL

MARKUP LANGUAGES

The HTML markup language is considered by many to be Tim Berners-Lee's key contribution to the Web architecture. HTML was actually derived from the mother of markup languages, SGML. SGML was also used to create XML, the markup language many consider to be the Web's predominant communication language.

SGML

Berners-Lee developed HTML using the **Standard Generalized Markup Language (SGML).** SGML is a comprehensive set of international standards that describe the rules for marking up electronic text and ensuring that electronic documents can be *device-independent*, or transportable, from one hardware and software environment to another. This characteristic makes it possible for information to be used and shared by people without concern for the type of computer or device being used.

More About IT
IT is infamous for its acronyms which frequently seem to refer to more than one thing. SGML is an early example of this having originated at IBM in 1969 as the *Generalized Markup Language* (GML) by a team of Goldfarb, Mosher and Lorie (GML). GML was given *Standard* status by the International Standards Organization (ISO) in 1986.

SGML's complexity and overhead have limited the number of environments where SGML is fully deployed. Parts of SGML, however, have been used to create other markup languages, notably HTML and **XML (eXtensible Markup Language).** While both HTML and XML are derivatives of SGML, they are fundamentally different. In simple terms, HTML is an application of SGML while XML is a subset of the SGML specification (see Figure 6.6). As a subset of SGML, XML can be used to create other markup languages and other applications, such as XHTML which we will be discussing later in this section. We will also discuss XML which has unofficially become the *lingua franca* of Web communications.

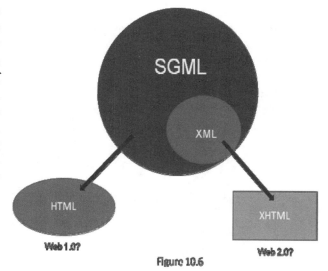

Figure 6. 6 SGML, the Mother of Markup Languages

HTML

Markup languages are not programming languages like C++ or Java. HTML, for example, uses words and symbols, called **elements**, to identify structures, or pieces, of an electronic document. Titles, headings, tables and lists are just a few examples of the types of structures found in documents and all of these structures can be identified using HTML elements. HTML elements are often referred to as "tags" but **HTML tags** are literally the symbols that signal the beginning and ending of an HTML element. The syntax of a typical HTML element, shown in Figure 6.7, can include the following components:

- a *start tag* marking the beginning of an element
- optional *attributes* and their associated *values*
- the *content* that is to be displayed
- an *end tag* marking the ending of an element

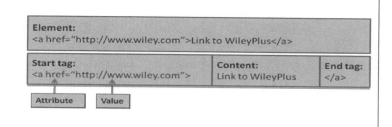

Figure 6.7 – An HTML Element

A learning objective of this chapter is to give you some familiarity with markup languages. Since HTML is currently the prevalent markup language of the majority of web documents, we have provided a simple example of a web page for BT's Rentals (Figure 6.8a) that was created in HTML. The actual HTML code used to create the BT's Rentals web page is shown in Figure 6.8b below. In Tutorial 6: An Introduction to XHTML, found at the back of the book, you can compare this web page to similar page created in XHTML. In Tutorial 6, you will also have an opportunity to create an XHTML document and to validate your XHTML code, using an on-line validator. An XHTML validator is essentially an efficient, automated method of checking the code to see if it is syntactically correct. If there are syntax errors, the validator helps pinpoint the problems.

HTML and XHTML files are typically saved in *text* format with either a *.htm* or *.html* extension. For example, the code for BT's Rentals web page was created in Notepad, the built-in text editor that comes with the Windows operating system. Notepad, like many other **text editors**, saves documents, by default, in *text* format. To be recognized as a web page to the browser, web documents need a filename that is followed by either the .htm or .html extension. For example, the BT's Rentals filename could be *BTsRentals.htm* or *BTsRentals.html*. In Tutorial 6, you will find examples and instructions on using your text editor to create simple XHTML documents.

Figure 6.8a Sample HTML document for BT's Rentals

```
<html>
<head>
<title>BT's Equipment Rentals</title>
</head>
<body>
<h1>BT's Rentals</h1>
<center><h3>Attention Contractors and Homeowners!!!</h3></center>
<hr>
<h3>
<ul>
<li>Lawn & Garden * Trenching * Drilling & Breaking</li>
<li>Painting * Remodeling * Plumbing</li>
<li>Heating & Cooling</li>
</ul>
</h3>
<h4>For the Best Selection of Rental Equipment in San Diego County.
Visit us now at 2 locations</h4>
<center><table border=1>
<tr>
<th>Downtown</th>
<th>Encinitas</th></tr>
<tr>
<td>3959 Pacific Highway</td>
<td>203 Rancho Santa Fe Rd.</td></tr>
<tr>
<td>619-299-4300</td>
<td>760-753-1148</td></tr>
</table></center>
<p>
For more information <a href="mailto:BThomas@BTsRental.com">click here</a>
</body>
</html>
```

Figure 6.8b Sample HTML code for BT's Rentals Web Page

A primary objective of early HTML was describing the logical structure of a document. In the BT's Rental example, see how the <title> tag is used to identify the title of a web page (the text that appears in the web page title bar). Also note the <ul> tag that is used to describe the unordered (bulleted) list structure that appears on the web page and the <table> tag that is used to identify the table structure shown in the sample HTML document. All of the elements used in the BT's Rentals example are described in Tutorial 6.

As HTML evolved, physical layout elements were introduced that describe how the structures and the words of a web document were displayed (for example, tables can be centered <center> and words can be italicized <i>). With the ability to describe both structure and display elements, HMTL is capable of describing the look, the feel and the action of a Web page. This capability however, does not come without some cost. At a minimum, it requires increasingly sophisticated (some say bloated) browsers that support the growing functionality associated with HTML.

Without the upgraded browsers and sophisticated plug-ins, the usability and accessibility of a web site can be affected. This explains why you still see warnings on some web sites that state that the site is best viewed with a particular browser.

More About IT

Besides the choice of a browser, the configuration of the browser, or browser settings, can also affect how a web page appears to viewers. All browsers can be configured to suit individual needs and preferences and frequently these settings will affect how a web page will appear or behave in the browser. Often people change their preferences for security reasons; for example, to enable a pop-up blocker or to prohibit computer code, such as JavaScript, from running in the browser. Additionally, most web developers understand how the screen resolution of computer monitors will also influence the appearance of a webpage. Pages viewed on higher resolution monitors generally take up less of the screen area than pages viewed on monitors with lower resolution.

Obviously, the choice of browser, the browser's configuration, and the resolution of the monitor used by website visitors are all beyond the control of the developer of a website. However, good website developers attempt to anticipate all of the issues that can affect the experience of users and strive to design sites to appear and function uniformly to *all* potential site visitors. This includes website visitors with visual, hearing, cognitive, physical and/or aging disabilities as well. Increasingly, **accessibility standards** are being applied to business websites to ensure that people with disabilities have the same access to information or services as individuals without disabilities.

No organization was specifically responsible for managing the development of HTML until the **World Wide Web Consortium** (**W3C**) was formed in 1994. Even after the W3C took responsibility for HTML development, the browser developers did not interpret the HTML guidelines uniformly. These issues were compounded by new versions of HTML being released almost every year (Table 6.2). The enduring outcome of all of this is that the World Wide Web is currently composed of millions of *legacy* web pages that contain various HTML syntax idiosyncrasies. For example, HTML allows the use of both upper and lower case elements. Additionally, not all browsers enforce the use of balanced tags (markup tags that have both an opening tag and a closing tag).

HTML version	Date Introduced	Description
HTML 1.0	1989	First public version of HTML
HTML 2.0	1995	First version to be supported by all graphical browsers
HTML 3.0	1996	Proposed, never adopted
HTML 3.2	1997	Added support for creating tables and interactive form elements
HTML 4.01	1999	Added support for style sheets and improved accessibility for people with disabilities.
XHTML 1.0	2000	Reformulated version of HTML 4.01 in XML
XHTML 1.1	2002	Modular-based XHTML
XHTML 2.0	2007	Working draft

Table 6.2 – Versions of HTML and XHTML

These legacy pages have generally required browser developers, sensitive to the vagaries of HTML, to develop browsers that are very forgiving but also very bloated. This has resulted in usability and accessibility issues for people who are trying to access the web using the newer, smaller web-enabled devices and for many people with physical limitations who may have difficulty navigating a website with a mouse or seeing anything but large text on a web page.

Usability and Accessibility Issues of HTML

Initially, HTML's growing scope was not viewed as problematic as web browsers also evolved and were being specifically developed to interpret HTML's markup tags in unique and compelling ways. Unfortunately, the increased functionality associated with the evolution of HTML and web browsers resulted in bloated browsers and countless web pages that are syntactically inconsistent. This has impacted the usability and accessibility of the Web.

The growing functionality of browsers was generally accompanied by an increase in the system requirements for devices running the higher powered browsers. For many desktop and notebook computer users, these issues may have been negligible because their systems typically had the CPU power and the memory to run the forgiving, full-featured browsers. However, faster CPUs and more RAM are not the typical options offered on the increasingly popular hand-held devices, such as 3G cell phones, that many people are using today to access the Web. These lightweight devices have limited system resources and they are heavily dependent on web sites and web pages that behave in an efficient and consistent manner.

The Web's increasing functionality and robust multi-media capabilities also created some unanticipated accessibility issues. For example, people who use hand-held devices and people with physical disabilities often experience similar barriers when interacting with the Web. Cell phone users, for example, often have a hard time navigating a Web site if the navigation requires the use of a mouse because cell phones typically only have alphanumeric keypads. Similarly, desktop computer users with physical disabilities may have difficulty navigating a Web site if they can't use a mouse.

XML

The W3C responded to the need for a simple, standardized version of HTML by creating a new *framework* for defining documents and describing the data within them in a standard way, regardless of the device being used. This new framework, the **eXtensible Markup Language (XML),** is considered a **meta-language** because it can be used to create other applications and other markup languages. The XML framework does not have a fixed set of markup tags like HTML, nor does it describe how a web page looks or how it behaves. Instead, each XML application and XML-related markup language has the ability to define it own markup tags. This is possible because XML provides the syntax that allows users to uniquely describe what the words in a document *are.* Adhering to this syntax results in what is generally referred to as a "well-formed" XML document. The consistent syntax of well-formed XML documents makes them more portable than HTML documents and is the reason many Web developers today have made XML the *de facto* markup language for Web communication.

> More About IT
>
> Besides *well-formed* XML documents, there are also *valid* XML documents. SGML requires the use of something called a Document Type Definition (DTD) which describes the structure of a SGML document. DTDs require some effort to create and are one of the reasons SGML was considered so cumbersome. To create a *well-formed* XML document, you are not required to create a separate DTD. You can create a well-formed XML document by simply following the XML syntax rules. However, if you do create a set of rules, or DTD, and you make your document conform to those rules, it is considered a *valid* XML document.
>
> If you use the XHTML tutorial at the back of the book, you will be guided to create an XHTML document that should conform to one of three DTDs associated with XHTML. To ensure it does conform, or validate, you can check your document using one of the XHTML validators available on the web.

Many people today are unaware of the ubiquity of XML but in reality XML can be found in systems that we use every day. For example, XML is the underlying file format of the 2007 versions of Microsoft Word, Excel and PowerPoint. XML is format that is often used to transfer digital pictures from a camera to a computer. Digital music is often organized and stored in XML. Of particular interest to this chapter is the fact that XML is used in many Web 2.0 applications. Later in this chapter we will take a closer look at XML, specifically how it is used in the Web 2.0 application known as Really Simple Syndication (RSS), what many consider to be the 'glue' of many Web 2.0 applications.

XHTML

One of the first applications of XML was the **eXtensible Hypertext Markup Language (XHTML),** a reformulation of HTML using XML. XHTML is an attractive web development alternative to HTML primarily because of the idiosyncrasies of HTML. Generally, the differences between XHTML 1.0 and HTML 4.01 are considered relatively minor, in part, because most web browsers can interpret XHTML pages and XHTML can be read by all XML enabled devices. The significant difference between HTML and XHTML 1.0 documents is that XHTML documents must be well-formed and that all elements are explicitly closed. Additionally, XML, hence XHTML, requires all element and attributes names to be lowercase.

Tutorial 6 provides basic instructions for creating web pages using XHTML. Familiarity with a markup language such as XHTML or HTML is an important skill for web developers today. Those who understand the syntax and the idiosyncrasies of a markup language are more likely to leverage the power of the graphical development tools to create cutting-edge web resources. Personally, basic knowledge of HTML will give you the ability to create your own web pages and to customize the pages you generate using templates and forms found on sites such as Facebook and MySpace, without any investment in special software.

While HTML proficiency is not a primary learning objective of this chapter, understanding the syntax of a markup language will help you better understand how organizations are using markup languages to create communication efficiencies with customers and suppliers.

Cascading Style Sheets

As we discussed earlier in the chapter, HTML's growing mix of presentation elements and structural elements often resulted in web pages that were complex and difficult to maintain. Additionally, the usability of some web resources was jeopardized by the idiosyncrasies of HTML. **Cascading Style Sheets (CSS)** were introduced by the W3C in 1994 to help separate the presentational markup, such as font colors, font sizes, background styles, from the structural markup. Generally, CSS allows developers to move much of the presentational information to a separate stylesheet, which generally results in considerably simpler HTML. CSS also allows the same markup page to be presented in different styles for different display methods, that is, on-screen, in print, and by speech-based browsers. While an extensive discussion of Cascading Style Sheets is beyond the scope of this book, it should be noted that the W3C has shown its preference for CSS by *deprecating* the use of the original HTML presentational markup. In other words, certain HTML presentational elements such as <b> and <u> have been formally superseded and are being phased out of use.

LEARNING CHECK
Be sure you can * identify the components of an HTML element * discuss the difference between HTML and XML * explain XHTML

WEB 2.0

Web 2.0, the so-called second generation of the Web, began in 2005. However, the beginning of this generation is not associated with a specific event or with the introduction of new technology as was the case with Web 1.0. Instead, Web 2.0's origination has been attributed to a change in the way the Web is used. **Web 2.0** is considered the era of web-based communities and community-generated content via blogs, social networking sites and wikis. It is also the era of hosted web applications and web services, such as RSS feeds and mashups that have brought us much closer to the objective that originally inspired Tim Berners-Lee and his colleagues at CERN, namely, to facilitate collaboration among communities of people.

 View an engaging YouTube video called "Web 2.0" at http://www.youtube.com/watch?v=6gmP4nk0EOE].

> **More About IT**
>
> *"The famous judicial assessment of pornography applies equally to Web 2.0: It's tough to define, but people know it when they see it. Textbook examples include global group hugs like MySpace and Friendster, file-sharing forums like Flickr and the Pirate Bay, and every one of the Net's 90 million blogs. But a precise definition is elusive.*
>
> *Sometimes Web 2.0 points to a set of technologies that lets sites share and manipulate each other's content, chiefly XML's flexible tagging scheme and the RSS automated-syndication standard. For instance, Hype Machine automatically assembles a virtual radio station out of MP3 files it scours from obscure music blogs, making it, in effect, a specialized user interface for thousands of disparate pages. But Web 2.0 can also mean sites and services that turn community into content, from pledge-night vomit pics on Facebook to the public-access reference entries on Wikipedia. The most convincing examples fuse these two strands, combining metadata and social networking. Take del.icio.us, which lets users tag and share Web bookmarks.*
>
> *What these sites have in common is a tendency to treat the Web less like a TV channel or magazine, which convey information, and more like an operating system or computer, which generate it. Except that this computer gets its processing power from the humans plugged into it."* (Source: http://*www.wired.com/culture/geekipedia/magazine/geekipedia/web_2_0*).

In this section, we survey the most popular Web 2.0 technologies that have had an impact on business processes and/or that are transforming the way businesses approach collaboration and knowledge sharing today.

Many Web 2.0 collaborative applications began their existence as consumer-oriented applications and the majority of the earliest consumers were young people. FaceBook and MySpace, the popular social networking applications, can be counted among the collaborative applications of the Web 2.0 era. The jury is still out on just how much these particular applications have aided business but a definite by-product of their use is the number of young people entering the workforce with well-developed Web 2.0 skills and habits. Increasingly, young Web 2.0-savy employees are introducing their organizations to a new generation of applications that often complement traditional business communication and collaboration processes.

Text messaging, or SMS (Short Message Service), is one example of a favorite communication medium for many people today. Text messaging is also becoming a legitimate business communication tool, particularly for mobile workers. Figure 6.9 is an example of how a business traveler may use Google's SMS service to find current exchange rates. Table 6.3 lists a few other SMS services and that are being used in business.

Figure 6.9 Using Google's SMS Service to find Currency Conversion Rates

Activity	Service Provider
Access quick access to information: - check flight status - currency conversion - driving directions	http://4INFO.net http://google.com/sms
Check a calendar	http://calendar.google.com
Add items to to-do lists Create reminders	http://gubb.net http://30boxes.com http://www.rememberthemilk.com
Quickly arrange a team meeting	http://twitter.com http://dodgeball.com
Get email by text message	

Table 6.3 – Business use of SMS Services

Twitter®

The number of Web 2.0 applications and services is dynamic and a detailed description of the current list of popular Web 2.0 applications is beyond the scope of this book. However, in the Opening Vignette at the beginning of this chapter, we referred to Twitter® (Figure 6.10), an interesting Web 2.0 communication application that was launched as a friendly, consumer-oriented service to help people stay connected. Twitter evangelists have now brought the service into the business and the political environment. **Twitter** uses SMS, email and a blog to immediately notify "followers" of short messages, called "tweets," and to access the "tweets" (updates) of those who we are "following." For business, Twitter has been used to instantly notify team members of a meeting and to provide immediate information updates and feedback to the team. Twitter has also been increasingly popular with politicians, notably during the 2008 presidential election, where it has been used to notify supporters of rallies and provide instant information to those following an apparent Web 2.0-savvy candidate.

Figure 6.10 – Twitter logo

Blogging

Twitter® is the micro-variation of a **blog**, or **Web log**. Blogs are asynchronous, Web-based discussions that typically focus on a particular topic, company, product or service. Blog owners generally allow just about anyone to participate in the blog and as a result blogs have become a popular Web 2.0 communication tool for individuals, businesses and other organizations. A blog is a very efficient and effective medium for sharing information, views and opinions. Blogs have their roots in the electronic bulletin boards that were popular in the early 1980s that were accessed by dial-up modems. VaxNotes, from Digital Equipment Corporation (DEC), was another early asynchronous discussion system that was used for collaboration and communication, particularly among researchers, in the period that preceded the microcomputer and the Web.

Today, there are millions of blogs on almost any topic imaginable.   According to Technorati.com, a popular index of blogs, there are three types of bloggers (see Figure 6.11):

- **Personal** - blog about topics of personal interest.
- **Professional** - blog about professional and industry interests but not officially representing a company.
- **Corporate** - blog about their company in an official company capacity.

Figure 6.11 – Types of Bloggers

Distinguishing a personal or professional blog from an official organizational web site becomes more difficult as the size and influence of a blog grows. It is important to remember, however, that the material found in a blog is typically not fact-checked, is usually someone's opinion, and blog posts need not be true. Despite this, many businesses have embraced blogging because of its ability to provide another level of service to customers. Blogs give customers access to information topics from a variety of perspectives, both official and unofficial, and they provide companies with a mechanism for obtaining customer suggestions and feedback.

More About IT

What is the difference between Twitter and a blog? Twitter is a service designed for quick, frequent communication between friends, family and co-workers. Twitter limits updates, or tweets, to 140 characters which allows "tweets" to be made using SMS. Blogs do not limit the size of a posting and are typically accessed via a web browser. Twitter updates are immediately passed to "followers" via SMS and email and immediately appear on the Twitter website. Blog updates appear immediately on the blog website but notification is not necessarily automatic. Blogs often use another Web 2.0 technology called RSS to alert participants of updates. Notification of tweets can also be made using RSS.

RSS and Atom

Today, the acronym RSS is usually associated with the term **Really Simple Syndication**. However, Really Simple Syndication, RDF Site Summary, and Rich Site Summary are all terms that have shared the acronym RSS. **Atom** can be considered another version of RSS. Generally, all of these terms refer to a technology that facilitates the sharing and syndication of website content, by subscription.   In simple terms, RSS and Atom allows subscribers to "pull" web content to their computers automatically as new information is made available on websites that use **RSS** (or Atom) **feeds**. We will refer to this category of Web 2.0 technology as RSS for simplicity.

There has been tremendous growth in the number of available RSS feeds in the last few years. Syndic8.com, one of the leading RSS feed directories on the web reported approximately 450,000 worldwide feeds in February 2006. This was nearly ten times the number of feeds available at the same time in 2004. Many of these feeds can be attributed to blogs. Bloggers seemed to be the first to understand the efficiencies associated with RSS, especially the ability of RSS to alert their readers to new blog content.

Lately, businesses have begun to realize the value of RSS. Marketing departments, for example, are turning to RSS as their email campaigns become less effective. People are reducing their intake of commercial email, in part because organizations are increasingly relying on spam blockers to filter unsolicited email. RSS avoids spam filters and other delivery threats because recipients have to *opt-in*, or subscribe, to RSS content. RSS provides other business benefits as well. For example, RSS generally makes information timelier as subscribers are notified of new content at regular intervals. Since this new content comes to the consumer, rather than the consumer going to the content, more content can be consumed. RSS effectively gives marketers another channel to build brand awareness. Perhaps this is the reason some consider RSS to be one of the most powerful Internet marketing tools available today.

RSS has also been adopted by project teams to facilitate communication among team members. Assignments and project updates can be fed to team members via an RSS channels specifically set up for the project. Additionally, many of the collaborative activities of a project are benefiting from the communication efficiencies and security provided by RSS compared to multi-recipient email. For example, Basecamp, a web-based project management tool, uses RSS to share and syndicate project documentation such as design documents and status reports. In the More About It section below you can how a business such as BT Rentals can employ an RSS feed.

More About IT

Recall the website discussed earlier in the chapter for BT's Rentals. Assume Brad Thomas, the owner of the rental equipment business said he hoped he could also use the BT Rental website to help sell "retired" rental equipment. He considered taking digital pictures of the retired equipment and including a dynamic photo gallery on his website of equipment to be sold. He could then notify his customers, by phone or email, that he has equipment for sale, or simply hope that his clients who may be interested in the equipment would see the pictures when they view his webpage. Today, both of these methods can be problematic: individual phone calls are time consuming and often it is difficult to speak directly to the person you are trying to reach; email, particularly email sent in 'bulk', is increasingly treated as spam and is either filtered or is not delivered at all. Additionally, it is unrealistic for customers to check a web site if the site changes only periodically. These problems are what make a technology such as RSS so appealing for marketing purposes today. RSS will allow Brad to notify his customers (those who subscribe) automatically every time he has something for sale.

An example of a simple RSS feed is shown in Figure 6.12(a). Most RSS feeds are XML files that include a <**channel**> element that describes the RSS feed itself and one or more <item> elements that describe the web resources that are available to subscribers. Each <item> in the example contains a <title>, a <link> and a <description> of the web resource. Since RSS and Atom are XML-based, different versions of the application refer to different Document Type Definitions (DTD) and therefore may also include different <item> descriptors.   Figure 6.12(b) shows how the sample RSS feed appears to subscribers in IE7.

```
<?xml version="1.0" encoding="UTF-8" ?>
- <rss version="2.0">
  - <channel>
      <title>Easton, George 930am or 11am</title>
      <link>http://rohan.sdsu.edu/~geaston/easton7.xml</link>
      <description>This is an RSS feed created by George Easton</description>
      <language>en-us</language>
    - <item>
        <title>George Easton Web Page</title>
        <link>http://rohan.sdsu.edu/~geaston/george_easton.html</link>
        <description>This is a personal web page by George Easton</description>
      </item>
    - <item>
        <title>George Easton Expense Report</title>
        <link>http://rohan.sdsu.edu/~geaston/yourname_expense_report.htm</link>
        <description>This is the Expense Report web page by George Easton.</description>
      </item>
    - <item>
        <title>IDS180 Web Page for grades</title>
        <link>http://ebiz.sdsu.edu/180spring2008</link>
        <description>You can check your grade in IDS180 by clicking on this link</description>
      </item>
  </channel>
</rss>
```

Figure 6.12(a) – RSS Feed

Easton, George 930am or 11am

George Easton Web Page

Wednesday, April 16, 2008, 2:58:14 PM ➡

This is a personal web page by George Easton

George Easton Expense Report

Wednesday, April 16, 2008, 2:58:14 PM ➡

This is the Expense Report web page by George Easton.

IDS180 Web Page for grades

Wednesday, April 16, 2008, 2:58:14 PM ➡

You can check your grade in IDS180 by clicking on this link

Figure 6.12(b) – XML Code for RSS Feed

The subscriber to an RSS feed requires an application that can interpret the XML code of the RSS file. Originally, many of these applications were discrete, installed or web-based applications called **newsreaders**, **aggregators** and **RSS feed readers**, such as Bloglines® and Google Reader. Today, most web browsers, including Firefox and IE7, and some web portals, such as My!Yahoo®, have integrated XML functionality. If you attempt to access an RSS file using client software that is not equipped to process XML, you will only see the XML tags, not the working RSS feed. Once you subscribe to an RSS feed, your RSS client software will periodically check the RSS file on the provider's website for content updates. If there is a new <item> added to the RSS feed, new web content is available. The RSS reader "pulls" the headlines and story excerpts of the new content to the subscriber's computer along with a hyperlink to the full content. It is important to note that the content may be on the provider's website or on a website located elsewhere. If the content is located on another website, the provider is 'really simply syndicating' this content. Figure 6.13 below shows the components of an RSS feed and provides a sampling of a number of popular web sites that offer their content via RSS technology and an assortment of the popular RSS aggregators that people are using to subscribe to RSS feeds.

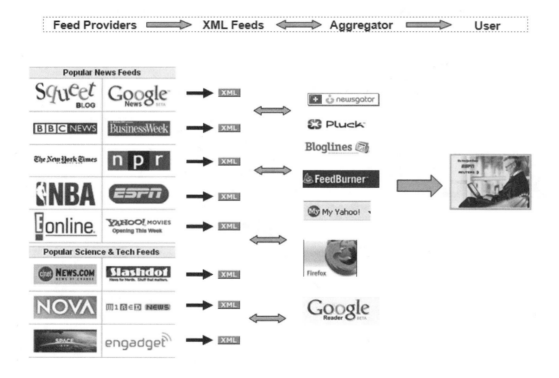

Figure 6.13 – The Components of an RSS Feed

We have been discussing RSS as a technology for publishing regular updates of web-based content to subscribers. For companies such as BT's Rentals, it permits the instant distribution of content updates to consumers. There is also a significant consumer advantage of using RSS. Essentially, consumers who subscribe to RSS feeds have the ability to review a large number of websites in a very short time possible. The existing volume of information available on the World Wide Web is already overwhelming to many of us. The situation becomes particularly acute for those time-challenged individuals who are professionally and/or personally compelled to comb the growing number of websites that harbor potentially pertinent information. RSS may be one solution that can help address the issue of information overload.

Mashups

Many young people are familiar with music mashups, the music that is created, typically, by remixing the vocal track of one song with the music track of another song. Digital technology, desktop software and bootlegged music have made music mashups relatively easy to produce and have inspired a growing number of would-be artists. For example, *Glass Octopus* is a music mashup of Blondie's *House of Glass* and the Beatles' *Octopus's Garden* by DJ Lobsterdust (Figure 6.14).

Figure 6.14 - *Glass Octopus music mashup*

The software equivalent of music mashups exists among the Web 2.0 technologies and it has inspired some would-be software developers. Software **mashups** are web-based applications, tools, widgets, or resources that blend data from more than one source. HousingMaps.com (Figure 6.15), the first and one of the best known software mashup, for example, is a mix of housing data from craigslist.com and Google maps.

Figure 6.15 – The First Mashup: HousingMaps.com

Today there are about 3400, live, mashup-based applications in existence according to ProgrammableWeb.com, a clearinghouse of mashup information. Many of these mashups are the 'push-pin-over-graphical-map' type of tool that some consider to be consumer-grade, that is, lightweight applications. Some of this criticism comes from the fact that mashups are replacing Excel as the new end-user development platform of the Web 2.0 era. The ease at which mashups can be created has generated a flurry of bottom-up application development efforts in companies of all sizes. Yahoo Pipes, shown in Figure 6.16, is a sophisticated, drag-and-drop, end-user mashup development platform that is helping overcome this stigma. With tools such as Pipes, mashup developers are taking aim at real business problems and enterprise-wide processes.

Figure 6.16 - Yahoo Pipes

There are an increasing number of enterprise mashups and mashup platforms available for businesses. IBM, for example, is developing a mashup "for a home improvement store that allows a logistics manager to drag and drop weather reports and maps and hardware inventory data into a mashup that shows which stores need rock salt, shovels and snowblowers." IBM, SAP, Microsoft and Saleforce.com are currently the most prominent companies that offer mashup products. There are however, many smaller companies competing in the mashup space.

While the value of business mashups grows, many organizations are informally becoming acquainted with this particular Web 2.0 technology by creating ad-hoc, self-service mashups using RSS feeds and other sources of data. Figure 6.17 shows how organizations can progress to more sophisticated mashups using tools such as Yahoo Pipes and Microsoft Popfly and other mashup tools. Figure 6.18 contains a table of sixteen mashup development tools that purportedly can be used to create Enterprise 2.0-grade mashups.

Figure 6.17 Mashup Architecture

Figure 6.18 Mashup Development Tools

The growing interest and popularity of mashups can be attributed to a number of things:
- mashups do not require anything but a web browser and a mashup URL to run.
- mashups have been very effective in leveraging earlier investments in Web applications allowing others the ability to reuse code (e.g., APIs).
- mashups deliver business intelligence and decision support tools to users that were previously considered too expensive or too impractical.
- Mashups are the 21st century analog of the spreadsheet. They have the potential to allow all of us to become "application developers."

However, mashups do have some critics and ironically, they often come from IT departments. Mashups, like many end-user apps, have generally been panned by IT departments as:
- Lightweight
- often of questionable integrity
- developed without corporate approval
- insecure
- not controlled by the IT department
- end-users developing mashups require help understanding the compliance, e-discovery and risk perspectives

LEARNING CHECK
Be sure you can * explain the difference between Web 2.0 and Web 1.0 * explain how Blogs are used by companies * explain mashups

E-COMMERCE

The World Wide Web is primarily responsible for the boom in **e-commerce**, the buying, selling and exchanging of goods and services electronically, or in a *virtual* marketplace. The Web has certainly become the favorite virtual marketplace of consumers. From 2001 to 2006, retail e-commerce, or *e-tail* sales, increased at an average annual growth rate of 25.4%, compared with a

4.8% growth rate for total retail sales. In 2007, e-tail sales in the US was estimated at $127.7 billion.

Web-based e-commerce actually represents a relatively small proportion of total e-commerce revenue. Private communication networks and the Internet also support standardized business transactions using a technology called **Electronic Data Interchange (EDI)**. EDI technology is losing ground to the Web and technologies such as XML as both the marketplace and the mechanism for e-commerce and **e-business**, the broader set of business activities and business processes supporting e-commerce. Because the terms e-commerce and e-business are similar, we use them interchangeably throughout this section. The Web technologies are an increasingly appealing alternative for both e-commerce and e-business because they are universal, inclusive, and less costly.

In this section, we are interested in understanding how businesses are implementing and leveraging the e-commerce capabilities of the Web. We begin by discussing the common types of e-commerce and the various revenue models used today on the Web. We also discuss *search engine optimization*, the methods and strategies businesses use to ensure that their websites will appear in search engines queries. We conclude the section with a brief discussion of the e-payment technologies.

Types of e-Commerce

A common way to classify e-commerce is by the market relationship that exists between those involved in the transaction. There are three major types of market relationships:

- **Business-to-consumer (B2C)** relationships are the electronic equivalent of retail. B2C transactions typically occur between businesses and individuals. Amazon.com is the world's largest on-line retailer. Figure 6.19 lists the top ten US e-tailers.

Figure 6.19 – Top Ten US e-tailers

- **Business-to-business (B2B)** relationships are the largest form of e-business by dollar volume. B2B transactions occur between two, or more, businesses; typically, with one business supplying parts and/or services to the other. B2B e-commerce transactions accounted for 93% of *all* B2B revenue in 2007.
- **Consumer-to-consumer (C2C)** relationships are formed when an individual sells to other individuals. EBay, the most popular C2C marketplace on the Web, had approximately 84.5 million active users worldwide in early 2008. In 2007, the total value of sold items on eBay was nearly $60 billion. Figure 6.20 provides market statistics for three of eBay's most popular product categories.

Figure 6.20 – eBay Statistics

EBay is the intermediary and virtual market for millions of goods offered at auction every day.   Most auction sites, such as eBay, have limited liability if buyers or sellers experience problems related to their transactions. EBay transactions that are settled using PayPal, eBay's electronic payment service, are generally protected from fraud, the ever-present risk in a virtual marketplace.

E-Commerce Revenue Models

A revenue model generally describes how a business earns revenue and generates a profit. There are a number of e-commerce revenue models that have been developed but most companies that are using the Web rely on at least one of the following models to achieve their revenue objectives.

Sales revenue model: revenue based on the direct sale of goods and services from the manufacturer or retailer to the customer is called the sales revenue model. E-tailers, such as Amazon.com, Dell Computer, Lands' End are just a few of the companies that rely on direct sales to customers to generate revenue.

Subscription revenue model: e-commerce web sites that charge a fee for membership or require a subscription to access content that is available on the site use the subscription revenue model. *The Wall Street Journal*, for example, currently costs $89 per year to access the complete on-line version of the newspaper, WSJ.com.

Advertising revenue model: many web sites, especially web portals, display advertisements and banner ads on the site to generate revenue. The revenue generated by using the advertising revenue model is typically determined by a metric such as **CPM,** *cost per thousand impressions*; **CPC,** *cost per click*; or **CPA,** *cost per action*. For example,
- a $1.00 CPM ad will generate $1.00 for each 1000 times the ad displays
- a CPC ad generates revenue, usually between five cents and fifty cents, each time a user clicks on the ad. As with a CPM ad, the revenue may only accrue for the first unique click from a particular user.
- a CPA ad generates revenue each time a user completes a specified action, such as completing a survey. There are two basic types of CPA ads:
    - **Cost per lead ads:** generate revenue each time a user provides contact information. These programs typically pay somewhere between 50 cents and $3.00 per signup.
    - **Cost per sale ads:** generate revenue each time a user buys a product. The commission is usually a percentage of the sale price.

Google's AdSense programs (www.google.com/adsense) are an easy way to become familiar with the advertising revenue model. AdSense works by placing unobtrusive Google ads on your website that are related to the content on your site (Figure 6.21). According to AdSense, this gives you a way to both "monetize and enhance your content pages." AdSense uses both the cost-per-click and a cost-per-impression techniques for calculating revenue earned.

Figure 6.21 – Google's AdSense Program

Transaction revenue model: most e-commerce websites are capable of processing transactions. Those that charge a fee for processing each transaction processed are relying on the transaction revenue model. At eBay, for example, each auction generates a small fee to eBay, from the seller, if the auction is successful in selling the item. Many brokerage firms, including E-Trade and Fidelity, execute stock trades via their websites, usually for a transaction fee. These transaction fees are the currency of the transaction revenue model. Figure 6.22 below shows the transaction fees assessed individuals and businesses when PayPal is used as the method of payment in a transaction.

Figure 6.22 – PayPal Fees

Affiliate revenue model: this revenue model depends on websites to steer, or refer, business to an affiliate's website. Typically this happens through ads and links placed on websites that refer to the affiliate website. The affiliate agrees to pay a referral fee if a sale results from the referral. Often the fee is a percentage of the sale revenue.

Search Engine Optimization (SEO)

"If you build it, will they come?" This twist on the famous expression from the movie *The Field of Dreams* is a legitimate question for any business that has, or is considering, a web presence. There are a number of techniques available to help improve the odds that visitors and customers will indeed come to your website. One of the most effective techniques to ensure website visitors is to optimize a website so it will rank higher on the major search engines. This is called **Search Engine Optimization (SEO),** or **Search Optimization.** SEO relies on both "organic," or unpaid, and paid approaches to improve the chances that your website will rank high with the major search engines.

There are many search engines that exist today, although most web searches are handled by four main search engines: Google, Yahoo!, MSN, and Ask.com, respectively. Figure 6.23 lists forty-five different search engines that are currently in use, but there are actually many others.

About.com	Go.com	Northern Light
AM-MA	Google	Open Directory
All the Web	HandiLinks	Overture
Alta Vista	Hotbot	Profusion
AOL	InfoGrid	REX
Ask Jeeves	Internet Sleuth	Scrub the Web
Beauco Up!	IWon	Search.com
BOTBOT.com	Kanoodle	Snap.com
Cyber411	LookSmart	Teoma Search
Dogpile	Lycos	Vivisimo
Excite	Mamma	Webcrawler
Fast Search	Metacrawler	What-U-Seek
Find Info	Metafind	Wise Nut
Galazy	MSN	Yahoo!
GigaBlast	Netscape	Yahooligans!

Figure 6.23 – Search Engines

Generally, search engine developers have created unique algorithms that comb and analyze an index, or directory, of web page information to determine which web pages will be displayed from a search engine query. Most search engines can be classified as either *crawler-based* or *human-powered directories*. Crawler-based search engines, such as Google, add to the index automatically using **spiders**, or crawlers, that find a web page, read it, and follow the links on the page to other pages within the website. Everything the spider finds is indexed. Human-powered directories, as the name implies, rely on people to submit the web site information that is processed by the search engine algorithms.

There are two types of factors that can influence the relevancy, or ranking, of web pages analyzed by the major search engines. O*n-page factors* are the things that can be manipulated by the webmaster, such as **keywords**, the words and phrases that help search engines index your website. O*ff-page factors* are the relevancy measures that are not easily manipulated by the webmaster, including **link analysis** and **clickthrough** measurement.

Keywords strategically placed in HTML code often help optimize your site for search engines. For example, search engines that find

- keywords in the HTML title tag of the web page may enhance the relevancy of a web page to the search topic.
- keywords at or near the top of a web page are usually considered more relevant because web pages typically describe their relevant topics from the start.
- keywords that appear with a higher frequency on a web page typically indicate greater relevancy of the web page to the search topic.

> **More About IT**
> Search engines may also exclude web pages from their index if they detect search engine "spamming." This type of spamming occurs when a keyword appears repeatedly, perhaps hundreds of times, in a web page specifically to increase the page's perceived relevancy to search terms.

Link analysis is an off-page search engine measurement that analyzes how web pages are linked to each other. This analysis helps search engines determine

- more about a particular web page by understanding what web pages are linking to that page.
- whether the web page is "important" based on the importance of pages linking to the page.

Another off-page search measurement is **clickthrough**. This provides search engines with relevancy information by monitoring which web pages people actually click on for particular search terms. High-ranking pages that aren't attracting web site visitors are usually re-evaluated and vice-versa.

View these videos on Search Engine Optimization:

- http://www.youtube.com/watch?v=jq4rUcmALhY

- http://www.youtube.com/watch?v=PpctGId-65U

- http://www.youtube.com/watch?v=65PQpHcAonw

LEARNING CHECK
Be sure you can * identify the different types of e-commerce * describe the e-commerce revenue models * explain search engine optimization

Wrapping IT Up

The World Wide Web has become the universal interface of the Internet and it has changed the way business is viewed and conducted, both locally and globally. Everyone everywhere seems to be relying more and more on the Web for everyday tasks and business activities. For a growing number of individuals and companies, the web browser is the Internet's operating system. In this chapter, you learned why browsers have attained that prominence and the role they have played in the evolution of markup languages such as HTML.

You have also seen how local brick-and-mortar businesses, such as BT's Rentals, have realized the necessity of a Web presence simply to stay competitive. Brad Thomas, BT's owner, recognizes that many of his potential customers are exclusively using Web search engines, such as Google and Yahoo, rather than traditional printed directories such as the *Yellow Pages* and newspaper advertisements, to help them find the nearest rental location, to locate a particular piece of equipment, and/or to search for best rental rates in the area. Brad was compelled to become familiar with techniques that can optimize BT's Rentals presence on the Web, making sure potential customers see his site in their searches.

The Web has also helped many business owners worldwide realize that their products and services need not be constrained by geographic and temporal locations. The Web has extended the reach and the operating hours of businesses, large and small, and given countless businesses the ability to compete in the global marketplace. The Web has also extended reach and efficiency of individuals who are relying on Web 2.0 communication technologies, such as RSS, to stay connected to colleagues and to dynamic web content that is personally and professionally pertinent.

Study Questions Summary

1. What are the key components of the Web?
   - The Web is a comprehensive Internet service that is inherently dependent on Internet technologies such as packet switching, TCP/IP, and URLs
   - The Web also is dependent on markup languages, particularly HTML and XML for communication.

2. What are markup languages such as HTML?
   - HTML is a derivative of hypertext and SGML.
     - Hypertext is a user-controlled document navigation system.
     - SGML is a meta-language that allows electronic documents to be device-independent and describes how electronic documents can be 'marked up' for formatting.
   - HTML elements are text, pictures, lines and links that appear on a web paged and the tags are the instructions that are interpreted by the browser to display the elements.

3. What is Web 2.0?
   - Web 2.0 refers to the second generation of the Web.
   - Web 2.0 signified a change in the way the Web was being used.
   - Web 2.0 technologies and applications are known for their collaborative properties and features.

4. What is Search Engine Optimization?
   - SEO are the tools and techniques that can be implemented to increase the probability that a Web search engine will return a particular website.
   - There are on-page and off-page factors that can be employed in SEO
     - On-page factors primarily relate to the use of keywords
     - Off-page factors primarily relate to link analysis

Key Terms

Page Number references are included in parentheses

Accessibility standards (181)	Hypertext Markup Language (HTML) (172, 178)	Spiders (197)
Aggregator (190)	HTML elements (178)	Standard Generalized Markup Language (SGML) (177)
Blog (186)	HTML tags (178)	Text editors (179)
Cascading Style Sheet (CSS) (184)	Hyptertext Transport Protocol (HTTP) (175)	Twitter (186)
Channel (188)	Mashups (191)	Uniform Resource Identifier (URI) (176)
eXtensible Hypertext Markup Language (XHTML) (183)	Meta-language (182)	Uniform Resource Locator (URL) (176)
eXtensible Markup Language (XML) (182)	Newsreader (190)	Web 2.0 (184)
Electronic data interchange (EDI) (194)	Really Simple Syndication (RSS) (187)	World Wide Web Consortium (W3C) (181)
e-Commerce (193)	RSS feed (187)	
Hypertext (175)	Search engine optimization (196)	

Multiple Choice Questions

1. Which of the following is Web technologies is credited to Tim Berners-Lee?
   - a. URLs
   - b. hypertext
   - c. HTTP
   - d. HTML

2. What was the meta-language used to create HTML?
   - a. XML
   - b. XHTML
   - c. NeXTStep
   - d. SGML

3. The first web browser was created by
   - a. Tim Berners-Lee
   - b. Microsoft
   - c. IBM
   - d. Marc Andreesen

4. The original name of the first web browser was?
    a. WorldWideWeb
    b. Nexus
    c. Mosaic
    d. Netscape Navigator

5. Which of the following is not a web browser?
    a. Safari
    b. Opera
    c. Firefox
    d. Google Reader
    e. Internet Explorer

Answers:
1. d   2. d   3. a   4. a   5. d

Projects

1. Today, most web developers agree that proficiency with a markup language such as HTML is a useful skill for everyone involved in web page design and website development. This is true even though most web professionals rely on specialized graphical web development tools (also called WYSIWYG tools for 'What You See Is What You Get'), such as Dreamweaver® and Expression®, that automatically generate HTML code. You are probably aware that many common software applications, such as Microsoft Word and Excel, will also generate HTML code using the "Save As" option.

Complete the following steps to gain a better understanding of HTML:

- Create the simple "Hello World" web page below using a text editor such as Notepad.
  ```
  <html>
  <head>
  <title>Hello World Web Page</title>
  <body>
  <h1>Hello World!</h1>
  </body>
  </html>
  ```

- Save the file locally (to your disk or USB drive) with any filename and an extension of .html (e.g., helloworld.html). Please pay attention to the *filetype*, or "Save as type" option of your HTML files. Most HTML documents require the .txt *filetype* with .html or .htm as the filename extension. In the figure below, the file is being saved to the Desktop as *helloworld.html* with the filetype as *.txt*.

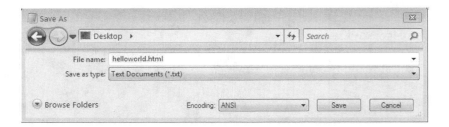

- View your page through your web browser by double clicking on the file on your desktop (or wherever you saved it).

- Copy and paste the web page you are viewing (not the HTML code) into Word or any other WYSIWYG editor and use the 'Save As' option to save the file as a web page.

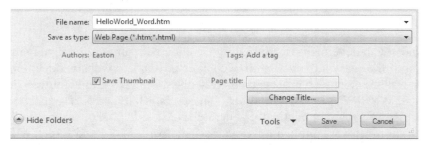

- View this new web page (named HelloWorld_Word.htm). Compare the appearance of the web page created by the WYSIWYG editor to web page created by the text editor. Generally, both web pages will look the same when viewed through your browser.

- Compare the HTML source code for each file. You can view the source code of most an HTML document in Internet Explorer using menu options View→Source.

As you will see, there is significant esoteric code generated by the WYSIWYG editor compared to what you entered into the text editor.

2. Use an RSS aggregator to subscribe to an RSS feed. Use more than one aggregator to view the same feed.

3. Use a text editor to create/copy a simple RSS file in XML (an example will be given in the chapter). Check your file against an RSS validator (http://validator.w3.org/feed). If you have sufficient priviledges on a website, upload your RSS file and the associated HTML file (it could be the HTML file you created in the project above) to a website. Subscribe to your own RSS feed using any RSS feed reader you wish.

4. Use Twitter or a Blog to communicate with a study group before an upcoming test. Have everyone in the group submit sample questions to the Blog before the group meets.

CHAPTER 7

Information Security and Cyber Crime

PLANNING AHEAD

After reading Chapter 7, you should be able to answer these questions in your own words:

STUDY QUESTIONS
What is information security?
What constitutes cyber crime?
What can be done to enhance cyber security?

LEARNING PREVIEW

The volume of *new* information created each year is growing exponentially. The new information created in 2002 alone was estimated to be equivalent to 37,000 new libraries the size of the Library of Congress. The 2006 estimate of new information was three million times the information in all of the books ever written. This is physically possible because most new information is born digital, that is to say, created in digital format. The efficacy of creating and storing vast quantities of natively digital information goes well beyond the cost of new libraries. Digital information is portable and replicable, meaning it is easy to access, copy and distribute using information systems and computer networks such as the Internet. Advancing the ability to access and distribute business information is undeniably desirable, for example, when it improves business decision-making, helps make commerce more efficient, and yields ideas that help people work more efficiently and effectively. There is however, a down-side to being digital. Digital information is only as secure as the people, the information systems and the computer networks that manage, access, store, and distribute the information. Not surprisingly, organizational and individual information resources are subject to constant risk today. Much of this risk comes from malicious, intentional acts that threaten the privacy of personal and sensitive information. Information security represents the safeguards and regulations that can help protect information assets from risks and threats that can expose, compromise, destroy or allow unauthorized access and use of personal and sensitive information. In this chapter, we review information security, specifically cyber security and the regulations enacted to help ensure information privacy and the security of digital information, information systems and computer networks.

OPENING VIGNETTE

Social Engineering, the USB Way

In early 2006, Steve Stasiukonis, VP and founder of Secure Network Technologies, Inc was hired by a credit union to assess the security of its network. The credit union was particularly concerned about employees succumbing to social engineering tactics because of previous problems with employees sharing passwords. The credit union was also concerned about employees using rogue USB drives that could introduce malware such as viruses and Trojan horses into the network that could compromise the information and information systems of the credit union.

Steve had used a variety of social engineering tactics to test the security of other networks. For example, he would hang out with the smokers, sweet-talk a receptionist, or commandeer a meeting room and jack into the network. This time, however, the credit union staff was aware that someone was going to test the security of their network so he decided to try a different tactic. He imprinted 20 inexpensive USB drives with a Trojan horse his firm created that when run, would collect passwords, logins and machine-specific information from the user's computer, and then email the findings back to his company.

Figure 7.1 – USB Drives: a threat to information security?

In order to get the USB drives in the hands of the credit union staff he scattered the drives in the parking lot, smoking areas and other places the employees frequented and then watched as the credit union employees found the devices. Steve was sure that the employees would plug the drives into their computers as soon as they got to their desks and view the image files that contained the malware. After three days, Steve confirmed that 15 of the 20 USB drives had been found by credit union employees and all 15 had been plugged into the credit union's computers.

Even this veteran security expert was amazed at the effectiveness of this social engineering tactic that exploited humans' innate curiosity. Email viruses and phishing expeditions take advantage of similar human tendencies. All the technology and filtering and scanning in the world won't address human nature which make it the single biggest risk to any company's secrets.

(Source: Compiled from Steve Stasiukonis, "Social Engineering, the USB Way," *Dark Reading*, June 7, 2006, http://www.darkreading.com/document.asp?doc_id=95556; accessed 1/2/2007).

Social engineering takes advantage of the most significant risk to information security today, human behavior. As the number and the sophistication of deliberate risks to personally identifiable information and to sensitive organizational information grows, the burden of combating these risks also increases. Organizations are starting to realize that this burden is much more than the tangible costs of fixing compromised systems and the lost productivity resulting from information security breaches. The intangible costs, such as lost sales, the loss of trust, and the liability associated with non-compliance to regulations enacted to ensure information security are also major concerns for almost every business today. In this chapter, we will look at information security and cyber crime. We also examine the security tools and practices that can help protect the privacy and sensitive information of individuals and organizations.

VISUAL ORGANIZATION OF CHAPTER

Study Question 1	Study Question 2	Study Question 3
Information Security	Cyber Crime	Cyber Security
• Information Security Risks • Information Security Regulations	• Malware • Social Engineering and Cyber Attacks	• 1st Level of Defense • Encryption • Access Controls • Cyber Security Suggestions
Learning Check 1	Learning Check 2	Learning Check 3

INFORMATION SECURITY

Today, most *new* information is natively digital. In other words, the information is *created* in digital format. Digital information can be organized, stored, accessed and distributed more efficiently than information existing in any other format. This is important, and arguably the cause, for the staggering volume of new information created annually. One estimate of the *new* information generated in the year 2006 alone was 161 Exabytes (one **Exabyte** is 1.074 billion gigabytes). To put this quantity in perspective, 161 Exabytes is roughly equivalent to 3 million times the information in all of the books ever written. At the current pace, the information added annually to the digital universe is expected to be nearly 1000 Exabytes by the year 2010.

This unfathomable quantity of information cannot be meaningfully managed were it not digital. The digital format makes information very portable and replicable giving employees, customers and business partners' easy access to the information at any time and from almost any place in the world via computers, portable wireless devices and computer networks such as the Internet. Unfortunately, the increasing volume of digital information and the accessibility afforded by information systems, wireless devices and computer networks, particularly the Internet, have also elevated the security risks associated with these information assets. These risks are costing US organizations approximately $67.2 billion each year according to the FBI.

Information security refers to the safekeeping of all information assets. A major component of information security is *cyber security* which centers on the stewardship of digital information, information systems, and computer networks. Many businesses and a growing number of individuals have learned, often with a great deal of agony and expense, that digital information is only as secure as the people, the information systems and the computer networks that access, store and distribute the information. Today, digital information and information systems that are presumed to be private and secure are regularly breached exposing sensitive and personal information to various risks that can compromise, alter, destroy or allow the use of information without authorization. In this section, we discuss these major risks to digital information and information systems and describe personally identifiable information, the type of information that is often targeted in a cyber security attack.

Information Security Risks

There is not a specific taxonomy, or classification system, for the various risks to digital information and information systems. Some of the risks are unintentional and the result of natural events, such as flooding and fire. Other unintentional risks that affect the security of electronic information are hardware or software-related problems, such as computer failure or software glitches. Increasingly, the risks and threats to information security are intentional acts that can expose, compromise, destroy or allow unauthorized access and use of personal and sensitive information. Regardless of the intent, organizations' must effectively plan for these inevitable occurrences by developing formal disaster recovery policies and routine backup procedures.

The most significant risk to information security today is the result of human action. Human behavior accounts for nearly 75 percent of all information security breaches in business today. Some of the information security risk associated with human behavior is unintentional, such as the curiosity of the employees in the opening case who were deceived by social engineering, or employees who naively leave passwords on Post-it notes beneath their computer keyboards. However, the intent of the majority of the human behavior that threatens information security today is unlawful and malicious and is usually carried out by disgruntled or fired employees, individual hackers, and organized crime groups who generally understand both the vulnerabilities and the value of information assets. We discuss the specifics of many of the intentional, malicious risks to digital information and information systems later in the chapter in the section entitled Cyber Crime. Regardless of the intent and the degree of malice, information security risks are increasingly a threat to information privacy and personally identifiable information.

 View an extreme example of the amount of information organizations could know about us at: http://aclu.org/pizza/images/screen.swf.

Personally Identifiable Information (PII) is sensitive business information that uniquely identifies individuals. Names, addresses, phone numbers, Social Security numbers and credit card numbers are typical personal identifiers collected and used by businesses and other organizations today to establish customer relationships, establish and verify identities, open financial accounts, extend credit, and complete business transactions. Besides its value to conduct business, PII also has market value. In other words, information that uniquely identifies customers and employees for one business is often used to solicit new business by affiliates and unrelated companies. Because PII is usually digital, and hence very portable, it is easily made available to other businesses, usually for a fee or some other consideration. At one time, PII passed legitimately from organization to organization with little regard for personal privacy or concern for how the information was subsequently used. Ostensibly, this information would be used for marketing purposes so other businesses or affiliates could contact individuals with offers and information about their products and services. Unfortunately, the abuses associated with personally identifiable information became more serious than just the annoying dinner-time telephone solicitations we once received regularly. Criminals discovered that having another person's identifying information made it relatively easy to acquire the identity of that person. Stealing another person's identity, or identity theft, has become the fastest growing crime in America.

Identity theft occurs when one person appropriates another person's personally identifiable information to get loans or acquire credit cards, withdraw money from a victim's financial accounts, or otherwise use another person's identity for fraudulent purposes. In 2006, approximately 9.9 million Americans were victims of identity theft according to the Federal Trade Commission. Identity theft is so prevalent that personally identifiable information has reached commodity status among the criminals who maintain the illegal secondary market for this information. The Treasury Department estimates the ill-gotten gain associated with identity theft is now comparable to the proceeds associated with the sale of illegal drugs. As with illegal drugs, organized crime controls much of illegal secondary market in personally identifiable information.

  View a video on what businesses can do to help prevent identity theft at: http://www.ftc.gov/infosecurity/

More About IT

If you are a victim of identity theft you should:
- immediately contact your credit card companies and banks and let know of the problem.
- contact the three major credit reporting agencies to notify them that you have had your identity stolen. They can flag your account with a "fraud alert" to limit the damage to your credit history.
- contact the Office of Social Security to inform them that your Social Security Number may be compromised.

If you are a victim of identity theft that involves your personal medical information you should also:
- contact your health insurance company as someone may be submitting medical claims under your name for services that are not yours. This could exhaust your health insurance and put erroneous health insurance information in your medical file that could cause you to fail an employment exam.

Other online references such as http://www.ftc.gov/bcp/edu/microsites/idtheft/

Despite the prominent role that human behavior plays in information security breaches many companies have yet to provide formal information security training for their employees. A great deal of the human risk to information assets could be reduced if:
- employees are able to identify sensitive business information.
- employees understand the information security procedures and information security controls of the company.
- procedures and controls are frequently monitored to ensure compliance.

Information Security Regulations

The risks to personally identifiable information and information privacy have generated significant debate over whether the federal government or state governments should regulate information security. Many believe that legislation at the federal level offers the most consistent protection for personal and sensitive corporate data. Others remain wary of federal laws and feel that legislation at the state level provides more freedom and better protection for this type of information. To date, a patchwork of federal, state and industry regulations have been enacted to help ensure the privacy of personally identifiable information and to enhance the security, control, and reliability of sensitive organizational information.

Federal legislation such as the Graham-Leach-Bliley Act, HIPPA, Sarbanes-Oxley, and numerous state laws such as California's SB-1386 have provisions that impose safeguards to help prevent sensitive digital information from being compromised, threatened, illegally used or destroyed. These safeguards generally involve a commitment to compliance at all organizational levels. Organizations choosing not to comply with information security regulations face fines and other prescribed penalties. These penalties, however, may be insignificant compared to the intangible cost of lost sales and the loss of customer and employee trust when personally identifiable information is mismanaged and personal privacy is put at risk. In this section we discuss the prominent information security regulations that have been enacted to help enhance information security, particularly cyber security and identity theft.

The **Graham-Leach-Bliley Act of 1999 (GLBA)** included a set of provisions specifically intended to protect consumers' personal information held by financial institutions. While the marketing value of personally identifiable information was not diminished by Graham-Leach-Bliley, the Act did give consumers more control over how their information was used by financial institutions. Certain provisions of GLBA are responsible for the many periodic privacy notices we receive today from financial institutions. For example, GLBA

- requires financial institutions to provide customers with an annual notice of their information sharing policies.
- gives consumer the right to "opt-out," or disallow financial institutions from sharing information with unaffiliated companies.

More About IT

The privacy provisions in the Graham-Leach-Bliley Act were initially in danger of being omitted from the Act because of the strong lobbying efforts against these provisions by the banking industry. However, a Victoria's Secret catalog is believed partially responsible for the passage of the Act with the provisions that now protect much of our personally identifiable financial information. Allegedly, a member of the House of Representatives started receiving the Victoria's Secret catalog at his Washington home. He claimed, however, that he never shopped at the Victoria's Secret store in Washington. To prove to his wife that he was not buying lingerie for other women, he traced how Victoria's Secret got his personal information. The congressman learned that Victoria's Secret bought his financial information from his Washington credit union. With that knowledge, he had no reservations of adding his support for the privacy provisions of the Graham-Leach-Bliley Act.

Figure 7.2 – Victoria's Secret and the GLB Act

The Graham-Leach-Bliley Act also specifically prohibited a particular type of **social engineering** attack called **pretexting**. Pretexting originally referred to the use of false, fictitious or fraudulent statements or documents to obtain information from a financial institution or from customers of a financial institution. A scandal at HP in 2006 helped expand the scope of pretexting by adding phone company records to the type of information that became protected by information security regulation. Patricia Dunn, HP's former chairman, used the phone records of reporters and board members, which were obtained by pretexting, to help determine a high-level leak of sensitive HP information. The scandal cost Dunn her job and prompted the **Telephone Records and Privacy Protection Act of 2006**. This act made it a federal crime for anyone, except law enforcement, to employ fraudulent tactics, to persuade phone companies to hand over information about customers' calling habits. We discuss other types of social engineering later in the chapter.

Until the Graham-Leach Bliley Act consumers had little control in how their financial information was being shared and used. The privacy provisions of the GLBA generally helped regulate the *legitimate* market for specific personally identifiable information but it did not specify safeguards to protect all personal information from the growing *illegitimate* secondary market that trades in personally identifiable information for unlawful purposes, particularly identity theft.

The **Health Insurance Portability and Accountability Act of 1996 (HIPAA)** is a set of regulations requiring doctors, hospitals and other health care providers to provide safeguards that ensure the confidentiality and integrity of all personally identifiable information they hold. The healthcare industry maintains a significant amount of personally identifiable financial and medical information. As we discussed earlier, unauthorized access to financial information allows identity thieves the opportunity to obtain credit illegally. Unauthorized access to personally identifiable health information has been used by criminals to file fraudulent claims for payment of medical services that were never provided. HIPPA also includes provisions for financial audits, reporting, information technology security and accountability controls, conflicts of interest, and corporate governance at public companies. Non-compliance with HIPAA regulations can result in fines up to $100,000 and up to ten years in jail.

The **Sarbanes-Oxley Act of 2002 (SOX)** is the result of the financial scandals at public companies such as Enron, WorldCom, and Global Crossing that resulted in losses of billions of dollars and the trust of investors in financial markets. While the overall objective of the Sarbanes-Oxley Act is corporate governance and accurate financial disclosure, the Act imposes important information security requirements such as access controls and other information technology safeguards that are critical for the compliance of the Sarbanes-Oxley Act. Additionally, SOX requires all public companies to submit an annual assessment of their internal financial auditing controls to the Securities and Exchange Commission (SEC). Compliance with SOX has been a significant challenge for many companies because it represents a new financial accounting process that requires public companies to generate financial reports with traceable source information. Corporate officers who fail to comply with SOX, or who submit false information, are subject to fines of up to $1 million and ten years in prison.

The **Federal Information Management Act of 2002** was implemented to provide a comprehensive framework for ensuring the effectiveness of information security controls and government wide oversight of information security risks.

The **Homeland Security Act of 2002** created the Department of Homeland Security which has the federal responsibility to work with the private sector, state and local governments, and the public to protect the nation's information, including the Internet.

The **Security Breach Notification Act (SB-1386)** is California's regulation that requires businesses to formally notify each customer if their personal information *may have been exposed* by an information security breach. California was one of the first states to enact cyber security legislation. Today, thirty-six states have notification laws similar to SB-1386 which, at a minimum, alerts consumers of the possibility that their personal information may have been compromised and suggests possible actions the victims can take. The Federal Trade Commission created a sample notification letter that businesses may use in the event of an information security breach of personally identifiable information. This sample letter is shown below in Figure 7.3.

SAMPLE NOTIFICATION LETTER CREATED BY FTC

Dear _____:

We are contacting you about a potential problem involving identity theft.
[Describe the information compromise and how you are responding to it.]

We recommend that you place a fraud alert on your credit file. A fraud alert tells creditors to contact you before they open any new accounts or change your existing accounts. Call any one of the three major credit bureaus. As soon as one credit bureau confirms your fraud alert, the others are notified to place fraud alerts. All three credit reports will be sent to you, free of charge, for your review.

Equifax   Experian   TransUnionCorp

800-525-6285   888-397-3742   800-680-7289

Even if you do not find any suspicious activity on your initial credit reports, the Federal Trade Commission (FTC) recommends that you check your credit reports periodically. Victim information sometimes is held for use or shared among a group of thieves at different times. Checking your credit reports periodically can help you spot problems and address them quickly.

If you find suspicious activity on your credit reports or have reason to believe your information is being misused, call [insert contact information for law enforcement] and file a police report. Get a copy of the report; many creditors want the information it contains to absolve you of the fraudulent debts. You also should file a complaint with the FTC at www.ftc.gov/idtheft or at 1-877-ID-THEFT (877-438-4338). Your complaint will be added to the FTC's Identity Theft Data Clearinghouse, where it will be accessible to law enforcers for their investigations.

We have enclosed a copy of *Take Charge: Fighting Back Against Identity Theft*, a comprehensive guide from the FTC to help you guard against and deal with identity theft.

[Closing]
Your name

Figure 7.3 Sample FTC Notification Letter

Figure 7.4 below shows the states that have laws that require information security breach notification. An interesting difference between the state regulations is the trigger each state uses to determine whether or not to notify potential victims of a security breach. In California, the personal information that triggers notification under SB-1386 includes a person's name (first name or initial and last name) plus *any* of the following:

- Social Security number
- Driver's license or California Identification Card number
- Financial account number or credit/debit card number with any Password or PIN required for access to the account.

The different triggers used by the states that determine notification of information security breaches are part of the debate on whether the federal government or the individual states should regulate information security. For example, some breaches that compromise the personally identifiable information of people from many states may trigger notifications only to victims from a few of the states.

Figure 7.4 Notification triggers by State

Depending on the size of the information security breach, formally notifying each person affected by an information breach can be a significant expense. Considering just postage, an information security lapse the size of the one at UCLA in 2006, where hackers broke into a database containing personal information on about 800,000 UCLA students, faculty and staff members, would cost in excess of $300,000. Obviously, the actual cost to notify each individual in such situations is significantly more than the $.41 cost of postage today. Some security experts estimate that actual cost for notification is between $65 and $85.

Besides the expense of notifying potential victims of an information security breach, businesses are increasingly being hit with significant fines and penalties for mismanaging personal information. An infamous example is the 2005 security breach at ChoicePoint, a data aggregator that compiles, stores, and sells information. ChoicePoint acquires information such as credit reports, court records, property tax assessor files, bankruptcy records, vehicle registration records, etc on virtually every U.S. adult. ChoicePoint uses this information to create and sell a variety of consumer reports including tenant rental history, insurance claims, and employment background checks to numerous organizations including the media, debt collectors, employers, loan officers, law enforcement and others. In 2005, some of these "others" were discovered to be Nigerian criminals posing as legitimate businessmen. These criminals were able to obtain the personal financial information of 163,000 people from ChoicePoint specifically to commit identity theft. ChoicePoint was fined $10 million in civil penalties and $5 million in consumer redress to settle charges by the Federal Trade Commission that information security and information management procedures violated consumers' privacy rights.

More About IT

If your landlord, prospective employer, or insurer ever used a ChoicePoint report to learn more about you, you are entitled to a free copy of the report. You can obtain information on how to order these reports at www.choicetrust.com

You can also receive a free copy of your credit report each year from each of the three major credit reporting services, Experian, TransUnion and Equifax. Staggering your requests for your free credit reports allows you to check your credit history every four months for free. For information on how to order your free credit reports go to http://annualcreditreport.com.

The largest information security breach to date was revealed in May 2007. The TJX Companies Inc., the parent company of Marshalls, T.J. Maxx, Home Goods and A.J. Wright stores allegedly compromised more than 45 million credit and debit card numbers of its customers in 2006. By September 2007, TJX had spent nearly $125 million cleaning up this information privacy problem that has been attributed to an inadequately-secured wireless network in one of its stores. The breach allegedly occurred at a Marshall's store in Minnesota that used Wireless Equivalent Privacy (WEP) to encrypt its network of hand-held price checking devices, cash registers and store computers. The weaknesses of WEP have been well known since 2001 and are discussed later in the chapter. These weaknesses were apparently exploited by cyber criminals sitting outside the store with a good WiFi antenna and a laptop computer. Once Marshall's wireless network was breached, it was relatively easy to access a central TJX database that contained credit- and debit-card numbers of millions of their customers. The TJX hackers also got personal information such as driver's license numbers, military identification and Social Security numbers of 451,000 customers.

The intrusion at TJX was notable not only for its size but also because it was the first time that an information security breach was *directly* tied to specific instances of credit card fraud. Banks and credit unions around the country were forced to block and reissue thousands of payment cards because of the TJX breach. In order to offset their expense, the banks and credit have sued TJX. TJX was also sued by stockholders for its failure to provide more information about the security breach. Some experts estimate that this particular security breach, which could have easily been prevented, will ultimately cost TJX over $1 billion, including reduced revenue from lost business.

Federal and state regulatory actions are just part of the response to the growing number of information security breaches that involves personally identifiable information. The Payment Card Industry has also imposed information safeguards on the personal financial information held by its merchants.

Figure 7.5 PCIDSS Supporters

The Payment Card Industry, which includes Visa, MasterCard, and American Express, has established a set of information security requirements for all companies that accept these payment cards for products and services. These regulations are called the **Payment Card Industry Data Security Standards (PCIDSS)**. All companies that processes, stores, or transmits credit card data must comply with PCI Data Security Standards. Non-compliance with PCI standards can result in a $50,000 for a first violation. Table 7.1 below provides a general overview of the information security requirements in the PCIDSS and a brief description of how each standard can be implemented.

Payment Card Industry Data Security Standards (PCIDSS)	
PCI Standard	**Implementation of Standard**
Protect Cardholder Data	• Encrypt transmission of cardholder data across public networks
Maintain a Secure Network	• Install and maintain a firewall that is configured to protect data
Maintain a Vulnerability Management Program	• Keep OS and software applications patched and use up-to-date anti-virus software
Implement Strong Access Controls	• Restrict access to data to those who need to know • Assign unique IDs to each person with computer access • Restrict physical access to cardholder data
Regularly Monitor and Test Networks	• Log and monitor all access to network resources and cardholder data • Regularly test security systems and procedures
Maintain an Information Security Policy	• Create and enforce an information security policy

Table 7.1 Overview of PCIDSS requirements

Ironically, compliance with the federal, state and industry information security regulations seems to be almost as challenging for many organizations as non-compliance. The number and cost of information security breaches such as those that occurred at ChoicePoint and TJX are just two of the *reported* information security breaches that have occurred in the last few years. Security experts estimate that many breaches go unreported, perhaps because of the costs associated with regulatory compliance and perhaps because of the intangible costs, such as loss of customer trust and lost sales that may result from public acknowledgement of an information security breach.

There is another perspective and set of regulations that pertains to the stewardship of digital information that companies must incorporate into their information security plans. **The Federal Rules of Civil Procedure, Rule 26** focuses on the *discovery of electronic information* (**eDiscovery**), rather than the privacy of the information. As of December 1st 2006, every company whose employees use real-time communications - email, instant messaging, even VoIP conversations – needs to be able to produce accurate records of those communications. Failure to comply with the eDiscovery regulations can mean fines and other penalties. Morgan Stanley, for example, was fined $1.5 billion for failing to produce electronic information as part of a civil litigation procedure.

The increasing volume and value of digital information, the numerous vulnerabilities of information systems and computer networks, the natural behavior of the humans that control these information resources and the regulations that govern the use of all forms of electronic information and communication will make information security an extremely challenging business undertaking for quite some time. Another reason that absolute information security is unlikely is because many of the criminals who trade in personally identifiable information are more sophisticated, have better tools and skills, and have greater incentive than their predecessors in cyber crime. In the next section, we discuss cyber crime, the intentional threats and risks to digital information, information systems and networks.

LEARNING CHECK
Be sure you can * describe 'personally identifiable information' * discuss the financial and medical implications of identity theft * describe what is included in an information security breach notification * describe how the Graham-Leach-Bliley Act helps protect personal financial information *

CYBER CRIME

The *intentional, malicious* risks to digital information, information systems and networks are generically called cyber crime. **Cyber crime** actually refers to a continuum of illicit activities that compromise, threaten or illegally use electronic information, information systems and computer networks. Cyber crime evolved from annoying electronic pranks undertaken by computer pranksters, or hackers, to lucrative, illegitimate business ventures underwritten by organized crime. The increasing value of digital information shifted the intent of cyber crime from prank to profit giving sophisticated criminals and organized crime ample motive to exploit security vulnerabilities in information systems and computer networks. The global reach and availability of high-speed Internet access has also made it easier for cyber criminals to remotely exploit computer and network vulnerabilities in search of valuable corporate financial data, intellectual property and personally identifiable information.

More About IT

Some of the original threats to digital information systems and computer networks were carried out by **phone phreaks** who could mimic the tones used by the telephone company in order to make free long distance calls. Phone phreaking has been traced to a blind eight-year old and Cap'n Crunch cereal. Joe Engressia, the eight year old, discovered that when he whistled at a particular frequency (2600 Hz) he could manipulate his telephone system. 2600 Hz was the frequency used in the late 1950s by some telephone companies to route telephone calls. A whistle offered in boxes of Cap'n Crunch cereal was also capable of producing the 2600 Hz tone. It did not take long until phone phreakers started using this whistle to make free long distance calls. Steve Jobs and Steve Wozniak, the founders of Apple Computer, are two of the most notable phone phreaks.

Cyber criminals are no longer merely pranksters who use telephone tones to illegally infiltrate an information or communications system. Instead, their tools and tactics include malicious computer code, or malware, the vulnerabilities of software and hardware, and social engineering to attack information systems and gain unauthorized access to personally identifiable information and other sensitive organizational information.

In this section we examine many of the tools and tactics of cyber criminals to better understand these risks. This understanding can be useful in helping you develop policies and practices that will help increase the security of your computers and networks and reduce your risk of becoming a victim of a cyber crime.

Malware

Malware, or malicious computer code, is a term that has become synonymous with a continuum of software tools that are intentionally designed to infiltrate and/or damage computers and computer networks without the owner's consent. On one end of the malware continuum are the annoying, but generally benign, pop-up advertisements known as *adware*. On the other end of the this continuum are malicious computer programs, such as *spyware viruses, rootkits, and bots* that can monitor our keystrokes, take control of our computers to generate spam, attack other information systems and steal or destroy our digital information. **Cookies**, which store information on your computer, generally help web sites serve users better by "remembering" certain information about the user. For example, shopping carts typically use cookies to remember what items are being purchased before "checkout." Advertising banners may also rely on cookies to keep track of the ads you see on a website. Cookies are not malware but when they are unknowingly shared with third parties, the information will most likely be used for advertising purposes.

Malware can be distinguished not only by its intent, but also by how it propagates or infects computer systems and networks. Some malware propagates via user interaction; for example,
- when you open an email attachment that contains malware.
- when you click on the "I Accept" or "I Agree" button of the free software you download from the Internet. The license agreement you accepted frequently includes obscure verbiage that asks for your permission to place malware on your system.
- when you participate in file-sharing activities through peer-to-peer (P2P) networks like Kazaa, Morpheus , iMesh, eDonkey, Gnutella, LimeWire and Grokster you often acquire more than just pirated songs, games and movies. File-sharing and P2P networks are very effective at propagating malware.

Other malware is self-propagating; it doesn't need users to help spread it to others. This type of malware usually exploits computer and network security vulnerabilities, such as a buffer overflow or an unpatched system. We discuss these vulnerabilities later in the chapter. In the next section, we discuss the more common types of malware.

Types of Malware
A computer **virus** is computer code that infiltrates a computer and performs an unanticipated, unauthorized operation on the computer system or information stored on the system. Viruses often make their presence known by presenting text, video, and audio messages. Some viruses are malicious and can delete files or reformat hard disks. Other viruses may not do any damage but even these types of viruses take up system resources that can cause performance problems. Computer viruses were the first malicious software to infect the PC and they are the most common type of malware. Computer viruses are so named because their behavior is similar to a biological virus which passes from person to person without the users consent. Computer viruses, unlike worms, typically use a host file to spread. For example, a macro virus may use an Excel file as its host. Sending the Excel file as an email attachment can easily spread the virus.

The global risk level of viruses for January through August of 2007 is shown in Figure 7.6. The spike in viruses in mid-April 2007 was caused, ironically, by users who were duped by malicious spam that convinced users their computers had been infected during a recent, well-publicized attack of the Storm worm. The spam also offered a patch, or remedy, to remove the malware, which actually was itself a variant of the Storm worm.

Figure 7.6 Global Virus Activity for January – August 2007
(Source: http://www.f-secure.com/security_center/virus_statistics.html; accessed 8/23/2007).

A **worm** is a specific type of virus that propagates over networks without user action to infect other computers. The earliest microcomputer worms and viruses were typically written as pranks, or recreationally, by **hackers** who usually had no criminal intent. Viruses and worms that were written with malicious intent began appearing in the late 1990s. The authors of malicious malware are referred to as **crackers**.

The Storm worm was originally unleashed onto the Internet as an **executable** e-mail attachment disguised as an e-greeting card. Executable files typically have *.exe* as the filename extension and execute, or run, when they are clicked on. Spammers have recently started using other tactics for spreading malware such as the Storm worm. The latest tactic is to use spam to direct victims to phony websites, disguised as popular sites such as YouTube. A sample of this type of spam is shown in Figure 7.7.

```
From: User gxcrusq
Sent: Monday, August 27, 2007 3:50 AM
To: aeaston@mail.sdsu.edu
Subject: who is that your with?

this i not good. If this video gets to her husband your both dead. see for
yourself... http://www.youtube.com/watch?v=ZWRG9LZxZNf
<http://71.197.141.181/>
```
Figure 7.7 Example of spam used to direct users to a phony website

One of the most efficient worms ever released was called **Slammer** (also called SQL Slammer Worm, DDOS.SQLP1434.A, W32/SQLSlammer, Sapphire, W32/SQLSlam-A). Slammer's intent was not particularly vicious; it did not destroy files or corrupt the operating system of computers. Instead, Slammer's infamy is related to the speed at which it propagated. The map in Figure 7.8 shows how much of the world was affected by the Slammer worm within 30 minutes after its release on January 25, 2003.

Slammer essentially overloaded computer networks (as in a Denial-of-Service attack, which we discuss later) causing many computer networks to lose connectivity as their bandwidth was saturated by local copies of the worm. For more information about how Slammer works see the More About IT section below.

Figure 7.8 – Slammer Worm infections 30 minutes after release

<u>**More About IT**</u>

Slammer used UDP (User Datagram Protocol), an Internet protocol similar to, but faster than TCP, to deliver the relatively simple program that flooded networks worldwide in a matter of minutes. UDP can carry a short message in a one-way packet (TCP requires two-way acknowledgement before communication). Slammer masqueraded itself as a query inside a UDP packet to gain access to computers running Microsoft's SQL Server database. (Many Microsoft applications have MS SQL code built-in). Once inside, the worm attempted to create a **buffer overflow**, a bug common in many software applications. Buffers, or memory, can overflow when a data string that is too long for the buffer is allowed to be written into memory. The excess data essentially can overwrite the program's code. Slammer took advantage of this bug to insert a small program that would repeatedly generate random IP addresses and then send itself via UDP packets to these addresses. Slammer was apparently not designed to be destructive but because it was able to commandeer about 75,000 computers running MS SQL in a very short time, each generating countless UDP packets that were being sent over networks, the worm effectively created a denial of service attack on IP addresses worldwide.

It should be noted that Microsoft distributed the patch that would have prevented Slammer six months before Slammer was released. Slammer is a good example why patching is important. We discuss patching later in this chapter.

A **Trojan Horse** is essentially a virus that presents itself as one program while it is actually another. A seemingly innocent program, such as a screensaver found on the Internet, could be a Trojan Horse that has a payload, or malware, programmed to do something else. Some Trojan Horse payloads have been known to modify and destroy data, erase hard drives and attempt to locate and steal passwords and personally identifiable information.

The security consultant in the opening case who was hired to infiltrate the credit union's computer network imbedded his Trojan Horse within a picture file and placed the file in what the security industry refers to as a road apple. A **road apple** relies on both physical media (the USB drives in the case) and social engineering (employee curiosity) to gain access to a network. Road apples can be considered one type of **blended threat,** or malware that combines the features of viruses, worms, Trojan Horses, and other malware with known computer and Internet vulnerabilities. These multiple threats are often difficult to detect and defend, can spread rapidly, and can cause significant damage.

Spyware is a general term for the software that delivers advertising to your computer, makes changes to the configuration of your computer or collects personal information from your computer *without your consent or understanding*. Spyware can also add unwanted components to your Web browser or change the browser's start page and it is usually very difficult to undo these changes. Spyware includes adware, keyloggers, rootkits, and bots which we discuss later in this section.

Computers are frequently contaminated by spyware during the installation of software downloaded from music or video file sharing programs. Whenever you install software on your computer, carefully read the End User License Agreement (EULA) and privacy statement for the inclusion of suspicious software. For example, take a look at Figure 7.9, an excerpt from the EULA of Joost™, a new, free, way of watching TV on the Internet. It is difficult to know exactly what the 3rd-party "widgets" will do once they are on your computer. The key to keeping spyware under control is to understand what such software will do before you agree to install it on your computer.

Figure 7.9 – Joost EULA regarding 3rd party widgets
(Source: Joost Software End User License Agreement, http://www.joost.com/eula.html; accessed 8/20/2007).

Adware is probably the most benign type of spyware, Adware is short for *advertising-supported software*. Adware automatically displays or downloads advertising material to a computer while the computer or an application is being used. Adware is typically not intended to be destructive but it is often annoying and it can degrade the performance of computer systems much like spyware.

  View a video by Microsoft about spyware at:
http://www.microsoft.com/protect/videos/Spyware/SpywareGenericHi.html

Keyloggers are a special type of spyware that is typically marketed as a tool to monitor the computer usage of children. With this type of surveillance software installed on a computer, parents can review everything their children types on the computer, including instant messages, website addresses and email. Keyloggers have utility beyond keeping children safe on the Internet. Suspicious spouses have installed keyloggers to catch an unfaithful mate and employers use them to monitor the computer habits of employees. Unfortunately, cyber criminals can also use keyloggers to capture personal information such as our credit card numbers and the usernames and PINs we use for online banking.

It is not always easy to know if your computer system is infected by spyware. One clue to the presence of spyware is the performance of your computer system. Spyware often degrades the performance of a computer; sometimes to the point that it is unusable. If you think your computer may be infected, there are a number of spyware removal tools that may help you remove the malicious code. Table 7.2 lists a few popular spyware and detection and removal programs. Security experts often recommend running more than one spyware removal tool as they typically use different techniques for identifying spyware.

Anti-Spyware Programs	
Ad-Aware	http://www.lavasoftusa.com
AVG Anti-Spyware	http://www.grisoft.com
Spyware Search and Destroy	http://www.safer-networking.org
Spysweeper	http://www.webroot.com
Windows Defender	http://www.microsoft.com/athome/security/spyware

Table 7.2 Popular Spyware Detection and Removal Programs

A **rootkit** is program code that establishes "root" access to a computer. Root access is similar to administrative access. This level of control allows the rootkit code to hide processes and network usage from users and system administrators. Cyber criminals rely on rootkits to sustain the control of computers that have been injected with spyware. Generally, the longer the spyware goes undetected, the more lucrative it is for cyber criminal.

More About IT

Rootkits became relatively well known in 2005 after Sony included a rootkit program on its music CDs to hide its new copy protection technology. Sony programmed the rootkit to install when a Sony CD was played on a computer's CD drive. When the CD was first inserted in the drive, a license agreement appeared on screen. If the listener accepted the license agreement the copy protection rootkit installed on the hard drive. The rootkit was effective at hiding all traces of the copy protection technology but it was also capable of hiding malware and other malicious code. Virus authors quickly took advantage of Sony's rootkit. A short time later, Sony reluctantly acknowledged the rootkit and suspended production of the CDs containing that particular copy-protection technology.

A **Botnet** is a network of computers that are all infected with malware called a **bot**. A bot is computer code that performs a repetitive task such as spreading malware, sending spam, or creating a distributed denial of service attack, which is discussed in the next section. An individual computer in a botnet is known as a **zombie** and the person controlling the botnet is known as a **bot herder**. The only difference between a bot and a worm is the bot herder who unifies botnets and manages the command and control (C&C) servers that actually commands the bots. Bot herders have historically used Internet Relay Chat (IRC), the Internet service that supports real-time group communication, for their command and control servers; each botnet uses a different IRC channel. Bot herders have started to switch to peer-to-peer (P2P) protocols to communicate with their botnets as P2P technology is not dependent on a single communications server. Figure 7.10 below shows a recent distribution of the active botnet C&C (command and control) servers.

Figure 7.10   Botnet Command & Control Servers
(Source: Shadowserver Foundation, http://www.shadowserver.org; accessed 8/20/2007).

 View a BusinessWeek article with interesting animation describing how botnets spread viruses, send e-mail spam and conduct distributed denial of service attacks at: http://images.businessweek.com/ss/05/05/hacker_botnet/index_01.htm.]

More About IT

In May 2007, one of the top 10 spammers in the world, Robert Soloway, was arrested for using botnets with millions of zombies to distribute millions of spam emails. If Soloway is convicted, he faces up to 65 years in jail. It is not clear whether Soloway built, rented or bought the botnets he used for his spamming efforts. Many cyber criminals today have found it more cost effective to rent botnets for a few days to accomplish their cyber crime. Shadowserver estimates the current cost of a botnet for a one or two day spam event to be about $1000. The estimated rent of a botnet of 10,000 zombies for a Distributed Denial of Service event is $500-$1000. Until recently, cyber criminals could purchase a botnet for approximately $5000 according to Shadowserver. Now, competition from Russia has apparently reduced the price to as little 25¢ per zombie.

Some security experts believe that the botnet epidemic is responsible for almost all of the spam on the Internet today. That means that for each piece of spam, there is a hijacked computer at the other end. Nowdays, much of the bot-generated spam is **image spam,** which uses a graphic, rather than text, to convey the spammers' objective. Spam with a graphic is generally more likely to be read and more difficult to filter than spam with just text. Furthermore, spammers are apparently no longer content trying to entice people into buying Viagra and other medications online. Much of the image spam received today is related to stock manipulation schemes where spammers attempt to pump up the price of a thinly traded stock by extolling its potential value, and then dumping the stock as soon as the price rises. This scheme is known as "pump and dump" in the financial industry. Stock spammers have been known to increase the price of some stocks 200-300 percent in two to three weeks.

Social Engineering and Cyber Attacks

Social engineering is a special type of information security attack. Instead of attacking the physical hardware and software of a computer or network system, social engineers attack people, more specifically, the human weaknesses and the behaviors of people, who may provide them access to something of value, including money and personally identifiable information. For example, we saw that the security consultant in the opening case was successful because he exploited the human tendency of curiosity. Most of us also have a natural tendency to trust. We trust the email that says our account information at e-Bay needs to be updated. We trust that the website where we update this information is actually an e-Bay website. These human tendencies are the reason humans will always be the most vulnerable component of any information security effort.

There is another aspect to social engineering that has played a role in a number of information security breaches. Many people are simply not aware of the value of the information under their care. As a result, some personally identifiable information may not have adequate safeguards. Some social engineers depend on this fact and employ tactics such as *shoulder surfing* to memorize access codes of ATM users and *dumpster diving* to harvest discarded bank statements.

Many cyber attacks are initiated using social engineering tactics. *Phishing*, *Pharming* and *Pretexting* (which we discussed earlier) are three types of attacks that explicitly depend on social engineering to be effective. Another common cyber attack is called the Denial-of-Service attack.

A **Denial-of-Service (DoS) Attack** is an attempt by attackers to prevent others from using the services of a computer or computer network. DoS attacks can essentially disable or make a computer or a network unavailable to others by consuming resources that are needed to operate. For example, a DoS attack could be carried out by a script or simple program on the infected computer that repeatedly makes copies of itself. Left unchecked, the copies could ultimately consume all of the disk space on the computer. Intruders have also attempted to consume disk space by generating an excessive numbers of email messages and by intentionally generating errors that must be logged in log files. In general, anything that allows data to be written to disk can be used to execute a denial-of-service attack, particularly if there are no bounds on the amount of data that can be written. **Distributed Denial-of-Service (DDoS) Attacks** are often carried out by a group of zombies, unified and controlled as a botnet that simultaneously attack a computer or network and overwhelm its resources.

Phishing is a social engineering attack that relies on 'spoofed' emails and fake websites to steal personally identifiable information from unsuspecting victims. Phishing emails are typically spam, generated and sent automatically by botnets. The email templates used for phishing however, are often dubiously-appearing correspondence from a bank, e-tailer, or credit card company. Cyber criminals often hijack the brand names and logos of legitimate companies to create the email so it appears legitimate. Usually the 'spoofed' email impersonally and vaguely describes a problem with an account that must be corrected immediately. The email also provides a hyperlink to a seemingly legitimate corporate website where the problem can be fixed. However, the hyperlink will usually take the victim to a 'spoofed' website created specifically to capture personally identifiable information, such as Social Security Numbers and credit card numbers.

Some phishing efforts appear to be very credible and it is easy to understand why someone with an account at one of the banks or credit card companies may be fooled, or phished, into giving up some personally identifiable information. Cyber criminals have even offered protection against phishing as a way to get potential victims to give up personally identifiable information (Figure 7.11). However, most phishing emails contain clues that will help you spot a phishing expedition. For example, phishing emails usually:

- begin with an impersonal greeting such as "Dear Customer," instead of a personal greeting such as "Dear Brad Thomas. "

- contain misspellings, poor grammar and/or poor punctuation.

- ask that you click on a link to a website. If you check the URL associated with this link it will often display an IP address for the domain, instead of the company name. If a company name does appear, you must still expect that the URL will lead to a spoofed web site.

Figure 7.11 Phony Anti-Phishing Scheme

Figure 7.12 (a) is an actual phishing email and two screenshots of a spoofed site (b & c). Figure 7.12 (d) is screenshot of the real CapitalOne site. It is not hard to see why many people are fooled by phishing efforts.

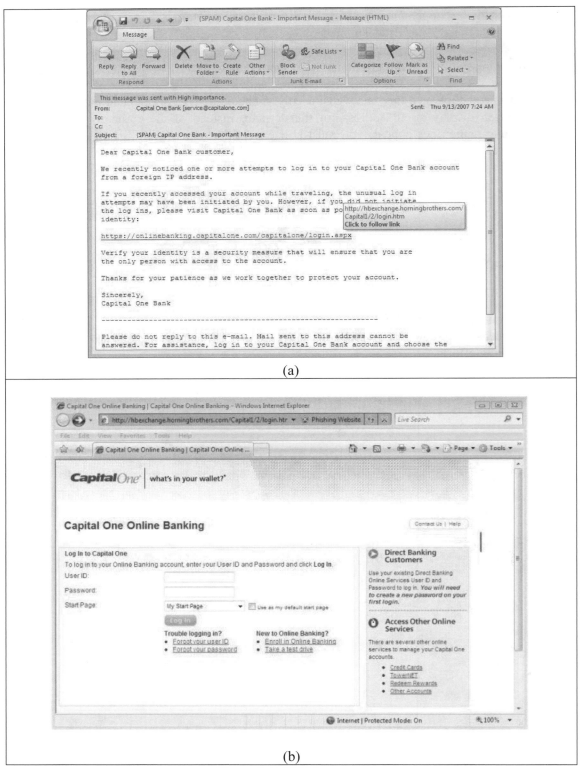

(a)

(b)

Figure 7.12 Phishing examples

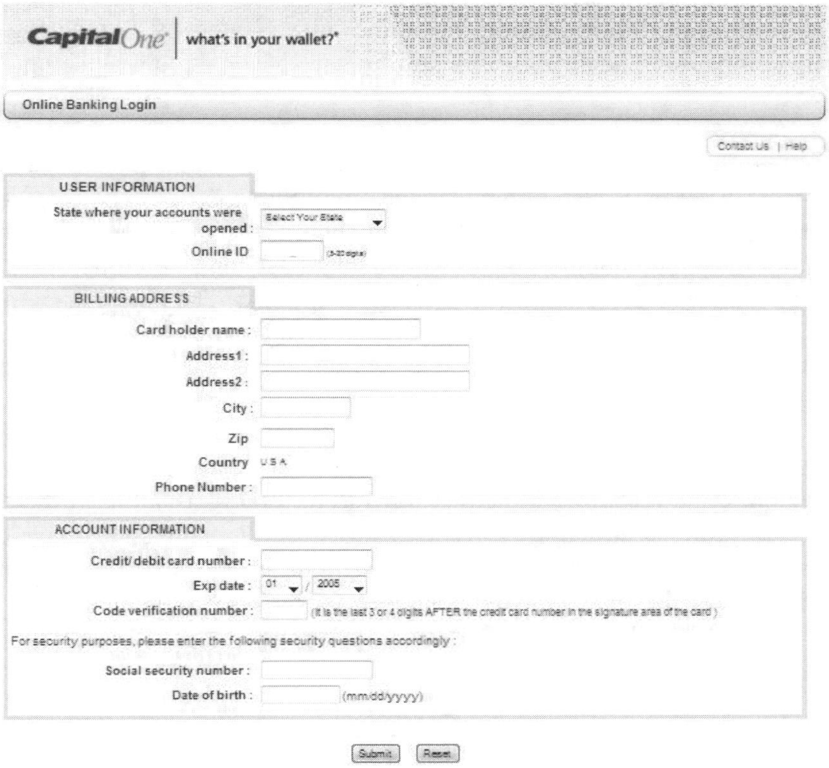

(c)

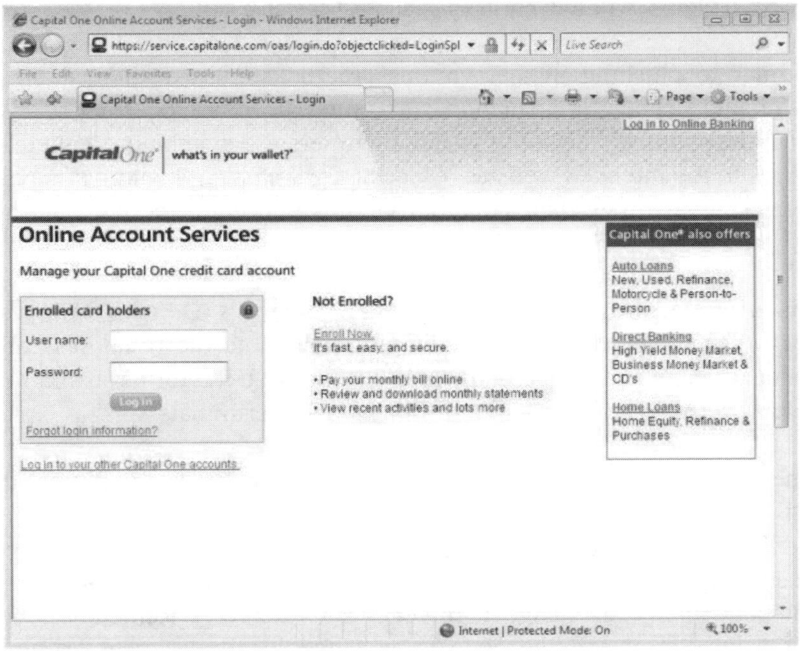

(d)

Figure 7.12 (continued) Phishing examples

Test your phishing IQ by taking an online quiz created by Sonicwall, a network security company. The quiz URL is http://www.sonicwall.com/phishing/.]

Phishing-by-phone is a new twist to the phishing scam that has also been catching some unsuspecting victims. This scam is also initiated by an email that appears to be from a legitimate business. However, instead of providing a link to a 'spoofed' website, the email provides the potential victim with a telephone number to call to update an account. Victims often realize too late that the telephone number they called was not really their bank. The phishing-by-phone scam relies on VoIP technology so scammers can use the actual area code of a company referenced in the phishing expedition. With VoIP products such as Skype, you can obtain a phone number with almost any area code you desire.

The Anti-Phishing Working Group (www.antiphishing.org) maintains an updated list of the latest phishing techniques and resources to help you avoid becoming a victim of the scam. One phishing technique the group reported recently was the flurry in domain name requests that contained the name, or reference, to a recent or impending disaster. Many of these requests were later linked to fraudulent websites that solicited donations for the disaster victims.

Figure 7.13 Anti-phishing best practices checklist

Pharming is similar to phishing in that victims are tricked into relinquishing personally identifiable information and financial information. Pharming, however, does not rely on email to get potential victims to the spoofed website. Instead, pharmers use a technique called *DNS cache poisoning* to get victims to the intended website. Once at the website, phishing and pharming are again alike and cyber criminals hope their potential victims will enter the personal information they are seeking.

DNS cache poisoning requires pharmers to hijack a victim's Domain Name server and change the IP address of the bank website or credit card website to the IP address of the bogus website. With this accomplished, a victim could enter the correct URL for her bank, for example, but be sent to fraudulent website created and controlled by cyber criminals.

Until recently, the difficulty of hijacking a Domain Name server was a sufficient deterrent to keep the incidents of pharming relatively low. Unfortunately, **Drive-by-Pharming** has made it easier to hijack a DNS server. Drive-by-Pharming is a cyber attack that allows you to take control of a DNS server *simply by visiting or viewing a particular web page* that contains malicious JavaScript code that can change a router's DNS server. Remember, our Internet browsers can interpret JavaScript and the code is executed locally. Cyber criminals embed JavaScript code in HTML documents to perform a number of malicious tasks. This technique is often referred to as *Cross-Site Scripting*. Drive-by-Pharming is just one example and the reason why many Internet security experts suggest we disable JavaScript in our browsers.

The popularity of WiFi networks has given cyber criminals another relatively easy way to hijack DNS servers and engage in Drive-by-Pharming. This can occur when the administrator of a wireless network neglects to change the default password that is used to configure the access point of the wireless router. It is common knowledge that the default passwords for these devises are usually the same for all products within a product line. It also well known that these passwords are readily available on the web. Having administrative access to the router or wireless access point makes it quite easy to hijack the device and make the DNS changes needed for Pharming. In the next section, we provide some simple tips for cyber security, the safeguards that can be implemented to help ensure the privacy and security of organizations' digital information assets.

LEARNING CHECK
Be sure you can * discuss how malware can infect computers and information systems * describe botnets* describe social engineering * describe phishing and pharming*

CYBER SECURITY

Cyber security refers to the stewardship of digital information, information systems, and computer networks. Digital information is only as secure as the people, the information systems and the computer networks that access, store and distribute the information. Digital information and information systems that are presumed to be private and secure seem to be breached regularly exposing personal and sensitive information to various risks that can compromise, alter, destroy or allow the use of personal or sensitive information without authorization. However, there are a number of tools and tactics that are available to help mitigate much of the risk to our information assets. The first level of defense is to ensure our computers and applications are configured with the most recent security patches and anti-malware files. Encrypting information and access controls are two other common tactics that businesses use to help safeguard digital information resources. In this section, we discuss these defensive tactics.

1st Level Defense

Security Patches
Today, information about hardware and software security vulnerabilities are communicated over the Internet, typically as a **security advisory** put out by the software developer or by the organizations that discover the vulnerability. Sometimes the **security patch**, or program code that will fix the vulnerability, is available with the advisory; sometimes the patch is released at a later time. For example, all but the most critical Microsoft patches are released on **Patch Tuesday**, the second Tuesday of each month. Ideally, patches are applied as soon as they are available in order to minimize the risk of infection or other potential damage.

<u>**More About IT**</u>

Microsoft introduced the practice of releasing security patches once a month to help system administrators of large deployments of Microsoft products better manage the patch process. Regular monthly patchings help system administrators make sure all systems are up-to-date. Tuesday was chosen as patch day because some patches create other system problems. In such situations, system administrators still have the remainder of the week to uninstall the patch and find a *workaround* to the situation.

Most organizations now have "patch policies" that plug security holes as soon as they are known and a patch is available. However, malware writers are very aware that it takes almost a month before even half of the vulnerable systems are patched. This gives malware writers time to acquire the patch, 'reverse engineer' it, and then write code to exploit it. If they are successful, another new security hole has been created. **Zero-day attacks** are exploits that takes advantage of vulnerabilities known only to malicious users and for which there is no known patch.

Besides adhering to a strict security patch policy, organizations and individuals are strongly encouraged to install and maintain anti-malware programs for additional first-level defense against the various virus and spyware risks so prevalent today. Organizations typically obtain company-wide license agreements with anti-virus vendors such as Symantec (www.symantec.com), F-Secure (www.f-secure.com) and AVG (www.grisoft.com) to help manage the cost, the installation and the maintenance of this type of security software. Grisoft also has a free edition that is available for individuals. There are plenty of resources available to explain and resolve problems associated with malware. For example, US-CERT (United States Computer Emergency Readiness Team) is a good source of information for all forms of malware, anti-virus and anti-spyware programs.

Many of these resources are actively involved in the effort to understand malware and to create mechanisms to defend against it. One tool these organizations use to learn more about malware is a honeypot. A **honeypot** is essentially a trap, disguised as normal network resource that is used to entice and watch how both cyber criminals and their malware tools behave. Malware such as viruses, worms and Trojan Horses typically carry some malicious payload or have been programmed for some unlawful or destructive outcome. The Slammer worm, for example, created so much network traffic that it effectively created a denial-of-service attack, making networks worldwide unusable.

Encryption

Encryption is one of the most common information security techniques employed today to protect the privacy and integrity of digital information and to ensure private, secure communication. Encryption refers to the process of transforming original information into something unreadable using a secret, reversible technique or algorithm. Two common encryption algorithms used for information security today are:

Shared or Secret-Key Encryption - This technique uses a single (shared) or secret key (algorithm) to work. The message is encrypted with the secret key and then sent. The receiver of the message decrypts the message with the same shared key. This encryption technique is sometimes referred to as *symmetric* encryption and it is the basis of the Data Encryption Standard

(DES) that is used by the National Institute of Standards and Technology (NIST) for commercial and unclassified applications.

Public-Key Encryption – This technique uses one key for encryption and another related, but mathematically-obscure, key for decryption. Using this technique, you distribute your public key to anyone interested in communicating with you. They would encrypt their message to you using your public key. When you received the message, you would be the only one who could decrypt it since only you have your private key (you know the mathematically-obscure relationship). This is the basis of RSA (Rivest, Shamir, & Aldeman, the MIT mathematicians who developed it). This encryption technique is widely used in software applications and for digital signatures.

Public-key encryption is also called *asymmetric* encryption because a pair of keys is required for the encryption scheme to work. Since both keys are required, it really does not matter which key is applied first. This makes pubic-key encryption a very robust information security tactic as long as the private encryption key remains secret. Public-key encryption
- ensures the privacy and confidentiality of a message since it cannot be read by anyone except the receiver.
- assures the integrity of a message since it cannot be altered after it has been encrypted.
- authenticates, or proves, the identity of the receiver
- allows for non-repudiation, or proof that the sender really sent the message. In other words, using a private key to encrypt a message is the electronic equivalent of signing the message; anyone can check the signature using the public key.

Secure Socket Layer (SSL) is a protocol developed in 1996 for securing data transmission across the Internet. This protocol relies on Public-Key encryption and the Public-Key Infrastructure (PKI), or Certificate Authorities, who verify the identities of individuals and servers and create digital certificates to ensure secure communication. Conceptually, a digital certificate is similar to your signature card on file at your bank (which is similar to the Certificate Authority). If you write someone a check, they can take it to your bank and cash it if the signature on the check matches the signature card (and assuming you have enough money in your account to cover the check). Certificate Authorities don't cash checks, or get involved in the finances of a transaction, but they will tell you if the signatures match, and hence, verify your identity.

Unfortunately, some hackers have found a way to undermine SSL. Internet Explorer and other browsers install with a number of digital certificates from certificate authorities that are considered trustworthy. Hackers have begun creating their own digital certificates and installing them in the susceptible victims' browsers. The phony digital certificates essentially tell the victims browsers to trust malicious web sites.

Access Controls

An information security breach is often the result of **unauthorized access and unauthorized use** of an information asset, such as personally identifiable information. Many organizations now require employees to sign a formal **Acceptable Use Policy** before they are granted access to organizational information assets. In some organizations, reading the Acceptable Use Policy is the extent of the organization's information security training.

Acceptable Use Agreements are important for communicating the rules and regulations associated with information resources. However, these agreements provide little deterrent for a cyber criminal and those determined to gain access to personally identifiable information and other sensitive organization information. The next level of information security involves the use of **access controls**, or hardware and software control mechanisms that can be implemented to further enhance cyber security.

Authentication

Authentication in information security terms refers to verifying the identity of a person. The most common authentication techniques for information security today involve three factors:

- something a person *knows* - usernames, passwords, PINS, other *shared secrets*
- something a person *is* – biometric identifiers: fingerprints, retinal scans
- something a person *has* – identity card, token, smart card

Shared secrets such as passwords, biometric devices and possessed objects all are effective and commonly used to help secure the information assets of an organization. In this section we discuss usernames and passwords, the common biometric identifies, and some of the possessed-object that are used for authentication.

Passwords are the most common *shared secrets* used for authentication today. There are also other shared secrets techniques organizations may use to prove a person's identity. For example,

- ask a question that only the customer can answer. For example, what was the name of your first pet? This is often used if a person forgets a username or password.
- display a group of pictures and ask the customer to pick the shared secret picture. This technique is increasingly being used in conjunction with a username and password. My!Yahoo and other online services can be configured to use a variation of this shared secret technique.

Organizations that authenticate using passwords should encourage their employees to choose strong passwords. Table 7.3 below shows the estimated time to crack a password of numbers or letters using a computer. The times are based on a computer capable of guessing passwords at a rate of 10,000 guesses per second.

Password of Numbers				Password of Letters ABCDEFGHIJKLMNOPQRSTUVWXYZ or abcdefghijklmnopqrstuvwxyz		
0123456789						
Length	Combinations	Time to Crack		Length	Combinations	Time to Crack
2	$10^2 = 100$	Instant		2	$26^2 = 676$	Instant
3	1000	Instant		3	17,576	< 2 Secs
4	10,000	Instant		4	456,976	46 Secs
5	100,000	10 Secs		5	11.8 Million	20 Mins
6	1 Million	1½ Mins		6	308.9 Million	8½ Hours
7	10 Million	17 Mins		7	8 Billion	9 Days
8	100 Million	2¾ Hours		8	200 Billion	242 Days
9	1000 Million	28 Hours		9	5.4 Trillion	17 Years

Table 7.3 Estimations of Time to Crack a Password

Biometrics use identifiers designed to authenticate the identity of someone based on physiological and behavioral traits. Today, the most common physiological traits used for authentication are fingerprints, eyes, and facial features. The most common behavioral traits used today for authentication are signatures and keystrokes.

Biometric authentication is commonplace in an increasing number of organizations. Our university requires students to authenticate using their palm print in order to gain access to the campus recreation center. Many companies now require that notebook computers used by employees be equipped with fingerprint authentication. However, there is still much debate on the use of biometric identification in many environments. For example, the use of fingerprint scanners in elementary schools are questioned for both health and privacy reasons. It is unlikely that the controversy over the use of biometric devices will subside soon because of the fundamental security/privacy tradeoff inherent in the use of these devices. In the meantime, biometric technology continues to improve and the applications for biometric devices continue to expand

Possessed objects are another way to authenticate an identity. Most of us possess, or carry, at least one object that is recognized as valid identification. This may be a driver's license or our university ID. However, fake, altered, borrowed or stolen ID cards undermine the credibility of these this type of object for authentication. There are possessed objects that do provide a higher level of security and are regularly used in the authentication process. These objects include Smart Cards and Tokens.

- Smart Cards typically store identification information that is accessible by a reader. Increasingly Smart Cards are used to store financial and health information and other information on a microprocessor embedded in the card. Smart Card require readers to access the information on the card and to update the card with new information if necessary.

- Token-based authentication is an increasingly popular way to securely access remote systems and servers. Tokens are typically small, handheld devices that either have a small display screen or that plug directory into the USB port of a computer. Both types of tokens have a unique serial number and a *shared-secret*. When a person tries to gain access to an information resource, the token uses the secret to prove that the user is legitimate. One of the best known token systems is SecurID from RSA Security (RSA, if your recall, is synonymous with public-key encryption).

Authentication that is based on only one of the factors described above is called **single-factor authentication**. Generally, single-factor authentication is less of a deterrent for cyber criminals than **multi-factor authentication**, the use of a combination of these factors.

Firewalls

Firewalls are used to prevent unauthorized access to digital information resources. This distinction is attributable to both the location of a firewall, (between a Wide Area Network and a Local Area Network, or PC) and the importance of the device for protecting information assets from harmful intrusion. Firewalls can be implemented in both hardware and software. Home and small office environments with a broadband connection to the Internet often only rely on hardware that integrates router and firewall technology into single device as shown in Figure 7.14. These devices offer protection at the LAN level using *network address translation* (NAT) to hide the IP address of LAN computers. Software firewalls can also be implemented at the PC level. Microsoft's Vista and WindowsXP (with Service Pack 2), for example, have personal firewalls built into the operating system.

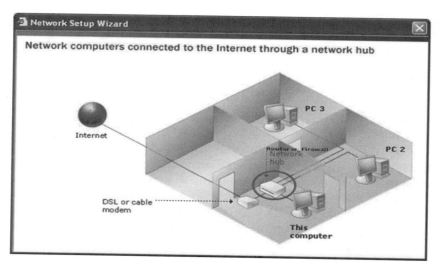

Figure 7.14 Integrated router and firewall

Using both a firewall at the LAN level and a personal firewall at the PC level are another level of information security for both organizations and individuals. Most security experts today recommend a multi-level approach to cyber security.

Cyber Security Suggestions

There numerous things that can be done to help raise the level of information security in organizations. Here are a few that were discussed in this chapter:

- Develop a multi-level security policy. As example, don't just rely on anti-spyware and anti-virus to keep malware-free.
- Identify what is installed and plugged into on your system. Identify what is needed. Resolve the difference. Prevent unauthorized applications from being installed on the system.
- Secure WiFi Networks and disconnect rogue access points.
- Require long passwords
- Use encryption for all confidential data if feasible. Insist on encryption for portable devices.
- Ensure all of your systems are patched.
- Install anti-virus and anti-spyware tools and configure the tools for automatic updates. Scan for and remove malware.
- Reduce the profile of important resources. For example, don't keep confidential files in a folder labeled "Confidential."
- Make sure employees are able to identify sensitive business data and that they understand the information security procedures and controls of the company.
- Monitor the environment to ensure compliance; institute and enforce penalties for non-compliance.
- Lock up important and sensitive documents. If they are no longer needed, shed them.

LEARNING CHECK
Be sure you can * describe the access controls used for authentication * describe encryption * discuss authentication

Wrapping IT Up

It is quite clear that the information security issues are bound to increase with the increasing volume and the value of electronically stored information. The portability of electronic information is also contributing to the number of information security breaches occurring each year. Today, sensitive and personal information is stored not only on hard drives in desktop and notebook computers, but also on newer devices with storage capacity such as memory cards, USB drives, PDAs, MP3 players, and cell phones. Generally, most of these newer devices that can store personal and sensitive information are more portable and potentially less secure than conventional storage media such as hard drives and magnetic tape.

As number and the sophistication of deliberate risks to personally identifiable information and to sensitive organizational information grows, the burden of combating these risks also increases. Organizations are starting to realize that this burden is much more than the tangible costs of fixing compromised systems and the lost productivity resulting from information security breaches. The intangible costs, such as lost sales, the loss of trust, and the liability associated with non-compliance to regulations enacted to ensure information security are also major concerns for almost every business today.

Study Questions Summary

1. What is information security?
   - Information security refers to the safekeeping of information assets.
   - Information security can be enhanced by understanding the security risks.
   - Information security is an objective of an increasing number of federal, state and industry regulations.

2. What constitutes cyber crime?
   - Intentional, malicious acts, or attacks, that threaten digital information, information systems and computer networks are considered cyber crime.
   - The intentional distribution of malware such as a computer virus, worm, spyware, and/or bots is also cyber crime.
   - The use of social engineering tactics to gain access to sensitive or personal information is considered cyber crime.

3. What can be done to enhance cyber security?
   - The first level of defense is to keep software applications "patched" and anti-malware programs up-to-date.
   - Cyber security is also enhanced by encrypting all important digital communication.
   - Access controls add another level of defense for securing digital assets.

Key Terms

Page Number references are included in parentheses

Access controls (229)	Federal Rules of Civil Procedures, Rule 26 (214)	Personally Identifiable Information (PII) (206)
Adware (219)	Firewall (232)	Pretexting (209)
Authentication (230)	Graham-Leach Bliley Act of 1999 (GLBA) (208)	Road apple (218)
Biometrics (231)	Hacker (217)	Root kit (220)
Bot (220)	Health Insurance Portability and Accountability Act of 1996 (HIPAA) (200)	Sarbanes-Oxley Act of 2002 (SOX) (210)
Botnet (220)	Homeland Security Act of 2002 (210)	Security Breach Notification Act (SB-1386) (210)
Cookie (216)	Honey pot (228)	Security patch (227)
Cracker (217)	Identify theft (207)	Social engineering (221)
Cyber Crime (215)	Information security (205)	Spyware (218)
Cyber Security (227)	Key logger (219)	Telephone Records and Privacy Protection Act of 2006 (209)
Denial of Service (222)	Malware (216)	Trojan horse (218)
Distributed Denial of Service (222)	Patch Tuesday (227)	Virus (216)
eDiscovery (214)	Payment Card Industry Data Security Standards (PCIDSS) (213)	Worm (217)
Encryption (228)	Pharming (226)	Zero-day attack (228)
Exabyte (205)	Phishing (222)	Zombie (220)
Federal Information Management Act of 2002 (210)	Phone phreak (215)	

Multiple Choice Questions

1. What organization is responsible for the largest reported information security breach to date?
   a. ChoicePoint
   b. UCLA
   c. the Federal government
   d. Marshall's

2. What is the estimated cost to formally notify each victim of an information security breach?
   a. the cost of postage
   b. $10-$20
   c. $25-$40
   d. $65-$85

3. What type of attack is associated with the Slammer worm?
   a. Spam
   b. Denial of Service
   c. Phishing
   d. Pharming

4. Which of the following is not an entry point for malware?
   a. E-mail attachments
   b. USB drives
   c. Downloading files found on peer-to-peer networks
   d. Entering data on a web form

5. What made the Slammer worm notable?
   a. The significant destruction of data it caused
   b. The speed at which it propogated
   c. The amount of personally identifiable information that was compromised.
   d. The time it took to distribute the "patch" to prevent the worm.

Answers:
1. d   2. d   3. b   4. d   5. b

Review Questions

1. List things you can do to help prevent malware infections.
2. What communication technology do you expect will make compliance with the Federal Rules of Civil Procedure, Rule 26 particularly difficult? Why?
3. What is the reasoning for "patch policies" such as "Patch Tuesday?"
4. Was the Slammer worm the work of a botnet? Why or why not?

Projects

1. Describe the information security notification regulations for your state. Include in your description the notification triggers.

2. Identity theft is a well-documented concern for U.S. citizens. Do you feel that the protection of personally identifiable information is a federal or state issue? Why?

3. Use Excel and the information in the Password tables in the chapter to estimate the resilience of passwords you devise. Use the example below to help you get started.

Possible Passwords		
Password	**Combinations**	**Time to Crack**
Michal	308.9 Million	8½ Hours
Land3rz	3.5 Trillion	11 Years

4.   The Office of Financial Aid & Scholarships has become aware of a potential fraud scheme involving persons who are contacting students and telling them that they've won a scholarship or grant. To get the money, the student is instructed to give their bank account number so that the money can be directly deposited. They also tell the student that there will be a one-time processing fee charged as well as a membership fee to remain eligible for the funds each year. What would you do? Why?

5.   If botnets have a cost to rent or own, what are the benefits? Can you find any information about the return on investment of a botnet?

6.   What are some of the privacy concerns associated with biometric authentication? How have companies that offer biometric ID products addressed these concerns?

TUTORIAL 1

Spreadsheet Basics

PLANNING AHEAD
After reading Tutorial 1, you should be able to answer these questions in your own words

STUDY QUESTIONS
What is a spreadsheet?
How do you work with formulas and functions?
How can you format and print a worksheet?

LEARNING PREVIEW

In this Tutorial you will be introduced to the basic skills necessary to develop your own spreadsheet-based solutions. Although this tutorial will certainly introduce you to a variety of skills in using a spreadsheet, it is not designed to be an exhaustive list of spreadsheet capabilities or skills.

VISUAL ORGANIZATION OF TUTORIAL

Study Question 1	Study Question 2	Study Question 3
Spreadsheet Overview	Working with Formulas and Functions	Formatting and Printing a Worksheet
• Worksheets and Workbooks • Tabs and Groups • Cell Data and Formulas • Accessing Help	• Entering and Viewing Formulas • Order of Operations • Absolute and Relative Cell Addressing • An Overview of Functions	• Formatting Data • Printing
Learning Check 1	Learning Check 2	Learning Check 3

SPREADSHEET OVERVIEW

A **spreadsheet**, or spreadsheet program, is a computer application designed to help organize data, perform calculations, format information, chart results, manage tables and develop reports. A spreadsheet program gives you the flexibility to solve a variety of business problems by entering data, formulas and functions. It was this flexibility that led the Lotus 1-2-3 spreadsheet program to become the "killer application" for the IBM PC. Today, spreadsheets are the most commonly used application by managers and executives to help them solve business problems and make decisions. Spreadsheets are often used in budgeting, data analysis, and inventory management. In this tutorial you will review the basics of working with a spreadsheet. The examples introduced in this textbook will be developed using Microsoft Excel 2007. However, the focus is on introducing common spreadsheet functionality that should be transferable across different spreadsheet programs.

It is assumed that you have some basic computer literacy skills in working with computer applications. For example, you should be familiar with how to start computer programs, use the Ribbon in Microsoft Office applications to perform basic functions, save files, copy, paste and delete data. Additionally it is assumed that you have some familiarity with the most basic operations in Excel. For example, you should know how to do the following skills:

- Save workbooks into different folders
- Enter data into a cell
- Print your spreadsheet including using print preview
- Adjust margins, page layout, etc. for printing
- Copy, paste and move cells
- Insert and delete rows and columns
- Edit the contents of a cell
- Use help in Excel

In this section we will briefly review parts of the Excel work environment to establish a common vocabulary. If you are brand new to working with computer applications, or are unfamiliar with some of the skills listed above, you should review some of the introductory tutorials and help available at the Microsoft Office website.

More About IT

In 1979, Dan Bricklin and Bob Frankston created the first electronic spreadsheet program, Visicalc. Originally created to work on an Apple II computer, this software application moved the Apple II from a recreational toy into a computer in demand by business professionals. The original version was limited to 254 rows and 63 columns. Compared to the spreadsheets of today, it was clunky and lacked much functionality. But at that time, this was the first software application that allowed people who didn't know how to program a computer to enter data and have meaningful results be returned.

Worksheets and Workbooks

When you start Excel, the Excel Program Window launches. This window is shown in Figure T1.1.

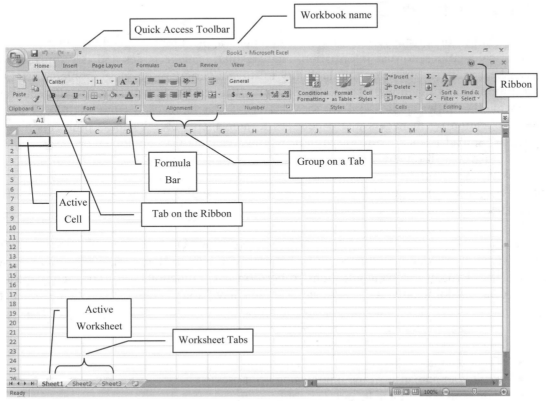

Figure T1.1 The Excel Program Window

The spreadsheet is the backbone of any project done in Excel. In Excel, the spreadsheet is more commonly referred to as a **worksheet**. To help you organize your data, Excel allows you to store data on different worksheets. The name of each worksheet is indicated on the **Worksheet Tab**, located at the bottom of the window. The worksheet you are currently viewing is designated as the **Active Worksheet**. The tab of the active worksheet will have a bolded sheet name. The complete project is stored in a **Workbook**, which is a collection of different worksheets. The **Workbook Name** is shown in the blue bar at the top of the program window. Recall that the workbook is the same as the file in which your project is stored.

The **Ribbon** and the **Office Button** provide the same functionality you find in other Microsoft Office 2007 Applications. Use the choices in the Office Button to select tasks you can do with your document such as Opening, Saving and Printing. Frequently used tools can be found on the Quick Access Toolbar. Ribbon **tabs** have been designed to contain task-oriented icons and tools. Within a Tab, the icons have been further organized into **Groups**. For example, the Center Icon can be found in the Alignment Group on the Home Tab. In Tutorials 2 and 3 you will learn more about some of the unique tools available in Excel.

Worksheets are organized by **rows** and **columns**. The intersection of a row and a column, such as B2, is called a **cell**. Did you know that an Excel 2007 worksheet can have up to 1,048,576 rows and 16,384 columns of data? This means you potentially could have 17,179,869,184 cells filled with data!

The **Active Cell**, A1 in Figure T1.1, is the cell in the worksheet that you are working on. It is always identified by the dark border surrounding the cell. The contents of the active cell are displayed in the **Formula Bar**.

Tabs and Groups

Excel provides some flexibility in how you organize your work environment and in how you choose to accomplish tasks. Often you will have several different ways to accomplish the same task. The worksheet shown in Figure T1.2 is used to record and calculate employee travel expenses for a business. We will use this example to illustrate a few tools and navigation features.

> *Practice:*
> Download the Employee Travel Expense Report spreadsheet from Blackboard so that you can explore these features in Excel. It may be helpful to perform the tasks explained in the next few paragraphs.

In Figure T1.2, look at the **Home Tab**. It contains seven different groups of tasks, such as the **Editing Group**. If you adjust the size of the window shown on the screen to become smaller, Excel will automatically reduce the number of icons shown in each group. Icons that are no longer visible can be viewed by opening up the group that was reduced.

> *Practice:*
> Adjust the window size of the Employee Expense Report spreadsheet. Find one of the groups that became smaller in size. Click the arrow in that group to view all the choices.

You can minimize the Ribbon to show just the row with the tab names (i.e. Home, Insert, etc.) by selecting the **Customize Quick Access Toolbar** icon and clicking **Minimize the Ribbon**. Some groups have a **Dialog Box Launcher** icon which will provides access to additional options through a related dialog box or task pane.

> *Practice:*
> Click on the Dialog Box Launcher in the Alignment Group. The Format Cells dialog box should have opened, providing you with additional choices. Close the dialog box when you are finished.

Additionally, some tabs only appear on the ribbon based on the task you are performing (e.g. creating a chart.) These are called **contextual tabs**. These tabs will appear under a new Tools area that is added to the right side of the ribbon. You will learn more about contextual tabs in Tutorials 2 and 3. Throughout this book we will use the convention of **Tab Name > Group Name > Option Name** to provide instruction on how to complete different tasks.

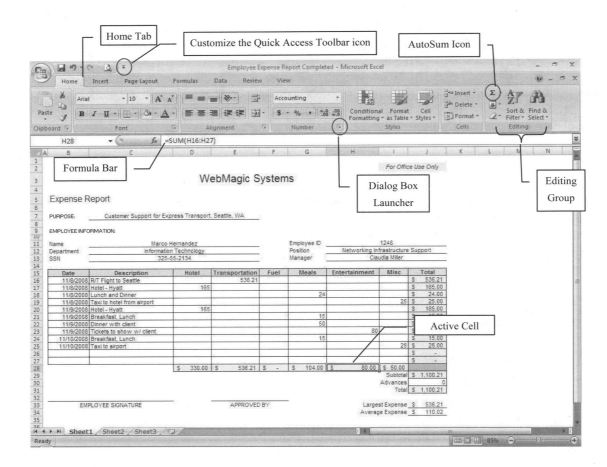

Figure T1.2 An Excel worksheet for employee travel expenses

Next, in Figure T1.2, look at cell H28, the **active cell.** The contents of the cell is a formula (shown in the **formula bar**) to add together all of the entertainment expenses for this trip. The cell itself shows the result of that calculation. In this example the formula used is the SUM function. Excel provides several different ways to enter this formula into the cell. Right now we will concentrate on two methods available by selecting tools from the Home Tab and Formulas Tab on the ribbon. As you continue to work with Excel you will learn about additional methods for entering formulas. While this flexibility can lead to confusion for beginning spreadsheet users, just remember that you don't need to become an expert on all ways to accomplish a task.

> *Practice:*
> Click on cell H28 and then click the Delete key to clear out the contents of the cell.
> Enter the SUM function using the following method:
>   Select the Home Tab > Editing Group > AutoSum Icon Σ▾ > Sum Function.
>
> Press Delete the clear out the contents of that cell. Now enter the SUM function using this alternate method:
>
> Select the Formulas Tab > Function Library Group > Insert Function > Sum

Remember that when you work with many software applications some of the more common choices can be easily accessed by "right-clicking" on the mouse. This is also true in Excel. When working on the active cell, some tasks, like Insert and Format Cells, will be available from this "right-click", shortcut menu in addition to being available on the ribbon. The choice of whether to access a task through an icon on the ribbon or the shortcut menu is left to you.

Cell Data and Formulas

A spreadsheet cell can contain data, formulas or a special type of formula called a function. There are several different types of data that can be entered. Any cell entry that contains letters, hyphens, or spaces is **Text Data**. In addition to entering the actual text-based data values in the worksheet, text data is also used to represent titles, column headings, and cell labels in a worksheet. Entries that are classified as **Numeric Data** can contain numbers and special characters such as dollar signs, commas, decimal points and percent signs. A special type of numeric data is a Date. When you enter a date, such as 11/27/09, into a cell, Excel will interpret that value as a date. This will allow you to perform date arithmetic by entering formulas which reference these values. For example, you can subtract one date from another to find out how much time has elapsed between those two different dates.

As you know, to enter data you simply need to click on a cell and then enter the text or numeric contents. While most people will simply enter the data directly into the cell on the worksheet, you can enter the data by typing it into the formula bar.

In addition to entering data into a cell, you can also enter a formula. A **formula** is a mathematical equation used to calculate a value inside your worksheet. Formulas must start with an equal sign (=). Formulas can include both cell references and constants. A **cell reference** is the unique address of a cell, identified by its column and row location. A **constant** is a value that doesn't change. In the formula =B2+C5*2, B2 and C5 are cell references while 2 is a constant. When you include a cell reference in your formula, your formula will use the value that is stored in that cell. While most of your formulas will involve numeric calculations, it is possible to write formulas that work with text data. For example, you can combine text data stored in two different cells together. As a result, sometimes the constant in a formula may be text.

Most spreadsheet designers recommend you minimize the use of constants in a formula. When you use constants in a formula, if the value needs to be changed it will require making modifications to the actual formulas. This could cause the spreadsheet user to accidentally change the formula, resulting in errors in the worksheet. Instead it is good practice to enter the constants into cells in a separate area of the worksheet, and then reference the cell that contains the value. You will learn more about this through the examples in Tutorials 2 and 3.

Accessing Help

Since this book is not designed to be an exhaustive reference for Excel, it will be important for you to utilize the help system inside Excel as an additional reference while you work on exercises in this tutorial.

The Help System is accessed by pressing the question mark icon 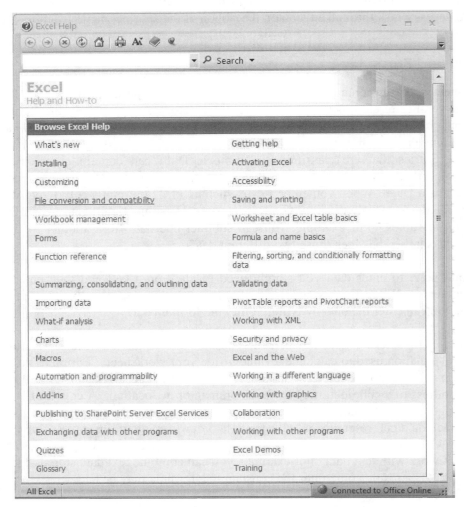 located in the upper right-hand side of the Ribbon.   Figure T1.3 provides an example of the help window that will open. You can either enter a specific word or phrase to search on in the Search Box or you can click on one of the topics to browse through the help information available.

Figure T1.3   The Help Window in Excel

LEARNING CHECK
Be sure you can *describe the pieces of a spreadsheet program window * explain the difference between a tab and a group * differentiate between text and numeric data and formulas* describe how to use the Help system

WORKING WITH FORMULAS AND FUNCTIONS

The capability of using formulas in a spreadsheet is one of the key factors that makes a spreadsheet such a powerful tool. But to take advantage of this power, you must know how to create valid and accurate formulas. In this section you will learn how to write formulas correctly. This involves a review of the Order of Operations, as well as learning about absolute and relative cell addresses. Additionally, as many formulas will use predefined functions, you will be introduced to some of the more commonly used spreadsheet functions.

Entering and Viewing Formulas

As you already learned, a formula can be entered by typing it directly into a cell or by entering it via the formula bar. When entering a formula you also have the choice of entering the cell reference by typing in the cell address, such as B2, or by clicking on that cell when you are entering the formula.

Practice:
Click on cell J33 in the Employee Travel Expense worksheet. (This is the cell that contains the largest expense. The formula in that cell is =MAX(J16:J27).

Click the Delete key to clear out the contents of the cell.
Enter the MAX function by typing in the formula directly:
 Click on cell J33 and enter =MAX(J16:J27)
 (Be sure to press enter when you are done to complete the formula.)

Press Delete the clear out the contents of that cell. Now enter the MAX function using the Point and Click method.

 Click on cell J33 and enter =MAX(
 Now click on cell J16
 Enter :
 Now click on cell J27
 Enter)
 (Be sure to press enter when you are done to complete the formula.)

- In Excel the result of a formula will display in the cell, as you have seen when working with the Travel Expense worksheet. When you click on a cell that contains a formula, the actual contents of the cell – the formula – will display in the Formula Bar. Sometimes you may wish to change the worksheet to show the formulas in the cells instead of showing the result of the formula. Displaying formulas instead of the values is often called **Formula View**. Formula View is most often used when you want to look at several formulas together to help figure out why something is not working correctly or when you want to print out the entire set of formulas used inside of a worksheet as documentation.

You can have Excel change to display the formulas inside of the cells instead of the results by pressing the **CTRL** key and the Tilde (~) key together, (**CTRL + ~**), or by selecting the **Formulas Tab > Formula Auditing Group > Show Formulas** option. Both the CTRL + ~ and Show Formulas task operate as a *toggle* – this means that to stop showing the formulas and return to the normal, or *value view,* you simply perform the same operation again (i.e. press CTRL + ~.)

You should be aware that when you switch to formula view, Excel will adjust the width of your columns. If you toggle back to the value view without making any changes, the original width of your columns will remain. The width that is used to show the formula may not be appropriate for the length of your formula and you may have to adjust the size manually. If you adjust the width, it will affect the width of the column when you return to the value view.

Order of Operations

One of the basic constructs in writing a valid formula is to understand how your spreadsheet will evaluate a formula. Luckily, Excel uses the same order of operations that are used in all basic math equations. Several years ago, maybe back in fourth or fifth grade, you learned about the **Order of Operations** , the rules for which calculations are done first when evaluating equations. Perhaps you learned the acronym PEMDAS (Please excuse my dear Aunt Sally.) Each of those letters really represents a mathematical operator (parentheses, exponents, multiplication, division, addition and subtraction.) Recall that formulas are evaluated from left to right. The operators are evaluated based on their precedence. If there are operators of equal precedence, they are evaluated in the order encountered from left to right. The order of operations is based on the precedence level shown in Figure T1.4. Since content inside of parentheses are evaluated first, you can use them to alter the way an equation will be evaluated. However, if you have several operations inside of parentheses, those operations will be evaluated using the precedence level as well.

Precedence	Operator	Description
1	()	Parentheses
2	^	Exponentiation
3	* and /	Multiplication and division
4	+ and −	Addition and subtraction

Figure T1.4 Order of Operations for formulas

<u>Understanding IT?</u>

Understanding the Order of Operations will be critical in having you write correct formulas. Look at the different formulas shown in Figure T1.5. Can you figure out the answer to each of the formulas?

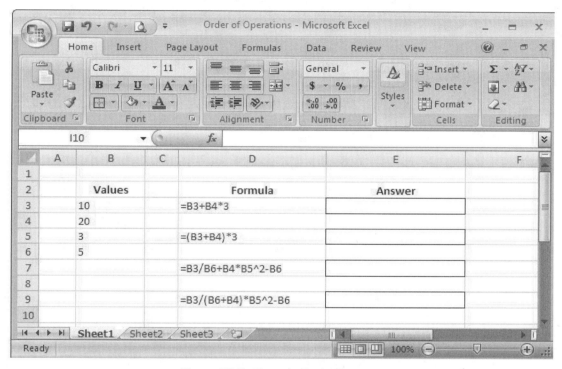

Figure T1.5 Formula Evaluation

Check your answers to the problems in Figure T1.5 at the end of the tutorial.

Absolute and Relative Cell Addressing

One of the powerful benefits of a spreadsheet is the ability to enter a formula in one cell and then copy that formula to other cells. Assuming you have entered the correct formula, you will save yourself much time and effort by copying the formula and having it automatically adjust to the new location. How do you know if you entered a formula correctly? Let's look at two examples shown in Figure T1.6.

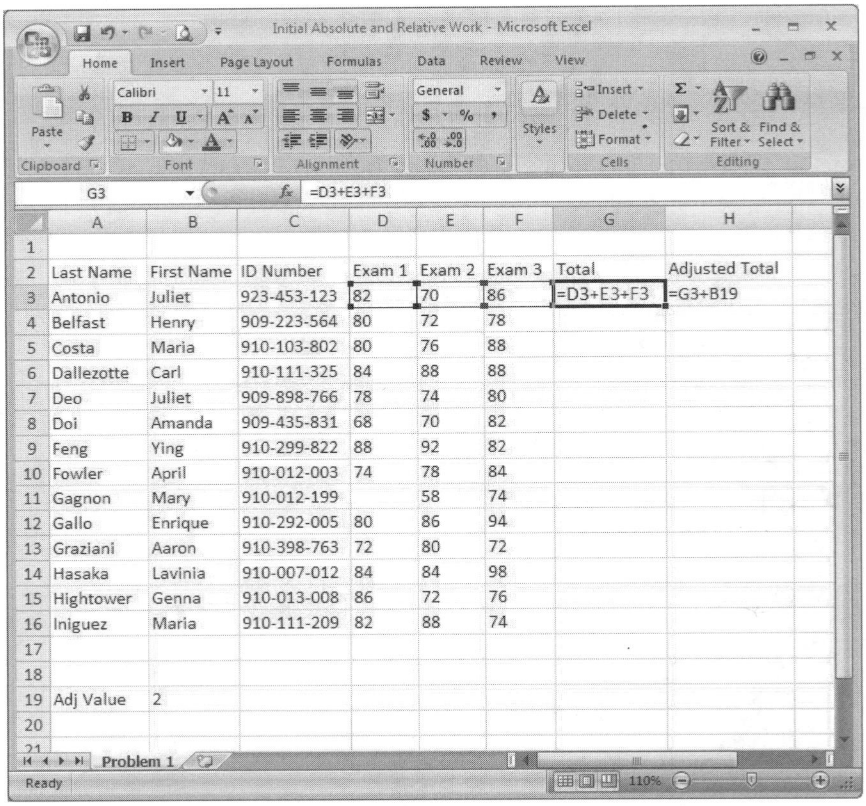

Figure T1.6 Example Formulas

The formula to calculate the Total points in cell G3 is **=D3+E3+F3**. This formula adds up Juliet's 3 exam scores to compute her total points. What should be the formula in cell G4, the one that would compute Henry's total points? The formula should be **=D4+E4+F4**.

Do you notice the outline border around cells D3, E3 and F3? If the active cell contains a formula, like that in G3, Excel provides a nice visual feature for formulas to help the user see what cells are included in a formula. Excel will color code the cell references in the formula and also outline the cells in the worksheet. This can serve as a useful visual indicator to help you verify that you have entered a formula correctly.

Let's look at the formula to calculate the Adjusted Total in cell H3: **=G3+B19**. In this worksheet, the instructor has decided to curve the class grades by adding 2 points to everyone's Total. The 2 points value is stored in cell B19 and it is identified with a label in cell A19. What should be the formula in cell H4, the one that would compute Henry's adjusted total? This formula should be **=G4+B19**. Notice that this formula is an example of storing a constant value in a cell instead of writing it into the formula. This way, if the instructor decides to add 3 points instead of 2, you only need to change the contents of cell B19 instead of changing the formula.

Now that you understand the basic formulas you need to have the worksheet calculate the Total and Adjusted Total for each of the students. You could enter the Total and Adjusted Total formulas into each of the cells in rows 4 through 16. However this can be very tiresome, not to mention impractical, when you have many rows of data. Additionally, it is possible that you might make data entry errors when entering the formulas. This could result in calculation errors. A better way get the formula into those cells is to use the Copy and Paste feature of Excel. The Copy and Paste icons are located on the Home Tab in the Clipboard Group. When you choose to copy and paste a formula, Excel will adjust the formula as it is pasted into the new cells. So let's look at Figure T1.7 to see what happens when the formulas are copied.

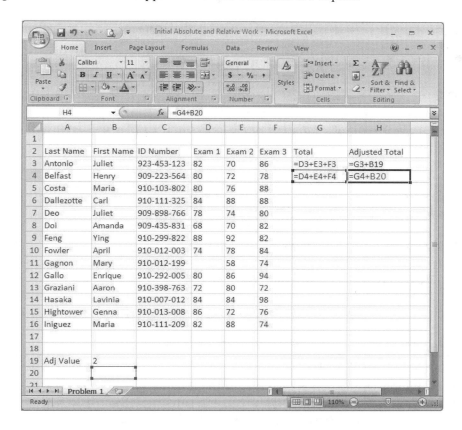

Figure T1.7 Result of Copying Two Formulas

Did the formula for calculating the Total adjust as expected from G3 to G4? Yes! It adjusted correctly so that the formula in G4 adds up Henry's 3 exam scores.

But what about the Adjusted Total formula in column H? We wanted the formula in cell H4 to read **=G4+B19**, but that didn't happen. Notice how the color coding indicator helps to highlight the problem. Let's explore why the copied formula is not correct.

In order to understand what happened when we copied the formula, you need to review the concept of absolute and relative cell references. Let's start with relative cell references. If a formula includes a cell reference, such as D3, it is called a **relative cell reference**. This means that when the formula is copied, the cell reference will adjust *relative to the new cell location* of the formula.

To understand how Excel interprets relative cell references, let's work through what the formula, **=D3+E3+F3,** in cell G3 really means. As we do this, it may be helpful to look at the visual view of the formula as emphasized in Figure T1.8.

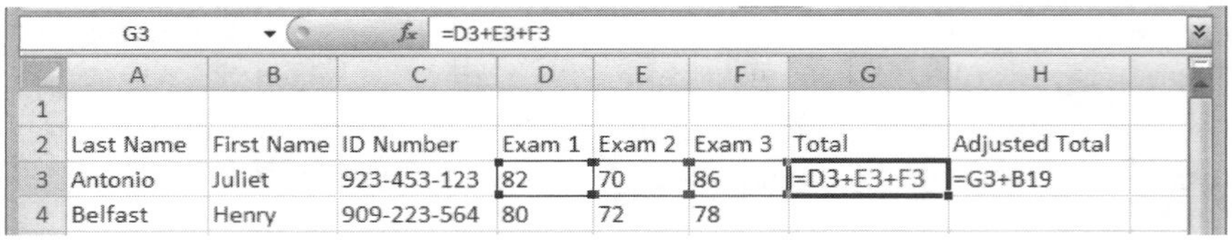

G3 =D3+E3+F3

	A	B	C	D	E	F	G	H
1								
2	Last Name	First Name	ID Number	Exam 1	Exam 2	Exam 3	Total	Adjusted Total
3	Antonio	Juliet	923-453-123	82	70	86	=D3+E3+F3	=G3+B19
4	Belfast	Henry	909-223-564	80	72	78		

Figure T1.8 Understanding the Formula

The formula, **=D3+E3+F3,** in cell G3 is interpreted as:

> ADD
> the contents of the cell 3 columns to the left
> [*D is three columns to the left of G*], and same row [*row 3 is the same row where the answer will be placed*]
> TO
> the contents of the cell 2 columns to the left
> [*E is two columns to the left of G*], and same row [*row 3 is the same row where the answer will be placed*]
> TO
> the contents of the cell 1 column to the left
> [*F is one column to the left of G*], and same row [*row 3 is the same row where the answer will be placed*]

When the formula is copied to G4, the formula adjusts so that it is interpreted relative to the location in G4:

> ADD
> the contents of the cell 3 columns to the left
> [*D is three columns to the left of G*], and same row [*row 4 is now the same row where the answer will be placed*]
> TO
> the contents of the cell 2 columns to the left
> [*E is two columns to the left of G*], and same row [*row 4 is now the same row where the answer will be placed*]
> TO
> the contents of the cell 1 column to the left
> [*F is one column to the left of G*], and same row [*row 4 is now the same row where the answer will be placed*]

This results in a correct formula, **=D4+E4+F4**, for this situation.

The same relative adjustments occurred when the formula to calculate the Adjusted Total was copied. Excel adjusted the formula relative to the new location which resulted in the formula **=G4+B20**. This is a perfect example to illustrate that Excel, or any computer application for that matter, will only do what you tell it to do. That is why it is so critical that you learn how to write accurate formulas.

Recall that the correct formula you want to have in cell H4 is **=G4+B19**. How can we get our spreadsheet to copy the formula from cell H3 the way you want? This is where absolute cell references come in. When you use an **absolute cell reference** Excel will NOT adjust the cell reference relative to the new formula's position. To indicate an absolute cell reference, you include a dollar sign ($) in front of both the column and the row of the cell address.

Let's change the Adjusted Total formula to use an absolute cell reference for the Adj. Value stored in cell B19. The new formula reads: **=G3+$B$19**. Notice that G3 is left as a relative cell reference because that part of the formula should still adjust when it is copied. Excel interprets the formula in cell H3 as follows:

> ADD
>> the contents of the cell 1 column to the left
>> [*G is one column to the left of H*], and same row [*row 3 is the same row where the result is being placed*]
> TO
>> the contents of always column B [*the B is absolute*], and always row 19 [*the 19 is absolute*]

When this formula is copied into cell H4, the formula adjusts so that it is interpreted the same way:

> ADD
>> the contents of the cell 1 column to the left
>> [*G is one column to the left of H*], and same row [*row 4 is the same row where the result is being placed*]
> TO
>> the contents of always column B [*the B is absolute*], and always row 19 [*the 19 is absolute*]

As a result, the formula in cell H4 becomes **=G4+$B$19**. This is exactly what we want.

In the example above, the $ was used in front of both the column and the row of the cell reference to indicate an absolute cell reference. Sometimes you only have a need to hold part of the cell reference as absolute. This is accomplished with a **mixed cell reference** – holding either the row or the column absolute. $C20 is an example of a mixed cell reference in which the column will hold unchanged at "C" but the row will adjust relative to the formula location. Because our formula was only copied down the H column, the formula could have been written as **=G4 + B$19**. In this case as we copy the formula down column H, we need to row to remain the same at 19 (which is why we make that part absolute). However, the column portion "B" is interpreted as "5 columns to the left of H." When the formula is copied down column H, even though the column reference could change since it is relative, it effectively stays the same since "5 columns to the left of H" will always stay at B. You will have a chance to practice with mixed cell references in the next **Understanding IT** exercise.

If you are writing a formula in a cell and will not be copying it into any other cells, you don't need to worry about choosing between absolute and relative cell references. In other words, the difference between absolute, relative and mixed cell references only matters when you copy the formula.

Before you do some practice, let's look at one more example to make sure you understand how a relative cell reference is interpreted. In this example we are going to work with a formula that has only one cell reference in it. While you most likely won't use a formula like this in an actual worksheet, it will help you gain a solid understanding of how relative cell references work.

Figure T1.9 shows the formula =E5 located in cell C4. The figure shows the worksheet in "formula view." The blue cells are locations into which we will copy this formula.

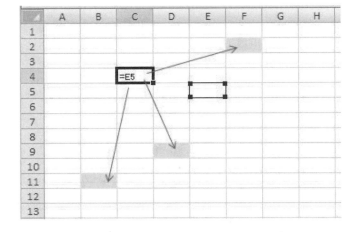

Do you remember how to toggle between displaying the formulas and the formula results?

Use CTRL + ~ to display the formulas.

Figure T1.9   Copying a Simple Formula

As you can visually see by looking at the outlined border of cell E5, the way relative cell reference in the formula in cell C4 is interpreted is:

= the contents of the cell 2 columns to the right
[*E is two columns to the right of C*], and 1 row below [*row 5 is one row below row 4*]

Now that you know the pattern, no matter where this formula is copied, it will always reflect the pattern of "two columns to the right" and "one row below."

- If the formula is copied into cell B11, you would find the cell that is "two columns to the right" and "one row below." The formula in B11 would read: =D12.

- If the formula is copied into cell D9, you would find the cell that is "two columns to the right" and "one row below." The formula in D9 would read: =F10.

- If the formula is copied into cell F2, you would find the cell that is "two columns to the right" and "one row below." The formula in F2 would read: =H3.

Now you have a better grasp of a formula with one cell reference. When you get a more complicated formula that has many cells in it, just remember to do each piece of the formula separately.

You might ask why you aren't getting any additional guided instruction with absolute or mixed cell references. Remember that the easiest formula to copy is one with absolute cells references. Since absolute cell references don't change, that is all you need to remember. When a formula with an absolute cell reference is copied, the cells in the formula that are absolute will remain exactly the same no matter where the formula is copied. As for mixed cell references, since they are a combination of absolute and relative, you just need to apply the rules for absolute and relative parts as you just have learned. Now you are ready to do some practice.

Understanding IT?

Gaining confidence in using absolute and relative cell references is a key component to being able to use spreadsheets effectively. Look at the different formulas shown in Figure T1.10. Can you figure out how each formula will appear after it is copied?

	A	B	C	D	E	F	G	H
1								
2								
3								
4		10	15	18	15			
5		15	15	17	20			
6		20	13	19	15			
7		30	18	15	20			
8						1		
9								
10					=C7		3	
11					=C7+D4+B5			6
12					=SUM(C4:D5)			
13					=SUM($B$4:D4)			5
14		4		2	=$C6+D7			
15								

Write the formula that will appear after each copy command is executed.
1. Copy E10 into F8.
2. Copy E11 into D14.
3. Copy E12 into G10.
4. Copy E12 into C14.
5. Copy E13 into H13.
6. Copy E14 into H11.

Figure T1.10   Copy Exercise for Absolute and Relative Cell References

Check your answers at the end of the tutorial.

An Overview of Functions

So far you have seen a few examples of formulas. Spreadsheets also provide a set of **functions**, predefined formulas to use for specific calculations. Earlier you saw an example of the SUM function. With many calculations, you can choose whether to create your own formula or use a predefined function as an alternative. For example, if you wanted to add up the cells from A1 to A6 you could either enter the formula =A1+A2+A3+A4+A5+A6 or =SUM(A1:A6). Often, using a function will allow you to write a formula that is easier to read. You can see the list of available functions in Excel by clicking the **Formulas Tab** > **Function Library Group** > **Insert Function** option. The Insert Function dialog box is shown in Figure T1.11. Excel groups the functions according to the type of function performed, such as financial or statistical.

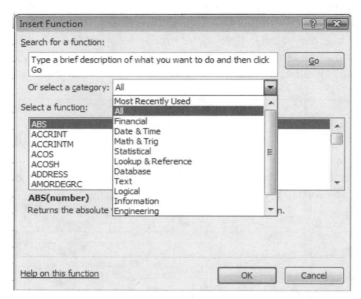

Figure T1.11 Insert Function Dialog Box illustrates the available function categories

Some of the most commonly used functions are listed in Table T1.1. The table shows the result of creating formulas to find the average, sum, maximum, minimum and count of the Exam 1 entries shown earlier in Figure T1.6.

Function	Description	Example	Answer
Average	Calculates the average of a range of cells	=AVERAGE(D3:D16)	80.5
Sum	Finds to total of a range of cells	=SUM(D3:D16)	1046
Max	Finds the largest number in a range of cells	=MAX(D3:D16)	88
Min	Finds the smallest number in a range of cells	=MIN(D3:D16)	68
Count	Counts how many numbers are in a range of cells	=COUNT(D3:D16)	13

Note: In the Count function, because D11 is blank it does not get counted as containing a number

Table T1.1 Commonly used functions

Many functions operate on a range of cells. A **Range** is a group or block of cells in a worksheet. The correct way to indicate a range is to specify the upper left-most cell, include a colon as a separator and specify the lower right-most cell. For example, the range B2:D4, for example, includes the cells B2, B3, B4, C2, C3, C4, D2, D3, and D4. In Table T1,1, the range used for all of the functions is D3:D16. This is because the individual student Exam 1 scores were stored in cells D3 through D16. As you work through Tutorials 2 and 3 you will be introduced to several powerful functions that can be used in Excel.

Complete the following exercise to gain some additional practice in working with formulas and functions.

Practice:

Open a new blank workbook in Excel. Enter the data shown below into the worksheet.

	A	B	C	D	E	F	G
1	Bookstore Inventory						
2							
3	Product	First Author	ISBN-13	Quantity	Cost	Total Cost	Retail Price
4	Accounting	Kimmel, Paul	978-0-470-37785-7	200	$ 139.97		
5	International Economics	Salvatore, Dominick	978-0-471-79468-4	300	$ 115.00		
6	Management	Schermerhorn, John	978-0-470-29437-6	175	$ 125.00		
7	Consumer Behaviour	Evans, Martin	978-0-470-99465-8	55	$ 46.00		
8							
9							
10	Profit Margin	30%					
11							

The total cost column should contain a formula that multiplies the Quantity times the Cost. In cell F4, enter =D4*E4

Copy the formula from F4 down through F7. If you are not familiar with the Fill Handle, explained in the tip below, you might want to try it out.

The Retail Price column should multiply the Cost by the Profit Margin (located in B10.)   This formula will require an absolute cell reference.

> *Did you know that you can use the F4 function key to toggle a cell reference in a formula?*

Use the F4 function key when you enter the formula for the Retail Price. In G4 enter =E4 * B10
After you have typed in B10 (before you press enter to finish the formula):
- Press F4, the B10 part of the formula will change to =$B$10.
- Press F4 again and it will change to =B$10.
- Press F4 again and it will change to =$B10.
- Finally if you press F4 one more time it will change back to =B10.

Note: Since you are copying this formula down the G column, it would be acceptable to either use the absolute cell reference of $B$10 or the mixed cell reference of B$10.

Copy the formula from G4 down through G7. Good work on this practice exercise. Save the file if you want to work with it more in the future.

Fill Handle Tip

Did you know you can use the Fill Handle to quickly copy a cell into consecutive locations? The **Fill Handle** is used to allow you to select a cell and then drag the fill handle to copy the cell contents down a column or across a row. The Fill Handle is circled in Figure T1.12.

Figure T1.12   The Fill Handle

LEARNING CHECK

Be sure you can *describe two ways to enter formulas * evaluate formulas using the order of operations * utilize absolute and relative cell references in formulas * switch between formula and value view in a worksheet * correctly write a formula using a function

FORMATTING AND PRINTING A WORKSHEET

To this point we have concentrated on reviewing information about what you can enter into a worksheet and different ways to enter that content. After you have entered the contents onto your worksheet, you will usually want to change the formatting of some of the cells in order to improve the appearance of the worksheet. In this section you will learn how to change the format of cell data and you will learn how to print the contents of your worksheet.

Formatting Data

Formatting involves changing the way that cell contents are displayed. Examples of formatting include changing fonts, colors, and the way numeric values appear. While it is often tempting to begin making modifications to the cell formats while you are creating the basic structure of the worksheet, it generally is best to wait until you have finished entering most, if not all, of the spreadsheet contents. This allows you to focus on the accuracy and functionality of the spreadsheet independently of how you might want the results to display.

Common formatting choices can be found on the Home Tab. Clicking the Dialog Box Launcher ▣ located in the bottom right corner of the different Groups (e.g. the Font or Alignment Groups) opens the **Format Cells Dialog Box** shown in Figure T1.13. This box allows you to choose a format category (this is the tab shown), adjust alignment (left, center, etc.), select font sizes and styles, and perform a variety of additional formatting options.

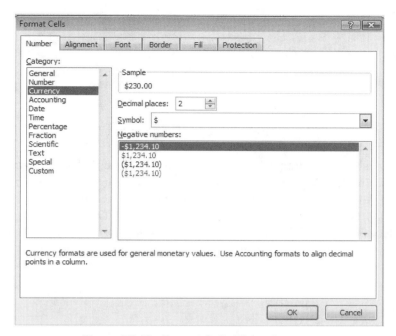

Figure T1.13 Format Cells Dialog Box

In the Cells Group on the Home Tab, one of the choices is Format. Selecting this choice will open the Format Cells drop down list. In addition to providing several other formatting options, the part of this list illustrated in Figure T1.14 show the choices available to adjust the height of a row and/or the width of a column.

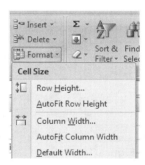

Figure T1.14 The Format Drop Down List

Printing

In many cases you will need to print a copy of your worksheet. Printing can be found under the Office Button. To print your spreadsheet you would select the **Office Button > Print** option. This is a common choice in all Microsoft Office programs. In Excel you may find it helpful to use the **Print Preview** option to ensure that your page will print as desired. Changes to the print layout can be made via the **Page Layout** tab, shown in Figure T1.15. The **Page Setup Group** can be used to adjust many common settings including selecting the paper orientation and setting the margins.

Figure T1.15 Page Layout Tab

Figure T1.16 shows the **Page Setup Dialog Box** that opens if you select any of the Dialog Box Launchers. In the Page Setup dialog box you can insert headers and footers on the **Header/Footer Tab**, and print settings related to the worksheet can be set on the **Sheet Tab**. The sheet tab allows you to include **row and column headings** and **gridlines** on the printed page. Unless you select this option, the grid that is visible on your screen will not appear on the printed page. Including the grid is most useful for spreadsheet documentation and for helping to make large lists of data more readable.

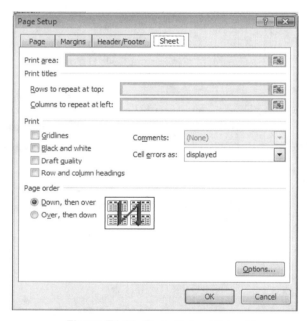

Figure T1.16 Page Setup Dialog Box

Another useful feature for spreadsheet documentation is the ability to print the formulas that are used in a worksheet. Recall that you can toggle, or switch, back and forth between viewing the spreadsheet values and the spreadsheet formulas with the **CTRL** + ~ key combination. Figure T1.17 shows a **Print Preview,** including **Row and Column Headings** and **Gridlines**, from a worksheet in that has been switched to display the spreadsheet formulas.

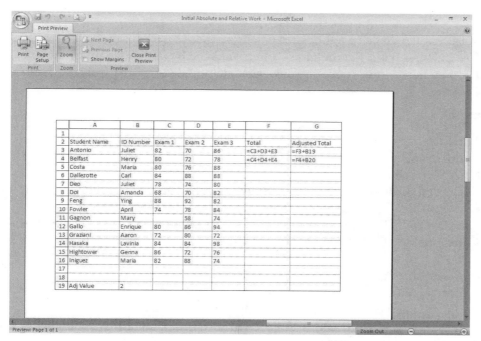

Figure T1.17   Print Preview of a Formula View with Gridlines and Row and Column Headers

LEARNING CHECK

Be sure you can *describe how to launch the format cells dialog box * adjust the row height and column width of a cell * explain how to use the page setup window to adjust print settings

PRACTICAL APPLICATION

Wow! We have covered a lot of the basics of spreadsheets in this section. This is a good time to have you stop and review the concepts just introduced. Complete the exercise below to ensure that you can apply the concepts covered in this Tutorial.

Fit for Life is a small business that provides individualized physical training and lifestyle support to clients. One of the tools the business provides to their clients is a spreadsheet that the clients will complete to record their food consumption. Open Excel so that you can build the sample spreadsheet shown in Figure T1.18.   If you are uncertain about how to accomplish each of the listed tasks, be certain to take advantage of the **Excel Help** System. For example, if you are not certain how to put a border around a cell, click the Help Icon ⊚ and enter **Cell Border** into the search textbox.   Use the specifications below to complete the worksheet.

Create the basic structure:
- ➤ Enter the "**Calorie and Fat Percentage Log**" and the "**Summary**" titles.
- ➤ Enter the column headings shown in row 2. Don't worry about formatting any of the cells at this point.
- ➤ Enter the data values in the **Day**, **Food**, **Calories Consumed** and **Fat Grams** columns.

In the Calorie and Fat Percentage Log area enter formulas to perform the following calculations:
- ➤ The **Calories from Fat** (column E) are calculated by multiplying **9** by the **Fat Grams**.
- ➤ The **Fat Percentage** (column F) is calculated by dividing the **Calories from Fat** by the **Calories**.

In the Summary area enter formulas to perform the following calculations:
- ➤ **Total Calories Consumed** should total all the **Calories Consumed** in column C.
- ➤ **Total Grams of Fat Consumed** should total all the **Fat Grams** in column D.
- ➤ Enter **9** in Cell I4.
- ➤ The **Total Calories of Fat Consumed** is calculated by multiplying **9** by the **Total Grams of Fat Consumed.**
- ➤ The **Overall Fat Percentage** is calculated by dividing the Total **Calories of Fat Consumed** by the **Total Calories Consumed.**

Format your worksheet as shown:
- ➤ Widen columns as necessary; format cells as shown.
- ➤ Wrap cells as necessary for the column headers. (Select the cell that contains text to wrap. Select the **Home Tab > Alignment Group > Dialog Box Launcher > Alignment Tab > Wrap Text** option.)
- ➤ **Center Across Selection** the titles "Calorie and Fat Percentage Log" and "Summary" as shown. (Select the cells over which to center. Select the **Home Tab > Alignment Group > Dialog Box Launcher > Alignment Tab > Text Alignment > Horizontal > Center Across Selection** option.)
- ➤ Add **a border** around the cells as shown.
- ➤ Add background shading to cells as desired.
- ➤ Remove the **gridlines** in the worksheet (**Page Layout Tab > Sheet Options Group > Gridlines > Uncheck View** option.)
- ➤ Change the name of your Sheet tab so that it reads "**Calorie and Fat Log**".
- ➤ Delete Sheets 2 and 3 as they are not needed.

Print your completed spreadsheet
- ➤ Add a custom header to the worksheet that contains "Fit for Life."
- ➤ Add a custom footer to the worksheet that has the current date.
- ➤ Change the orientation to landscape and force the printout to fit to one page.
- ➤ Print a report showing the spreadsheet values.
- ➤ Print a report showing the spreadsheet formulas (include gridlines and row and column headers on this printout.)

Save your worksheet. You will use it in Tutorial 2.

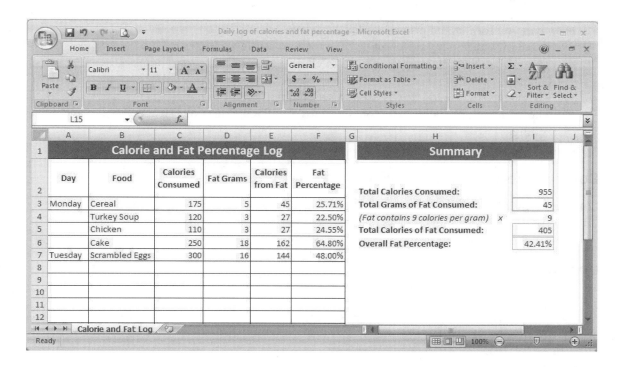

Figure T1.18 Caloric Intake Log built in Excel

WRAPPING IT UP

In this Tutorial you learned the basics about spreadsheet programs. You learned to differentiate formulas from numbers and text. Additionally, you learned how to write a well-structured formula so that it can be correctly copied within your worksheet. In Tutorials 2 and 3 you will look at how spreadsheets can be used for several common business tasks.

Study Questions Summary

1. What is a spreadsheet?
   - Spreadsheet applications are designed to organize data, perform calculations, format information, chart results, manage lists and develop reports
   - Worksheets are a collection of rows and columns of cells that contain data and formulas
   - The Excel Menus and Toolbars provide flexibility for accessing common tasks

2. How do you work with formulas and functions?
   - Writing valid formulas requires a solid understanding of the order of operations
   - Selecting the correct combination of absolute and relative cell references will allow a formula to be copied correctly throughout a worksheet.
   - Functions, such as Average or Sum, are predefined formulas used to complete a specific task

3. How can you format and print a worksheet?
    - Excel provides many different options for formatting cell entries
    - The format cells dialog box is used to choose a format category, adjust alignment of cell contents, select font sizes and styles, and select additional formatting options.
    - The page setup dialog box is used to set common print options
    - The page setup dialog box contains tabs for Page, Margins, Header/Footer and Sheet settings

Solutions to Tutorial Activities

UNDERSTANDING IT?

> *Order of Operations pg. 247*
> *70, 90, 177, -1.4*

UNDERSTANDING IT?

> *Copying Absolute and Relative pg. 253*
> 1. =D5
> 2. =B10+C7+A8
> 3. =SUM(E2:F3)
> 4. =SUM(A6:B7)
> 5. =SUM($B$4:G4)
> 6. =$C3+G4

Key Terms

Page Number references are included in parentheses

Absolute Cell Reference (251)	Formula (243)	Range (254)
Active Cell (241)	Formula Bar (241)	Relative Cell Reference (249)
Average Function (254)	Formula View (245)	Row (241)
Cell (241)	Function (253)	Spreadsheet (239)
Cell Reference (243)	Max Function (254)	Sum Function (254)
Column (241)	Min Function (254)	Tabs and Groups (241)
Constant (243)	Mixed Cell Reference (251)	Text Data (243)
Contextual Tab (241)	Numeric Data (243)	Workbook (240)
Count Function (254)	Order of Operations (246)	Worksheet (240)
Fill Handle (255)	Page Setup Dialog Box (258)	
Format Cells Dialog Box (256)	Print (257)	

Multiple Choice Questions

1. To view formulas in Excel you use what key combination?
    a. Ctrl + =   b. Alt + ~   c. Shift + PrtScrn   d. Ctrl + Shift   e. Ctrl + ~

2. Given the formula =A1+A2*A3-A5/2, what will the result be assuming the following cell contents: A1=2, A2=3, A3=4, A4=5, A5=6?
    a. 11   b. 17   c. -1   d. -5   e. 4

3. G5:K10 is best referred to as a _____.
    a. range   b. selection   c. cell group   d. reference

4. You have the following formula: =B3-C5+E3 in cell E6. If you copy the formula into cell D8, what will the contents of D8 be?
    a. =B5-C7+E5   b. =A5-B7+D5   c. =A3-B5+D3   d. =B3-C5+E3

5. What is the result of typing the D5*2 into a cell in Excel?
    a. The entry is invalid and an error message will show
    b. The result of multiplying D5 and 2 will show
    c. The result is the same as typing in =D5*2
    d. The text D5*2 will shown in the cell
    e. Both B and C are correct

Answers:
1. e   2. a   3. a   4. b   5. d

Review Questions

1. What is the difference between a formula and a function?
2. List and describe three different types of formatting you might use in a worksheet.
3. When writing a formula, why is it recommended to use cell references instead of hard-coding in the values?
4. Briefly explain the differences between absolute, relative and mixed cell references.

TUTORIAL **2**

Developing Business Systems with Spreadsheets

PLANNING AHEAD

After reading Tutorial 2, you should be able to answer these questions in your own words

STUDY QUESTIONS

What are some common functions and features in a spreadsheet?
How can you improve the functionality of a spreadsheet by controlling user input?
How do you develop and implement a spreadsheet-based system?

LEARNING PREVIEW

In Chapter 3 you learned the process organizations use to develop information systems. In this tutorial you will learn how to apply that process as you develop several business applications using a spreadsheet. In the earlier chapters you also gained some familiarity with spreadsheets by working on the different activities. Now you are ready to start building your own spreadsheet-based solutions. This tutorial assumes that you are familiar with the basic skills of using a spreadsheet that were covered in Tutorial 1. With that in mind, the focus of the tutorial is not to teach you an exhaustive list of spreadsheet capabilities and skills. Rather the tutorial is geared toward helping you understand how to use a spreadsheet to solve business problems.

VISUAL ORGANIZATION OF TUTORIAL

Study Question 1	Study Question 2	Study Question 3
Functions and Features	Improving Functionality by Controlling User Input	Steps to Creating a Spreadsheet
<ul><li>Logical Functions</li><li>Conditional Formatting</li><li>Creating a Column Chart</li><li>Statistical Functions</li><li>Creating a Pie Chart</li></ul>	<ul><li>Data Validation</li><li>VLookup Function</li></ul>	<ul><li>Analyze the business problem</li><li>Develop the spreadsheet framework</li><li>Enter the formulas</li><li>Verify for completeness and accuracy</li><li>Document</li><li>General Guidelines</li></ul>
Learning Check 1	Learning Check 2	Learning Check 3

FUNCTIONS AND FEATURES

In Tutorial 1 you were introduced to the concept of a function. In this section we will explore several different functions and features that are available when working with spreadsheets. These functions will include statistical capabilities, data management capabilities, logical analysis, and graphing. To help you learn how these functions are used, they will be explained in the context of two different examples. While these examples cover several different uses of spreadsheets, they are not an exhaustive list of the types of business tasks where you may find creating a spreadsheet to be beneficial.

Example 1: Calorie Intake Spreadsheet

In this first example you are going to enhance the Calorie Intake Spreadsheet you created in the Practical Application at the end of Tutorial 1. Build that spreadsheet now if you did not do so earlier. In this tutorial you will learn how to add the following features to this spreadsheet:
- Logical functions to check if cells have anything entered into them
- Conditional formatting to have Excel automatically display the result in a different format based on a condition
- A column chart to visually display the fat as a percentage of total calories

Figure T2.1 shows how the completed spreadsheet will look. You will get to the graph shortly, but for now let's look at column E and column F.

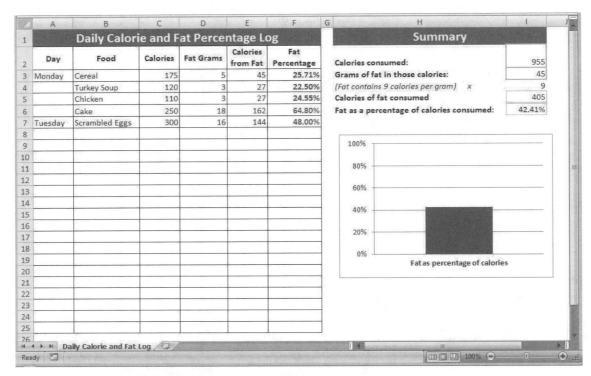

Figure T2.1   The revised Calorie Intake spreadsheet

Practice:

Open the Calorie Intake spreadsheet you created in the **Practical Application** activity in Tutorial 1.

Over the next few pages you will perform a variety of steps to add functionality into the spreadsheet.

Logical Functions

You want to build spreadsheets that don't require your user to have to edit or copy any of your formulas. When you built your spreadsheet earlier, did you only enter formulas in cells E3 through E7, and F3 through F7? That may have seemed logical based on the data shown in your assignment. However, you can't be certain how many different rows your user will need to enter their entire food intake. Additionally, you don't want your user to have to enter or copy formulas since that introduces the possibility for errors. As a result, you will want to copy the formulas in E3 and F3 down to the end of your entry space (row 25).

Practice:

If you didn't do this when you built the original spreadsheet, copy the formula in E3 down through cell E25 and copy the formula in F3 down though F25.

Uh-oh! Do the cells in column E that now have a formula show a 0? This is because in the rows where you did not have a value in column D, Excel interprets the empty cell as a 0 for calculation purposes. Do the cells in column F that now have a formula show #DIV/0!? This message occurs because the formula in column F uses the contents of cells in column C as the denominator. For the rows where C is empty, Excel uses a value of 0, which generates the "divide by zero" error messages.

Overall, this doesn't look very nice. You certainly don't want to give your clients a spreadsheet that shows zeros or a "divide by zero" error message when the user hasn't filled in any values in a row in the worksheet. It can lead them to believe that the spreadsheet has an error or that the user has done something wrong. How can you fix this problem?

Fortunately, you can use a logical function to control user input. **Logical functions** are used to have Excel evaluate a condition and perform an action based on the result. In this case we will have Excel only display the calculation result when the cells in the row have a data value inside of them. Excel offers several logical functions. In this section we will learn about the IF, AND, and OR logical functions.

The IF Function
We will concentrate on the **IF Function** first. The IF function is used to perform a logical test on the contents of a cell.

The general form of an **IF** function is:

=IF(Logical_Test, Value_if_true, Value_if_false)

*The Logical Test can be any condition returning a TRUE or FALSE

*The Value if True or Value if False can be a formula, a numeric value, or a text value. Text values must be enclosed in quotes.

Let's now learn how we can use the IF function to solve the problem with our formula in column E.

Correcting the Calories from Fat formula (column E). We will use the following IF formula in cell E3:   =IF(D3<>0,D3*9,"")

Examining the formula:

Formula Contents	Part of Formula	Explanation
D3<>0	Logical test	This is the question we want Excel to evaluate. In our example we want to check to see if D3 has a value not equal to 0. Note: In Excel an empty cell is interpreted the same as if it has 0 inside of it
D3*9	Value_if_true	If there is something besides 0 in cell D3, then do the calculation *Explore: Why don't you write =D3*9, since it is a formula and you learned earlier that all formulas start with the equal sign?* *When your formula contains multiple equations/formulas, only the very first formula begins with the equal sign.*
""	Value_if_false	If cell D3 doesn't have something inside it, then leave the cell blank. (Note: quotes with nothing inside will leave the cell empty)

Practice:
Enter the formula **=IF(D3<>0,D3*9,"")** into cell E3. Because row 3 has data values in the other columns, you aren't able to determine if your formula works correctly yet.

Copy the formula in E3 down through cell E25. The zeroes in E8 through E25 should have been replaced with empty cells.

Before we move on to fixing column F there are two items to consider. First, there are different ways that you could have structured the logical test. We will explore the ISBLANK function.

Extending your Knowledge – The ISBLANK Function

Excel offers several IS functions that are classified under the Information category of functions. All of the IS functions check a specific value and return an answer in the cell of either "True" or "False". The **ISBLANK** function is used to check if a cell is empty.

The general form of the **ISBLANK** function is:

=ISBLANK(Value)

*The function returns a True if the Value is Blank

*The function returns a False if the "value" is not blank

While IS functions can be used by themselves, they are often combined with an IF and serve as the logical test portion. Using the ISBLANK function in our example, we could have written our formula for E3 as follows:

=IF(ISBLANK(D3),"",D3*9).

Notes on this new equation:

*The contents of the Value_if_true and Value_if_false parameters switched because of the way the logical test was phrased.

*Remember to only use one equal sign at the very beginning of the equation. Just as we didn't put an equal sign before D3*9, we won't put an equal sign before ISBLANK.

The second consideration involves the error message. Did you notice that the error message in column F switched from #DIV/0! to #VALUE! This occurred because you changed the formula in column E to use the new IF function. For rows where D is blank, the new formula now leaves an empty cell in column E instead of a cell with 0. As a result, the error no longer is caused by trying to divide by 0, but instead by trying to divide by an empty cell. Let's move on to fix the error.

Correcting the Fat Percentage formula (column F). Look at the formula in F3. Currently it reads **=E3/C3**. Can you figure out a way to adapt that formula by incorporating the IF function to solve the error message?

Practice:
Enter the formula **=IF(D3<>0,E3/C3,"")** into cell F3. This new formula appears to work.

Copy the formula in cell F3 down through cell F25.

Does the formula look like it works in all of the rows? Unfortunately there is a problem with this formula that isn't visible right now. You have a logic error in your formula.

> *Practice:*
> Delete the 175 calories in cell C3 leaving that cell empty. What happened to your result in cell F3? It no longer works – you should see the #DIV/0! error message.

Why did your error message change? Look at your value_if_true calculation. It references both cells E3 and C3. When C3 doesn't have an entry, the calculation no longer works correctly. A similar problem will occur if cell D3 doesn't have an entry. Don't worry; the formula will work correctly with a slight modification. Logically, what should happen is you should check that C3, D3 and E3 all have something inside of them. This is known as a **compound condition** -- two or more separate conditions combined with either AND or OR. Unfortunately you can't ask a compound condition directly in an IF statement.

The AND Function

Excel provides another logical function to remedy this situation, the AND Function. The **AND Function** is used to evaluate up to 255 different logical tests – thankfully we only have 3 in our example. The general form of an AND function is:

> =AND(Logical1, Logical2,Logical3,...)
>
> * Logical1, logical2, etc. are separate conditions, or tests, that can each be evaluated as either TRUE or FALSE. You can have up to 255 different logical conditions.
>
> * The AND function returns TRUE if all logical tests are TRUE
>
> * The AND function returns FALSE if one or more logical tests are FALSE

In the formula for column F there are three conditions to test: C3<>0, D3<>0 and E3<>0. The AND function would be written as: **=AND(C3<>0,D3<>0,E3<>0).**

Enter **=AND(C3<>0,D3<>0,E3<>0)** into cell F3.

> *Practice:*
> Enter the formula **=AND(C3<>0,D3<>0,E3<>0)** into cell F3.

Does F3 now display the word FALSE? What just happened? Since you deleted the 175 from C3, the condition C3<>0 evaluates to FALSE because it is empty. D3 contains 5; E3 contains 45. Thus D3<>0 evaluates to TRUE and E3<>0 evaluates to TRUE. However, since all arguments are not TRUE the AND function returns a FALSE.

> *Practice:*
> Change cell C3 back to 175.

Does cell F3 now read TRUE? While you are not quite finished, you are making great progress.

Finishing the formula:

Now that we have checked that the AND function is working correctly, our last task for the formula in cell F3 is to combine the AND with the IF. The general form of combining the two is:

=IF(AND(Logical1,Logical2,..),Value_if_true, Value_if_false)

* The AND serves as the "logical test" of this IF statement.

* Remember not to use the =sign in front of the AND. Only the very first part of an equation begins with an equal sign.

Practice:
Enter the formula **=IF(AND(C3<>0,D3<>0,E3<>0),E3/C3,"")** into cell F3

Examining the formula:

Formula Contents	Part of Formula	Explanation
AND(C3<>0,D3<>0,E3<>0)	Logical test	This is the question we want Excel to evaluate. In our example we want to check to see if cells C3, D3 and E3 all have a value not equal to 0.
E3/C3	Value_if_true	If there is something besides 0 in cells C3, D3, and E3then do the calculation
""	Value_if_false	If cell D3 doesn't have something inside it, then leave the cell blank

Practice:
Copy the formula from Cell F3 down through F25.

The error messages in F8 through F25 should have been replaced with empty cells.

Extending your Knowledge – The OR Function

Excel offers another Logical function named **OR**. Like the And function, the OR function can be used to evaluate up to 255 different logical tests.

The general form of the **OR** function is:

=OR(Logical1, Logical2,Logical3,...)

* Logical1, logical2, etc. are separate conditions, or tests, that can each be evaluated as either TRUE or FALSE. You can have up to 255 different logical conditions.

* The OR function returns TRUE if any of the logical tests are TRUE

* The OR function returns FALSE if all of the logical tests are FALSE

*Examples include: (Assume A1 contains 5, A2 contains 10 and A3 contains 15)
=OR(A1=5,A2=10,A3=15)   Evaluation = TRUE
All three conditions are true, which meets the criteria that at least one of the individual conditions is true

=OR(A1=6,A2=10,A3>A2)   Evaluation = TRUE
Even though A1=6 is False, since the other two conditions are true, this meets the criteria that at least one of the individual conditions is true

=OR(A1=6,A2>A3,A3="Red")   Evaluation = FALSE
Since all three tests are false, the overall equation evaluates as false

Conditional Formatting

Before you leave column F, look at the blue and red colors used in the fonts of the cells shown in Figure T2.1. The developer of the spreadsheet wanted to emphasize, by using different font colors, whether the Fat Percentage was above 30% of Total Calories. Excel offers a feature called **Conditional Formatting**. Conditional formatting allows Excel to apply different cell formats based on the contents of the cell. Let's add conditional formatting to your worksheet.

Practice:
Select the range of cells F3 through F25.

Select the **Home Tab** > **Styles Group** > **Conditional Formatting** option.

Select **Highlight Cell Rules** > **Greater Than…**

The Conditional Formatting dialog box shown in Figure T2.2 will appear.

Figure T2.2   The Conditional Formatting Dialog Box

Practice:
Enter 30% in the textbox below "Format cells that are GREATER THAN."

Select **Custom Format** in the drop down selection of the With box. Set the font color to Red and select Bold.

With the same cell range selected choose **Conditional Formatting** again and select **New Rule**.

The New Formatting Rule window should appear as shown in Figure T2.3. Make the following selections and entries:

Practice:
Select **Format only cells that contain** as the **Rule Type**.

Complete the **Rule Description** entries to match Figure T2.3. The Preview font should show a Dark Blue color with Bold style.

Select OK when complete.

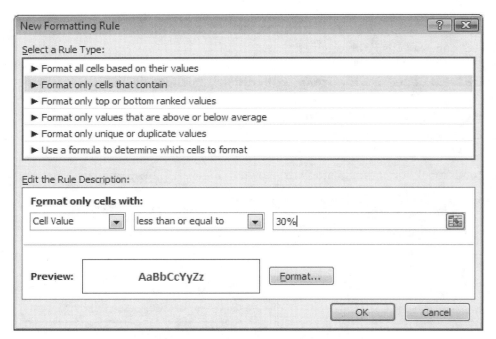

Figure T2.3 The completed conditional formatting dialog box

The Fat Percentage cells will now automatically change color based on the cell contents. If you want to see all of the rules you have created for a cell range you can select Manage Rules from the Conditional Formatting choices. This will also allow you to edit or delete existing rules.

> *Practice:*
> Apply the same conditional formatting to the Fat as a Percentage of Calories Consumed cell in the Summary area.

Creating a Column Chart

The last task you need to complete on the worksheet is to create the column chart. Charts provide users with a graphical view of the data. In Excel, you can easily create a chart by working with the icons in the **Charts Group** located on the **Insert Tab**.

To create a chart, begin by selecting the data that you want to graph. For this chart you want to graph cell I6, the "fat as a percentage of calories" cell in the summary area.

> *Practice:*
> Select cell I6.
>
> Select the **Insert Tab > Charts Group > Column > 2D Column > Clustered Column** option. This option is shown in Figure T2.4.

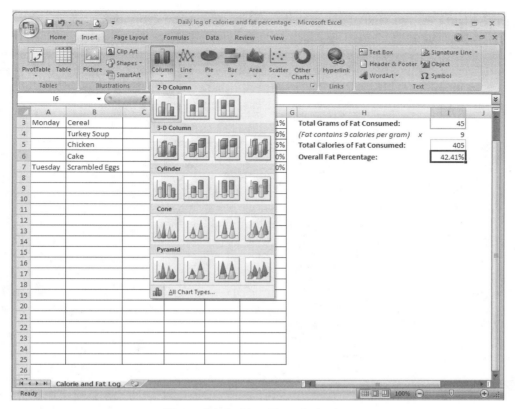

Figure T2.4 Chart Type Selection

Excel automatically creates the chart for you and inserts it as an object in your worksheet. The chart will initially look similar to Figure T2.5. After a chart has been created, three new contextual tabs, containing the Chart Tools, become available on the Ribbon. These new tabs contain tools for Design, Layout and Format options. The Design tab is used to make changes to the *source data* used to create the chart. The Layout tab is used to add titles and data labels. The Format tab is used to change colors and styles. Since the chart in Figure T2.5 doesn't look like the finished chart you want, you will need to edit the chart.

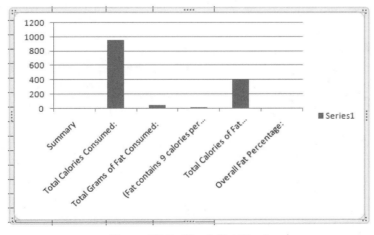

Figure T2.5 The Initial Chart

Edit the Data Range. Excel completed the Data Range entry for you based on you selecting cell I6 before inserting the chart. The data you have selected to graph is also known as the **source data**. Since you chose a clustered column chart, Excel assumed that you wanted to compare several different cells in column I (instead of just one) and also assumed that the labels for those cells were in column H. If you had selected more than one cell, Excel's estimate of the data range would be more accurate. However in this case you will make a change.

Practice:

Click the Chart to select it. Notice at the right-side of the Ribbon that Excel added Design, Layout and Format contextual tabs under a Chart Tools area.

Select the **Design Tab > Data > Select Data** option. The Select Data Source dialog box will appear, as shown in Figure T2.6. Notice that Excel has estimated that the data range is $H$1:$I$6.

Change the Chart Data Range to read ='Calorie and Fat Log'!$I$6:$I$6. *Note: The 'Calorie and Fat Log' references the Sheet Name. If you named the sheet something different, then you should adjust the entry as appropriate.*

Click OK to continue.

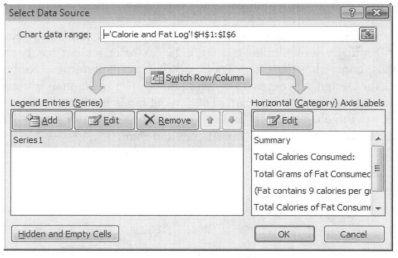

Figure T2.6 The Select Data Source Dialog Box

Edit the Chart Layout. The next step is to modify the layout options for the chart. For example you can enter a title for the overall chart and axes, change the placement of the legend, and add labels onto the columns in the chart. Make the following changes using tools on the Chart Tools **Layout Tab**.

Practice:

Select the **Labels Group** > **Axis Titles** > **Primary Horizontal Axis Title** > **Title Below Axis** option. Enter "Overall Fat Percentage" into the title.

Select the **Axes Group** > **Axes** > **Primary Horizontal Axis** > **Show Axis without Labeling** option. This will remove the 1 currently showing in the chart.

Select the **Labels Group** > **Legend** > **None** option. This will remove the Series1 legend shown.

Select the **Axes Group** > **Axes** > **Primary Vertical Axis** > **More Primary Vertical Axis Options** option to open the **Format Axis** dialog box. Make the following changes to adjust the scale of the Axis.
-   For the Axis Options choices, change the settings so that they match those shown in Figure T2.7.
-   For the Number choices, change the Decimal places to 0.

Click Close when finished.

Figure T2.7   The Format Axis Dialog Box

Edit the Chart Format. The next step is to modify the color of the column. These settings can be found on the Chart Tools **Format Tab**.

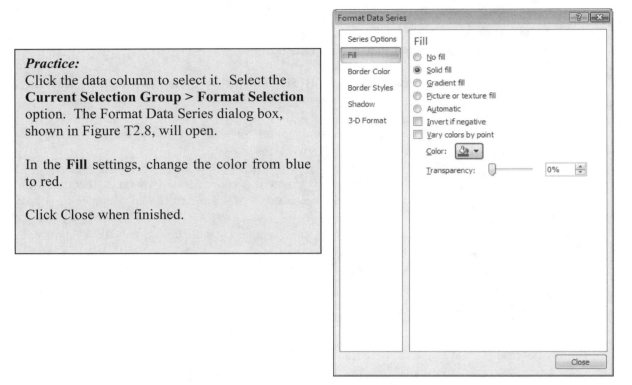

Practice:

Click the data column to select it. Select the **Current Selection Group > Format Selection** option. The Format Data Series dialog box, shown in Figure T2.8, will open.

In the **Fill** settings, change the color from blue to red.

Click Close when finished.

Figure T2.8 Change the column color in the Format Data Series Dialog Box

Your worksheet should now look similar to the one shown in Figure T2.9.

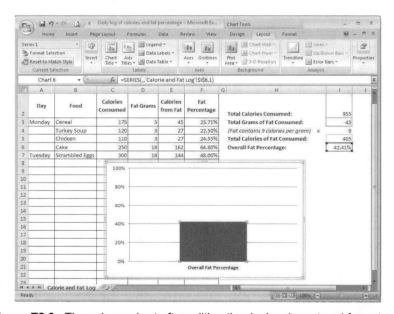

Figure T2.9 The column chart after editing the design, layout and format

> *Practice:*
> Use the sizing handles to adjust the size and shape of the chart area, and move the chart to the desired location so that it will match the one shown in Figure T2.1.

You now have a spreadsheet that is easy to use. In Example 1, you learned spreadsheet skills in creating logical functions, using conditional formatting, and creating graphs. You will have a chance to reinforce these skills in some of the end of tutorial exercises.

Example 2: Demographic Analysis Spreadsheet

It is important for businesses to collect data about their customers and to analyze that data to determine underlying changes in customer habits, interests, etc. When the business happens to be education, you will find that professors need to collect and analyze data about their students. In the information systems discipline it is important to analyze changes in incoming skill levels. This helps to ensure that the material taught is current with the needs of the students. Figure T2.10 shows the completed contents of the Section 2 Student Demographic Analysis workbook, which displays some summary information about student demographics from one class section. Cells C457 through C460 display statistics computed on the Age of students in the 2:00 class section. Notice that this calculation is based on 450 students who completed the survey. The graph shows the spreadsheet skill levels for those same students. This is a tremendous amount of data. In this example you will learn how to work with large data sets.

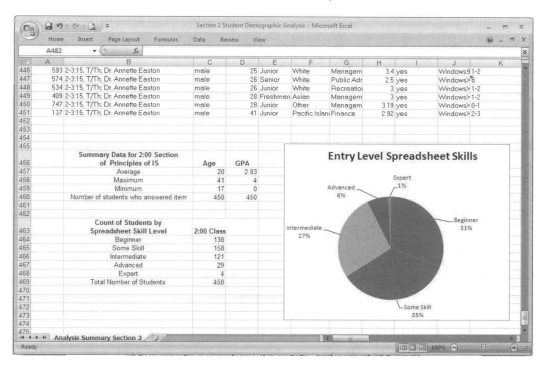

Figure T2.10 Demographic Data Analysis

> *Practice:*
> Download and open the **Section 2 Demographic Analysis** Spreadsheet from Blackboard.

This spreadsheet shows data from only one of the class sections that completed the survey. In reality, the professors have captured data from all of the sections.   In Tutorial 3 you will learn how to manage a workbook that organizes the student records by class section onto different worksheets. By having you concentrate now on this smaller subset of data, you can focus on becoming familiar with some of the spreadsheet skills without worrying about multiple worksheets. By creating the summary shown in Figure T2.10 you will add the following enhancements to the spreadsheet:

- Statistical functions to summarize data
- A pie chart to visually display the summarized data

Prepare the Summary Area.   Notice that the data in the worksheet extends through row 451. In this example, you will create the framework for the summary area several rows below the data area.

> *Practice:*
> Enter the column headings and labels for the summary area cells as shown in Figure T2.10.
>
> Use the Format Cells dialog box to adjust the appearance of the column headings and labels by selecting options on the Format Cells dialog box.
> - Remember that clicking the Dialog Box Launcher will open the Format Cells dialog box.
> - Settings to control the alignment and wrapping of cell contents are found on the Alignment Tab of the Format Cells dialog box.

How do you get the label "Summary Data for 2:00 Section of Principles of IS" to display on two lines within the same cell?

Wrapping Text Tip

Did you know you can check the "Wrap Text" box on the Alignment Tab of the Format Cells Dialog Box?   This is shown in Figure T2.11. This wraps the text based on the width of the column.

If you want to control the exact placement of the *line break*, where the text will wrap, you can specify the break point. This is done by pressing **Alt + Enter** at the point you want to wrap the text.

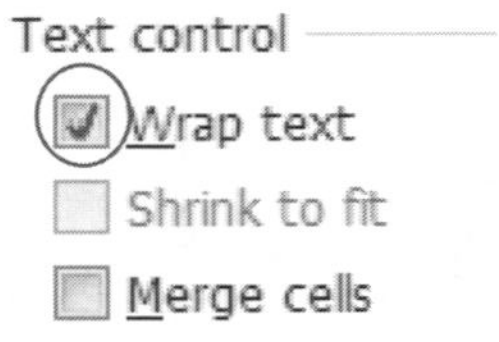

Text control
☑ Wrap text
☐ Shrink to fit
☐ Merge cells

Figure T2.11 Wrap Text Check Box

> *Practice:*
> Click on cell B456. This cell should contain the label "Summary Data for 2:00 Section of Principles of IS"
>
> Place your cursor after the word "section." Press the Alt key and the Enter key together. The text should now wrap.
>
> Press enter to leave that cell.
>
> Wrap the text in cell B463 using the same method.

While Excel will usually adjust the row height accordingly, you may need to make adjustments to fine tune the visual display. With the summary area framework now complete, you can begin to enter the appropriate formulas to display the results.

Statistical Functions

As you know, Excel provides a variety of statistical functions. The Average, Minimum, Maximum and Count functions needed to analyze the summary data for Age and GPA were illustrated in Tutorial 1.

> *Practice:*
> In the upper summary area (rows 456 through 460), enter the Average, Maximum, Minimum and Count functions in the respective cells in the Age and GPA columns of the summary area.
>
> *If you need to review the correct way to write these functions, refer back to Table T1.1 or use the Help feature in Excel.*

The second summary area is used to display the results of a question that students answered related to how they would rate their skill level with spreadsheet skills. The students had to choose one of five different skills levels. The summary area totals the answers by each of the skill levels. These results can be obtained using the **CountIF** statistical function.

The CountIF Function

The CountIF function combines a logical test with the count function to count how many cells in a range meet the specified criteria. The general form of the CountIF is:

=CountIF(range,criteria)

* The range contains the cells that should be counted. Note: If your formula is to be copied to other cells, pay attention to the need for absolute cell references when defining the range

*The Criteria contains the value that specifies which cells will be counted. The value can either be a number, expression, cell reference or text. Criteria that include text or expressions must be enclosed in quotation marks (e.g. ">54"). It is often recommended to use a cell reference in your criteria instead of hard-coding the criteria. This allows you to isolate data values from the formula. In this case, using a cell reference in your criteria will allow you to easily copy the formula from the first cell into the other cells.

*Examples include:
=CountIF(A1:A10,"A")
this will count how many cells in A1 through A10 contain the letter "A".

=CountIF(A1:A10,2)
this will count how many cells in A1 through A10 contain the number 2.

=CountIF(A1:A10,C18)
this will count how many cells in A1 through A10 contain the value stored in cell C18.

Your formula should look through the data entered in the Spreadsheet column. This is column V. What is the range of data to use in the formula? Since the first row has column headers, the range will start in V2 and continue through V451.

Complete the following **Understanding IT** exercise to reinforce your comprehension of the CountIF function, along with refreshing some general skills in working with formulas.

Understanding IT?

Explore each of the following formulas. Answer the specific questions posed for each formula shown:

=COUNTIF(V2:V451, "Beginner")

1. Will this formula work correctly in cell C464? Why/Why Not?

2. Do you think that if you copy this formula into cell C465, you will get the correct answer for the "Some Skill" students? Why/Why Not?

3. After copying the formula from C464 into C465, what will be the formula in C465?

=COUNTIF(V2:V451, "Beginner ")

4. Will this formula work correctly in cell C464? *(Note that the criteria includes an additional space after the word beginner.)*

5. Write a formula that will solve the problems identified in Question 2.

6. Is there a variation you can use when indicating the range in your formula for Question 5 that will also work?

Check your answers to the problems at the end of the tutorial.

As you learned in the Understanding IT exercise, there are several ways to write a correct formula for cell C464. However some will have limitations related to copying the formula. In this case, you also saw that you could write a valid formula using either Mixed or Absolute Cell References for Range. We will use the Absolute Cell Reference option in our example.

Practice:
Enter the following formula into cell C464: **=COUNTIF($V$2:$V$451,B464)**

Copy this formula into cells C465 to C468.

Enter a formula, using the Sum Function, to determine the total in cell C469.

Excel has several functions like the CountIF that combine a function, like the Count, with the logical capabilities of the IF function. Two of the more common functions, the AverageIF and SumIF, are introduced in the Extending your Knowledge boxes.

Extending your Knowledge – The AverageIF Function

AverageIF – This function will *average* a range of cells that meet the specified criteria.

=AverageIF(range, criteria, [average_range])   Function Category: Statistical

* The range contains the cells that should be averaged.

*The Criteria contains the value that specifies which cells will be averaged. Like the criteria in the CountIF, the value can either be a number, expression, cell reference or text.

*The Average_range is an optional parameter. *Note: When describing the general format of a function, optional parameters will always be included within square brackets.* The Average_range parameter specifies the actual set of cells to average. If it is not included, the cells in the range are averaged. The Average_range parameter would be used when you want to use the cells in the range to determine "what" rows meet the criteria, but the actual cell contents to be averaged are located in a different range. This is illustrated in the second example below.

*Examples:
Assume your worksheet contains rows of employee data. Column A contains the employee ID, Column B contains the Division to which they are assigned, and Column C contains their annual salary.

   =AverageIF(C1:C75,">35,000")
        this will average of all the salaries for employee who earn more than $35,000.

   =AverageIF(B1:B75,"Central",C1:C75)
        this will average of all the salaries for employees who are in the Central division.

Extending your Knowledge – The SumIF Function

SumIF – This function will *sum* a range of cells that meet the specified criteria. This works very much the same as the AverageIF function.

=SumIF(range, criteria, [sum_range])   Function Category: Math & Trigonometry

* The range contains the cells that should be summed.

*The Criteria contains the value that specifies which cells will be summed.

*The Sum_range is an optional parameter. It specifies the actual set of cells to sum. If it is not included, the cells in the range are summed. The Sum_range parameter would be used when you want to use the cells in the range to determine "what" rows meet the criteria, but the actual cell contents to be summed are located in a different range. This is illustrated in the second example below.

---

*Examples:
Assume your worksheet contains rows of employee data. Column A contains the employee ID, Column B contains the Division to which they are assigned, and Column C contains their annual salary.

=SumIF(C1:C75,">35,000")
this will total of all the salaries for employee who earn more than $35,000.

=SumIF(B1:B75,"Central",C1:C75)
this will total of all the salaries for employees who are in the Central division.

You will have a chance to work with the AverageIF and SumIF functions in the end of tutorial exercises. For now, let's return to finishing the Demographic Analysis Worksheet.

Creating a Pie Chart

The last task on this worksheet is to create a pie chart to visually display the distribution of spreadsheet skills. Creating a pie chart is very similar to creating the column chart in the calorie intake spreadsheet. The pie chart you will create does not display a legend, but instead shows the category names as data labels and includes the percentage on the chart.

Practice:
Select the cell range for the data to be graphed. Include the cells that have the labels in your range. Did you select B464 through C468?

Select the **Insert Tab > Charts Group > Pie > 2D Pie > Pie** option.

On the Layout Tab make the following changes:
- Add a Chart Title
- Remove the legend
- Choose **More Data Label Options** from the **Data Labels** icon. The Format Data Label dialog box, as shown in Figure T2.12, will appear. Choose to display the Category Names, Percentage, and Leader Lines. Position the label at the Outside End.

Figure T2.12   Format Data Label Dialog Box

Your worksheet should now look similar to the one shown in Figure T2.10. Make any necessary adjustments to adjust the chart size or placement. Some of your pie pieces may not show the *leader lines* – the lines that connect a category label to the piece. Excel automatically displays leader lines only when the label placement is away from the pie piece. Save your Workbook.

You now have a spreadsheet that uses statistical functions to compute summary data and graphically displays that data. In Example 2 you learned spreadsheet skills in creating statistical functions and creating a pie chart. You will have a chance to reinforce these skills in some of the end of tutorial exercises.

LEARNING CHECK

Be sure you can *describe how to use logical functions like IF, AND, and OR * create a column chart * use statistical functions like CountIF to analyze data * create a pie chart

IMPROVING FUNCTIONALITY BY CONTROLLING DATA INPUT

In the last section you were introduced to several logical and statistical functions, along with learning how to create two different types of charts. In this section we will explore ways to make a worksheet less prone to user error and easier to use by automating some tasks. To help you learn these new features, they will be explained in the context of an example.

Example 3: Customer Order Form Spreadsheet

For smaller businesses, or tasks, you can use a spreadsheet to help automate the ordering process. Hair Today is a small retail business that supplies hair care accessories to a variety of clients. They have been entering orders on paper-based forms, but are finding that they are often quoting the wrong prices to customers. This causes unneeded confusion and a loss of potential revenue. To minimize these problems, they would like to have an electronic order form built that will allow them to only pick products that they currently sell, and have the system look up and automatically complete the entry for the unit cost. Additionally the order form uses formulas to calculate the extended price, subtotal, discount, tax and total. This increases the accuracy of the overall order process. After talking with the owners and reviewing their business processes, the systems analyst has created the screen design (shown in Figure T2.13) for their new system. Notice the use of a drop down list for the Item Description.

The last project you will work on in this tutorial is to build the order form for Hair Today shown in Figure T2.13.   You are going to create a new workbook to build this project. This project will help you learn how to include the following features in the order form:
- Data validation to create a drop down list
- Data validation to restrict data entry values
- Lookup functions to automate calculations on the form.

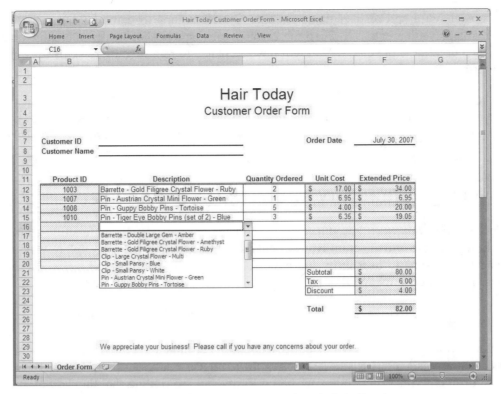

Figure T2.13 A customer order form built in Excel

Practice:

Open a new workbook in Excel.

On Sheet1 enter the titles and labels in rows 1 through 11. Remember to use "Center Across Selection" in the alignment for the Titles.

Don't enter any of the data values shown in Figure T2.13 or the needed formulas. You will learn how to do that in this section.

Remove the gridlines from the worksheet and add the border around the appropriate cells.

Enter the labels for Subtotal, Tax, Discount and Total. Add the customer message in row 29.

Enter the =NOW() function in F7 so that the order form will always enter the current date when an order is entered.

Rename the Sheet1 Tab where you have entered the form structure to read Order Form.

Delete the tabs for Sheet2 and Sheet3.

Don't worry if the formatting of all the cells is not completed. That can be finished towards the end of the project.

When developing a worksheet it is important to think about the overall layout. One of the principles of good spreadsheet design is to create an area in your worksheet where you include all of the constants used in your spreadsheet. Recall that constants are the data values that are not calculated and are often referenced elsewhere in the worksheet. In this example the sales tax rate and discount rate would be considered constants. Additionally, in this assignment you will be entering a list of product information related to the products that Hair Today sells. In order to add all the desired functionality into the order form, enter the information shown in Figure T2.14 into your spreadsheet. Experts offer different recommendations as to whether these constants and assumptions should be isolated onto a separate worksheet. Since we have not yet covered working with data on multiple sheets, the assumptions and constants will be entered on the same worksheet.

> *Practice:*
> Enter the comments, labels, and assumptions data shown in Figure T2.14 in your spreadsheet. Enter this data several rows below the customer message in row 29.

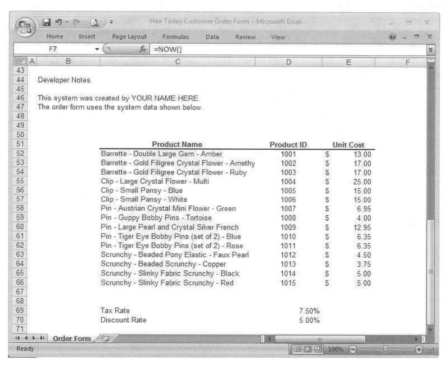

Figure T2.14 The Assumptions and Data that will be used in your spreadsheet calculations

Data Validation

Data Validation is a powerful feature offered in Excel to help control what data your user can enter. This is very helpful in preventing data entry errors. For example, when you provide your users with a drop down list of State Names, the user won't be able to misspell a state or enter a state that doesn't exist. In the Customer Order Form spreadsheet you will use data validation to create a drop-down list and to restrict data entry values.

Your first task will be to restrict the item description cells (C12 through C20) to only allow users to choose products that are shown in a drop down list. The product information that you just entered will be used to populate the drop down list choices.

Drop-Down List Data Validation

> **Practice:**
>
> Select cells C12 through C20 – This is the cell range to which we will apply the Data Validation
>
> Select the **Data Tab** > **Data Tools Group** > **Data Validation**> **Data Validation** option
>   The Data Validation dialog box, as shown in Figure T2.15, will be displayed.
>
> Complete the following choices on the Settings Tab so that your choices match those shown in the figure.
>   Allow: choose **LIST**
>   Source: =**$C$52:$C$66** – this is where you define the range of your possible choices.
>   Note: The source matches the cell locations of the product data entered from Figure T2.14.
>
> Select **OK** when finished.

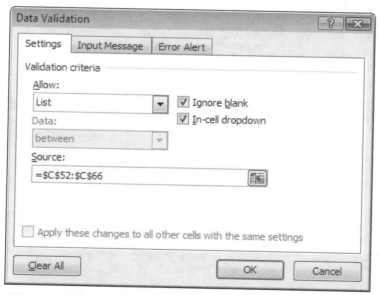

Figure T2.15 The completed Data Validation Dialog Box for a drop down list

Keep in mind that you do not include the top row where you have "labeled" your list in the range. Also note that you must start your source entry with an = sign. Make the range absolute so that it will be correct for all of your Item Description cells.

Practice:
Select cell C12. Do you see the drop down arrow appear in the right hand corner of the cell?
Pick one of the products to add to your order.

Your second task is to add a different type of data validation to the cells in the Quantity
Ordered column. This validation will restrict the amount entered to whole numbers, with a range
of 1 through 100.

Type and Range Restriction Data Validation

Practice:
Select cells D12 through D20 – This is the cell range to which we will apply the Data
Validation

Select the **DataTab > Data Tools Group > Data Validation** option
        The Data Validation dialog box, as shown in Figure T2.16 will be displayed.

Complete the following choices on the Settings Tab so that your choices match those shown in
the figure.
        Allow: choose **Whole Number**
        Data: choose **between**
        Minimum: enter **1**
        Maximum: enter **100**

Select **OK** when finished.

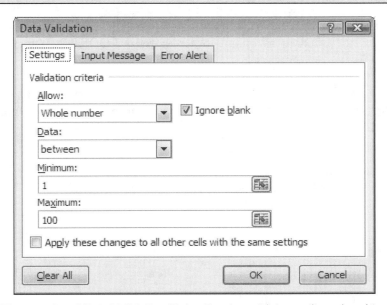

Figure T2.16 The completed Data Validation Dialog Box to restrict quantity ordered to whole numbers

Practice:
Enter 5 into cell D12. Enter X into D12.

Did you get an error message? If you don't like the default message provided by Excel you can change it on the Error Alert Tab of the Data Validation dialog box.

VLookup Function

In order to automate as much of the order form as possible, the owners of Hair Today want the order form to automatically fill in the product ID and the unit cost when an item is selected. This can be accomplished using the **VLookUp function** in Excel. The VLookUp function looks for a match in the first column of an array or table and then moves across the row to return the value of a corresponding cell. The general form of a VLookUp function is:

=VLOOKUP(lookup_value, table_array, col_index_number,[range lookup])

* The Lookup_value is the cell in your worksheet that you want to look up in the table

* The Table_Array is the range of rows/columns that contain the VLookUp Data Table

* The Col_Index_Num is the number of the column in the VLookUp Table that has the resulting value [the left most column is 1, the next column is 2, etc.]

*The Range Lookup is an optional parameter (indicated by the brackets.) You use the range_lookup to indicate whether you want the VLookUp to find an exact match or an approximate match bv entering True or False. If you omit the Range Lookup parameter, Excel treats it the same as if you had entered True.

  If you specify TRUE, Excel will look for an exact match, but will return an approximate match if an exact match is not found. The approximate match is the next largest value that is less than the lookup value. When using the TRUE parameter, the table array must be sorted in ascending order or the VLOOKUP may not give the correct answer.

  If your specify FALSE, then Excel will **only** look for an exact match. When using the FALSE parameter your table array values do not have to be sorted in ascending order. If an exact match is not found, the error code #N/A is returned.

Create the formula for the Product ID cells. Let's analyze the VLookUp formula that will be used in cell B12:   **= VLOOKUP(C12,$C$52:$E$66,2,False)**

Examining the formula:

C12 – this is cell you want to look up. In this case it is the Item Description for the row

$C$52:$E$66 – this is the table array, the area in the worksheet where you store the list of all the possible items. Recall that in the Data Validation above you used part of the table array (C52:C66) to populate the drop down list. It is always a good idea to reuse as much as possible when creating spreadsheets. Since the table array location will not change, it is important to make it an absolute reference so that you can copy the formula correctly.

2 – this is the column index number. Your table array has 3 columns (the product name, product ID, and the unit cost.) The product name is the left most column (1). Since you want the VLookUp to return the correct product ID, use the second column as the column index number.

False – you are looking for an exact match in the table.

Practice:
Enter the formula   **= VLOOKUP(C12,$C$52:$E$66,2,False)** into cell B12.

Did it find the correct product ID for the product you had selected in C12?

Practice:
Copy the formula in B12 to the rest of the Product ID cells

What happens to the product ID cells of rows where you have not selected an item? Does it display **#N/A**? This means that Excel cannot find a match, which is understandable.

Can you think of a way to fix this problem? It is useful if you can learn to "borrow" from other solutions and adapt them as needed to current situations. Have you encountered a similar problem earlier? Recall that you used the IF function to see if a cell was empty. Now you can use it to check if the item description cell is empty. If it is empty, then leave the product ID cell empty, otherwise perform the VLookUp. How might that formula look for cell B12?

=IF(C12="","",VLOOKUP(C12,$C$52:$D$66,2,FALSE))

The formula is simply an IF function. In this case the logical test is whether C12 is empty (C12=""). If that test is TRUE, then we want cell B12 to remain empty (""). If that test is FALSE (e.g. C12 has a description in it, then perform the VLookUp function.

Practice:
Enter the formula shown above into cell B12. The formula now should work correctly in all instances.

Copy the formula in cell B12 to the remaining Product ID cells. The #N/A should have been removed from the affected cells.

Notice the power and flexibility that you have in Excel to combine different functions to accomplish sophisticated tasks.

Be sure to save your worksheet. Your worksheet is not yet finished, but it should look closer to the one shown in Figure T2.13. You will complete the rest of the worksheet in one of the end of tutorial exercises. You now have a spreadsheet that helps minimize data entry errors and controls when functions will display a result.

In this section you learned a variety of spreadsheet skills that can be used to create a robust spreadsheet application. You explored how to have Excel validate date entry, helping to improve data accuracy. You also saw how Excel can automatically enter values for you based on the VLookUp function. In addition you learned how to combining two functions. You will have a chance to reinforce these skills in some of the end of tutorial exercises.

LEARNING CHECK
Be sure you can *use data validation to create a drop down list * use data validation to restrict the type of data that can be entered * explain how the vlookup function works

STEPS TO CREATING A SPREADSHEET

Through the work you have done so far in this tutorial, you can get a sense of how complex it can be to develop a spreadsheet-based information system. In Chapter 2 you were introduced to the Sarbanes-Oxley Act, which requires corporations to enact a variety of controls related to financial reporting. This includes verifying the accuracy of all of their spreadsheet based systems. Spreadsheets are susceptible to a variety of errors. These include entering the wrong value or referencing the wrong cell, entering an incorrect formula due to a mistake in reasoning, and leaving out a critical part of the spreadsheet. To avoid these problems it is critical that spreadsheet developers follow basic guidelines. You had a chance to see some of these potential problems as you worked on the different spreadsheets in this tutorial. Spreadsheet development is usually not as formalized as following the phases in the SDLC, however you will most definitely benefit if you follow a structured development process as described below.

Analyze the Business Problem

Understanding what the spreadsheet needs to do is the first step in creating a solution. This is essentially the "analysis" phase. While on the surface this may seem quite easy, this is usually where beginning spreadsheet developers stumble. It will be important for you to have a clear understanding of "what" the purpose of the spreadsheet is; this includes understanding what each formula is supposed to do. Only after you are clear on the purpose will you be able to start creating the solution – developing the actual Excel formulas. In this analysis phase, the complexity of the problem, and how the solution fits into the business, will influence how many users in the company you meet with, the extent of existing documentation you review, and the formality of the documentation you will be required to create.

Develop the Spreadsheet Framework

Once you have a clear understanding of what the system needs to do, you can begin to focus on how to design the solution. Obviously our discussion is centered on solutions where you have determined a spreadsheet would be the appropriate application. Designing the solution includes identifying the needed outputs of the system including whether they will be screen-based, printed, or some combination, identifying inputs that will be provided by the user, and creating a worksheet layout that minimizes user errors and maximizes the effectiveness of the system. Presenting quantitative information is challenging, so it is important to choose a layout and format to help the user understand the spreadsheet. Due to the nature of a spreadsheet application, it is quite common to use a prototyping approach to development. This would include building part of the system, receiving feedback from your user, making adjustments, and adding functionality.

Creating the spreadsheet framework involves deciding on the layout of the worksheet. Some of the common decisions made at this stage include choosing appropriate titles and labels, selecting the placement of different areas, identifying assumptions and isolating them in the worksheet, determining whether to use multiple worksheets and choosing formatting characteristics such as font style, font size, color selection, displaying gridlines, etc.

Enter the Formulas

Formulas are the power within a spreadsheet. You should write formulas that are simple and easy to read. Use functions as appropriate. Use references to a separate assumptions area instead of hard coding in constants. A benefit of this is that when the constant values change, you don't need to go back and change a formula. Instead, you just change a value in a cell.

Because some formulas can be very long and complex, it is important to provide a set of documentation notes that explains how and why certain formulas were structured as they are. Don't forget that when someone else uses your spreadsheet several months from now, they will not know why you did things. A poorly designed spreadsheet can cause frustrations for users and cause wasted time in performing calculations.

Verify for Completeness and Accuracy

Once you have entered all of your formulas you must test them to verify that they produce the correct results. You should enter test data and compare the results to what you know the answer should be. If you have copied formulas, be sure to check the result of the original formula and the copied formula to ensure that the correct combination of absolute and relative values was used.

When creating test data you want to make sure that you use enough to test a variety of situations. This is especially important when you have a logical function. You will want to enter test data for each of the possible conditions to check that each condition comes up with a correct result. For example, in the Calorie Intake spreadsheet you should verify that the formula in column F that calculates the Fat Percentage produces the correct answer, but also that it leaves the cell empty if the Calorie cell is empty. Another test you should do for that formula is to see what happens if someone enters text data into the calorie cell. Open up that spreadsheet and change the

175 calories in cell C3 to the word "ten". What happens to the result of your formula? Did it display #VALUE!? This is a perfect example of the need for testing. You built the function to check if the cell had a value in it, but you didn't control for text data. You will have a chance to correct this problem in the End of Tutorial exercises.

In addition to checking formula results, you will want to check the overall spreadsheet for completeness and accuracy. Spell check titles and labels. Verify accuracy of any constants entered into an assumption area. Check that column widths and formatting are appropriate. For example, enter a value that is larger than you might expect to ensure that you don't end up with ##### displaying in a cell that is not wide enough. If your user will be printing the results of the spreadsheet, you must be certain to check the Page Settings so that a Print Area is defined, the Orientation and Scaling are correct, and a Header and Footer are included as needed. Additionally, if color has been used in the spreadsheet to provide information, you need to check that a black and white printout still conveys the same meaning.

Document

Documentation describing the purpose, design and functionality of a spreadsheet is a critical part of the overall spreadsheet development process. The amount of documentation will vary depending on the complexity of the overall spreadsheet. As mentioned earlier, the Sarbanes-Oxley Act requires corporations to enact a variety of controls related to financial reporting including verifying the accuracy of all of their spreadsheet based systems. Documentation is one part of this process.

Documentation generally includes information about the purpose of the spreadsheet, any specific features built into the spreadsheet such as data validation, macros, worksheet protection, etc., the comments describing what the different functions and formulas do, information about the author, and a version history that describes any changes that have been made on the spreadsheet. It is important to include information about assumptions you made in designing the spreadsheet and any limitations you encountered.

When deciding what should go into your documentation, think about it from the perspective that the documentation should help a future developer understand what the current spreadsheet does, and why it was built a certain way. Look back at the Demographic Analysis Spreadsheet you worked on earlier in this tutorial. You were not provided with very much documentation to explain what each column represented. If someone gave you that spreadsheet and asked you to perform more data analysis, it would be very difficult. For the Demographic Analysis Spreadsheet, it would be important for the documentation to contain a copy of the original survey questions including the possible answer choices.

When completing your documentation you need to decide where to put the documentation. It could be included on separate documentation worksheets, in the File Properties of the spreadsheet, or in a separate documentation file. If the documentation is not too extensive then it is usually best to keep it within the spreadsheet file.

General Guidelines

Most of the guidelines suggested here have been introduced through examples that you worked on in this tutorial. They are summarized here to provide a checklist as you continue to gain experience in developing your own spreadsheet solutions.

- Align cells for readability
- Use appropriate formatting to aid the reader in understanding cell content
- Use formatting to distinguish cells for input data from cells showing results of formulas.
- Simplify formulas
- Use an assumptions area to enter constants used in the worksheet
- Don't use constants in formulas – reference them
- Use uniform column widths
- Use mixed-case for column labels
- Avoid using Merge and Center. This can cause problems later on in trying to locate cell contents. Instead use "Center Across Selection." Recall that this is found on the Format Cells dialog box > Alignment tab > Horizontal Text Alignment.

In this section you studied the different steps involved in a structured spreadsheet development process. As you have seen from the work you performed during the tutorial, it is easy to make mistakes when building a spreadsheet. Learning how to minimize your chance for creating errors during the development process, as well as learning how to minimize the chance that your users will make mistakes while using the spreadsheet, will help you create efficient and effective spreadsheets.

LEARNING CHECK
Be sure you can *describe the steps to creating a spreadsheet * explain the importance of ensuring that a spreadsheet produces correct results * explain the importance of documentation

WRAPPING IT UP

In this tutorial you learned about spreadsheet programs and how businesses use them. You have seen the complexities involved with creating and managing large amounts of data inside of a spreadsheet and have a better understanding of how to use them to solve common business problems. You have seen how systems development concepts can be applied to creating prototype systems using spreadsheets. In the next few tutorials we will explore additional ways to manage data through additional features of spreadsheets, programming, web tools and databases.

Study Questions Summary

1. What are some common functions and features in a spreadsheet?
   - Logical functions, such as =IF, can be used to have excel evaluate the contents of a cell or cell range
   - Conditional formatting can be used to apply different cell formats based on the contents of a cell

- Statistical functions, such as average, max, and min are useful in summarizing large sets of data
- Graphs can be used to provide a visual summary of the data

2. How can you improve the functionality of a spreadsheet by controlling user input?
   - Data validation can be used to create a drop down list to limit the choices available to a user
   - Data validation can be used to check if a value entered into a cell meets criteria that has been established for data entry values
   - Lookup functions allow Excel to compare cell values against a set of entries, and determine the appropriate result
   - You can combine functions together, for example you can use the VLookup inside of the IF statement

3. How do you develop and implement a spreadsheet-based system?
   - Sarbanes-Oxley has increased the focus on companies to provide verification that all of their spreadsheets provide accurate results
   - Understanding the business problem is the critical first step before you start building a spreadsheet solution
   - The design phase of a spreadsheet system includes developing the spreadsheet framework and creating the formulas
   - Identifying a robust set of test data is important in ensuring that your spreadsheet works in a variety of situations
   - Documentation of your spreadsheet design provides important information when modifications need to be made in the future

Solutions to Tutorial Activities

UNDERSTANDING IT?
Exploring the CountIF pg. 282-283

1. Yes the formula will work correctly. The range is valid and the criteria is correct.

2. This formula will not give the correct answer in cell C465.
   - The range uses Relative Cell References. Relative Cell References will change when the formula is copied. This will result in incorrect results.
   - Since the criteria is hard-coded, if you copy the formula down to cell C465 you would need to edit the criteria to count the "Some Skill" students.

3. The formula in C465 would be: **=COUNTIF(V3:V452, "Beginner ")**
4. No. Assuming that the word Beginner (as entered in the cells in V2:V451) was entered without a space, then Excel will not think that "Beginner" is equal to "Beginner ".
5. The formula **=COUNTIF($V$2:$V$451,B464)** works.

   This formula fixes the two problems. Absolute Cell References will not adjust when copied, ensuring that the range remains the same. Additionally, the criteria now references the cell B464, which contains the criteria "Beginner."

6.   The formula =**COUNTIF(V$2:V$451,B464)** works.

This formula uses Mixed Cell References. Because we are only copying the formula down column C (from C464 to C468), it is not necessary to hold the column Absolute.

Key Terms

Page Number references are included in parentheses

AND Function (270)	Data Type Restriction (291)	OR Function (272)
AverageIF Function (284)	Data Validation (289)	Pie Chart (285)
Column Chart (274)	Drop-Down List (290)	Source Data (276)
Compound Condition (270)	IF Function (267)	SumIF Function (285)
Conditional Formatting (272)	ISBLANK Function (269)	VLookUp Function (292)
CountIF Function (281)	Logical Functions (267)	Wrap Text (280)

Multiple Choice Questions

1.   In Excel, if a cell shows ##### it means that _____.
   a.   Your formula has a syntax error
   b.   The row is too short to show the number at the current font size
   c.   The column is too narrow to show all the digits of the number
   d.   Either B or C

2.   You have a spreadsheet that contains one row of data for each customer. The columns contain data such as the Customer ID, Customer name and city. If you wanted to find out how many customers provided the information about the city that they lived in (they didn't' leave the value in their City column blank), what Excel function could you use for that column?
   a.   Count   b.   CountA   c.   CountIF   d.   CountIFS

3.   What Excel feature can you use if you want to automatically change the font color and size of different cells based on the contents of the cell?
   a.   Conditional formatting
   b.   Data validation
   c.   Statistical functions
   d.   Absolute cell addressing

4.   What is wrong with the following function: =IF(A1>A2,MAX(B1:B25),"Decline")
   a.   The MAX function; a function cannot be an argument in another function
   b.   The word "Decline"; text cannot be used as an argument in a function
   c.   The word "Decline"; it will cause an error because it is inside of quotation marks
   d.   Nothing is wrong with the function as written

5. What is the result of typing the D5*2 into a cell in Excel?
   a. The entry is invalid and an error message will show
   b. The result of multiplying D5 and 2 will show
   c. The result is the same as typing in =D5*2
   d. The text D5*2 will shown in the cell
   e. Both B and C are correct

6. In the worksheet shown below, =Vlookup(G6,E15:G19,3) has been entered into H6. What will display in cell H6 as the result?

	A	B	C	D	E	F	G	H	I
1									
2	Student Gradebook								
3									
4							Adjusted		
5	Student Name	Exam 1	Exam 2	Exam 3	Total	Average	Average		
6	Barbara	65	80	85	230	77%	79%		
7	Mark	80	78	81	239	80%	82%		
8	Anthony	62	75	80	217	72%	74%		
9	Carlos	70	77	79	226	75%	77%		
10	Raquel	65	72	60	197	66%	68%		
11	Jacob	91	86	93	270	90%	92%		
12									
13									
14	Adjustment Percent	2%							
15					0	Fail	F	0.0	
16					0.6	Pass	D	1.0	
17					0.7	Average	C	2.0	
18					0.8	Above Avg	B	3.0	
19					0.9	Excellent	A	4.0	

   a. 2.0
   b. Average
   c. C
   d. An error message
   e. None of the above

Answers:
1. c   2. b   3. a   4. d   5. d   6. c

Review Questions

1. What is the difference between a formula and a function?
2. Explain what each of the following error messages indicates:
   a. #N/A
   b. ####
   c. #DIV/0
3. What is the IF function used for?
4. Explain why you needed to combine the AND inside of the IF in the Calorie Intake Worksheet?

5. What is the VLookUp function used for?
6. Describe the importance of data validation.
7. List and briefly explain the steps to creating a spreadsheet.
8. Pick three different standard types of Excel charts. Describe what each chart type is used to display and provide an example of when you might use each type.
9. Briefly explain the differences between the following Excel functions: Count, CountA, CountBlank, CountIF, and CountIFS. Use the Excel Help feature to assist you in finding the answer.

Projects

1. Complete the Customer Order Form Worksheet.
    Functionality requirements:
    - Enter a formula in the Unit Cost column that will look up the correct price based on the product that was selected. Ensure that the formula does not display an error message if a product has not yet been selected. Hint: Use the formula for the Product ID column as a model.
    - Enter a formula to calculate the extended price. Copy the formula into all of the cells in the entry area. Ensure that the formula does not display an error message when a product has not yet been ordered on a particular row.
    - Compute the subtotal
    - Calculate the tax owed on the subtotal. Remember that the tax rate is stored in the assumptions area. Don't hard-code the tax rate into the formula
    - Calculate the discount. Remember that the discount rate is stored in the assumptions areas. If the subtotal is greater than $75.00 the customer earns a discount, otherwise the discount is 0.
    - Compute the overall order total.

    Formatting requirements (use *HELP* if you are not certain how to complete all of the following tasks):
    - Remove the gridlines from the worksheet
    - Add borders to define the data entry spaces (e.g. for customer number) and to show the grid area for entering items on the order.
    - Format all dollar values as currency

2. Build the following spreadsheet to calculate the total number of calendar days that an employee was employed on the Carson Middle School Project and the total number of actual days that they worked on that project.

Carson Middle School Project				
Employee	Start Date	End Date	Days Between	Workdays Between
Margaret Williams	7/10/2007	3/30/2008	264	189
Drew Dougherty	7/12/2007	12/5/2007	146	105
Laura Carp	8/15/2007	3/1/2008	199	143
Roger Morales	11/1/2007	1/10/2008	70	51

- Use a simple arithmetic formula to calculate the difference between the end date and the start date to determine the "Days Between" value.

- Use the Networkdays function to calculate the number of days that an employee actually worked on the project. Assume that there were no sickdays and no scheduled holidays during the time period. Use the Help feature to learn more about the Networkdays function.

3. Open the Calorie Intake Spreadsheet you created earlier in the tutorial. As you will recall, the formula for the Fat Percentage (column F) was designed to not perform the calculation unless the cells involved in the formula had a value in them.

   What happens if someone has entered "text" data into the cells involved in the formula?

   In cell C3, type the word "xxx" into the cell. Did the value in cell F3 change to display #VALUE!? This is because your formula didn't control for a user entering text data.
   There are two ways that you can control this error.
   Use data validation to prevent your user from entering text data.
   OR change the formula so that also checks to see if the value is not text data.

   Change the formula in cell F3 to do option 1. Change the cells in C4, D4, and D5 to use data validation.

   Which choice do you think is a better solution? Why?

4. Research the impact of Sarbanes-Oxley regarding the need to verify the accuracy of spreadsheets. Write a one-page summary of your findings.

TUTORIAL **3**

Extending Spreadsheet Development

PLANNING AHEAD
After reading Tutorial 3, you should be able to answer these questions in your own words

STUDY QUESTIONS
What features can you use to help manage large sets of data?
How do you work with multiple worksheets?
How can you analyze data using PivotTables?

LEARNING PREVIEW

In Tutorial 2 you learned how organizations use spreadsheets as one tool to develop information systems applications. You explored some of the basic skills used in creating a spreadsheet. You also learned how the systems development concepts can be applied to the steps that a spreadsheet developer should use to ensure that they are building correct spreadsheet solutions. Ideally, you followed those steps when you were working on some of the projects at the end of Tutorial 2. These steps become even more critical when you begin to work on problems that require larger and more complicated spreadsheets. In this tutorial some of the spreadsheets will involve hundreds of rows of data, more than 30 columns, multiple worksheets, and more complicated equations. Analyzing the business problem, thinking critically about the best way to organize and develop the spreadsheet framework, and creating and documenting accurate formulas are skills that must be further developed and practiced to ensure that you learn how to build spreadsheet-based information systems that work correctly. In this tutorial you will learn additional skills that will help you solve more complex business problems using a spreadsheet.

VISUAL ORGANIZATION OF TUTORIAL

Study Question 1	Study Question 2	Study Question 3
Data Commands	Multiple Worksheets	PivotTables
• Sorting Data • Calculating Subtotals • Working with Tables	• Using Different Worksheets • Using Functions to Recode Values • Referencing Cells on Separate Worksheets • Named Cell References	• Creating a PivotTable • Completing the Row, Column and Value Areas • Refining the PivotTable
Learning Check 1	Learning Check 2	Learning Check 3

DATA COMMANDS

Spreadsheets are often used to manage large quantities of data. Excel provides several different tools to help manage data. Let's start by exploring some of the options on the Data Tab. In Tutorial 2 you completed some statistical analysis and graphing on the data related to Student Demographics. You will use a modified version of the Demographic Analysis Workbook for several activities in Tutorial 3.

Example 1: Complete Demographic Analysis Spreadsheet

> *Practice:*
> Download the **Complete Demographic Analysis** spreadsheet from Blackboard and open it. A screen shot of that spreadsheet is shown in Figure T3.1.

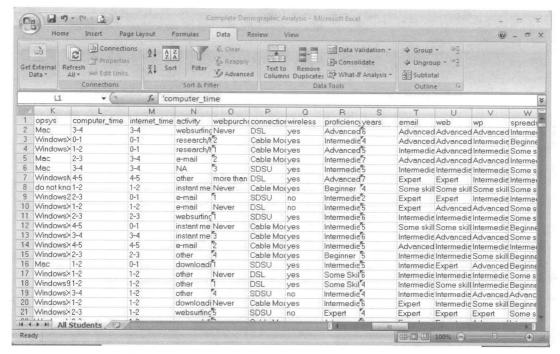

Figure T3.1 Complete Demographic Analysis Worksheet

Before you jump into the Data Tab options you need to spend some time understanding the contents of the Complete Demographic Analysis spreadsheet. Recall that the first step in developing a spreadsheet-based information system is to analyze the business problem. In this case you need to find out about the contents of the spreadsheet data and what analysis needs to be accomplished. The spreadsheet contains data about students in a class very similar to yours. The data was collected so the faculty in the College of Business can analyze changes in the technology skills of incoming students. At the beginning of the semester each student completed a survey in which they answered questions related to their background in using a variety of computer applications and technology-oriented products. Figure T3.2 shows several of the questions that were answered by the students.

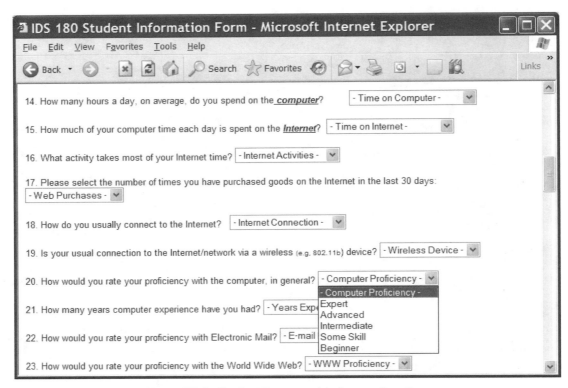

Figure T3.2 Student Demographic Survey Questions

After looking at the survey questions, you can now see that the columns shown in Figure T3.1 correspond to the set of survey questions shown in Figure T3.2 (e.g. column L is question 14, column M is question 15, etc.) Navigate around the worksheet looking at the column headings and different row values. Some of the data may be intuitive to figure out, such as **Sex**, **Age** and **Major**. But other data, such as **Webpage** in column AM may not be so clear. By the way, the question in column AM is "Have you ever created a webpage?" Hopefully you can see the importance of including documentation that explains the contents of your worksheet. It would be extremely difficult for you to make much progress on analyzing this data if you were not provided with more information about the different columns of data. You can access a complete description of all of the survey questions and possible answer choices on Blackboard. As you explore the demographic spreadsheet, notice that 624 students, in 3 different class sections (The professor column), completed the survey. As a result, the worksheet contains 624 rows of student data. In this tutorial you will help do some analysis work on this spreadsheet data.

Sorting Data

When you have large amount of data, you will frequently wish to sort the data to help in organizing the contents. A quick way to sort data is to select a cell in the column you wish to have sorted. You can then select the Sort A to Z or Sort Z to A icons from the Sort & Filter Group on the Data Tab. This will work correctly if your data range does not have any blank rows or columns because Excel will recognize that the surrounding rows and columns should remain together. You can also choose to sort by selecting the Sort icon from Sort & Filter Group on the

Data Tab. When you sort following this method you are provided with the ability to sort on text, numbers, dates and colors using up to 64 different levels in a single sort.

Practice:
Select a cell inside of the data range.

Select the **Data Tab > Sort & Filter Group > Sort** option to sort the data in the demographic worksheet by **Major** (A to Z) and **Age** (Largest to Smallest.)
When you select the Sort icon, a Sort dialog box will appear, as shown in Figure T3.3. The Dialog Box automatically has one sort level added. Based on the way our data is organized, each sort level will represent a column of data.

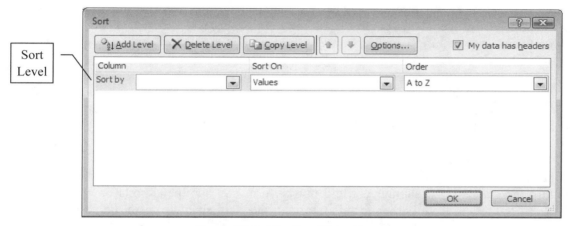

Figure T3.3   The Sort Dialog Box

In the Sort dialog box you will indicate the different sort *criteria*, or conditions, you wish to use. Each criteria will be placed on a different sort level. Excel will also estimate the data range and whether the first row contains column headers. If Excel did not estimate the data range correctly, **Cancel** the sort. In that situation you will need to select the range of data prior to starting the Sort command. The most likely reason why Excel would not estimate the correct range is that your data contains many blank cells or blank rows. Assuming that the correct range was identified, complete the sort by making the following selections:

Practice:
1st sort level: Sort by Major; on Values; Order A to Z.

Click the Add Level Icon

2nd sort level: Sort by Age; on Values; Order Largest to Smallest

Click **OK** to perform the sort.

You will need a sort level for each column of data you want to use in your sort. Excel will begin by sorting the data based on the first sort level. A second sort level will only be used in cases of a tie on the first level. In our example, the sort on Age will only be done in cases where there is more than one student in a particular major.

Keep the data in this sorted order as you will use it in the next section. Sorting can be useful to help provide some structure to your data. Typically Excel will ignore the case of the text entered into the cells when it performs a sort. However if you wish to perform a **case sensitive** sort you can designate that choice by selecting the Options button on the Sort dialog box and selecting the Case Sensitive option.

Calculating Subtotals

Often you will want to calculate subtotals based on different groupings of data. You could perform a sort and then insert new rows in which you could enter formulas to perform the calculations. However that wouldn't be a good choice because these rows would affect your ability to sort in the future since they would be treated as if they were regular rows of data. If you removed the new rows, you would no longer have the subtotals available.

A much better choice is to use the Subtotal feature to automatically calculate subtotals and grand totals on different fields in your data range. Before you insert the automatic subtotals, you need to sort the data on the column(s) by which you want to subtotal.

Create a subtotal to count how many students have selected each major. Since the data will be grouped by major make certain that you have sorted the data by the major column before starting the subtotal. Assuming you did not perform any additional sorts or make any other changes to the data from earlier in this tutorial, your data should already be sorted on major. Once you have the data sorted correctly, follow these steps to create the subtotals:

Practice:
Select any cell in the data range

Select the **Data Tab > Outline Group > Subtotal** option. This will open the Subtotal dialog box.

When the subtotal dialog box first displays, Excel automatically marks the settings to create a subtotal on the last field (column) in your data range. Sometimes that is the correct field. However when that is not the case, uncheck that last field and choose the correct field. You can have subtotals performed on more than one field. Also notice that the default function is Count. If you wish to perform another function, choose the correct one from the list.

Practice:
Complete the Subtotal dialog box so that the selections match those shown in Figure T3.4

Click OK to create the subtotals.

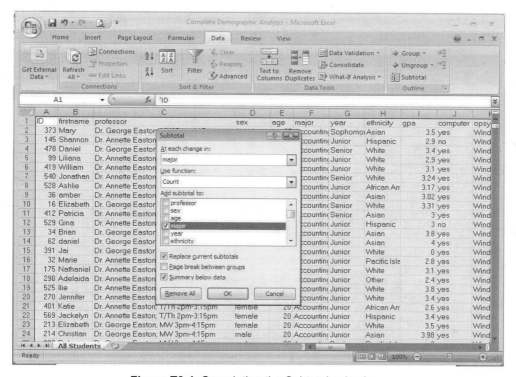

Figure T3.4 Completing the Subtotal selections

Figure T3.5 shows the results of the subtotal. Given the quantity of data, you will need to scroll down to row 64 in the worksheet to see the results. Notice that Excel has inserted a new row at each change in the major and has calculated the subtotal. When subtotals have been calculated Excel also creates an Outline structure so that you can control how much detail you wish to see.

The 1 2 3 **subtotal outline** symbols [1][2][3] are located near the row numbers on the left side of the spreadsheet. When subtotals are first generated, the view displays all of the data rows, the subtotal rows and the grand total row (button 3.) If you click the **1** button you will see only the grand total row. The **2** button shows the rows containing subtotals and the grand total. The **3** button shows each of the individual rows, the subtotals and the grand total. Select each of these buttons to see the effect. If you were going to print out a report of these subtotals you should adjust the column width of column E to display the full text of the different major choices.

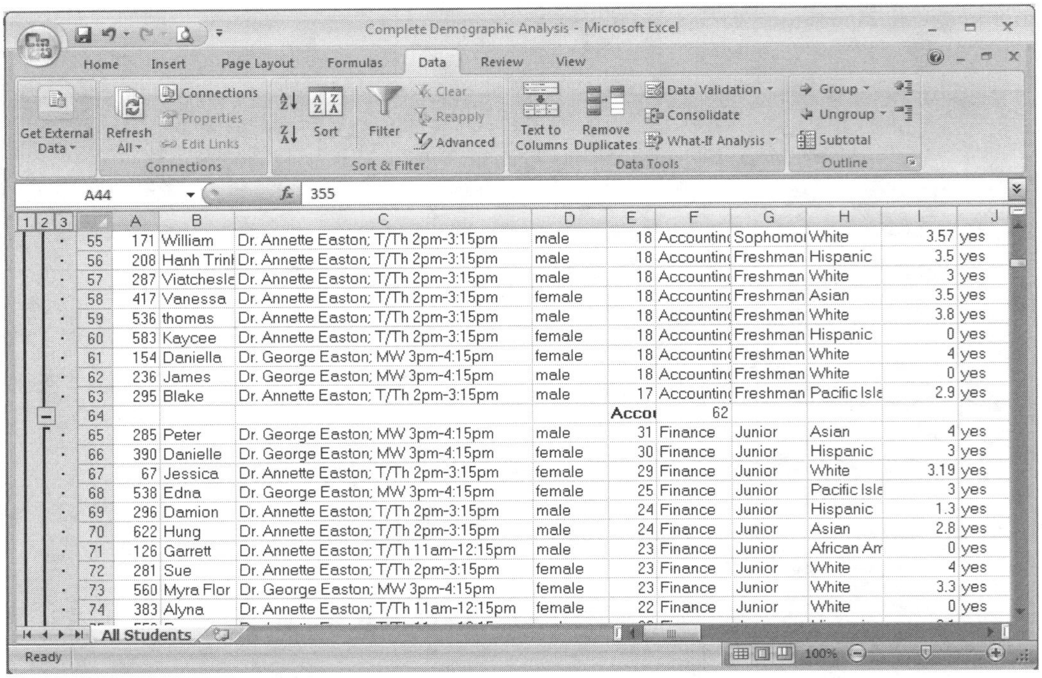

Figure T3.5 Subtotals are used to count how many students are in each major.

Complete the following **Integrate IT** exercise to reinforce your understanding about subtotals.

Integrate IT

➢ Create a new subtotal that in addition to showing the subtotals by major, will also include subtotals by gender within that major. Before performing the subtotal think about how the data must be sorted and what field you will select for the "At each change in" selection. How many male finance majors did you find? How many female international business majors did you find? Once you have the answer to these questions remove the current subtotals by selecting **Remove All** on the **Subtotal** dialog box.

➢ Create a new subtotal that will show the average GPA for each sex. Hint: Don't forget to remove the subtotals (from the prior subtotal command) before performing a new sort. Remember that you can Undo tasks if you make a mistake by selecting **Undo** on the **Quick Access Toolbar**. What is the average GPA for females? For males?

➢ Remove all subtotals and save your workbook.

Check your answers at the end of the chapter.

Subtotals are a great feature when you need to print reports that show totals. However when you have large quantities of data, Excel can be very slow to process the subtotals. Additionally, you have to remember to remove the subtotals when you are done. Otherwise you will have the subtotals included in the data range. Remember that you can remove subtotals by selecting **Remove All** on the **Subtotal** dialog box. Finally, if you have created a *Table* out of your data (tables are explained below), subtotals will not be available as a choice. You would first need to convert your table back into a data range.

Working with Tables

A **table** is simply a range of data that contains similar data stored in rows and columns. The data format of the demographic analysis workbook would be appropriate for defining as a table. Each row represents information about one student, and each column represents a piece of data about the student. A table provides you access to table features to sort, filter, query and manipulate the data. **Drop-down filters** are automatically added to the header row of a table. The drop-down filter is also called **Autofilter**. If records are added or deleted from the table, Excel automatically updates the table definition. Additionally, calculated columns and total rows can be easily created.

Before you can actually define a table in Excel, you must set up the data so that is will work as a table. There are several guidelines to follow:
- The first row in the range must contain labels, or field names, that describe the contents of each column.
- The field names can be a maximum of 255 characters long.
- Shorter field names are easier to remember.
- Leave a least one blank row below the data table and any other data below the table.

Create a table in the Demographic Analysis spreadsheet by performing these steps:

> *Practice:*
> Select the data, including the row of field names
>
> Select the **Insert Tab > Tables Group > Table** option. The Create Table dialog box, as shown in Figure T3.6, will appear.
>
> Confirm the data range and Click OK.

Figure T3.6 The Create Table Dialog Box

Figure T3.7 shows an example of what your worksheet will look like after the table has been created. Notice that a new Table Tools Design Tab has become visible on the Ribbon. This is another example of a contextual tab. Inside the table a formatting style has automatically been applied. You can change the formatting style by making another selecting in the Formatting Styles Group. Filter drop-down lists were automatically added to the header row. These arrows give you the ability to filter out records based on different criteria.

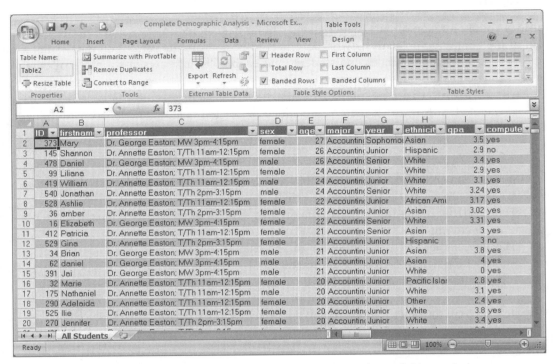

Figure T3.7 AutoFilter drop-down arrows appear when a list is created

---

Practice:
Click the arrow in the Age column. The Auto-Filter drop-down list options, as shown in Figure T3.8, will display.

Notice that you can choose to sort the data, select number filters, and show only certain choices (certain age values). If you select the number filters choice, the second list of choices will appear. In this second list you can select comparisons (such as greater than), show the top 10, or create custom criteria by which to filter the data.

Practice:
Deselect the check box for "Select All" in the area with the list of age values and select the check box for 17.

You should now be viewing only the records for 17 year old students. If you look at the row indicators at the left of the spreadsheet, do you see gaps in the row numbers? This indicates that some of the rows do not meet the criteria and are being hidden from view.

Practice:
Click on the arrow in the GPA Column and select Custom Criteria from the number filter option.

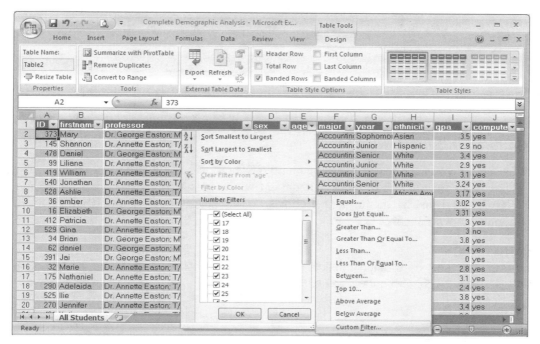

Figure T3.8 Choices available on the AutoFilter drop-down list

Figure T3.9 shows an example of a completed custom criteria window that will show only students who have a GPA <= 1.3 or >= 3.7.

Practice:
Enter the custom criteria shown in Figure T3.9 and select OK.

Since you did not remove the "age = 17" filter, the GPA filter is applied only to that narrower subset of data. You should have five 17-year old students with a GPA of 0 showing in the results.

Practice:
Click on the GPA filter and Clear the filter.

Click on the Age filter and Clear the filter.

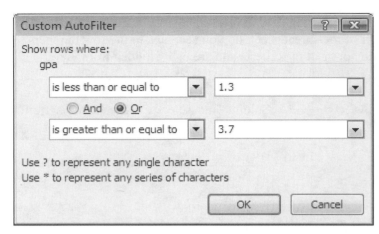

Figure T3.9 Custom AutoFilter allow the user to specify the criteria about which records should display

If you no longer want the data to be used as a table you can convert the table back into a range by selecting the **Table Tools Design Tab > Tools Group > Convert to Range** option.

In this section you have learned about using the Data tools to help you work with large sets of data. Being able to quickly sort through data, find records that are pertinent, and calculate subtotals are critical tasks. In the next section you will learn about working with data that is stored on multiple worksheets.

LEARNING CHECK
Be sure you can *sort data using multiple sort keys * correctly use subtotals in a worksheet * create tables * create custom criteria to filter a table

MULTIPLE WORKSHEETS

Up to now, the majority of your work has been with data stored on only one worksheet. When an organization has large quantities of data, they will often look for different ways to organize the data to make it more manageable. Because Excel gives you the capability to use more than one worksheet, some people choose to organize the data so that different segments of the data appear on different worksheets. Recall that at the bottom of the spreadsheet window you see the different worksheet tabs. When you open a new workbook, by default, Excel includes three sheets. You can insert an additional worksheet to the right of your existing worksheets by clicking the **Insert Worksheet tab** at the bottom of the screen. You can insert additional worksheets before an existing worksheet by selecting the worksheet and then selecting the **Home Tab > Cells Group > Insert > Insert Sheet** option. The number of worksheets you are allowed is limited by the available memory on your computer. Recall that in Tutorial 2 you learned how to remove an extra worksheet by selecting the **Home Tab > Cells Group > Delete > Delete Sheet** option. You also practiced renaming a worksheet by **right-clicking** the tabname on the sheet you wish to rename and then selecting **Rename**. As you begin to use multiple worksheets more extensively you will notice that selecting the **Home Tab > Cells Group > Format** option provides additional worksheet formatting options including **Hide**, **Unhide**, and **Tab Color**. Use these as needed to control the overall format of your workbook.

Let's explore multiple worksheets, and learn a few additional features, by continuing to work on the Demographic Analysis Workbook.

Practice:
Open the **Complete Demographic Analysis** spreadsheet if you have closed it from earlier.

You are going to learn the following skills by enhancing this workbook:
- Segregate the data onto different worksheets
- Use the Vlookup function to recode data values
- Create named cells
- Create formulas that work across different worksheets

The college faculty would like the data in the Complete Demographic Analysis spreadsheet to be grouped by class section but also would like to be able to provide some overall analysis. In order to complete this data analysis you will need to work with multiple worksheets. Planning the overall layout is important to ensure that the information produced is readable. Additionally, because there are so many rows of data, it will be critical to correctly use absolute and relative cell references so that you can copy your formulas. Imagine how long it would take if you had to enter a separate formula into each of the rows of data.

Using Different Worksheets

The first activity to accomplish is to prepare the worksheet by putting data for each class section onto a separate worksheet tab.

Practice:
Insert three new worksheets into the workbook. Each worksheet will contain data for a particular class section.

Rename the worksheet tabs to read *TTh 11am*, *TTh 2pm*, and *MW 3pm*.

Move the *All Students* tab so that it is to the right of all of the other tabs.

Now we are ready to put the data for each class section onto the separate tabs. How do you get only the correct records for each section? One way would be to sort the data. You could then copy and paste the records for each class section. An alternate way is to use the Filter command. The Filter command selects the records that meet your criteria. Records that don't meet the specified criteria are hidden from view.

We will use the Filter command to segregate the data. The Filter command is found in the **Home Tab > Editing Group**. Earlier you saw that if you defined your data range as a Table, Excel would automatically turn on the drop-down filters. Now we will explore how to use the Filter when you have not turned your data into a Table.

Practice:

Turn on the Filter by selecting the **Home Tab** > **Editing Group** > **Sort & Filter** > **Filter** option.

Click on the drop-down arrow in the Professor column and select *Dr. Annette Easton; T/TH 11am – 12:15 pm.*

> You should now be viewing only the records for the 11 am class.

With the filter still in effect, select all of the data (all the rows and columns, including row one with the column labels.)

> You can easily select all of the data by clicking on the Select All button ▣ in the upper left hand corner of the worksheet.

Copy and paste that data onto the TTh 11am worksheet.

Repeat this process to filter and copy the appropriate records to the TTh 2pm worksheet and the MW 3pm worksheet.

Notice that you have kept all of the 624 student records on the All Students worksheet because you simply copied the selected groups onto the different worksheets. If you filtered, copied and pasted correctly you should have ended up with 214 students on the TTh 11am worksheet, 212 on the TTh 2pm worksheet and 198 on the MW 3pm worksheet.

Practice:

Turn off the Filter by selecting **Sort & Filter** > **Filter** from the **Editing Group** on the **Home Tab**.

Using Functions to Recode Values

Columns T through Z contain self-assessment ratings provided by the students for various technology skills such as Word Processing and Spreadsheets. The faculty would like to determine an *aggregate self-assessment rating score* by combining the ratings on each individual assessment skill. The individual assessment skills have been entered as text (e.g. "Beginner"). This prevents you from simply adding the ratings together. Instead you will first need to convert the text-based rating (e.g. "Beginner") into a numeric value (e.g. 1). You can then add together all of the individual ratings to determine the aggregate self-assessment rating score.   The individual ratings should be converted into the numeric rating as shown in Table T3.1.

Description Coding Values

Description	Rating
Expert	5
Advanced	4
Intermediate	3
Some Skill	2
Beginner	1

Table T3.1   Data values for performing the self-assessment conversion

Now that you understand "what" you need to accomplish, you can focus on figuring out "how" you can do this task. How can you automate the conversion of these descriptions into numeric ratings? Have you worked with any functions that could be applied here? Complete the following **Understanding IT** activity to develop two possible solutions.

Understanding IT?

Figure T3.10 shows a small portion of the larger worksheet you are completing for student demographics. Sometimes it is easier to apply a new skill if you first focus your attention on a subset of the entire worksheet.

You need to create a formula for cell F2 that will convert the self-assessment text-based rating in C2 into the correct numeric-based rating. Can you think of a function that could be used to assign a web rating of 3 (in cell F2) based on the choice in the web assessment cell of the description/word "Intermediate" (in cell C2)? You actually have learned two different functions that can be used in this situation. Let's explore both of them, and then discuss what might be a better choice.

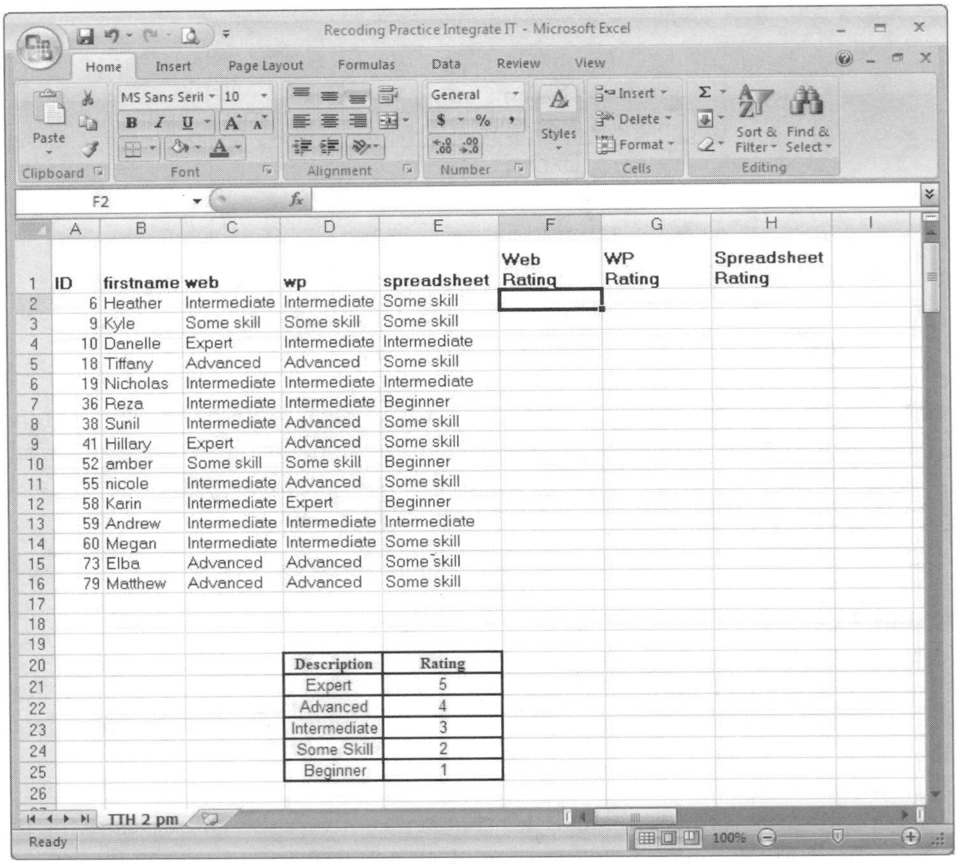

	A	B	C	D	E	F	G	H
1	ID	firstname	web	wp	spreadsheet	Web Rating	WP Rating	Spreadsheet Rating
2	6	Heather	Intermediate	Intermediate	Some skill			
3	9	Kyle	Some skill	Some skill	Some skill			
4	10	Danelle	Expert	Intermediate	Intermediate			
5	18	Tiffany	Advanced	Advanced	Some skill			
6	19	Nicholas	Intermediate	Intermediate	Intermediate			
7	36	Reza	Intermediate	Intermediate	Beginner			
8	38	Sunil	Intermediate	Advanced	Some skill			
9	41	Hillary	Expert	Advanced	Some skill			
10	52	amber	Some skill	Some skill	Beginner			
11	55	nicole	Intermediate	Advanced	Some skill			
12	58	Karin	Intermediate	Expert	Beginner			
13	59	Andrew	Intermediate	Intermediate	Intermediate			
14	60	Megan	Intermediate	Intermediate	Some skill			
15	73	Elba	Advanced	Advanced	Some skill			
16	79	Matthew	Advanced	Advanced	Some skill			

Description	Rating
Expert	5
Advanced	4
Intermediate	3
Some Skill	2
Beginner	1

Figure T3.10 Recoding the Descriptions into Numeric Values

<u>Solution 1</u>

In Tutorial 2 you learned that the IF Function can be used to perform a logical test. Could the IF work in this situation? Conceptually the question that needs to be answered is: If the description is "beginner" then assign a 1 else if the description is "some skill" then assign a 2 else if the description is "intermediate" then assign a 3, etc. Can you figure out a way to write that question in Excel?

In the examples in Tutorial 2 where we used the IF function, there was only one question that needed to be answered. For example, "If the description is "beginner." We never had multiple questions. However we did see examples of using a function inside of another function – for example we put a VLookUp function inside of an IF function. We can extend this thinking to the situation we have here. We can put an IF function inside of another IF function. This is called a **Nested IF**.

The general form of a **Nested IF** function is:

=IF(Logical_Test1,Value_if_true1, IF(logical_Test2, Value_if_true2, value_if_false2))

This piece represents the Value_if_false portion of the IF.

Sometimes it is helpful to first write out a nested IF in an outline form to trace the logic:

IF logical_test_1 then
    Value if true1
Else
    IF logical_test_2 then
        Value_if_true_2
    Else
        Value_If_False2
End IF

How many logical tests can you nest in Excel? A formula in Excel can contain up to 64 different nested functions? The example showed above nests two functions.

Question 1: Using outline form, write the logic that would compare the contents of cell C2 (the web description) to the five possible choices and assign the correct numeric rating.

> ➤ Before you proceed, *check your answer at the end of the tutorial.*

Did you get the correct answer? Were you able to see that the outline incorporated the IF statement four times. This means that when the statement is converted into a nested IF, it will use four of the 64 nestings allowed.

Question 2: Convert the outline form into an IF statement that could be entered into cell F2. Remember that the "=" sign is only used to start the equation; it isn't included on the subsequent functions.

> ➤ Before you proceed, *check your answer at the end of the tutorial.*

When actually writing the IF statement it would be better to reference the cell locations that store the words "Beginner", etc. and the corresponding code values of 1, 2, etc. than to hardcode the words into the IF statement. For example, an IF statement that only performs the beginner conversion would read: =IF(C2=D25, E25, ""). Recall that you learned that using the cell references helps minimize the chances for spelling errors and will avoid the users having to make changes to the formula if the values in the conversion area changed.

While the Nested IF statement will work, there are some limitations. First if you had more than 65 different ratings you would not be able to use the IF function because you would exceed the maximum number of functions that can be nested. Second, and more importantly in this case, the Nested IF function is complicated to read. Chances are that you could more easily introduce a logic error which would be hard to detect.   So what is another option to use instead of the IF function?

Solution 2

In Tutorial 2 you learned that the VLookUp Function can be used to look for a matching value. Could the VLookUp provide an easier way to perform this task? Recall that the general form of the VLookUp is:

=VLOOKUP(lookup_value, table_array, col_index_number,[range lookup])

The VLookUp requires a table array where Excel will look to make the comparison. Cells D21 through E25, on Figure T3.10, can work as this array.

Question 3: Write a VLookUp function that could be entered into cell F2.

> Before you proceed, *check your answer at the end of the tutorial.*

Did you remember to set the last parameter, the Range_Lookup, in the Vlookup function to false? Setting this parameter to FALSE does not require you to sort the list of descriptions in alphabetical order and will only return an Exact Match when doing the comparison.

Do you think that the VLookUp provides a formula that is easier to read and debug? Keep in mind that when creating spreadsheets you often will have several ways to write a formula. As you develop your spreadsheet solutions, remember to compare your options and make choices that will aid in creating a well designed spreadsheet. Having completed this review, you are now ready to return to the demographic analysis spreadsheet.

Before you can write the VLookUp function in your demographic analysis spreadsheet, you need to decide where to locate the table array. In the **Understanding IT?** exercise you just completed, the table array was included below the rows of data. However, you have data stored on three different worksheets. It would be redundant to store the table array on each sheet and would cause the potential for problems if any changes weren't made on each separate copy of the table array. You could also store the table array on only one of the class section sheets, but that probably isn't the best way since the table array is used by all of the section sheets. A better way would be to store the table array on a new, separate worksheet. This worksheet could store any data values needed by all of the section sheets, and could also be used for any calculations that are performed on the overall data analysis. This sheet could also hold any documentation notes about the workbook. Figure T3.12 shows an example layout for this new worksheet.

Prepare the new worksheet by completing these steps:

Practice:
Insert a new worksheet

Rename the worksheet Data Analysis

Enter the worksheet framework as shown in Figure T3.12. The Spreadsheet Skills by Section and the Distribution of Overall Proficiency areas in the worksheet will be completed after you complete the recoding to determine the aggregate self-assessment rating score.

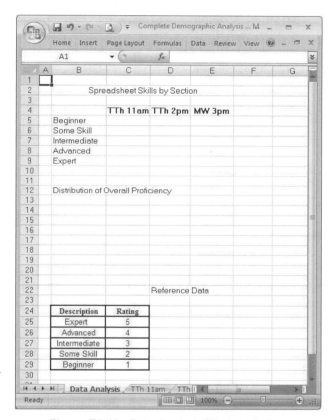

Figure T3.12 Data Analysis Worksheet Tab

The table array that will be used in the VLookUp functions is now located in cells B25 through C29 on the Data Analysis worksheet. Remember that row 24 contains labels for the table array, but the labels should not be included in the formula when you specify the table array reference. When you entered the description values into column B, make certain that you didn't add any extra spaces before or after the words. Excel treats those spaces as being part of the cell entry. As a result, when the VLookUp compares the word "Expert" to the word "Expert ", they will not be equal – even though for all practical purposes they look to be the same. This kind of error can be very hard to find. With the table array created you now need to learn how to use this table array location in a formula on a different worksheet?

Referencing Cells on Separate Worksheets

The formulas used so far have all included cell references to cells located on the same worksheet as the formula. When you write a formula that references a cell located on a different worksheet you must include the worksheet name along with the cell reference. The format includes the Sheet name, an exclamation point, and the cell reference. An example of the proper notation is: **Sheet1!D2** or **Sheet2!H5:J8**. If the worksheet name contains spaces, like **Data Analysis**, the sheet name must be written inside of single quotation marks, e.g. **'Data Analysis'!H7**.

Recall that the data in the demographic spreadsheet that needs to be converted includes the ratings for *email* through *OS_proficiency* (columns T through Z.) Before you can enter the VLookUp function to perform the conversion, you will need to insert the new columns that will hold the corresponding rating value. Complete the following tasks on the TTh 11am worksheet:

Practice:
Insert 8 new columns to the right of column Z

In row 1, insert appropriate labels, such as *email Rating*, for each of these new columns. Column AH will hold the aggregate, or overall, rating.

The next task is to develop the VLookUp function that will be used in cell AA2 to convert the email description in cell T2 into the corresponding numerical rating. Use the VLookUp function you created in the Understanding IT? exercise as your model to create your solution.

Did you come up with the following formula?
        =VLOOKUP(T2,'Data Analysis'!B25:C29,2,False)
Remember to pay close attention to the proper placement of the quotation marks around the sheet name. Ideally you can write one formula and figure out a way to have it adjust correctly when copied across into columns AB through AG and down from row 2 through the remaining student records. Will the formula shown above copy correctly?

While the reference to a sheet name, such as 'Data Analysis' is an absolute reference, hopefully you recognized that the range specified for the table array ('Data Analysis'!B25:C29) needs to be made absolute. The updated table array reference should now read: 'Data Analysis'!$B$25:$C$29. If you make that adjustment, the formula would work to copy across into columns AB through AG and down through the remaining rows. However, before you enter that formula and copy it to the rest of the worksheet let's look at one other modification that could improve the readability of the formula.

Named Cell References

The formulas you have written and used so far have all included cell references, such as C2. Excel also provides the ability to name a cell or range of cells. A **name** is a word or phrase linked with a cell or cell range. When you name a cell you can then choose to use the name of the cell in a formula instead of the cell reference. For example, a formula that reads =TaxRate*SubTotal is more understandable than one that reads =A57*F30.

Names can be up to 255 characters long. They must start with a letter, _ (underscore), or \ (backslash) character. The remaining characters can be letters, numbers, periods, or underscore characters. Names cannot include spaces, punctuation or hyphens. Names are not case sensitive. Using a combination of upper and lower case characters can make names with multiple words easier to read.   For example, SocialSecurityNumber is easier to read than SOCIALSECURITYNUMBER.

Names are created with a scope. The **scope** is the location within which the name is unique, and can be used without further qualifying the name. The scope is either a specific worksheet or the entire workbook. So what does all of that mean? If you create a name of TaxRate with a scope of Sheet1 you can write a formula on Sheet1 that uses the unqualified name of TaxRate. If you want to reference the TaxRate from Sheet1 on a different sheet you will need to qualify the name. This means that you have to include the sheet name in addition to the cell name. For example: Sheet1!TaxRate. Because TaxRate had a scope of Sheet1, you could assign that same name to a different cell on a separate sheet. If a name has a scope of the workbook you will not need to specify a sheet name when it is used. Excel does allow you to create and use the same name at both a worksheet and workbook level scope – this has the potential to cause confusion. If you choose to use the same name with different scopes, the worksheet level name takes precedence. To help you avoid a potentially confusing situation don't use the same name at both a workbook and a worksheet level. No matter the scope, it is important to point out that names use an absolute cell reference. This means that if you enter a formula using a name, and copy that formula, the name is treated as an absolute cell reference.

When creating a name you can either use labels that you have already entered into a cell as the name or create your own name during the definition process. There are several ways to create a name. We will cover two methods available on the **Formulas Tab**.

- **Using an existing cell label as the name:** If the cell(s) that you want to name already have a cell label next to them that you want to use as the name, begin by selecting the range including the cell label. Select the **Formulas Tab > Defined Names Group > Create from Selection** option. A dialog box similar to Figure T3.13 will appear. Mark the appropriate check box to indicate the location of the label(s).

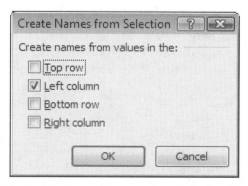

Figure T3.13 The Create Names from Selection Dialog Box

- **Create a new name:** If the cell(s) that you want to name do not have an existing label, you can define a new name. Begin by selecting the cell(s) that will be associated with the new name. Select the **Formulas Tab > Defined Names Group > Define Name >**

Define Name option. A dialog box similar to Figure T3.14 will appear. Enter the name you wish to assign to the cell(s) and indicate the name scope.

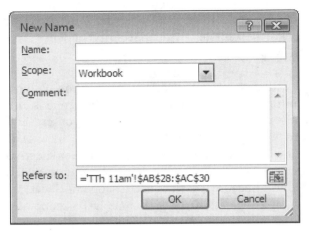

Figure T3.14   The New Name from Selection Dialog Box

Enter the Formulas to Perform the Rating Conversion
In the demographic analysis workbook define a name for the table array cell range.

Practice:
Select cells B25 through C29 on the Data Analysis worksheet.

Select the **Formulas Tab > Defined Names Group > Define Name > Define Name** option

Enter the name Rating_Values.

Set the Scope to Workbook.

Click OK.

Assigning a name, such as Rating_Values, to this cell range provides much more information as to the contents of the cells compared to 'Data Analysis'!$B$25:$C$29. Now you are ready to modify the VLookUp function you developed earlier to incorporate the range name. On the TTh 11am worksheet perform the following tasks:

Practice:
Enter =VLOOKUP(T2,Rating_Values,2,FALSE) in cell AA2.

Copy the formula across the remaining columns

Select cells AA2 through AG2.

Use the fill handle to copy this range down through the remaining rows.

Save your workbook.

So far we have only been working on the TTh 11am worksheet. You need to perform this same conversion on the other two section worksheets.

Practice:

Following the same steps as outlined earlier, insert the necessary columns onto each worksheet.

Copy the vlookup functions from the second row of the TTh 11am worksheet into the second row of the other two section worksheets. Since each worksheet has an identical layout, you don't need to write a new vlookup function for the other sheets. Instead, copying the formula will save time.

Copy the formulas down to the remaining rows of each of those worksheets.

After completing the other sheets it may seem like you did quite a bit of duplicate work, such as adding the columns into each of the sheets. Why didn't we add the columns into the *All Students* worksheet before filtering and copying the data onto the class section sheets? Most systems developers recommend against altering the original source data to avoid the possibility of any corruption. An alternative would have been to make a copy of the entire source data onto a new sheet and then add the extra columns before filtering and copying from the new sheet. This "extra work" helps you to see that it is important to think through the most effective and efficient ways to create your complete spreadsheet.

Calculate the Aggregate Total

Column AH will be used to hold the aggregate total. With the conversion of each of the individual text-based descriptions into a corresponding numeric value completed, you can now add the individual scores together.

Practice:

In each worksheet, enter the appropriate formula to complete this calculation to sum the individual scores together.

Copy it down through all necessary rows.

You will use this Aggregate total column for further analysis in one of the projects at the end of the tutorial.

Complete the following **Integrate IT** activity to reinforce your understanding of named cell references and formulas that reference data on separate worksheets.

Integrate IT

In Tutorial 2 you learned how to use the CountIF function to combine a logical test with the count function. Incorporate the new skills you have learned about named cell references and formulas that reference data on separate worksheets to complete this activity.

> ➢ On the Data Analysis tab, write the CountIF formulas needed to complete the Spreadsheet Skills by Section area. Incorporate the following requirements into the formulas:
>   • Use a named cell reference for the range. This will require you to name the range on each section worksheet
>   • Use a named cell reference for the criteria.
> ➢ Create a clustered column chart to compare the ratings across the three sections. Place the chart to the right of the data values on the Data Analysis worksheet.

Your completed worksheet should look similar to Figure T3.15. Save your workbook. You will add the remaining analysis areas at the end of the chapter.

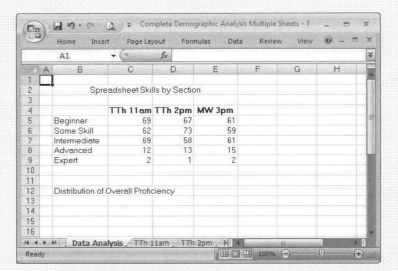

Figure T3.15   The Completed Spreadsheet Skills Section on the Data Analysis Worksheet

    In this section you have learned about working with data on multiple worksheets. You explored how to filter data, add worksheets, write formulas that reference cells on different worksheets and to define named cells. You also practiced using some of the skills to help you solve different business problems. Incorporating these features in spreadsheets will help you build more effective, and manageable, solutions. In the next section you will learn about another tool available to help you organize and summarize data.

LEARNING CHECK
Be sure you can *use autofilter to select subsets of data * effectively work with data on separate worksheets * write formulas that reference data on separate worksheets * use named cell references

PIVOT TABLES

Using multiple worksheets provides one way of organizing data so that you can perform calculations based on these different groupings. Another tool for organizing and summarizing large amounts of data is the PivotTable. A **Pivot Table** easily helps you make comparisons, determine trends, and reveal relationships among different data items. Using a PivotTable allows the user to focus on the data they are interest in – grouping, filtering and summarizing selected data items and then drilling down on details from summary area. PivotTables can help answer questions about the data stored in a spreadsheet. For example if you have a spreadsheet with data about product sales, it would be good to know which products sell best in different regions of the country. Another question you could ask of your data is which managers have the most profitable salespeople. Determining the questions you want to have answered is part of the analysis portion of spreadsheet development, the "what" part. Once you know the questions, your next step is to figure out "how" to accomplish the task in Excel. PivotTables provide an easy way to answer these questions. The PivotTable, or PivotTable Report, presents the data in a tabular format. Excel also provides the capability to create a PivotChart Report, which allows the user to view a graphical representation of the PivotTable data. In this section you will work with a new example spreadsheet to learn how PivotTables can help analyze data.

Example 2: Gourmet Foods Distribution Spreadsheet

Figure T3.16 shows the master data list for the Gourmet Foods Distribution Company. Let's get started by opening the spreadsheet.

Practice:
Download the Gourmet Foods spreadsheet from Blackboard and open it.

You will use this spreadsheet to learn how to use PivotTables to analyze data. PivotTables are created by selecting the **Insert Tab > Tables Group > PivotTable** option. Before you create your first PivotTable, it is important to review some rules related to preparing your data list. Notice that the first row in the Sales Data Master List worksheet contains column labels. The PivotTable requires that the first row contain these headings/columns labels since it will use them to create the list of fields for the PivotTable. Remove any empty rows or columns in the data range that you will be analyzing. Verify that the cells in each column all contain the same type of data – you can't have some cells in a column with numeric data and others in that same column with text data. Ensure that your spreadsheet meets these rules. As you were browsing through the data, did you notice that there are 446 rows of data that you will be working with?

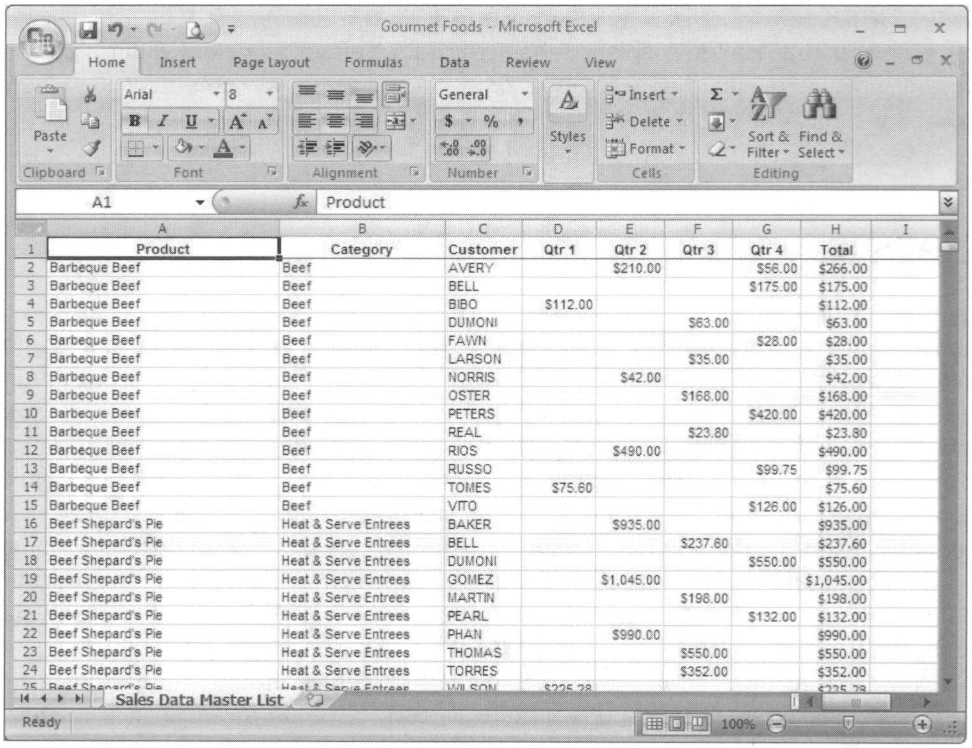

Product	Category	Customer	Qtr 1	Qtr 2	Qtr 3	Qtr 4	Total
Barbeque Beef	Beef	AVERY		$210.00		$56.00	$266.00
Barbeque Beef	Beef	BELL				$175.00	$175.00
Barbeque Beef	Beef	BIBO	$112.00				$112.00
Barbeque Beef	Beef	DUMONI			$63.00		$63.00
Barbeque Beef	Beef	FAWN				$28.00	$28.00
Barbeque Beef	Beef	LARSON			$35.00		$35.00
Barbeque Beef	Beef	NORRIS		$42.00			$42.00
Barbeque Beef	Beef	OSTER			$168.00		$168.00
Barbeque Beef	Beef	PETERS				$420.00	$420.00
Barbeque Beef	Beef	REAL			$23.80		$23.80
Barbeque Beef	Beef	RIOS		$490.00			$490.00
Barbeque Beef	Beef	RUSSO				$99.75	$99.75
Barbeque Beef	Beef	TOMES	$75.60				$75.60
Barbeque Beef	Beef	VITO				$126.00	$126.00
Beef Shepard's Pie	Heat & Serve Entrees	BAKER		$935.00			$935.00
Beef Shepard's Pie	Heat & Serve Entrees	BELL			$237.60		$237.60
Beef Shepard's Pie	Heat & Serve Entrees	DUMONI				$550.00	$550.00
Beef Shepard's Pie	Heat & Serve Entrees	GOMEZ		$1,045.00			$1,045.00
Beef Shepard's Pie	Heat & Serve Entrees	MARTIN			$198.00		$198.00
Beef Shepard's Pie	Heat & Serve Entrees	PEARL				$132.00	$132.00
Beef Shepard's Pie	Heat & Serve Entrees	PHAN		$990.00			$990.00
Beef Shepard's Pie	Heat & Serve Entrees	THOMAS			$550.00		$550.00
Beef Shepard's Pie	Heat & Serve Entrees	TORRES			$352.00		$352.00

Figure T3.16 Gourmet Foods Master Data List

Creating a PivotTable

The first PivotTable you will create will summarize the total sales for each product. Before you begin, select a cell inside of the data list. This will let Excel know where the data is.

Practice:
Select the **Insert Tab > Tables Group > PivotTable** option. The Create PivotTable dialog box, as shown in Figure T3.17, will be displayed.

Complete the following choices in the Dialog Box so that your choices match those shown in the figure.

- Select a table or range: Because you had selected a cell within the data range before you began, the table/range should be already completed. Verify that the range displayed in correct. If the range is not completed, you can select the entire range, including the column headers, now.

- Choose to place the PivotTable report in a **New Worksheet.** This will keep the analysis results separate from the master data.

- Select **OK** when finished.

Figure T3.17 The Create PivotTable Dialog Box

Completing the Row, Column and Value Areas

After completing the wizard your worksheet should match that shown in Figure T3.18. Notice that the ribbon now shows two new contextual tabs, Options and Design, available for working with the PivotTable Tools. Initially your PivotTable displays only an empty layout framework. To answer an analysis question, in the **PivotTable Field List** window you will drag fields from the **Field List** section into the four different areas in the **Layout** section. As you drag the fields into the different areas in the layout section, the PivotTable report will be updated. A PivotTable is a dynamic object within your worksheet. This means that you can modify it many times to see different views of your data.

The different areas in the layout section control where the data fields appear in the completed PivotTable. **Row Labels** display the different values of a data field in separate rows. If you were to move the customer field into the row area, you would see one row for each customer. **Column Labels** display the different values of a data field in separate columns. If you moved the customer field into the column area, you would see one column for each customer. The **Values** area is where data values are summarized. Usually this area will contain numerical data. If you move one of the Quarter fields into the Values area you would see summarized data for that quarter, such as count, sum, or average. You will determine which summary value you wish to display. Put fields into the **Report Filter** area when you want to be able to narrow down the data values that are displayed in the entire report. For example, if you created a report to view the buying patterns of products over the four quarters, you may want to filter this to show only selected customers. You can move fields from the Field List into the different areas by dragging the field names, right clicking on the field name and selecting the appropriate area, or by clicking the check box. Clicking the check box will put the field into the default area of the layout section.

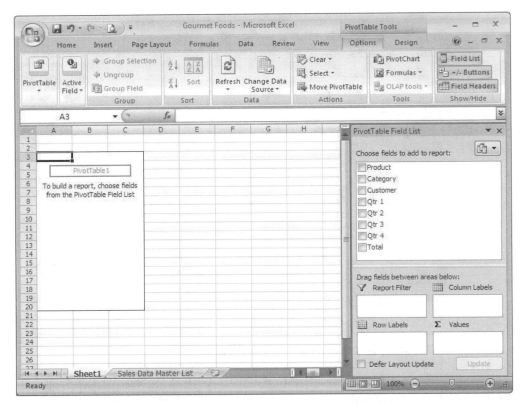

Figure T3.18 PivotTable Inserted on a New Worksheet

When setting up your PivotTable you will want to use the areas that make your PivotTable easy to read and understand. You don't have to use all of the layout areas. It will take a little bit of practice to get comfortable understanding the different areas and how best to use them. Generally it won't matter whether you decide to put a field in a row or a column – the data shown is the same. However if you have fields with very long names, or many different possible values, it usually will be more readable to include those field in the Row area instead of the Column area. This will create a table that is longer but narrower, which most people consider easier to read.

Finish building the PivotTable to summarize the total sales for each product by dragging the appropriate fields into the layout areas.

Practice:
Drag the **Product** field to the **Row Labels** area.

Drag the **Total** field to the **Values** area.

For this PivotTable you will not use the Report Filter or Column labels sections. After dragging these two fields your Sheet1 should look like the one shown in Figure T3.19.

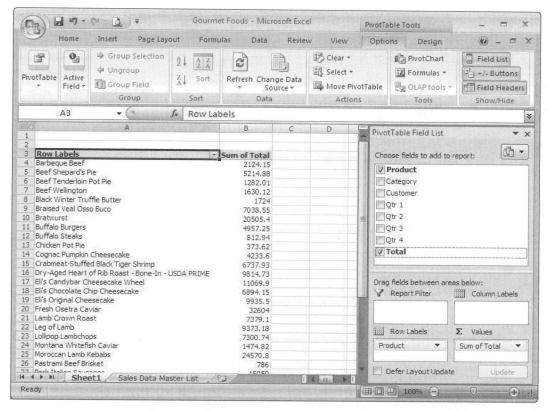

Figure T3.19 PivotTable after fields have been dropped into the row labels and Values areas

Refining the PivotTable

Format the amount in the total column to show Currency Format with zero decimal places. This can be accomplished by performing the following tasks:

Practice:
Select the drop-down arrow next to *Sum of Total* in the Values area.

Select **Value Field Settings**. The Value Field Settings dialog box, shown in Figure T3.20 will appear. Notice that you can choose to change the summary function, if necessary, in this dialog box.

Select **Number Format** and then select the appropriate settings.

Remember that after your PivotTable has been created you can still make changes to it. To remove a field, select the drop-down arrow for that field name and select **Remove Field**. To move a field to another layout area, select the field and drag it to the other area. If you right click inside of the PivotTable you can activate the short cut menu which provides additional formatting options. If you close the field list and want to display it again, select the **PivotTable Tools Options Tab > Show/Hide Group > Field List** option.

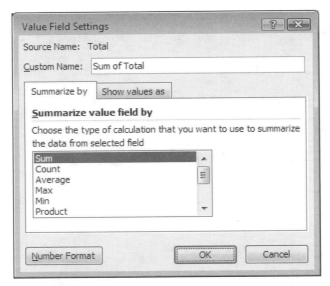

Figure T3.20 The Value Field Settings Dialog Box

Gourmet Foods management would like you to modify the report so they can see what category each product belongs to. Modify the PivotTable so that it groups the products within the category.

Practice:
Drag the **Category** field on top of the Product field in the Row Labels area.

Your revised table should match that shown in Figure T3.21. If the Categories are showing below the Products simply click the drop-down arrow for the Category field and select Move Up.

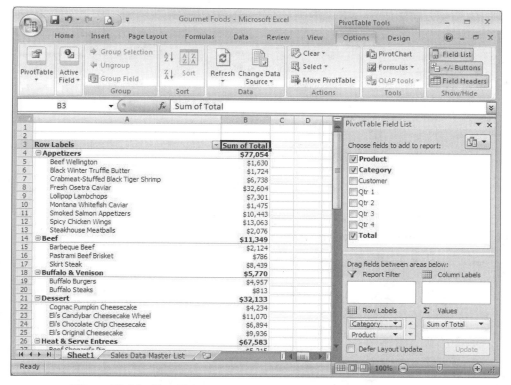

Figure T3.21 PivotTable showing totals by product within categories

In the PivotTable report, notice the minus outline symbol next to each Category name. Clicking on the symbol will hide the details of each product showing only the total for that category. The symbol changes into a plus outline symbol which will expand a collapsed category. Also notice the drop-down arrow next to Row Labels in the PivotTable report. This arrow opens a dialog box where you can choose sorting and filtering options. Click on the **drop-down arrow** for row labels. A dialog box, similar to Figure T3.22, will appear.

Figure T3.22 PivotTable Sort and filter options

Complete the report by performing the following tasks:

> **Practice:**
> Select Field: Category. Select the correct check boxes to display only **appetizers, dessert** and **heat & serve entrees**. Select OK to confirm these choices.
>
> Select the Row Labels Drop-down arrow again.
>
> Select Field: Product. Select **Value Filters > Top 10**. In the Top 10 Filter (Product) dialog box change the filter selection to show the top 3 instead of 10. Select OK.
>
> Select OK to finish.

Your completed PivotTable report should be similar to Figure T3.23.

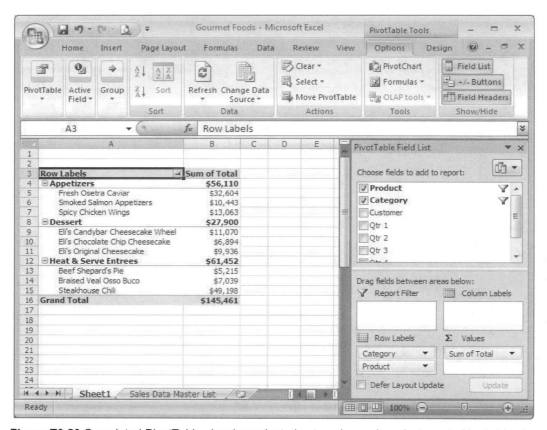

Figure T3.23 Completed PivotTable showing selected categories and products sorted by total sales

In just a minute you will have a chance to practice these skills in an **Integrate IT** exercise. But before you proceed, there are a few things to keep in mind. First, spending time analyzing the data before you decide to drag fields will be very helpful. PivotTables can become quite complex and the more you can do to understand the best way to present the data the more effective your spreadsheet will be. Second, most elements in Excel, such as formulas and graphs, automatically update themselves when data values change. Unfortunately PivotTables do not automatically update. You can update the PivotTable by selecting **PivotTable Tools Options**

Tab > **Data Group** > **Refresh** option. Finally, don't be afraid to experiment. Try placing different fields in the different layout areas to see the effect and to help you determine the best way to organize your data.

Integrate IT

Create a second PivotTable in your Gourmet Foods workbook. This PivotTable will analyze customer buying patterns over the four quarters. The completed PivotTable should be similar to that shown in Figure T3.24. Complete the following steps to create this PivotTable.

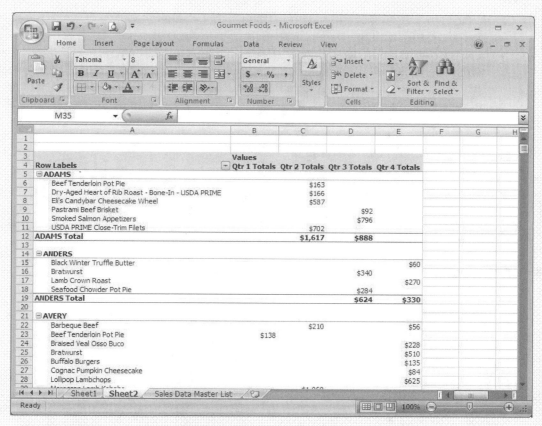

Figure T3.24 Completed PivotTable analyzing customer buying patterns over the four quarters

---

Create the PivotTable:

➤ Click in a cell in the data list in the Sales Data Master List worksheet

➤ On the **Insert Tab** in the **Tables Group**, select **PivotTable**.

➤ Make the following selections on the dialog box:
 • Confirm that the correct data range is identified.
 • Choose to put the PivotTable on a new worksheet.

Integrate IT (continued)

➤ Select **OK** to create the PivotTable.

➤ Drag the following fields into the PivotTable layout section:
  • Drag **Customer** to the Row Labels area
  • Drag **Product** to the Row Labels area, below the **Customer** field.
  • Drag **Qtr 1** into the Values area. Note that this will create a column labeled **Count of Qtr 1**. See Figure T3.25 for an example of how the PivotTable layout will appear at this point. We will change the Count function to a sum function in a few steps.

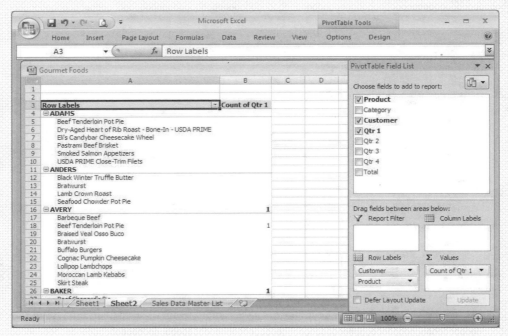

Figure T3.25 PivotTable after adding Qtr 1 into the Values area

  • Drag **Qtr 2** below *Count of Qtr 1* in the Values area. Figure T3.26 shows how the PivotTable should appear.
  • Drag **Qtr 3** below *Count of Qtr 2* in the Values area.
  • Drag **Qtr 4** below *Count of Qtr 3* in the Values area.

Integrate IT (continued)

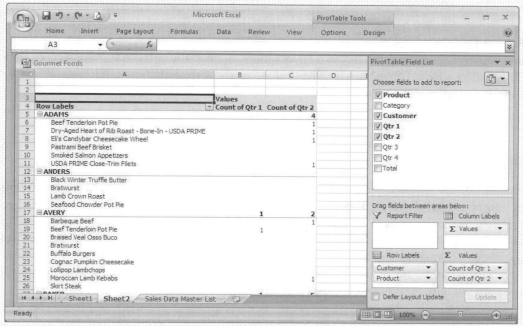

Figure T3.26 PivotTable after adding Qtr 2 into the Values area

Change the Field Settings and Layout of the PivotTable Report

➤ Select the cell that contains the **Count of Qtr 1** label. Right click and select **Value Field Settings**. Change the entry in *Custom Name* to read Qtr 1 Totals. Select **SUM** in the *Summarize value field by* list box. Select **Number Format**. Format the cells using Currency with zero decimal places.

➤ Repeat for the Count of Qtr 2, Count of Qtr 3, and Count of Qtr 4 labels.

➤ Select the **PivotTable Tools Layout Group Design Tab > Subtotals > Show all subtotals at bottom of group** option.

➤ Select the **PivotTable Tools Design Tab Layout Group > Blank Rows > Insert blank line after each item** option.

➤ Close the PivotTable Field List Window.

Your completed PivotTable should now match that shown earlier in Figure T3.24. Save your workbook.

In this section you have learned about to create a PivotTable to help you view and analyze large sets of data. You practiced building a PivotTable and using the different layout sections. Hopefully you have seen how a PivotTable can aid in summarizing data.

LEARNING CHECK
Be sure you can * explain the uses of a PivotTable * describe how the data range must be setup prior to creating a PivotTable * create PivotTables to show relationships among data * customize some of the default settings in a PivotTable

WRAPPING IT UP

In this tutorial you had a chance to see how important it is to understand the business problem before you begin developing a spreadsheet solution. The steps to creating a spreadsheet become more critical when you began to work on problems that required larger and more complicated spreadsheets. You saw the complexities of dealing with large worksheets and learned several approaches to organizing and analyzing this data. You further developed skills in creating and documenting accurate formulas. In Chapter 4 you will learn another way that organizations manage large quantities of data – through a database management system.

Study Questions Summary

1. What features can you use to help manage large sets of data?
   - Sorting is a useful technique to help you organize large sets of data
   - Excel allows you to sort data in ascending or descending order, or by color, on up to 64 different levels
   - The subtotal command will automatically create subtotals on one field for different subgroups of data
   - After creating a subtotal, you can choose three different outline views to control the level of detail displayed
   - Tables can be defined to provide filtering capabilities to your data
   - Tables require the first row to contain column headings/field labels. Although not required, it is a good idea to format the column headings so that they are easy to read
   - The drop-down filter allows you to select records that meet specified criteria
   - The custom filter option can be created to provide additional querying capabilities on your Excel table

2. How do you work with multiple worksheets?
   - Excel provides the capability to store data on many separate worksheets
   - Each worksheet has a unique name
   - When referencing cells on another worksheet you must include the sheet name along with the cell reference
   - Naming cells provides for formulas that are more easy to read and understand

3. How can you analyze data using PivotTables?
   - The PivotTable command is used to create the basic layout of your PivotTable
   - The layout section of a PivotTable contains drop areas for Report Filters, Column Labels, Row Labels and Value fields
   - You can typically choose to use either row or column drop areas interchangeable
   - PivotTables do not update automatically when the underlying data values change. To ensure up-to-date data it is a good idea to refresh your PivotTables when you open a worksheet
   - Once a PivotTable has been created you can further restrict the data values that are displayed by narrowing down the choices on the drop-down lists

Solutions to Tutorial Activities

INTEGRATE IT
Subtotals - pg. 310

1. To compute the first subtotals you need to sort the data in the demographic worksheet by **Major** (in ascending order) and **Sex** (in descending order.) You should have found 31 male finance majors and 22 female international business majors.

2. To compute the second subtotals you need to sort the data by Sex (you can select either ascending or descending.) Be certain to change the "Use Function" choice to Average. "Add the subtotal" to the GPA field. You should have found the females averaged 2.92 while males averaged 3.42. Don't forget that you can use the outline buttons to easily show both averages at the same time (select button 2.)

UNDERSTANDING IT?
IF and Vlookup logic to Recode the Self-Assessment Description - pg.317-320

1. The logic for the IF statement is as follows:

```
IF C2 = "Beginner" then
    1
ELSE
  IF C2 = "Some skill" then
        2
  ELSE
        IF C2 = "Intermediate" then
            3
        ELSE
            IF C2 = "Advanced" then
                4
            ELSE
                5
End IF
```

2. Write the =IF statement:
=IF(C2="Beginner",1,IF(C2="Some Skill",2,IF(C2="Intermediate",3,IF(C2="Advanced",4,5))))

3.   Write the =VlookUp statement:
=VLOOKUP(C2,D21:E25,2,FALSE)

Key Terms

Page Number references are included in parentheses

Autofilter (311)	Nested IF Function (318)
Cell reference on a different worksheet (322)	Pivot Table (327)
Drop-down filters (311)	Scope (323)
Field List (329)	Sorting Data (306)
Multiple Worksheets (314)	Subtotals (308)
Name (322)	Subtotal Outline (309)
Named Cell Reference (322)	Table (311)

Multiple Choice Questions

1.   Which of the following is a correctly written IF function to accomplish the following logic?

   If cell A5 is less than 25, then multiply B10 by 2
   If A5 is greater than or equal to 25 but less than 50, then multiply B10 by 20
   If A5 is greater than or equal to 50 and less than 75, then multiply B10 by 200
   For all other values in A5 multiply B10 by 250

   a.   =IF(A5>=75, B10*250, IF(A5<75, B10*200, IF(A5<50, B10*20, B10*2)))
   b.   =IF(A5<25, B10*2, IF(A5<50, B10*20, IF(A5<75, B10*200, B10*250)))
   c.   =IF(A5<25, B10*2, IF(A5 >=25 AND A5<50, B10*20, IF(A5 >=50 AND A5<75, B10*200, B10*250)))
   d.   =IF(A5>75, B10*250, IF(A5>50, B10*200, IF(A5>25, B10*20, B10*2)))
   e.   All of the above are true statements

2.   Which of the following is not a true statement about setting up your Excel data to work correctly as a table?
   a.   The first row of the range must contain labels
   b.   The field labels can be of any length
   c.   Shorter field labels are easier to remember
   d.   A table is created by selecting Table from the Table Group on the Insert Tab.

3.   Which of the following is a true statement about a named cell or range?
   a.   The scope of a name specifies the location within which the name is unique
   b.   When naming a cell it must be based on a label you have already entered into a different cell
   c.   Cell names are treated as relative cell references when they are copied
   d.   Cell names are case sensitive
   e.   All of the above are true statements

4. Based on the image below, which of the following is a true statement?

	A	B	C	D	E	F	G	H
1	Product	Category	Customer	Qtr 1	Qtr 2	Qtr 3	Qtr 4	Total
17	Beef Wellington	Appetizers	SMYTHE		$64.80			$64.80
32	Crabmeat-Stuffed Black Tiger Shrimp	Appetizers	SMYTHE	$1,472.50				$1,472.50
57	Fresh Osetra Caviar	Appetizers	SMYTHE			$1,216.00	$1,710.00	$1,577.00	$4,503.00
80	Lollipop Lambchops	Appetizers	SMYTHE					$625.00	$625.00
89	Montana Whitefish Caviar	Appetizers	SMYTHE			$775.00		$775.00
105	Smoked Salmon Appetizers	Appetizers	SMYTHE				$936.90	$936.90
128	Steakhouse Meatballs	Appetizers	SMYTHE				$119.25	$119.25
155	Pastrami Beef Brisket	Beef	SMYTHE			$110.00		$110.00
172	Skirt Steak	Beef	SMYTHE				$1,032.00	$1,032.00
189	Buffalo Burgers	Buffalo & Venison	SMYTHE			$1,389.60	$405.30	$1,794.90
201	Buffalo Steaks	Buffalo & Venison	WELLS	$8.64				$8.64
208	Cognac Pumpkin Cheesecake	Dessert	SMYTHE			$1,008.00		$1,008.00
219	Eli's Candybar Cheesecake Wheel	Dessert	WELLS			$920.00		$920.00
235	Eli's Chocolate Chip Cheesecake	Dessert	SMYTHE			$1,045.00		$1,045.00

   a. By looking at the row numbers you can tell that criteria has been applied to limit the data shown
   b. The data is filtered based only on the customer column
   c. The data is filtered based on everything except the customer column
   d. A and B are true
   e. A, B, and C are true

5. The image shown below illustrates which Excel feature?

	A	B	C	D	E	F	G	H	I
1	Product	Category	Customer	Qtr 1	Qtr 2	Qtr 3	Qtr 4	Total	
130		Appetizers Total						$77,053.55	
175		Beef Total						$11,348.89	
204		Buffalo & Venison Total						$5,770.19	
257		Dessert Total						$32,133.15	
310		Heat & Serve Entrees Total						$67,582.84	
361		Lamb Total						$41,323.08	
391		Sausages Total						$36,455.40	
408		Seafood Total						$11,602.80	
440		USDA Prime Steaks Total						$27,419.33	
457		Wagyu Beef Total						$4,887.00	
458		Grand Total						$315,576.23	
459									
460									
461									

Sales Data Master List

   a. Data table   b. Subtotal   c. Autofilter   D. Validation

6. In a VLookUp formula, if the contents of the lookup cell is blank, the formula will return _____.
   a. the result in the first row of the table array
   b. the result in the last row of the table array
   c. the #N/A message
   d. an empty cell

7. By looking at the formula: = (West!B10 + 'Mid States'!B10) * TaxRate, which of the following is a true statement?
   a. West, Mid States and TaxRate are named cells.
   b. West, Mid States and TaxRate are worksheet names.
   c. West and Mid States are worksheet names and TaxRate is a named cell
   d. The formula will not work because West must also be inside of quotation marks
   e. C and D are true

8. An Excel workbook contains 3 sheets with data values (one per store location) and 2 additional sheets, each containing Pivot Table. How many files are used by Excel use to store all of these sheets?
   a. 1
   b. 2
   c. 3
   d. 5

9. If the data in the worksheet shown below is sorted with a first level sort key of Department (Ascending), a second level sort key of Gender (Ascending) and a third level sort key of Salary (Ascending), what will be the name of the 1st person shown in the list after the sort?

	A	B	C	D	E	F	G	H
1	First Name	Last Name	Department	Title	Salary	Hire Date	Birth Date	Gender
2	Kevin	Grundies	Marketing	CSR	38,900.00	12/24/1999	3/4/1971	M
3	Oscar	Gomez	Marketing	CSR	43,500.00	2/16/2000	4/29/1977	M
4	Hillary	Flintsteel	Marketing	Staff	34,500.00	3/21/2000	8/22/1968	F
5	Maria	Andretti	Marketing	CSR	42,500.00	3/21/1990	8/20/1965	F
6	Sharad	Manispour	Engineering	Security Engineer	45,600.00	10/13/2001	2/4/1970	M
7	Roberta	Kuzweil	Management	Manager	63,000.00	6/16/1992	12/22/1958	F
8	Barbara	Grabowski	Management	Manager	75,700.00	10/13/1995	4/1/1965	F
9	James	Van Horn	Management	Manager	66,500.00	12/18/1996	2/3/1958	M
10	Artie	Lambros	Management	CSR	41,000.00	5/16/1993	7/13/1970	M
11	Melinda	English	Marketing	Manager	56,400.00	10/1/2000	2/14/1966	F
12	Edgar	Rolrock	Engineering	Security Engineer	53,300.00	2/8/2002	3/21/1970	M
13	Hillary	Cushner	Management	Staff	32,000.00	8/26/2004	5/6/1980	F
14	Luca	Pacioli	Engineering	Staff	42,300.00	8/24/2005	3/4/1983	M
15	Yuan	Chang	Engineering	Security Engineer	46,540.00	9/5/2005	2/12/1978	M
16	Nemesha	Mehta	Engineering	Security Engineer	65,000.00	10/1/2005	4/29/1980	F
17	Francine	Detweiller	Engineering	Security Engineer	56,700.00	10/10/2006	1/24/1984	F
18	Koshi	Yamamoto	Engineering	Security Engineer	49,600.00	11/16/1999	9/13/1976	F
19	John	Zumkowski	Engineering	Staff	33,000.00	4/18/1996	12/12/1976	M
20	Phyllis	Leonard	Engineering	Security Engineer	59,800.00	12/13/1997	7/20/1970	F
21	Samuel	Gates	Engineering	Security Engineer	66,300.00	4/11/1998	3/7/1963	M
22	Michael	Goldstein	Engineering	Security Engineer	51,000.00	7/6/1998	4/12/1975	M
23	Patti	Stonesifer	Engineering	Security Engineer	64,300.00	7/6/1998	3/21/1973	F
24	Joseph	Paterno	Marketing	Staff	32,000.00	5/14/2001	5/22/1981	M
25	Frederich	Bednarczyk	Engineering	Security Engineer	56,700.00	9/16/2003	5/3/1982	M
26	Carmen	Ortega-Molina	Engineering	Security Engineer	46,000.00	11/5/2001	11/17/1978	F
27	Svetlana	Kartashev	Human Resources	Staff	38,000.00	1/29/1997	10/28/1975	F
28	Alice	Rovik	Human Resources	Manager	43,000.00	12/30/1997	1/15/1976	F
29								

   a. Nemesha Mehta
   b. Hillary Flintsteel
   c. John Zumkowski
   d. Koshi Yamamoto
   e. Carmen Ortega-Molina

10. Using the data shown in the Pivot table below and the listing of fields (shown to the right), which of the following is a true statement?

2				
3		Values		
4	Row Labels ▾	Average of 2006	Average of 2007	Average of 2008
5	⊟Midwest	$20,919	$21,557	$25,013
6	Ancillary	$19,489	$20,075	$21,601
7	Food	$22,397	$22,707	$26,072
8	Fresh Food	$17,999	$18,032	$20,811
9	Hardlines	$22,167	$23,383	$28,376
10	Softlines	$18,097	$18,703	$23,626
11	Sundries	$25,368	$26,443	$29,589
12	⊟Northeast	$20,705	$21,661	$22,590
13	Ancillary	$19,256	$18,391	$17,060
14	Food	$22,682	$23,499	$25,199
15	Fresh Food	$16,220	$17,493	$18,004
16	Hardlines	$23,909	$24,106	$26,421
17	Softlines	$17,019	$17,293	$19,150
18	Sundries	$25,144	$29,184	$29,704
19	⊟Northwest	$19,885	$20,565	$22,954
20	Ancillary	$17,076	$17,431	$17,548
21	Food	$21,173	$22,165	$24,975
22	Fresh Food	$14,461	$15,358	$17,255

- a. The fields Region and Product Line are in the Row Labels area.*
- b. The Product Line field is in the Values area.
- c. The fields 2006, 2007 and 2008 are in the Report Filter area.
- d. Sum of 2006, Sum of 2007 and Sum of 2008 are in the Values area.

Answers:
1. b   2. b   3. a   4. d   5. b   6. c   7. c   8. a   9. e   10. a

Review Questions

1. Describe the relationship between the Sort and Subtotal tools.
2. Discuss how you can use a Data Table to help with filtering data.
3. Can the custom filter be used for any combination of criteria? Why or Why not?
4. In the Complete Demographic Analysis project you created a separate column to hold the numeric equivalent of each text rating. Then you added those together in the Aggregate Total column. You have decided that it isn't necessary to have separate columns to store each individual rating. Write a formula for the Aggregate Total column that will do the conversion and addition in one formula.
5. Compare and contrast the nested IF function to the VLookUp function.
6. What is the correct syntax to use when writing a formula that will reference cells on another worksheet?
7. Explain the advantages of naming cells or cell ranges.
8. List and briefly explain the contents of each of the four areas in a PivotTable.

9. Compare the use of the Subtotal tool to a Pivot Table.
10. Use the Excel Help to read about Pivot Chart. Describe the difference between a Pivot Table and a Pivot Chart.

Projects

1. Open the Complete Demographic Analysis workbook. Use subtotals to find the average age of students in each major.

2. In the Complete Demographic Analysis workbook, find the student with the highest GPA in each major. What technique did you use to accomplish this task? Are there any other ways you could have accomplished this task? Are any of the ways more efficient?

3. Create a PivotTables for the Complete Demographic Analysis workbook that will show the results of the following question: "Do the number of text messages sent each day vary based on the age and gender of the student?"

    Hint: The survey question asked students to select a range of how many text messages they sent each day (none, 1 to 5, 5 to 10, 10 to 20, and more than 20.) The field with the most choices should become your row field.

    Create a PivotChart to display this data. (Use Help to determine how to create a PivotChart from the PivotTable.) Analyze the resulting PivotChart. Think about the way this data is coded. Do you think that the PivotChart shows a clear view of how many text messages are actually being sent?

4. Select two fields in the Complete Demographic Analysis workbook that we have not analyzed in this tutorial. Create a PivotTable to show the relationship between those two fields.

5. SmartValue Warehouse Stores operates membership warehouse stores across the Unites States. While the transaction data is managed in corporate transactions processing systems, sales data is periodically downloaded to allow for management to perform a variety of analyses to track performance. Open the SmartValue Warehouse workbook provided by your instructor.
    a. Management wants to analyze the sales by Product Line across the different regions. Create a Pivot Table similar to that shown in Figure Q5 – 1.
    b. Remove the Product Lines from the Pivot Table so that you can compare the Net Sales dollars for each of the regions as a whole.
    c. Convert the Net Sales by Region Pivot Table (step b) into a Pivot Chart. The Pivot Table from step b and the Pivot Chart from step c should be similar to that shown in Figure Q5 – 2. Do you feel the Pivot Table or the Pivot Chart is easier to read to find the best performing region?

	Values		
2			
3			
4 Row Labels ▼	Average of 2006	Average of 2007	Average of 2008
5 ⊟Midwest	$20,919	$21,557	$25,013
6 Ancillary	$19,489	$20,075	$21,601
7 Food	$22,397	$22,707	$26,072
8 Fresh Food	$17,999	$18,032	$20,811
9 Hardlines	$22,167	$23,383	$28,376
10 Softlines	$18,097	$18,703	$23,626
11 Sundries	$25,368	$26,443	$29,589
12 ⊟Northeast	$20,705	$21,661	$22,590
13 Ancillary	$19,256	$18,391	$17,060
14 Food	$22,682	$23,499	$25,199
15 Fresh Food	$16,220	$17,493	$18,004
16 Hardlines	$23,909	$24,106	$26,421
17 Softlines	$17,019	$17,293	$19,150
18 Sundries	$25,144	$29,184	$29,704
19 ⊟Northwest	$19,885	$20,565	$22,954
20 Ancillary	$17,076	$17,431	$17,548
21 Food	$21,173	$22,165	$24,975
22 Fresh Food	$14,461	$15,358	$17,255

Figure Q5 – 1

	Values		
Row Labels ▼	Average of 2006	Average of 2007	Average of 2008
Midwest	$20,919	$21,557	$25,013
Northeast	$20,705	$21,661	$22,590
Northwest	$19,885	$20,565	$22,954
Southeast	$22,985	$23,002	$22,184
Southwest	$19,378	$20,108	$22,086
Grand Total	$20,858	$21,422	$22,901

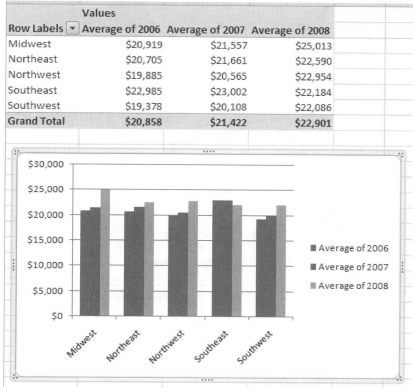

Figure Q5 - 2

TUTORIAL 4

Building a Simple Database

PLANNING AHEAD
After reading Tutorial 4, you should be able to answer these questions in your own words

STUDY QUESTIONS
How can you create a simple database system in Access?
How can you enhance your Access database system?

LEARNING PREVIEW

In Chapter 4 you learned how databases can be used by organizations to manage data. You learned about what a relational database is and the advantages a database can offer. You began studying about how to create a database by developing an Entity Relationship Model. In this tutorial you will expand on this foundation by learning how to build a database system using Microsoft Access. You will explore the primary objects in an Access database, including tables, forms, queries and reports. Finally you will learn how to add some enhancements into a database to increase the functionality.

VISUAL ORGANIZATION OF TUTORIAL

Study Question 1	Study Question 2
Creating a Simple Database System in Access	Enhancing your Database System in Access
• Creating the Database • Create the Student Table • Create the Student Form • Create a Student Query • Create a Report	• Access Field Properties • Customizing a Form • Compound criteria in a Query • Customizing a Report
Learning Check 1	Learning Check 2

CREATING A SIMPLE DATABASE SYSTEM IN ACCESS

What is Microsoft Access? **Microsoft Access** is a relational database management system (RDBMS) created by Microsoft. In Chapter 2 you had a chance to work with the Northwind Traders database, built using the MS Access database management system. You gained familiarity with different functions of a DBMS. By using the options provided in the Navigation Pane as your starting point you were able to add records into the database, view records and create reports.

While many larger companies will choose to use RDBMSs such as Oracle, Sybase, Ingres, or DB2, Access provides all of the tools needed to give you a chance to learn more about the database concepts illustrated earlier in Chapter 4. This section will teach you quite a bit about Access, however it is not designed as an extensive course in using MS Access. As you learned by working in Excel, there is often more than one way to accomplish a task. The same is true in Access. To allow you to focus on learning the key concepts, not all possible approaches to solving a task will be covered.

Example 1: University Registration Database System

To help learn about Access, you will build a simple prototype database system for the University Student Registration exercise you completed in the Understanding IT activity in Chapter 4. To help focus your learning about Access, you will start by creating only a small part of the system. In this section you will learn how to create a database, a table, a form, a query and a report. To start the project the first task is to create a database. In Access the concept of the database is the holding container that will store all of the different Access objects.

Create the Database

> *Practice:*
> Launch the Access DBMS
>
> Select **Blank Database**, under **New Blank Database**, on the **Getting Started with Microsoft Office Access** page.
>
> Enter Student Registration in the **File Name** box. Click on the Folder icon to select the correct folder in which to store your work.
>
> Select **Create** after you have entered the filename. Access will automatically add the extension of .accdb to your file.
>
> *Note: You cannot open an Access 2007 database using an earlier version of Access unless you first convert the database into an earlier file format using the Save As command.*

Your database will now be created. The database will open in Datasheet view and should resemble the screen shown in Figure T4.1.

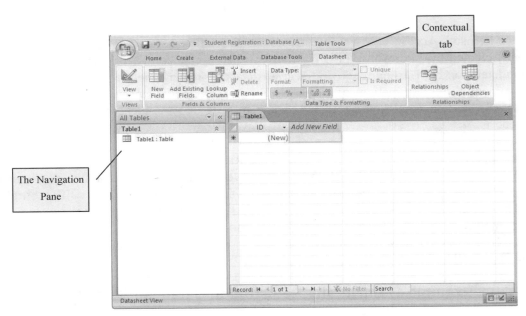

Figure T4.1   The Main Access Database Window

   The Ribbon in the Access Interface contains four primary tabs—Home, Create, External Data and Database Tools. Depending on the task you are working on you may see additional tools on the Ribbon. For example, in Figure T4.1 a Datasheet tab is available within Table Tools. The tabs associated with Table Tools are considered contextual tabs. Remember from your work with Excel that contextual tabs appear only when you are performing certain tasks.

   Now that the database is created, begin to create the different components of your database. For example you will need to create the different tables, forms, and reports needed in the system. In Access these components are called **objects**.   To create an object you will select that object type from the Create Tab. Once an object has been created it will appear in the Navigation Pane. The next few activities will help you learn about the primary objects in Access – the tables, forms, queries and reports.

Create the Student Table

A database **table** is a collection of records. In other words, the database table contains the actual data of your system. Without the tables, you would have little need for any of the other objects. From the ER Model, each of the entities created will become its own table. In Access when you create the database one table is initially created for your use. Additional tables can be built by describing each of the fields, basing it off a template, or by importing data from another source. We will build the student table by describing the fields. While you can describe the fields in Datasheet view, only the most common field properties are available. You will have more control if you switch to Design view.

Practice:
Select Table1.

Select the **Datasheet Tab > Views Group > View > Design View** option.

Access will prompt you to save the table.

Enter tblStudent.

When you name objects in your database, it is helpful to use a standard naming system. For example if you start all table names with a prefix of "tbl", you will be able to clearly identify that object as a table later on. This is extremely helpful when you have a database containing a large number of objects.

Because the first table was automatically created in Datasheet view, Access created a field inside of this table to serve as the primary key. We will want to use a different field as the primary key. As a result, we don't need the field that was automatically created.

Practice:
Select the ID field and select the **Design Tab > Tools Group > Delete Rows** option.

Access will prompt you to make certain you really want to delete a field that is designated as a primary key. Select Yes. Your database should look like that shown in Figure T4.2.

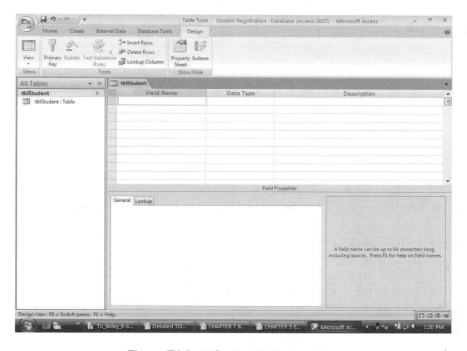

Figure T4.2   tblStudent in Design View

Define the database fields

You are now ready to define the fields needed in the student table. Table T4.1 contains the information about the fields that you will create in the Student table. In the ERD one of the fields was "address." Since it is a better design principal to separate the "address" into its different components, your table will have these as separate pieces.

Field Name	Data Type	Description	Size
StuID	Number	Unique student ID – 8 digits long	Long Integer
StuName	Text	First and Last Name	35
StuAddress	Text	Street address	20
StuCity	Text	City	10
StuState	Text	State	2
StuZip	Text	Zip Code	5
StuPhone	Text	Phone number	10
StuMajor	Text	Major abbreviation code for the major student is enrolled in	5

Table T4.1 Student Table Field Descriptions

> *Practice:*
> In the first row of the upper portion of the *Design View* of the tblStudent, enter the field name, data type and description for the StuID field. Use the choices provided in Table T4.1.
>
> In the Field Properties portion of the screen, enter the Field Size.
>
> Move to the row below StuID. Notice that as you navigate from one row to another, the Field Properties area of the table window changes.

Before you define the remaining fields, it is important to spend a few minutes learning about Field Names and Data Types.

Field Names
In Access a **field name** is used to uniquely identify each field within a table. There are two important rules you must be aware of when creating and using field names.
1. In Access a field name can be up to 64 characters long, including spaces.
2. Within a table, you can't use the same field name for different fields.

So what makes a good field name? First and foremost the name should accurately describe the contents of the field. This means don't name your fields Field1, Field2, etc. Many companies have guidelines or protocols for naming fields. Industry guidelines also are available, although they do vary over time. One guideline suggests beginning each field with the name of the Table (or an abbreviation of the table name) such as StudentName. Sometimes you will find recommended guidelines that conflict with each other. For example some developers suggest using an underscore to separate out words, such as Student_Address. Another developer might suggest using mixed case to separate words, such as StudentAddress. While there is not universal agreement, the most important rule is to decide on the protocol you will follow and then use it consistently.

Data Types

Access has eleven **data types**. A data type determines the type of data that can be stored, along with the different capabilities and storage sizes. The data types, along with a brief description of them, are shown in Table T4.2. The number data type has several subtypes that are selected via the FieldSize property. Those are shown in Table T4.3.

Data Type	Description
Text	Used to store text, combinations of text and numbers, such as an addresses, and number fields, like a phone number, that won't be used in a calculation. Can store up to 255 characters. Use the **FieldSize** property to set the maximum length of the field.
Memo	Used to store text with more than 255 characters or that requires stored rich-text formatting. Can store up to 65,535 characters.
Number	Used to store numbers that will be used in mathematical calculations. Use the **FieldSize** property to define the specific Number type and associated storage requirements. Table 4.10 shows a complete listing of the different number types.
Date/Time	Used to store dates and times. Stores 8 bytes.
Currency	Used to store numbers that represent currency values. This field type prevents rounding off during calculations. Stores 8 bytes.
AutoNumber	Used to have Access insert a unique sequential (incrementing by 1) or random number when a record is added. Stores 4 bytes; stores 16 bytes for Replication ID (GUID).
Yes/No	Used to store fields with one of two possible values, such as Yes/No, True/False, On/Off. This displays as a check box. Stores 1 bit.
OLE Object	Use for OLE objects (such as Microsoft Word documents, Microsoft Excel spreadsheets, pictures, sounds, or other binary data) that were created in other programs. OLE is a program-integration technology used to share information between programs. Stores up to 1 gigabyte (limited by disk space).
Attachment	Used to pictures, images, and Office files. (This is a new data type in Access 2007 and is preferred data type for storing images.) Stores up to 2 gigabytes for compressed documents.
Hyperlink	Used to store hyperlinks. Stores up to 1 gigabytes of characters, of which 65,535 can be displayed in a control.
Lookup Wizard	Used to convert your field into a combo box that allows you to choose a value from another table or from a list of values. This is not really a data type but instead starts a wizard to create the lookup field. Requires the same storage size as the corresponding field.

Table T4.2 Access Data Types (Adapted from Microsoft Access Help Information)

Setting	Description	Storage size
Byte	Used to store numbers from 0 to 255. No decimal precision allowed.	1 byte
Integer	Used to store numbers from –32,768 to 32,767. No decimal precision allowed.	2 bytes
Long Integer	Used to store numbers from –2,147,483,648 to 2,147,483,647. No decimal precision allowed. This is the default number type.	4 bytes
Single	Used to store numbers from –3.4 x 10^{38} to +3.4 x 10^{38} with a precision of 7 significant digits. .	4 bytes
Double	Used to store numbers from –1.797 x 10^{38} to +1.797 x 10^{38} with a precision of 15 significant digits.	8 bytes
Replication ID	Used to store a globally unique identifier (GUID) randomly generated by Access.	16 bytes
Decimal	Used to stores numbers from -10^{28} to $+10^{28}$ with a precision of up to 28 significant digits.	12 bytes

Table T4.3 Field Size settings for Number Data Types (Adapted from Microsoft Access Help Information)

With so many choices, how do you know what to select? You must consider how a field will be used to determine the best choice. As you review the list of data types remember that your choice of data type should incorporate two primary considerations:

1.   **Select a data type that allows for needed processing**. For example, although a "total amount" is certainly numeric, it should be defined as a currency data type to prevent rounding during calculations. Some database developers recommend storing fields that are made up of numbers, but never used in calculations, as a text field. This prevents you from using that field in error in a mathematical operation. However, you need to balance that benefit against limitations that may arise based on that choice. For example, numbers will sort differently if they are stored as text. The text values of 1, 2, 11, 29, and 1500 will sort based as a string of characters resulting in an order of 1, 11, 1500, 2, 29. If you need to sort a field consisting of numbers you should not store it as a text field.

2.   **Select a data type that uses the smallest possible Field Size**. This allows faster processing and requires less storage and memory. For example, assume you wanted to add a "Graduated" field that would store whether the student has graduated from the university. The graduated field could be:
    - Text with a size of 3 (allowing the words Yes or No.) This would require 3 bytes to store "yes." With 8 bits in a byte that total storage space is 24 bits.
    - Text with a size of 1 (allowing the characters Y or N.) This would require 1 byte to store the character for a total storage space of 8 bits.
    - Yes/No. This displays as a check box and requires 1 bit of storage space.

    For systems where you are storing large quantities of data the impact of this difference in the required storage size can become significant.

With this overview about the choices available when creating fields, you are ready to finish building the Student Table.

Practice:
Following the same steps you used to define the StuID field, create the remaining fields from Table T4.1.

After you have finished entering all of the fields, continue to the next step.

Select the StuID field and then select the **Design Tab > Tools Group > Primary Key** option.

How do you know which field would make a good Primary Key? You should look for a field that will have a unique value for each student. Since StuID is a unique identifier and will make a good primary key.

Save the Table by selecting the **Save** icon on the **Quick Access Toolbar** or on the **Office Button**.

Your system should now resemble the screen shown in Figure T4.3. When you create a table, or make changes to the structure of the table (change the field properties) you will primarily work in **Design View**. To see the contents (the actual student records) of your table you need to switch to **Datasheet View**. You will also use Datasheet view to add, delete and change the contents.

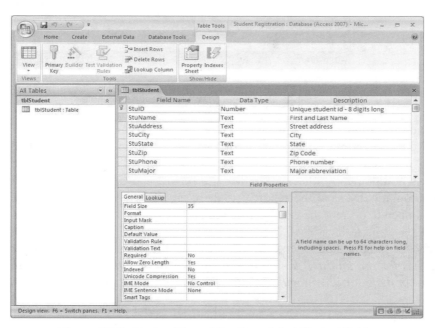

Figure T4.3 Design View of the Completed Student Table

Switch to the Datasheet View.

Practice:
Select the **Design Tab > Views Group > Datasheet View > View** option.

The Datasheet view, shown in Figure T4.4 allows you to view the records that have been entered into the table. If you want to make the columns wider, simply click and drag the column separator in the field. Currently you don't have any data in the table. You can also add new records, edit records, or delete records in this view. With the cursor positioned in the first record of the student table, you are ready to begin entering data values.

Note: In the Datasheet view, if you select the Datasheet Contextual Tab, you are allowed to make some changes to the table structure as well. For example, notice the options in the Data Type and Formatting Group in Figure T4.4.   As mentioned earlier, since the field property options are limited, the Design View is the recommended view to make table structure changes.

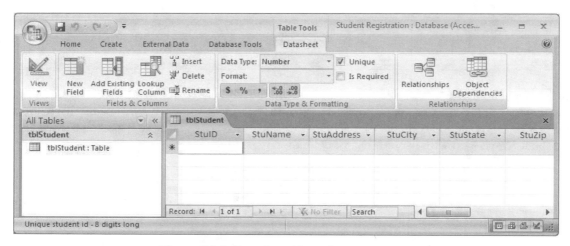

Figure T4.4 Datasheet View of the Student Table

How do you add the rows of data into your table? Enter the numeric or text data directly into each field. Use the *keyboard navigation arrows* or *tab key* to move between fields and records. After entering data into a record, when you leave that record (navigate to a field on another record), Access automatically checks whether the record can be saved. If there are no errors Access will automatically save the record. If there are errors, such as leaving a required field blank, you will need to correct the error before the record will be saved.

Table T4.4 shows sample data to enter into the Student Table. *Note: The phone number data shows the dashes for readability; don't enter the dashes in the phone number field when you add the data. Later in the tutorial you will learn how to have the dashes display in the field.*

StuID	StuName	StuAddress	StuCity	Stu State	Stu Zip	StuPhone	Stu Major
82210003	Jessica Williams	5433 Montezuma Ave	San Diego	CA	92117	858-259-4432	Bus
85312243	Henry Jericho	33220 Water Ave	Tucson	AZ	85109	805-943-4444	Engr
85429938	Joe Johnson	9 Main Street	Phoenix	AZ	85225	805-524-0443	Hist
86640093	Angela Rivera	2765 West Hills Dr	Cypress	CA	90630	213-987-3358	Psyc
87026754	Mike Bergstrom	6332 Artesia Blvd	Anaheim	CA	92806	714-635-4949	Bus
87210243	Eric Nelson	5246 Maple St	San Diego	CA	85715	619-555-2356	Engr

Table T4.4 Data Values for the Student Registration System

Practice:

Enter the data for the first three students (students 82210003, 85312243, and 85429938) in datasheet view. Be sure to enter the correct value in each field. Remember to enter the phone numbers without the dashes.

Save and close the table when you are finished.

Create the Student Form

A database **form** provides the ability to add, update, delete and view data. While these tasks can be done in datasheet view, a form usually provides a more user-friendly interface. A form can be customized to include instructions and command buttons. Additionally, you can place fields on the form in an order that eases data entry, and you can select a subset of the table fields to include on the form. There are several types of forms you can create in Access and several different ways to create the database forms. We will cover a few of the more common ways to create a form. A quick way to create a form is with the Form Tool. The Form Tool automatically creates a basic form all the fields from the source table or query. The Form Tool is accessed by selecting the **Create Tab > Forms Group > Form** option. A second way to create forms is to use the Form Wizard. The **Form Wizard** provides you with choices about the source table(s) or queries and you select specific fields along with your choice of common form layouts. The Form Wizard is accessed by selecting the **Create Tab > Forms Group > More Forms > Form Wizard** option. A third way to create forms is to use the Blank Form Tool. With the Blank Form Tool you design the form from scratch. The Blank Form Tool is accessed by selecting the **Create Tab > Forms Group > Blank Form** option. We will use the Form Wizard option.

Practice:
Select the **Create Tab > Forms Group > More Forms> Form Wizard** option.

Let's work our way through creating the student form using the wizard.

Select the fields to appear on the form.

In the first step in the Form Wizard, shown in Figure T4.5, you select the fields that will be on your form. The fields can come from Tables or Queries. Right now you only have one table, so you don't need to make a change to the *Table/Queries* drop down. You can add individual fields onto a form with the **Select Single Field** button ⟩ or add all of the fields onto the form with the **Select All Fields** button ⟩⟩.

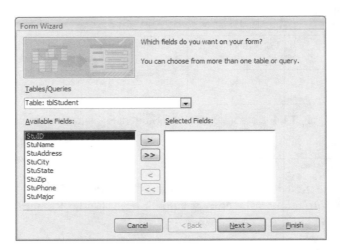

Figure T4.5   Selecting Fields - The first step of the Form Wizard

---

Practice:
Click on the **Select All Fields** button to move all of the fields from the *Available fields* window to the *Selected fields* window.

Click **Next** to continue.

Select the layout of the form.

In the second step in the Form Wizard, shown in Figure T4.6, you will decide on the form layout.

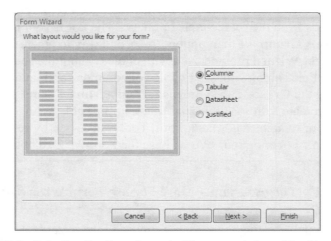

Figure T4.6   Selecting the Form Layout - The second step of the Form Wizard

Practice:
Select the radio button for *columnar* layout.

Click **Next** to continue.

Select the style of the form.
In the third step in the Form Wizard, shown in Figure T4.7, you will decide on the style of the form. Click on several of the style choices to preview the different options.

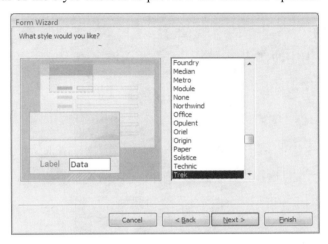

Figure T4.7 Selecting the Form Style - The third step of the Form Wizard

Practice:
Select *Access 2007.*

Click **Next** to continue.

Name and Save the Form.
In the last step in the Form Wizard, shown in Figure T4.8, you will name the form. The recommended prefix for form names is "frm."

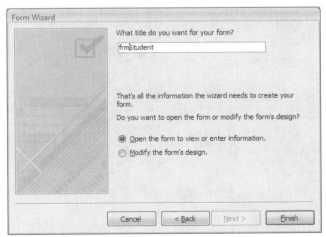

Figure T4.8 Saving the Form - The final step of the Form Wizard

> ***Practice:***
> Enter "frmStudent."
>
> Click on **Finish**.

The completed form is shown in Figure T4.9. Later in this tutorial we will add some enhancements to this form to make it easier to use and more attractive.

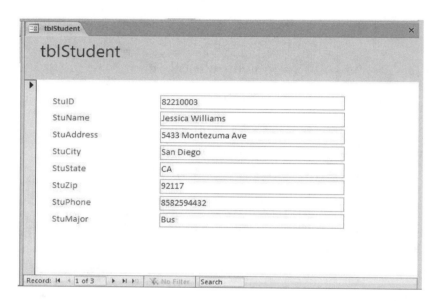

Figure T4.9 The completed Student Form

Enter the remaining student records.

> ***Practice:***
> Use the form you created to enter the remaining 3 student records shown earlier in Table T4.4
>
>   Use the navigation buttons to move among the different records. The navigation button functions are explained in Figure T4.10.

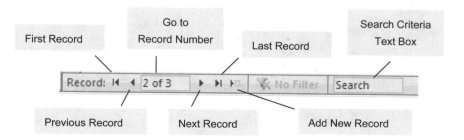

Figure T4.10 The Record Navigation Buttons

> *Practice:*
> Close the Student Form when you are done entering the records.

We will now learn how to write a query to find data that has been entered into your database.

Create a Student Query

A database **query** is a question about, or a request for information from, your database. Queries provide a powerful tool to be able to analyze the contents of your system. They can access information from multiple tables. While queries can be used to update or delete data based on certain conditions, the most common query is a **select query** – one that allows you to ask a question about that data. The results of a query are shown in datasheet view. If desired, you can create a form or report based on a query which will then allow for a more customized viewing experience. Access provides two ways to create a database query. In Design View you start with a blank query and decide on the tables, fields and criteria that will be part of the query. With the Wizard you can select tables and fields, but you are limited by not being able to provide selection criteria or to perform more advanced tasks such as updating data. We will use the Design View to create a select query.

> *Practice:*
> Select the **Create Tab > Other Group > Query Design** option.
>
> A new Select Query opens in design view and the Show Table dialogue box appears.
>
> Click **Add** to indicate the query will use the tblStudent table.
>
> Close the Show Table dialogue box.
>
> Since you only have the tblStudent, it was already selected. If you had created more tables you would first select the correct table before clicking Add.

Design the Query
Figure T4.11, shows the design view for a query. The top portion of the window shows the table(s) that will be used in the query. The bottom portion shows the fields that have been selected, along with any additional specifications such as a sorting order or selection criteria. You can adjust the height of the top or bottom windows by moving the divider bar. You can resize the table to show all fields at one time.

You will create a query that will show the student ID and student name for all students who live in California.   You may recall that from the 6 student records you entered (shown in Table T4.4) that 4 of the students live in California.

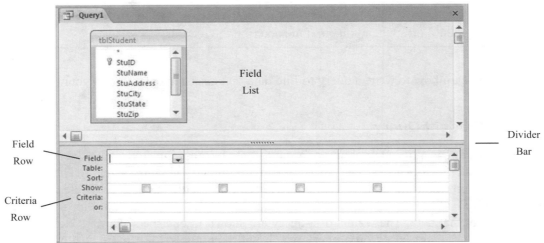

Figure T4.11 The Design View of a Query

Practice:
Drag the StudentID field to the first column in the Query Grid.

Drag StuName to the second column.

Drag StuState to the third column.

In the Criteria row for the StuState, enter "CA".

Uncheck the Show Box for the StuState column, since you don't want the StuState field to show in the query.

Access calls this graphical or drag-and-drop approach to building a query **Query By Example**. Your query grid should match that shown in Figure T4.12.

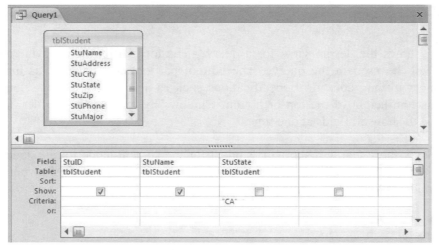

Figure T4.12 The Completed Design View of a Query

Finish the query

After you run the query, the results will show in datasheet view as shown in Figure T4.13. Notice that the StuName column is not wide enough to show the complete name. You can easily widen the column by using the mouse to click and drag the column larger.

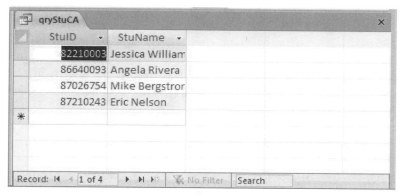

Figure T4.13 The Query Results

As you just learned, the design view mode of creating a query in Access uses Query by Example, a graphical interface for writing queries.   Behind the graphical interface, Access uses **Structured Query Language (SQL),** the most common language used to interact with databases. Users have the option of writing queries directly in SQL or using the graphical interface. Access converts the query by example queries into SQL. SQL queries use the Select keyword. In the Select statement you specify the fields you want to display, the table(s) that contain the fields, and any criteria used in the query.

An example of the Select statement for the query in Figure T4.12 is:
SELECT StuID, StuName
FROM tblStudent
WHERE StuState = "CA".

You can see the actual SQL code that is created by selecting the **Query Tools Design Tab > View > SQL View** option.   The code generated by Access for the query shown in Figure T4.14.

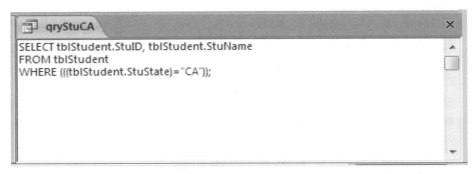

Figure T4.14   The SQL View of the Students in California Query

Notice in Figure T4.14 that Access uses a fully qualified field name (e.g. tblStudent.StuID) which includes the table name along with the field name. While you won't need to write the queries for your system directly in SQL, it will be helpful to understand SQL for some of the features you will want to include in your database.

Create a Report

A database **report** provides the ability to organize, view and print data. When viewing data in a report you are not able to change that data, unlike viewing it in a table or form. Using reports can be helpful when you want to protect your data from accidental changes. A report can be based on a table or a query, and can be customized to include titles, groupings, and summary fields. Additionally, fields can be arranged in any order on the report to improve readability. Access provides three ways to create a database report.

A quick way to create a report is with the Report Tool. The Report Tool automatically creates a basic report using all the fields from the source table or query. The Report Tool is accessed by selecting the **Create Tab > Reports Group > Report** option. A second way to create reports is to use the Report Wizard. With the Report Wizard, you are provided with choices about the source table(s) or queries and can select specific fields along with a choice of common report layouts. The Report Wizard is accessed by selecting the **Create Tab > Reports Group > Report Wizard** option. A third way to create reports is to use the Blank Report Tool. With the Blank Report Tool you design the report from scratch. The Blank Report tool is accessed by selecting the **Create Tab > Reports Group > Blank Report** option. We will use the Wizard to create our report. We will use the Wizard to create our report.

Practice:
Select the **Create Tab > Reports Group > Report Wizard** option.

Select the fields to appear on the report.
In the first step in the Report Wizard, shown in Figure T4.15, you select the fields that will be on your report. The fields can come from Tables or Queries. At this point your database contains the student table and the California students' query. Build your report based on the qryStuCA query. Add individual fields onto a report with the **Select Single Field** button or add all the fields onto the report with the **Select All Fields** button ⟩⟩.

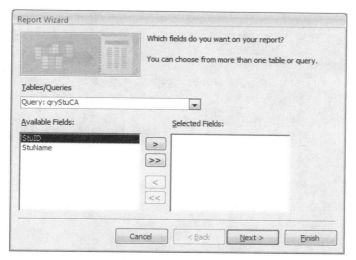

Figure T4.15 Selecting Fields - The first step of the Report Wizard

---

Practice:
Click on the **Select All Fields** button to move all of the fields from the *Available fields* window to the *Selected fields* window.

Click **Next** to continue.

Select any groupings for the report.
In the second step in the Report Wizard you can indicate that you want the records to be grouped according to selected fields. This would be appropriate if you were showing all of the student records, instead of just those in California, and wanted the results to be grouped by the state. In our example, grouping doesn't make sense.

Practice:
Click **Next** to continue.

Select any sorting for the report.
In the third step in the Report Wizard you can indicate that you want the records to be sorted according to selected fields. If you wanted the records to be in alphabetical order by the student name you could make that selection now. In our example, we will not sort the records.

Practice:
Click **Next** to continue.

Select the layout for the report.
In the fourth step in the Report Wizard, shown in Figure T4.16, you decide on the form layout.

Practice:
Select the radio button for *tabular* layout.

 Since this report only includes two fields, keeping a *portrait* orientation will be fine. For future reports you may choose to have a landscape orientation to allow a better spacing of fields.

Click **Next** to continue.

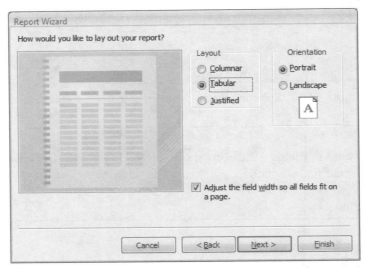

Figure T4.16 Selecting the Report Layout - The fourth step of the Report Wizard

Select the style for the report.
In the fifth step in the Report Wizard, shown in Figure T4.17, decide on the style of the report.

Practice:
Click on several of the style choices to preview the different options.

Select *Access 2007.*

Click **Next** to continue.

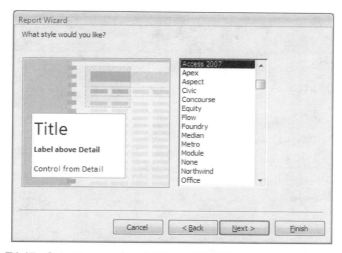

Figure T4.17   Selecting the Report Style - The fifth step of the Report Wizard

Name and Save the Report.

In the last step in the Report Wizard, shown in Figure T4.18, name the report. The recommended prefix for report names is "rpt."

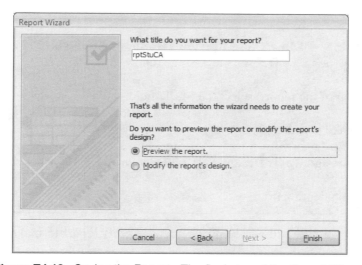

Figure T4.18   Saving the Report - The final step of the Report Wizard

Practice:
Enter "rptStuCA."

Click on **Finish**.

The completed report is shown in preview mode in Figure T4.19.

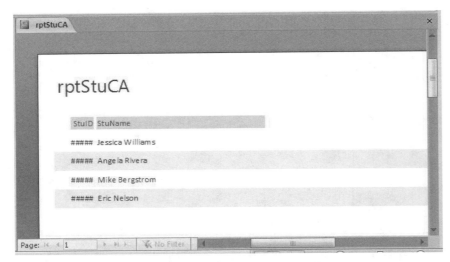

Figure T4.19   The completed Student Report

Fine Tune the Report Layout

Notice that for theStuID field, the Form Wizard did not set the column width large enough to see the entire ID value.

Practice:
Select the **Print Preview Tab > Close Preview Group > Close Print Preview** option.
   You should now be in the Design View of the report.

In the Detail Section of the report, select the StuID field.

Drag the field to make it wider.

Select the **Report Design Tools Design Tab > Views Group > View > Print Preview** option.

Save and close the student report.

Later in this tutorial we will add some enhancements to this report to make it easier to use and more attractive.

   In this section you started the process of creating a database application using Access. You learned how to create a database, as well as how to build many of the objects you will use in your application. Now you are ready to explore how to add more functionality into your system.

LEARNING CHECK
Be sure you can *create a database *understand the importance of selecting the correct field types when building a table *build a simple form, query and report *understand the differences between the different objects in Access

ENHANCING YOUR DATABASE SYSTEM IN ACCESS

You have a good start on some of the basics necessary to create a database using Access. In this section you will explore some of the features Access offers to enhance your database. These features include utilizing field properties to help ensure data integrity, customizing a form with additional objects, using compound criteria in queries and customizing a report. These enhancements will make your database system easier for your users.

Access Field Properties

You already learned that a DBMS can help with ensuring data integrity. For this to occur, you need to tell the DBMS what needs to be validated. When you defined the fields in the table you selected the field type and size, so the DBMS is already validating those rules.   The **field properties** allow you to indicate additional data integrity constraints. We will explore several properties you may choose to help ensure data integrity. Remember that the choice of which properties to ultimately use, and the settings to apply to those properties, will have been determined during the analysis and design phases of the systems development life cycle.

In the Student Table, you will learn to define a validation rule so that all Student Numbers will be 8 digits long and will all start with the number 8.

Practice:
Open *tblStudent* in Design View (In the Navigation Pane, right-click tblStudent and then click Design View.)

Select the *StuID* field.

Look at the properties for the StuID field. Most of the field properties are found on the *General Tab*, which is emphasized in Figure T4.20. A few are found on the *Lookup Tab*, which we will explore later in this tutorial.

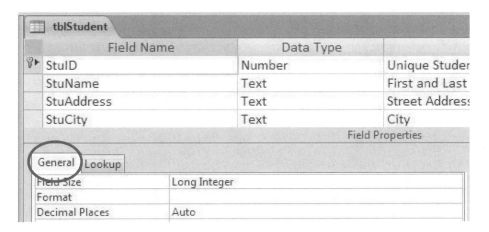

Figure T4.20   The General Tab of the Field Properties

Validation Rule and Validation Text

The **Validation Rule** property is used to enter specific requirements for the data in a field. These requirements might include defining a range of values for a number, or indicating that a field must start with a specific letter, or providing a list of possible answers. Access checks the validation rule when you leave the field and move to another field. Examples of entries for the validation rule property, along with an explanation of the effect are shown in Table T4.5.

Validation Rule	Explanation of Effect
<> 0	The value entered must not equal zero.
>=21	The value entered must be greater than or equal to 21.
Like "A???"	The value entered must be 4 characters long and begin with the letter "A". *Note: The ? wildcard character is used to match any single alphabetic character.*
Like "A*"	The value entered may have any number of characters (up to the field size limit) and must begin with the letter "A". *Note: The * wildcard character is used to match any number of characters.*
Like "2####"	The value entered must be 5 numeric characters long and begin with the number 2. *Note: The # wildcard character is used to match any single numeric character.*
"A" OR "B" OR "C" OR "D" OR "F"	The value entered must contain only one of the 5 possible choices listed (A, B, C, D, or F)
>= #1/1/2007# AND <#1/1/2009#	The value entered must be a date from 2007 or 2008

Table T4.5 Examples of Validation Rules

If the data entered does not meet the validation rule, a standard error message is displayed to the user. A customized error message can be created by entering the text you wish to display in the **Validation Text** property.

Practice:
In the properties window for the StuID field:

Enter   Like "8#######" in the **Validation Rule** property.

Save the table.
    Since your table already contains data, Access will display a warning message notifying you that the data integrity rules have changed. The message asks if you want to have Access check all of the existing data to make sure that it meets the new criteria.

Select **Yes**. This will ensure that your data meets the new criteria.

To see the effect of the standard error message complete the following steps.

> **Practice:**
> Switch to Datasheet View.
>
> Add a new record and enter a Student ID value of 32220001.

Did you receive a message similar to the one shown below in Figure T4.21? Do you think that your user would understand what that message means? Would they be able to figure out what they did wrong and how to correct it? Probably not. Utilizing the Validation Text property to create a custom error message helps the database system be more user-friendly.

Figure T4.21 An example of a Standard Error Message when using a Validation Rule

Before you can create a custom error message you will need to complete the practice below to correct the error caused by entering an invalid Student ID Number value.

> **Practice:**
> Press Ok to close the error message.
>
> Change the Student ID value to 80110207 and enter the data values shown below in the other fields:
>
> | | |
> |---|---|
> | **StuName:** | Tessa Varsonofieva |
> | **StuAddress:** | 3319 College Avenue |
> | **StuCity:** | Oceanside |
> | **StuState:** | CA |
> | **StuZip:** | 92054 |
> | **StuPhone:** | 760-237-9965 |
> | **StuMajor:** | Engr |
>
> Enter a custom message in the Validation text property by completing the following steps.
> - Switch to Design View.
> - Select the *Student ID* field.
> - Enter "The Student ID must be 8 digits long and begin with the number 8." in the **Validation Text** property.
>
> Save the table.

The effect of the new error message can be seen by switching back to Design View and entering an incorrect value.

Lookup Tab Properties

The field properties used so far have been found on the **General Tab**. Several additional properties found on the **Lookup Tab** allow you to make changes related to the type of display control. The **display control** indicates the type of control used on a form to display the field. Text or numeric fields initially have their control type set to a textbox. On the Lookup Tab you can change the display control to a list box or combo box. Both a list box and a combo box limit the possible choices to a predefined selection.

You just learned about using the Validation Rule property to limit the selection of choices. Why would you want to change the display control? With the Validation Rule property, the user first enters a value in the textbox. When the user leaves that field, the entry is checked against the Validation Rule. If the entry is not valid, Access displays an error message. This is an appropriate method to validate when the user is required to know the value they should enter (for example a User ID or Password.) In comparison, by using a list or combo box, the user is shown the list of valid choices and then selects from that list. This prevents the user from entering a value that is not valid. The main difference between a list box and a combo box is how each will appear on a form. Figure T4.22 illustrates the appearance of a list box and a combo box. Notice that the values for a list box appear at all times, while the combo box values will only appear when the user selects the drop-down arrow for that control. Additionally, with a combo box you can restrict the data entry to only those choices provided in the value list.

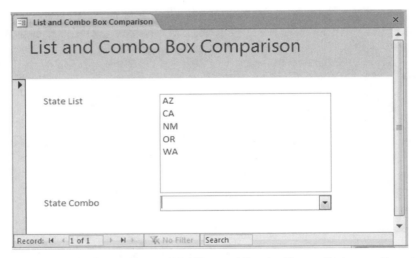

Figure T4.22   Comparison of List Box and Combo Box controls on a Form

In the Student Table, you will create a combo box for the State field. For this example, assume that the university is a regional university, with most of the students living in 5 western states. To help save time in the data entry, the university wants to use a combo box in the Student Table that provides the choices for the State field to the following states (AZ, CA, NM, OR, WA.) However, if a student lives in a different state they will still be allowed to enter a 2 digit code for a different state.

Practice:
Open the *tblStudent* in Design View.

Select the *StuState* field.

Select the **Lookup Tab**.

Select *Combo Box* in the **Display Control** property.

Select *Value List* in the **Row Source Type** property.

Enter   AZ; CA; NM; OR; WA in the **Row Source** property.

Save the table.

Switch to Datasheet view and navigate to the State field on one of the records.
    Does your combo box now appear showing you the choices of your 5 valid states?

Try to enter a state not on the list.
    This is allowed since you left the setting of *"No"* on the **Limit to List** property.

Default Value

The **Default Value property**, on the General Tab, is used to automatically enter a specified value into the field. This property is useful when most of your records would contain the same answer for a field. Having Access automatically enter the value can save your user time when entering the data. Of course, your user can change the value from the default if they wish.

Practice:
Open the Student Table in Design View.

Select the *StuState* field.

Enter "CA" in the **Default Value** property.

Save the table.

Switch to Datasheet View.

Notice that the last record of your table, where you would enter a new student, already has CA as the default value.

Customizing a Form

When you built the Student Form earlier, you learned how to create a basic form using the Form Wizard. While that provides a good starting point, in most cases you will want to customize the form. Some enhancements you can make include adding additional graphics or text, rearranging where the fields appear on the form, and changing the words in the labels. In Access the items that appear on a form are called **controls**. When the form was initially built, the wizard created textbox controls for the different fields and label controls to display the field name.

It is important for you to realize that the student form made earlier in this tutorial is based on the specifications of the student table in place at that time. If you later change the underlying table by adding or deleting fields, or changing field properties, some of the changes may not be automatically transferred to existing database objects, such as forms. In your case, the student table was changed after the student form was created. You changed the student table by adding a validation rule and text, adding a default value and creating a combo box. The specific changes made include:

- Adding a validation rule to restrict the Student ID to an 8 digit field beginning with an 8.
- Adding a default value of CA in the State field
- Changing the State field to a combo box display control

Let's see if these changes to the underlying structure of the table are reflected in the form.

Practice:
Open the *Student Form* in Form View.

Add a new record with the Student ID value of 223171.
    Notice that you should get an error message.

Look at the **State** field.
    Notice that the default value of CA does appear. However the control on the form
    is still a textbox, not the combo box that you indicated.

As you saw, the validation rule change carries forward to an existing form, as did a default value. However, the change in the display control does not carry forward to an existing form. While we could edit the existing form, at this stage in your learning about Access, the easiest way to ensure that the student form utilizes the most recent features built into the table will be to create a new form based on the new table.

Practice:
Select the existing *Student Form* and Delete it.

Use the Form Wizard to create a new Student Form, based on the student table.
    Be sure to include all the fields from the table onto the form.

When you have completed the wizard, open the new student form in design view.
    Your screen should appear similar to that shown in Figure T4.23.

Notice that the form is divided into three sections – the Form Header, the Detail area, and the Form Footer. The Form Header Section and Footer Section contain information that stays constant for all records. Company names, form titles and graphics are often displayed in the

Header Section while command buttons and instructions are often displayed in the Footer Section. The Detail Section displays the contents of a record. Currently your form has controls in the Form Header and Detail sections.

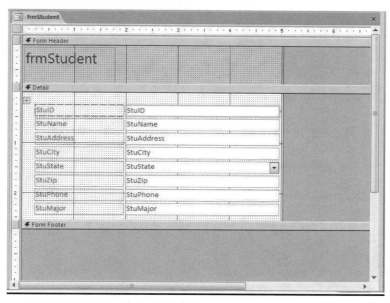

Figure T4.23   Design View of the Student Form

Enlarge the form

The first task is to make the form larger so that you have some working room. Modify the canvas so that your form looks similar to the one shown in Figure T4.24.

> **Practice:**
> Place the pointer at the right hand edge of the form.
>> The cursor will change from a white arrow into a black cross-hatch.
>
> Drag the cursor to the right to make the form canvas larger.
>
> Place the pointer at the top of the Form footer section separator.
>> It will change from a white arrow into a black cross-hatch.
>
> Drag it down slightly to enlarge the form canvas.
>
> Place the pointer at the bottom of the footer section separator.
>> It will change from a white arrow into a black cross-hatch.
>
> Drag it down slightly to create some room in the footer.

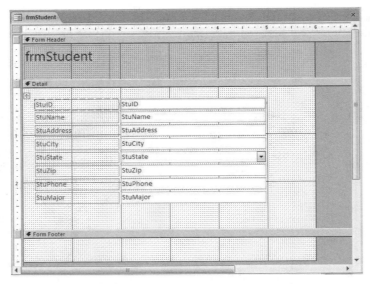

Figure T4.24   Enlarged Canvas of the Student Form

Editing the Background of a Section

The different sections of a form, along with many of the controls placed into a section, begin with a background color based on the style selected when the form was created. For example, if you choose the *Access 2007* style, your form should have a blue header section and the rest of the sections are white. You can change the background color by editing the properties of each section.

Practice:
Click in the Form Header section to select it.

Right click and select **Properties** to open the properties window.

Select the **Back Color** property and **click** the **ellipse** icon to open the color palette.
  Because you selected the *Access 2007* style when you created the form you should see that the Header is using the 6th color from the Access Theme Color section.

In the **Selection Type Section**, change from Form Header to Form Footer.

Change the **Back Color** property to match that of the Form Header section.

The completed Property Sheet window should match that shown in Figure T4.25.

  Note: *If you didn't choose the Access 2007 style, or if your theme colors are different, you can select another color to use for the Back Color of the Form Header and Footer sections.*

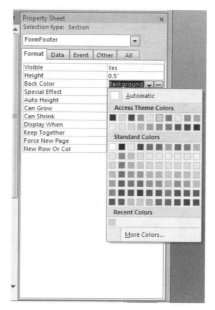

Figure T4.25 The Property Sheet Window for the Form Footer

Edit the Caption of Label Controls

When you created the form you included all of the fields from the Student Table. Access created a Text Box control for each field and a Label control that would identify each Text Box. Access uses the field name as the **caption**, or text shown, in the label.   The field name might be appropriate as the caption, but often you will want to use more descriptive text inside of the label. There are two ways that you can change the label text. First, you can select a label and then click inside of the label to edit the label text. The caption could also be changed by selecting the label, right-clicking to open the shortcut menu, and selecting the Caption Property. An example of the Properties window for the StuCity field is shown in Figure T4.26.   Practice editing some of the labels.

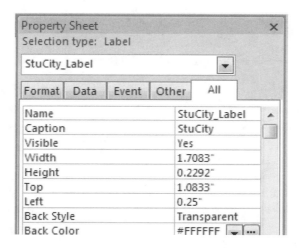

Figure T4.26 The Property Sheet for the StuCity Label

Practice:
Be sure that you are selecting the "label" control instead of the "textbox" control when performing these changes.

In the **Properties Window** for the StuCity label, change the **Caption Property** to read *City* instead of *StuCity*.

Edit the text directly inside of the StuZip label so that it reads Zip Code.

Using the Properties window, edit the Caption Property of the StuState label to read State.

In the **Form Header section** change the caption of the frmStudent label to read Beach Cities College.

Use the sizing handles to adjust that label so that all the text fits on one line.

Save your form so you don't lose your changes.

Add a Label into the Header Section

If you want to add additional controls, such as labels, buttons, or graphics, onto the form you will select the appropriate control from the **Form Design Tools Design Tab > Controls Group.** The Controls Group is shown in Figure T4.27. Several of the controls that we will use are emphasized.

Figure T4.27 The Controls Group

Create an additional Label for the Form Header section to identify the student form.

Practice:
Select the Label Control Icon.

Add a label into the Header Section - **Click** and **hold the click** in the header section below the Beach Cities College label. Then **drag** the mouse to adjust the size of the label control.

Enter "Student Information Form" directly into the label.
    If desired you can change the font type, size or alignment by selecting the label control and changing the appropriate formatting options.

Move Label and Text Box Controls

Access uses Control Layouts to give your form a uniform appearance. A **control layout** aligns the controls placed inside of that layout both horizontally and vertically on a form. Because you created this form using the wizard, all of the fields were placed into one control layout. This means that all of those fields will have the same size. Figure T4.28 shows the control layout for the Student Registration Form.

Practice:
Select the City Label.

Using the sizing handles, make the label smaller.
    Notice that all of the labels in that control layout adjusted.

Adjust the position of the label captions by aligning them all to the right.

Rearrange the different controls within a control layout by dragging a control to the new location. For example, you could drag the StuMajor control to appear above the StuPhone control.

To select the entire control layout, click the Layout Selector at the top left corner of the layout.

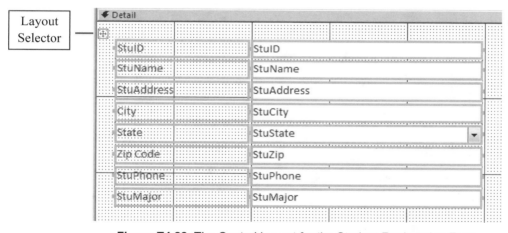

Figure T4.28 The Control Layout for the Student Registration Form

If you want to adjust the placement or sizing of individual controls you will need to move those controls to a separate control layout. Move the StuMajor controls so they appear to the right of the StuID controls.

Practice:
Select the StuMajor textbox control (the label will be selected with it automatically.)

Select the **Arrange Tab** > **Control Layout Group** > **Stacked** option.
    Access will create a new control layout with the StuMajor controls. Notice the new
    Layout Selector icon next to the StuMajor Label.

Make the StuMajor textbox and label smaller in size. Change the caption to Major.

Move the StuMajor textbox and label to the right of the StuID controls.

Adjust the form size and control placements so that your form resembles the one shown in
Figure T4.29.

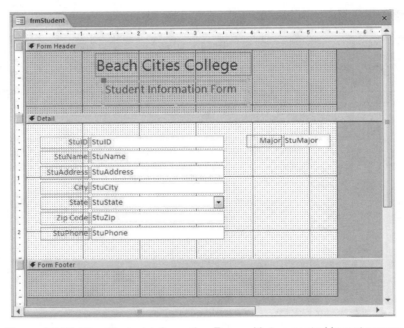

Figure T4.29 The Student Information Form with two control layout groups

Add a Command Button onto the Form

Command Buttons are used to automate the performance of different tasks. In most cases, a command button will make a task easier for your user to perform. For example, you can put a button on a form to print a record or form. Without the command button, the user would have to select the Print Command from the Office Button Menu. Examples of some other functions that command buttons can perform include opening a form, closing a form, adding a new record and opening a report. When you add a button onto the form you need to tell Access what function or event the button should perform. Using the Control Wizards to help build the event procedure greatly simplifies this task.

Create a Button to Print the Current Form.

Practice:

Before you add a button onto your form, ensure that the Control Wizards icon is selected. Once selected, it will appear orange, as shown previously in Figure T4.27.

Select the **Form Design Tools Design Tab > Controls Group > Button** option.

Click inside of the Footer Section of the form to place the button in the Footer Section. The **Command Button Wizard**, as shown in Figure T4.30, will open.

Select *Record Operations* in the **Categories** area.

Select *Print Record* in the **Actions** area.

Click **Next**.

Select the **Text** radio button and enter "Print Student Record" as the text to display in the caption.

Click **Next**.

Enter cmdPrintStuInfo as the name of the button.

Click **Finish**.

If the Font Color for the button is too light to be able to read the caption of the button, you can open the properties for the button and change the Fore Color property to Text Dark.

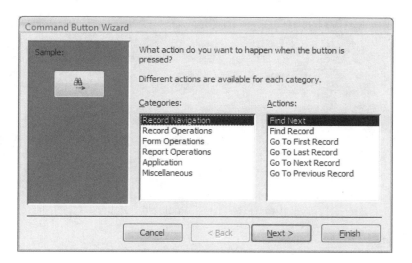

Figure T4.30 The Control Button Wizard Menu

Finish the Form

Add a second button onto the form that will Close the Form and a third button that will Add a New Student.

Practice:

Add the Close Button:

Select *Form Operations* in the **Categories** area and *Close Form* in the **Actions** area.

Decide on an appropriate caption.

Add the Add Student Button:

Select *Record Operations* in the **Categories** area and *Add New Record* in the **Actions** area.

Decide on an appropriate caption.

Complete the enhancements to your form so that it looks similar to the form shown in Figure T4.31.

Save the form.

Close the form when you are finished.

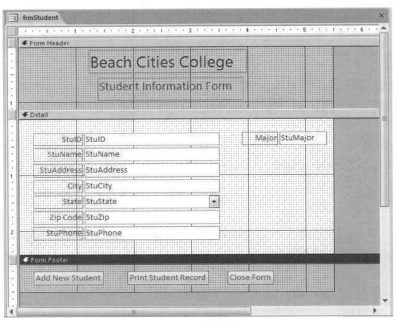

Figure T4.31 The Completed Form

Compound Criteria in a Query

Earlier you created a select query that would find students who lived in California. Recall that in the criteria row of the query grid, you entered the value you wanted to use as the criteria. Often you will need to create a query that answers a compound question – one that uses either an "and" or an "or", or both. For example, perhaps you want to find all the students who live in San Diego, California or in Phoenix, Arizona. To write a query to perform this task you will need use **compound criteria**, two or more different criteria values located in several different cells.

Build an AND Query

If you enter criteria into two or more fields on the same criteria row, Access interprets the query as an "and" query. For example, the query grid shown in Figure T4.32 can be used to find students who live in the city of "San Diego" and the state of "California."

> *Practice:*
>
> Create a new Query in Design View by selecting the **Create Tab > Other Group > Query Design** option.
>
> Add the student table into the query.
>
> Close the Show Table dialog box.
>
> Edit the query grid for your query so that it matches Figure T4.31.
>
> Run the query to ensure that it works.

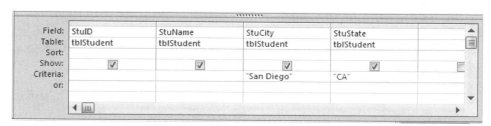

Figure T4.32 Creating an "AND" Query

Build an OR Query

If you enter criteria into two or more fields on different criteria rows, Access interprets the query as an "or" query. For example, the query grid shown in Figure T4.33 can be used to find students who live in "California" or in "Arizona."

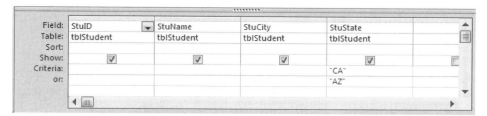

Figure T4.33 Creating an "OR" Query

Practice:
Change the *AND* query that you just created so that it will find the students records that meet this "OR" criteria.

Run the query to ensure that it works.

Finally, let's look at an example of a query that combines the "and" and "or" in one query. Returning to our example earlier, in order to find all the students who live in San Diego, California or in Phoenix, Arizona, you will need to use both the "and" and "or." Notice in the query grid shown in Figure T4.34, the query is looking for the city of "San Diego" and the state of "California" or the city of "Phoenix" and the state of "Arizona."

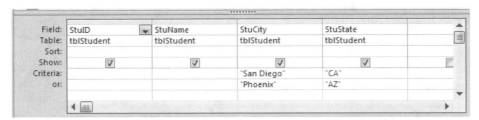

Figure T4.34 Combining an "AND" with an "OR" in a Query

Practice:
Change the *OR* query that you just created so that it will find the records that meet this criteria.

Run the query to ensure that it works.

Save and close the query.

In Tutorial 5, we will write more queries that will use further examples of compound criteria. Additionally, we will focus on some other capabilities of queries that allow users to enter the search criteria when the query is run and to create a query that performs a calculation based on existing data.

Customizing a Report

The Student Report created earlier provided an introduction to using the Wizard. While the wizard is a good starting point, often you will want to customize the report. Enhancements can include adding additional graphics or text, rearranging where the fields appear on the report, and changing the words in the labels.

Practice:
Create a new report using the wizard.

Base the report on the Student Table and add all the fields into the report.

Choose to group the report by the student major.

Don't sort on any fields.

Choose a stepped layout and a landscape orientation.

Choose the style you wish to use and enter *rptStudentsByMajor* for the report title.

Select the radio button to modify the report's design.

Click Finish. Your report should look similar to that shown in Figure T4.35.

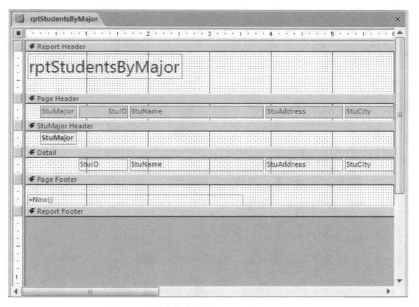

Figure T4.35 Initial report layout

The report layout uses controls similar to those in the form layout. You should be able to use the experience gained from working on the forms to help you modify the report. Make the following modification to the report in Layout View.

Practice:

In Layout View make the following changes:
Change the wording in the field labels to better reflect the data. For example, StuMajor would be better as Major.

Adjust the field widths so that the fields fit better on the report. For example, the major field is longer than needed.

Switch to Design View to make the following modifications:

Select the phone number data field.

Right click to open the shortcut menu and select properties.

Set the input mask property (found on the data tab of the property sheet window) to display as a phone number.

Choose to store the data without the symbols.

You may need to widen the field to be able to see all of the data.

Select the StuMajor Header section. Right click to open the shortcut menu.
        Your screen should be similar to Figure T4.36.

Open the Sorting and Grouping menu.

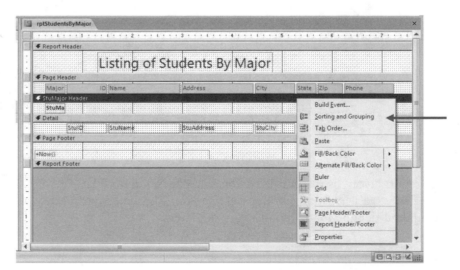

Figure T4.36 The shortcut menu for the StuMajor heading section

Practice:
In the Group, Sort, and Total section, as shown in Figure T4.37, click on More.

Figure T4.37 The Group, Sort, and Total menu

Practice:
In the expanded Group, Sort and Total section, shown in Figure T4.38, use the drop down arrow to change the second entry so that it displays *with a footer section*.

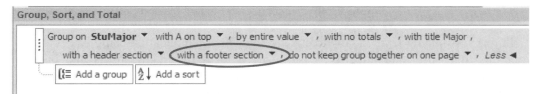

Figure T4.38 The Expanded Group, Sort, and Total menu

Practice:
Close the Group, Sort and Total section.
    Your report should now have a StuMajor footer section.

Expand the size of the StuMajor footer. In the StuMajor footer add two labels and place a copy the StuMajor textbox so that the contents appears similar to Figure T4.39.

Figure T4.39 The group footer section for the Student Major report

Practice:
Save the report.

Change to Report View.
    The completed report should appear similar to the report shown in Figure T4.40.

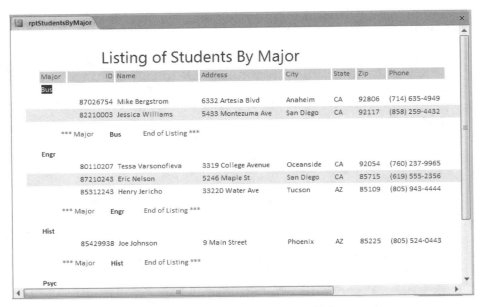

Figure T4.40 The completed Student Major report

In this section you learned how to enhance a database application using Access. You set field properties to ensure data integrity, customized a form by adding labels and buttons, created queries using compound criteria, and modified a basic report. You have done a good job learning these important skills. In Tutorial 5 you will learn how to create a more sophisticated database that includes several related tables, and objects based on a multiple tables. Additionally, you will learn how to link all of these separate forms and reports together into a complete database application.

LEARNING CHECK

Be sure you can *modify properties in a database table *add controls to a form *create a query using compound criteria *create and edit a report

WRAPPING IT UP

In this tutorial you learned about how to create a database system using the Access database management system. You practiced creating a database using Access. You built several different Access database objects including tables, forms, queries, and reports and learned how to improve their functionality. In the next tutorial you will learn how to build more complex database objects and to create a complete database application.

Study Questions Summary

1. How can you create a simple database system in Access?
    *   Access is a relational database management system developed by Microsoft.
    *   In Access, the database is created first and serves as the "container" to store all of the different database objects

- A database table contains the actual data and serves as the heart of the entire database system.
- Forms, queries and reports are examples of Access objects that are built to provide different ways to view and manipulate the data

2. How can you enhance your Access database system?
   - The Field Properties of an Access table can be used to help ensure data integrity
   - Fields can utilize drop-down lists to limit the possible data entry choices
   - The design of a basic form or report can be edited to alter the content and appearance of different controls placed on the form or report
   - Compound criteria can be used in a query to ask more complicated questions about the data

Key Terms

Page Number references are included in parentheses

Caption (375)	Design view (353)	Query by Example (360)
Command button (378)	Field names (350)	Report (362)
Compound criteria (381)	Field properties (367)	Select query (359)
Control (372)	Form (355)	Structured Query Language (SQL) (361)
Control layout (377)	Form Wizard (355)	Table (348)
Data type (351)	Microsoft Access (347)	Validation rule (368)
Datasheet view (353)	Object (348)	Validation text (368)
Default value property (371)	Query (359)	

Multiple Choice Questions

1. Which of the following is not an Access data type?
   a. currency
   b. text
   c. primary key
   d. number
   e. memo

2. The field properties are shown in _____ view.
   a. form
   b. design
   c. datasheet
   d. database

3. Which of the following is a TRUE statement about Access?
    a. Queries and reports are different types of Access objects
    b. In Access, only the tables, not the forms and reports, are stored in the database file
    c. An Access database contains only one table
    d. A new database can be created only through the Database Wizard

4. Which of the following is a true statement?
    a. Metadata are the descriptions about what data values represent and their format, and in Access they are called Table Data.
    b. Metadata are the descriptions about what data values represent and their format, and in Access they are called Properties.
    c. Metadata, also known as Properties in Access, are one of the three primary tasks of a DBMS.
    d. Metadata, also known as Table Data in Access, are one of the three primary tasks of a DBMS.

5. The most common language used for queries is _____.
    a. MS-Access
    b. structured query language
    c. query-by-example
    d. query manipulation

Answers:
1. c   2. b   3. a   4. b   5. b

Review Questions

1. Describe the two primary considerations for selecting a data type.
2. In Access, explain the difference between a table, form, query and report.
3. What is a validation rule and when would you use one?
4. What is a combo box and when would you use one?
5. What is metadata and how is it implemented in Access?

Projects

1. You are storing the Zip Code field as a Text data type, size 5. Could you use an Integer data type to store zip codes? Why/Why Not? Calculate the amount of storage space needed to store the zip code in its current data type and size compared to storing it as a long integer data type.

2. Using your student database, create a query to find all the students who are from Arizona and are Business or Engineering majors.

3. Using your student database, find the Student ID, Student Name and Phone number for all students who have phone number with an 805 area code. Hint: The criteria used in a query can be written like that used for validation rules. Refer back to Table 4.12 for some help.

4. Create a report based on that query.

5. You have been asked to create a database to track stock purchases and sales. The client has identified the following information they wish to have tracked.

> Stock Symbol
> Stock Name
> Date Purchased
> Purchase Price
> Number of Shares
> Date Sold
> Selling Price

   a. Although the client has told you that the Stock Symbol is a unique identifier, why can't you use that field as your primary key? What will you use as your primary key? Hint: you will need to add a new field to the table.
   b. Create a new database and create the Stock Table. Enter a validation rule to ensure that the Date Sold is greater than or equal to the Date Purchased. Include an appropriate error message.
   c. Which fields cannot be designated as "required?" Why? For all fields that can be required, set that appropriate property.
   d. Create a form to make data entry easier. Customize the form by adding buttons to "Enter a New Stock Transaction" and "Print the Current Stock Record."
   e. Enter 10 rows of test data. Have some of the entries be for stocks that have not yet been sold, some for stocks where the selling price was greater than the purchase price, and some for stocks where the selling price was less than the purchase price.
   f. Create a query to find all the stock that sold for less than the purchase price.
   g. Create a report, using the Report Wizard, which will show all of the records in your stock table.

TUTORIAL **5**

Developing Advanced Business Systems with Databases

PLANNING AHEAD

After reading Tutorial 5, you should be able to answer these questions in your own words

STUDY QUESTIONS

How do you create the physical database model?

How do you establish relationships?

How can you create a more complex database system in Access?

LEARNING PREVIEW

In Tutorial 4 you learned the basics about using the Microsoft Access database management system. In this tutorial you will continue to build your understanding about databases. You will learn how to develop a complete database system. You will begin by learning how to develop the complete set of database tables and how to establish the relationships between those tables. Next you will learn how to build queries, forms and reports that connect all of the tables together. Finally you will explore how the navigation pane can be used to work like a menu system.

OPENING VIGNETTE

Fighting Crime with Data

While fighting crime and terrorism still involves stakeouts, car chases, flying bullets, and a great deal of risk, some law enforcement agencies are incorporating technology in their battle plan. The Los Angeles Police Department's (LAPD®) Counter Terrorism and Criminal Intelligence Bureau is installing a new intelligence system that will allow investigators to identify and connect related pieces of intelligence, helping the Bureau deter and respond to terrorism attacks. The Bureau contains the Major Crimes Division (ATD) and the Emergency Services Division (ESD).

Major Crimes Division encompasses Criminal Conspiracy, Criminal Investigations, Intelligence Investigations, Surveillance, and Liaison Sections. Emergency Services Division (ESD) is comprised of Field and Community Support, Emergency Planning, Operations, and Hazardous Devices Sections. In short, the Counter- Terrorism Bureau is responsible for planning, response and intelligence activities for the LAPD.

A key problem in handling investigations is the difficulty of trying to find and bring together all the different sources of information. With over 9,300 officers, tips and leads get reported to different divisions and the lead investigator may never learn of the new information. Even within the Counter Terrorism Bureau coordinating data with 150 officers presents significant challenges. In the battle against terrorism, identifying that key piece of information that could prevent a terrorist attack is critical. On a larger scale, these concerns are echoed in one of the criticisms from the 9/11 Commission Report – that different agencies failed to bring together different pieces of information that possibly could have prevented the attack.

To help overcome these problems, the new system will connect the divisional units and provide investigators the ability to gather, analyze, and disseminate information as part of a comprehensive intelligence cycle. The system uses data mining, analysis, and visualization tools to allow police officers to search multiple intelligence databases simultaneously. The system will help officers make links between seemingly unrelated pieces of information. It also provides proactive notification and email alerts when patterns are identified.

Investigators will be able to easily drill down to data when they are searching for people, locations, or license plate numbers, no matter where the data is stored. For example, an officer could search for a Black Chevy Pickup Truck without having to specify that the value must be found in a "vehicle" field. The system will locate all references, including searching through Word documents that contain officer's case notes.

The one million dollar system is built by Memex, Inc. It uses a hybrid relational and open text-search database paired with an intelligence engine to compress data. This provides the power for the rapid searches. The database can help enforce business processes and data rules with data validation when data are initially entered, providing greater assurances that the results have value.

(Sources: Compiled from Sarkar, Dibya, "LAPD to implement intelligence, analysis system," *Federal Computer Week*, January 10, 2006, *http://www.fcw.com/article91928-01-10-06-web* accessed July 17, 2007; Havenstein, Heather, "LAPD turns to data analysis to fight terrorism," *Computerworld*, January 12, 2006; *www.lapdonline.org* accessed July 16, 2007; *www.memex.com* accessed July 17, 2007; and "Memex chosen to Provide intelligence system for LAPD", *Bapco Journal*, February 20, 2006; *http://www.bapcojournal.com/news/fullstory.php/aid/116/Memex_chosen_to_provide_intelligence_system_ for_LAPD.html. The LAPD acronym is a registered trademark of the Los Angeles Police Department.*)

In this tutorial you will learn more about the ideas introduced in this vignette. You will learn about larger database systems and how to create relationships across different tables in a database. You will explore different features within Access to help ensure data integrity and to make the database system more user friendly. Finally you will learn how to create a complete database application that links together all of the different pieces you have built. In addition to learning how to create these different database components, you will learn about some emerging trends with database technology, such as the use of business intelligence systems like the one in use by the LAPD. By the end of this tutorial you will be able to answer the following questions about this story:

- Describe how business intelligence systems work
- Describe the benefits that the LAPD is hoping to realize from their system
- How do organizations use data mining?
- This system could be viewed as one component of a knowledge management system. Are there cultural issues that must change related to law enforcement agencies for a broader implementation of knowledge management practices?

VISUAL ORGANIZATION OF TUTORIAL

Study Question 1	Study Question 2	Study Question 3
Creating the Physical Model	Creating Relationships in Access	Creating a More Complex Database System in Access
• Convert Entities to Tables and Assign Fields • Identify Primary Keys • Represent the Relationships • Store Additional Data Values • Decide about Calculated Attributes • Build the Physical Tables for the Hair Today Database	• Referential Integrity Choices • Define the Customer-Order Relationship • Define the Order-Line Item and Product-Line Item Relationships	• Build the One-Table Forms and Enter Sample Data • Create a Form using a Main Form – SubForm Association • Create advanced reports • Customize the Navigation Pane
Learning Check 1	Learning Check 2	Learning Check 3

CREATING THE PHYSICAL MODEL

Developing a database system involves creating not only the tables, but also the queries, forms and reports to provide a complete system. The starting point is to analyze the data needs. As you have seen, analyzing the data needs involves creating both the conceptual design of how the data will be organized as well as the physical design of how the actual tables will be built in the DBMS. The Entity Relationship Diagram was the tool you learned to use to create the conceptual design of the data. Once you have completed the ERD the next step is to create the specification for the physical tables, the ones you are going to build in your database. How do you know how many tables your database will need, or what fields go into the different tables? Let's explore the answer to these questions by returning to the Hair Today database.

To re-orient yourself with the business situation, review the original order form shown in Figure T5.1. Next, review the ERD shown in Figure T5.2. Remember that the ERD was created to show a conceptual model of the data represented in the order form. The Hair Today ERD included four entities: customer, order, line item, and product. Calculated attributes were included on the ERD. Additionally, while creating the ERD the designers realized that the Unit Cost attribute actually needed to be represented as two separate attributes – the Unit Cost in the Product Table and the Unit Price in the Line Item Table. This was necessary to store the distinction between the cost of the item today (the Unit Cost) and the Price of the item on a particular order (the Unit Price.)

Hair Today
Customer Order Form

| Customer ID | 12922 | | | Order Date | July 10, 2007 |
| Customer Name | Angela Escobar | | | | |

Product ID	Description	Quantity Ordered	Unit Cost		Extended Price	
1003	Barrette - Gold Filigree Crystal Flower - Ruby	2	$	17.00	$	34.00
1007	Pin - Austrian Crystal Mini Flower - Green	1	$	6.95	$	6.95
1008	Pin - Guppy Bobby Pins - Tortoise	5	$	4.00	$	20.00
1010	Pin - Tiger Eye Bobby Pins (set of 2) - Blue	3	$	6.35	$	19.05
				Subtotal	$	80.00
				Discount	$	4.00
				Tax	$	5.70

Total $ 81.70

We appreciate your business! Please call if you have any concerns about your order.

Figure T5.1 The Original Customer Order Form

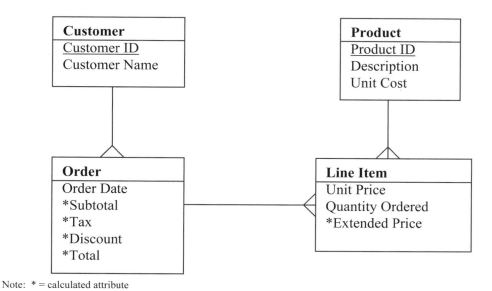

Note: * = calculated attribute

Figure T5.2 The Conceptual ERD for Hair Today

With the ERD completed, you might think that building the tables in Access would be the next activity. Not quite. Before you can build the tables in Access, you will need to create a physical model of the database. The **physical model** shows you the specifics of each of the required tables, including exactly what fields will be in each table and how the tables will be linked together. In this section you will learn how the ERD is converted into the physical model using the following steps:

- Each entity will become a table.
- All of the attributes in the entity will become fields.
- A primary key will be selected in each table, as a way to uniquely identify each record of data.
- Implement relationships

While converting the ERD into the physical model, attributes may be added to the tables for several reasons. First, if the entity did not have a unique identifier, one will be created at this time. Second, the relationships shown on the ERD are implemented via fields known as foreign keys. Finally, if the user desires storage of additional information, fields will be added. If you have shown calculated attributes on the ERD you will also need to decide whether they will be stored in the database table or calculated as needed. Ultimately the process of data modeling gets easier but it can appear to be a little messy as you work through this stage. Hang in there!

Convert Entities to Tables and Assign Fields

The first step of creating the physical model is to put each entity into a physical table format. Each attribute on the ERD become a field in the table. The notation shown in Figure T5.3 is a common way of writing the physical table descriptions.

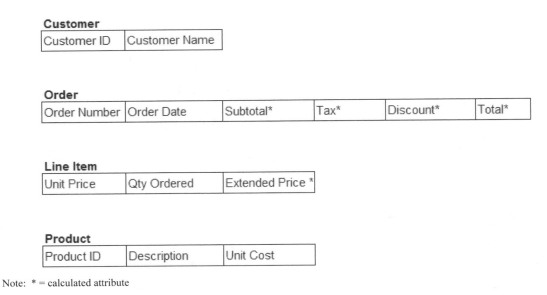

Customer

Customer ID	Customer Name

Order

Order Number	Order Date	Subtotal*	Tax*	Discount*	Total*

Line Item

Unit Price	Qty Ordered	Extended Price *

Product

Product ID	Description	Unit Cost

Note: * = calculated attribute

Figure T5.3 Physical Table Description

Identify Primary Keys

During the ERD creation, unique identifiers were selected for the Customer and Product entities. Primary keys will be indicated in the physical table description by underlining the field. But what is the primary key in the Order Table? Unfortunately the fields on the original order form didn't include a way to uniquely identify one order from the next. In this case we will need to add a field to serve as the primary key. Creating an Order Number field is a good solution. Deciding on the specific field type and size is a decision that will need to be made before the table can be built.

In the Line Item Table there also is not a unique identifier. Recall that the line item entity came about to break up the many-to-many relationship between Product and Order. Because of this, the primary key is going to be created when we incorporate the relationships in the next step.

Represent the Relationships

The process of converting relationships was introduced in Chapter 4. Recall that the relationships from the conceptual ERD are incorporated into the physical tables by adding attributes. For a one-to-many relationship, the relationship is incorporated by taking the primary key from the "one" side of the relationship and adding it as a foreign key into the "many" side of the relationship.

Following this rule, the one-to-many relationship between Customer and Order will result in adding the Customer ID of the Customer Table (the "one" side) into the Order Table (the "many" side) as a foreign key.

When building the ERD we solved the many-to-many between Order and Product by creating the intersection entity of Line Item. This resulted in the creation of two one-to-many relationships (between Order and Line Item and between Product and Line Item.) Following the conversion rule, those relationships will be represented by taking the primary keys from the Order and Product Tables and adding them into the Line Item Table. Since this is an intersection entity, those two foreign keys will work together as the primary key to uniquely identify each row of data. If a key is made up of more than one field, it is known as a **compound key** or **concatenated key**. To illustrate how a concatenated primary key works, Figure T5.4 shows a few rows of sample data for the Line Item table. Notice that product 1002 appears on three orders (10001, 10002, and 10004), but the combination of Order Number and Product ID is unique for the table.

Order Number	Product ID	Unit Price	Qty Ordered	Extended Price*
10001	1002	$ 17.00	2	$ 34.00
10001	1006	$ 15.00	1	$ 15.00
10001	1009	$ 12.95	1	$ 12.95
10002	1001	$ 12.00	3	$ 36.00
10002	1002	$ 17.00	1	$ 17.00
10003	1010	$ 6.35	4	$ 25.40
10003	1005	$ 15.00	1	$ 15.00
10004	1002	$ 17.00	1	$ 17.00
10004	1005	$ 15.00	2	$ 30.00

Figure T5.4 Sample Data for the Line Item Table

Figure T5.5 shows the physical tables that have been designed based on the work so far. Notice that primary keys are underlined and foreign keys are shown in italics. For clarity, lines show the link between the foreign key and the related table.

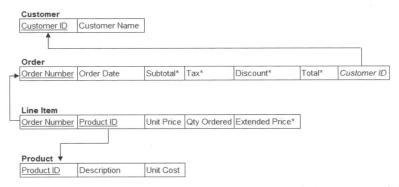

Note: * = calculated attribute

Figure T5.5 Physical Tables for the Hair Today Database

Store Additional Data Values

Attributes may also be added into the tables at this time to allow the system to capture and manage additional information. For example, although the Order Form only shows the Customer ID and Name, it makes sense that Hair Today would also like to store information about the customer address, city, state, and zip. Further, it will be better to store the first and last name separately. In the Product Table, Hair Today wants an attribute to store the color of each product. This will make it easier to query the database to find all "Tortoise" colored products, for example. They also want to store the inventory they have of each product – this could be represented as the quantity on hand.

Decide about Calculated Attributes

In Chapter 4 when the ERD was created, we intentionally left the calculated attributes of Extended Price in the Line Item entity, and Subtotal, Tax, Discount and Total in the Order entity. Because those values can be calculated, many database designers recommend that you do not store the actual fields in the database. Instead, when the information is needed on a form or report, create a calculated field to display the result. Following this recommendation, remove these four attributes from the physical tables. Figure T5.6 shows the final physical table layout based on the decisions made so far. At this point the physical table layout can be used to create the tables in your Access database.

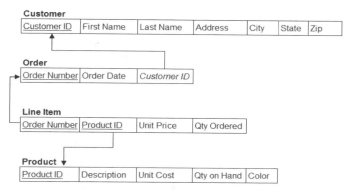

Figure T5.6 Physical Tables for the Hair Today Database

Build the Physical Tables for the Hair Today Database

The specifications for the four tables that will be included in your database are shown in Table T5.1. Remember that these specifications were determined during the analysis phase for this database system by interviewing users and reviewing existing forms, reports and data.

Practice:

Open Access and create a new blank database for Hair Today.

Build the Customer, Product, Order, and Line Item Tables using the field type, size, and other property setting specifications shown in Table T5.1.

If you need a review on how to create a database table in Access, refer to Tutorial 4.

When creating the tables, keep the following points in mind:
- Use a naming convention for field names of beginning with the table identifier (e.g. CustFirstName instead of FirstName.)

- Set the *required* property for all fields to "yes."

- Designate a primary key in each table. To designate a concatenated primary key in the Line Item table, select both the OrderNumber and the ProductID fields before selecting Primary Key. In Design View, select the FKOrderNumber field. Press and hold shift, and then select the FKProductID field. Then press the Primary Key icon. Both fields should now have the key symbol next to them.

- Save each table using the *tbl* prefix with an appropriate descriptive name (i.e. tblOrder.)

After you have built the four tables you should see them all listed in the Navigation Pane.

Customer Table Field Definitions - (tblCustomer)

Field Name	Data Type	Description	Size	Primary Key
CustID	Number	Unique customer ID – 5 digits long	Integer	Yes
CustFirstName	Text	First name of customer	15	
CustLastName	Text	Last name of customer	15	
CustAddress	Text	Street address	40	
CustCity	Text	City	20	
CustState	Text	2 digit abbreviation for state	2	
CustZip	Text	Extended zip code	9	

1. CustID – create a validation rule to check that the entries begin with a 1 and are 5 digits long. Create a custom error message if the user violates this rule.
2. CustState – set default value to "CA"; Change the Lookup tab properties to a combo box to restrict the possible choices to CA, AZ, OR, WA, NV, UT, NM, ID, CO, MT, or WY
3. CustZip – use the Input Mask Wizard (the ▣ icon) to select the Zip Code mask. Note: An input mask sets the display pattern for the field. The Zip Code mask makes the first 5 digits required and includes a hyphen to separate the first 5 digits from the last 4 digits.

Order Table Field Definitions - (tblOrder)

Field Name	Data Type	Description	Size	Primary Key
OrderNumber	Number	Unique order ID – 5 digits long	Integer	Yes
OrderDate	Date/Time	The date the order was placed		
FKCustID	Number	Foreign key from the Customer table	Integer	

1. OrderNumber - Create a validation rule to check that the entries are 5 digits long; Create a custom error message if the user violates this rule.
2. OrderDate - Set the format property to Medium Date; Set the default value to Date( ). Note: This will enter the current date into this field when a new record is added.

Product Table Field Definitions - (tblProduct)

Field Name	Data Type	Description	Size	Primary Key
ProdID	Number	Unique Product ID – 4 digits long	Integer	Yes
ProdDesc	Text	Name of the product	45	
ProdUnitCost	Currency	Current cost of the product		
ProdQOH	Number	Quantity on hand in inventory	Integer	
ProdColor	Text	Color of the product	12	

1. ProdID - create a validation rule to check that the entries are 4 digits long and begin with a 5. Create a custom error message if the user violates this rule.

Line Item Table Field Definitions - (tblLineItem)

Field Name	Data Type	Description	Size	Primary Key
FKOrderNumber	Number	Unique order ID – 5 digits long; foreign key from the Order table	Integer	Yes
FKProductID	Number	Unique product ID – 4 digits long; foreign key from the Product table	Integer	yes
LIUnitPrice	Currency	The price of the item on this order. Initially equals the UnitCost from the Product Table		
LIQtyOrdered	Number	The quantity requested for this item	Integer	

Table T5.1 Table Definitions for Hair Today

In this section you learned about how to convert the ERD created during conceptual database designing into a physical database model. You learned identifying primary keys, representing relationships and deciding which fields should be stored in the database. Additionally you had more practice building physical tables using Access. In the next section you will learn more about creating relationships.

LEARNING CHECK
Be sure you can *convert an ERD into a set of physical tables *convert relationships on an ERD into fields in a physical table *identify calculated fields in an ERD *create a validation rule for a field

CREATING RELATIONSHIPS IN ACCESS

The database design process you have followed resulted in a set of four database tables that will help minimize redundant data while helping to increase data integrity. Database relationships are necessary to bring all the information stored in separate tables back together again. The foreign keys are used to link the tables, but until the relationships are actually established in Access the tables will not be connected. In this section you will learn about the different choices that need to be made when creating a relationship, and then you will practice creating several different relationships.

Referential Integrity Choices

There are several steps to defining a relationship in Access. Begin by identifying which tables are to be related. Next specify which fields (the primary key and the foreign key) are linked together and the type of relationship (one-to-one or one-to-many.) After this is done decide how the relationship will be enforced.

The first decision is whether to enforce referential integrity. **Referential integrity** ensures consistency of data across related tables. If you enforce referential integrity it will:
- Prevent you from entering a value in the foreign key field (in the "many" table) that doesn't match an existing primary key value of the related ("one") tablePrevent you from deleting a record in the "one" table if there are associated records in the "many" table.
- Prevent you from changing the value in a primary key of the "one" table if there are associated records in the "many" table.

In most cases you will always enforce referential integrity. You will have to review business rules that have been identified to determine if you would not want to enforce referential integrity. In addition to enforcing referential integrity you also need to determine whether the required property for the foreign key field will be set to yes. In other words, it is appropriate to allow the foreign key field to be left empty/blank. This is also called a Null value. When the foreign key is left empty, the record won't be associated with a record in the "one" table.

Let's look at an example to see how enforcing referential integrity would work. Assume that at a veterinary office you have a one-to-many relationship between an owner table and a pet table. Figure T5.7 shows the Relationships window in Access (you will learn how to access and use the Relationships window a little later in the tutorial) for our veterinary office. Because the *Enforce Referential Integrity* box is checked, when an owner value is entered into the *owner* field on a pet record, the number must match one that already exists in the owner table. Additionally, you won't be able to change an *OwnerID* if that owner has pet records in the Pet table. Further, if an owner has pets in the Pet table, you will not be able to delete that owner. Notice in the Edit Relationships window that there are two other check boxes – Cascade Update Related Fields and Cascade Delete Related Records. Checking those boxes will override some of the referential integrity restrictions, as explained below.

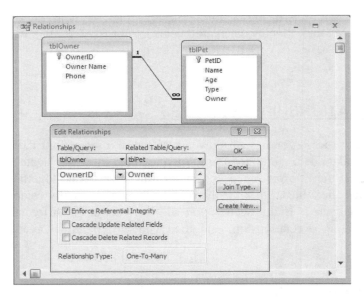

Figure T5.7 The initial relationship window, showing the Edit Relationships window, for the Veterinary Office

If you select **Cascade Update Related Fields**, Access will allow the primary key value to be changed in the "one" table and then will automatically update the value in the foreign key for all related records. In the Vet Office example, if a user changed an owner ID value in the Owner Table, the Owner foreign key in the pet table would be updated for any pet records assigned to the owner.

If you select **Cascade Delete Related Records,** Access will allow a record in the "one" table to be deleted even if there are related records in the "many" table and Access will automatically delete the related records. In the Vet Office example, if an Owner record is deleted, all pet records linked to that owner will also be deleted.

Making the correct choices when establishing relationships is very important, but how do you know what the correct choices are? This is where reviewing and understanding the business rules that exist for the company will become very important. As we work through several examples of creating relationships, you will get a chance to see different combinations of choices.

With this as background you are ready to begin creating the relationships. Relationships can be created directly in the relationship window. Another approach is to create the relationship by building a lookup field. In Tutorial 4 you created a lookup field which displayed a list of choices for the State field. In that example you entered the list of possible choices for the drop down list. Alternatively, you can have a lookup field where Access maintains the list of possible choices based on the values that are stored in another table in the database. The next section will show you how to build a relationship using a drop-down list.

Define the Customer-Order Relationship

In the Hair Today system, when your user enters an order they will need to assign the order to a customer. While the user could enter the Customer ID into a textbox, this would require the user to remember all of the possible Customer ID values. The possibility for data entry errors increases if your user has to enter the Customer ID, in addition to it being cumbersome to remember all the choices. The Hair Today system can be made more user-friendly by creating a drop-down list of existing customers. You will use the Lookup Wizard to help in this process. The **Lookup Wizard** is an access tool used to convert your field into a combo box that allows you to choose a value from another table or from a list of values.

Practice:

Open the Order Table in Design View.

In the FKCustID field, change the **Data Type** to *Lookup Wizard*.

Choose the radio button to have the lookup column lookup the values in a table or query.

Click *Next*.

Select the tblCustomer table as the table to provide the values for the lookup column. The wizard window should be similar to that shown in Figure T5.8.

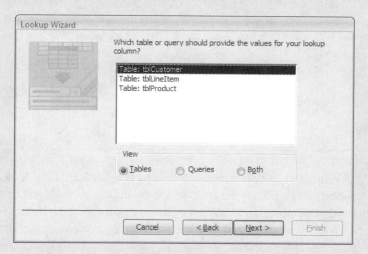

Figure T5.8 Selecting the table for the lookup column

Click *Next*.

Practice (continued):

Move the CustID field, as shown in Figure T5.9, from the list of available fields into the selected fields. This tells Access that the CustID field contains the matching values.

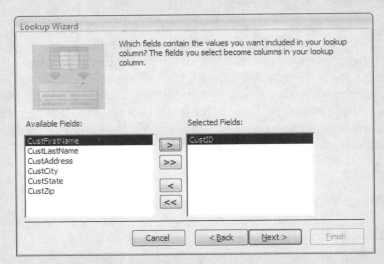

Figure T5.9 Selecting the field for the lookup column

Click *Next.*

Do not choose to sort on any fields. Click *Next.*

Adjust the column width to an appropriate size. Click *Next.*

In the last step of the wizard, keep the label as FKCustID. Click *Finish.*
    Access will provide a message indicating that the table must be saved before the relationship can be created.

Select "*YES*" to save the table.

On the **Lookup Tab**, change the Limit to List property to "*Yes.*"

Let's explore the relationship you just created. On the Lookup Tab, look at the contents of the **Row Source** property. The **Row Source** property indicates the source of the data for the field. The source could be a table, query or list of values you entered. Notice the Access created an SQL query based on the selections you made during the Lookup Wizard. The query is:

SELECT [tblCustomer].[CustID] FROM tblCustomer;.

This example illustrates why you should understand a little bit about SQL, even though you may still choose to use the Query By Example mode when writing the queries in your system.

Practice:
Save and close the Order Table.

When you created the lookup values above, you began the process of creating the relationship between the tables.

Practice:

Open the relationship window by selecting the **Database Tools Tab > Show/Hide Group > Relationships** option.

    The Customer and Order tables should display in the window, as shown in Figure T5.10. Notice the relationship line that connects the two tables.

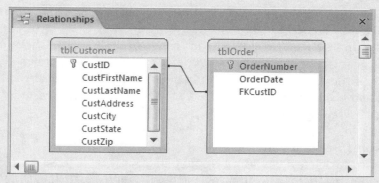

Figure T5.10 The relationship window after creating the lookup between tblOrder and tblCustomer

Click on the relationship line connecting the two tables.

Select the **Relationship Tools Design Tab > Tools Group > Edit Relationships** option.
    Figure T5.11 displays the Edit Relationships dialog box.

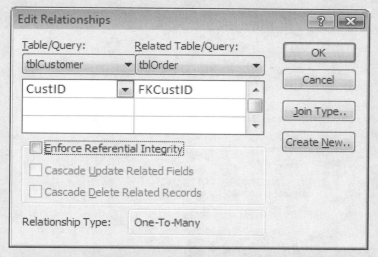

Figure T5.11 The Edit Relationship Dialog Box for tblCustomer and tblOrder

Because you created the lookup field Access has already established a one-to-many relationship between the Customer table (the "one" side) and Order table (the "many" side) based on the CustID field. At this point you will need to decide which of the three check boxes you want to select to ensure that your relationships work as intended.

Practice:

Check **Enforce Referential Integrity**.

In this instance, enforcing referential integrity ensures that when a customer number is entered in an order record, the customer number is one that already exists in the customer table. Once you have made this selection, the two other check boxes will become active. This will allow you to override the restriction on deleting records and changing values, if appropriate.

Check **Cascade Update Related Fields**.

For Hair Today, this selection will allow the change of the primary key value in the Customer table and then will automatically update the value in the foreign key for all related records in the Order table. For example, if the ID of a customer becomes compromised and needs to be changed, the CustID field in all related order records will be updated accordingly.

Do not check **Cascade Delete Related Records**.

Recall that **Cascade delete** will allow a record in the "one" table to be deleted even if there are related records in the "many" table and will automatically delete the related records. Does it make sense to allow Cascade delete in this situation? What if a customer calls you to say she is moving out of the service area for Hair Today? Should you delete the orders that she has placed? No. Those orders still happened and need to be stored in the database. A situation like this might indicate the need for another field on the customer table to store whether the customer is "Active" or not. To keep our example manageable we will not add that field now.

After selecting the choices just described, the Edit Relationships dialog box should appear similar to Figure T5.12.

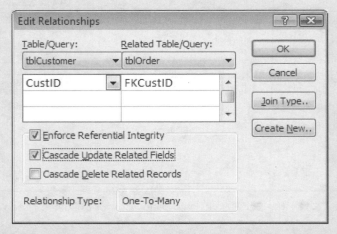

Figure T5.12 Completed Edit Relationship Dialog Box for tblCustomer and tblOrder

Click *OK* to confirm these choices.

Click the *Save* icon to save the relationships.

The Relationships window should show an updated relationship line that includes the one-to-many symbols, similar to Figure T5.13. The notation used by Access is a 1 on the "one" side and the infinity symbol to represent the "many" side.

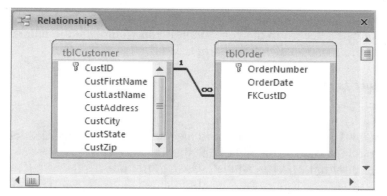

Figure T5.13   The Relationship window after referential integrity has been enforced

---

Practice:
Close the Relationship window.

Define the Order-Line Item and Product-Line Item Relationships

Following a similar process, you need to define the remaining relationships for your Hair Today database. When your users are selecting products to place on an order, the line item must be associated with both an order number and a product number. Create drop-down lists to make the selection of these values easier for your users and to help ensure data integrity within the system.

Define the Order-Line Item Relationships

Practice:
Create the Order-Line Item relationship to meet the following specifications:
1. Open the Line Item Table in Design View.
   - Use the **Lookup Wizard** to create a drop-down list on the FKOrderNumber field. This should lookup values in OrderNumber field of the Order table.
   - On the **Lookup Tab**, change the **Limit to List** property to "*Yes*." Save and close the table.

2. Edit the Relationship to Enforce Referential Integrity, Cascade Updates and Cascade Deletes. If the Line Item table does not automatically appear in the Relationship window, select the **Relationship Tools Design Tab > Relationships Group > All Relationships** option to update the tables shown in the window.

Be sure to save the relationship settings and close the relationship window when you are done.

In this situation, referential integrity is enforced because you don't want line items to be created for an order that doesn't exist. Likewise, if an order number happens to change values in the Order table, you would want that update to occur for all the line item records associated with the order. Finally, in this situation you will want to Cascade Deletes. If a customer calls to cancel an order (delete a record in the "one" table), you would want to automatically delete all of the line items that are associated with that order.

Define the Product-Line Item Relationships

Practice*:*

Create the Product-Line Item relationship to meet the following specifications:

1. Open the Line Item Table in Design View.
    - Use the **Lookup Wizard** to create a drop-down list on the FKProductID field in the Line Item Table. This should lookup values in ProdID field of the Product table.
    - On the **Lookup Tab**, change the **Limit to List** property to "*Yes.*" Save and close the table.

2. Edit the Relationship to Enforce Referential Integrity and Cascade Updates. If the Product table does not automatically appear in the Relationship window, select the **Relationship Tools Design Tab** > **Relationships Group** > **All Relationships** option to update the tables shown in the window.

Save and close the relationship window when you are done.

Referential integrity is enforced because you don't want line items to be created for products that don't exist. Likewise, if a ProdID happens to change values in the Product table, you would want that update to occur for all the line item records associated with that product. Finally, in this situation do not Cascade deletes. If Hair Today stops selling a product you do not want to automatically delete all of the line items that are associated with that product. In reality you would need to determine a mechanism to ensure that you don't sell any more of the product that has been cancelled, but that is beyond the scope of our example database.

In this section you saw how foreign keys are used to establish relationships. You learned about referential integrity, including deciding on cascading updates and deletes. Additionally, you learned how to create relationships in Access via the lookup wizard and the relationships window. Having established the relationships you will start to build database objects that utilize the connected tables.

LEARNING CHECK
Be sure you can *explain the impact of enforcing referential integrity, cascading updates and cascading deletes *use the lookup wizard in Access to establish a relationship between tables *use the edit relationships window to adjust settings

CREATING A MORE COMPLEX DATABASE SYSTEM IN ACCESS

The Hair Today database application will contain a collection of tables, forms, queries and reports. Now that you have built all of the tables needed for Hair Today and have established the relationships, you are ready to start building different database objects that will utilize the complete set of tables. This is where you will really see the power of a relational database. In this section you will build the set of forms needed to add, delete and update records. Next you will build several reports that will allow the Hair Today staff to better manage their business. Finally you will learn how to customize the navigation pane to help your users more easily perform tasks in the database system.

Build the One-Table Forms and Enter Sample Data

A database system typically includes several different forms. Some of the forms are based only on one table. For example, the form used to add customers into the database only uses fields from the customer table. Other forms may include data from multiple tables. To build an order form similar to the original order processing form you built in Excel will require data from each of your four tables. Building the forms involves deciding on a final layout that will be applied to all forms. After that is completed you then start to build the forms. When deciding which forms in your system to create first, it is often easiest to design the forms based solely on one table. For that reason we will focus first on building the Customer and Product forms. These forms will be used to add and modify customers and products, respectively.

Finalize the Layout of all Forms
During the system design stage of the SDLC you learned that the systems developer should create a mock-up of all the forms and reports that will be used in the new system. One important part of this process is to develop the basic structure that all forms and reports will contain. This includes deciding on common titles, font styles and sizes, graphics, colors, button designs, etc. For example, each form should have the Hair Today company title and logo in a common location. To save yourself the time and effort of redoing forms, these decisions should be made before you begin creating forms. An example of a sample form design for Hair Today is shown in Figure T5.14. As you can see in this figure, the sample form may start as a sketch of how a typical form will appear. In this sample we have decided that each form will have a Header section that contains the Hair Today title and a more specific form title, such as Customer Information Form. On the Master Form Layout in Figure T5.14, the "XXXX Form" label serves as a placeholder for the form title label. The record information will be in the Detail section. The caption of the form field Labels will be right justified. Finally, buttons will be located in the Footer section. Buttons will use text descriptors instead of icons, e.g. "Print the record" instead of showing a picture of the printer. The Detail section will have a white background color. The Header and Footer sections will have the same background color, which will not be white.

Since you will create several forms that will use this basic layout, it will save you time to create and save a master form that can then be used as a base for your other forms. This will save you from having to make the same property settings in several different forms. For example, you will need to set the Back Color property in the Form Header only one time on the form master instead of on each of the different forms.

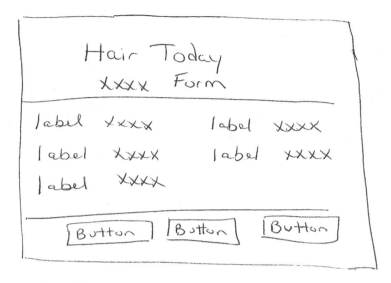

Figure T5.14   Example of Master Form Layout

Create the Master Form Layout

Previously you have used the Form Wizard to create basic forms. However, to create forms that use the layout shown in Figure T5.14 will require that the forms be created in Design View. This provides the most flexibility in placing and sizing objects on the form. Follow the instructions below to create the master form. Since the placeholder textboxes, labels, and buttons will need to be attached to specific data values or functions, it is not necessary to place any of them onto the form master. They are shown in Figure T5.14 so that you have an idea about their location.

Practice:

Select the **Create Tab > Forms Group > Form Design** option. A blank form will open.

Select the **Form Design Tools Arrange Tab > Show/Hide Group > Form Header/Footer** icon ▦ .

Adjust the size of the Form Header, Detail, and Form Footer sections so they are similar to that shown in Figure T5.14.

Use the **Form Design Tools Design Tab > Controls Group > Label** icon to add two labels into the Form Header section.

Change the **Back Color** property in both the Form Header and Form Footer sections to the same color.

Save the form as frmMaster.

Close the form.

After creating the Master Form layout it should appear similar to that shown in Figure T5.15.

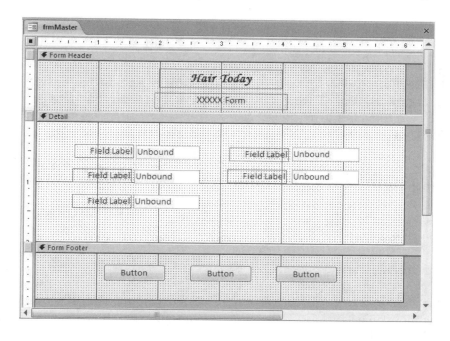

Figure T5.15 Master Form Layout built in Access

Create the Customer Form

Create the customer form so that it looks similar to the form shown in Figure T5.16.

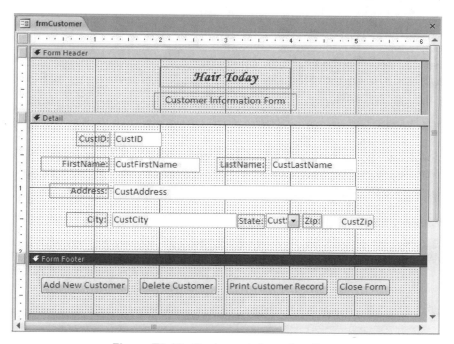

Figure T5.16 Customer Information Form

Practice:
Open the frmMaster form in Design View.

On the **Office Button** choose **Save As > Save Object As.** In the **Save 'frmMaster' to** textbox enter frmCustomer. This will create a copy of the master form for you to use.

Edit the XXXX Form label so that it reads "Customer Information Form."

Add the fields from the Customer Table onto the form by selecting the **Form Design Tools Design Tab > Tools Group > Add Existing Fields** option.

Expand tblCustomer to view the fields. Click and drag each of the fields into the approximate location shown in Figure T5.16.

Edit the label captions and alignment.
> You can perform the same action (such as aligning to the right) on several objects at the same time by selecting all of the objects (use the shift key to continue to select more objects) before pressing the align right icon. Fine tune the location of the different objects.

Use the the **Form Design Tools Design Tab > Controls Group > Command Button** icon to add four buttons to the form. Remember to have the Control Wizard selected before putting a button on the form. The buttons should have the following specifications:
- Add a New Customer (Record Operation category)
- Delete a Customer (Record Operation category)
- Print Customer Record (Record Operation category)
- Close the Form (Form Operations category)

Save the form when you are done.

Your completed form should look similar to the form shown in Figure T5.16. Close the form. Note: If you view the form in Form View you will not see any data values since you have not yet added any records into the tables.

Create the Product Form
Following the same instructions you used to create the Customer Form, create a product form based on the frmMaster form. The Product Form will be used to manage the inventory.

Practice:
Create a copy of the frmMaster form to be used as the Product Form.

Include all the fields from the product table on the form.

Edit the form so that your completed form is similar to that shown in Figure T5.17.

The Form label should read "Product Information Form."

Use the Command Button tool to add three buttons to the form with the following specifications:

Add a Product (Record Operation category)
Delete a Product (Record Operation category)
Close the Form (Form Operations category)

Save and close the form when you are done.

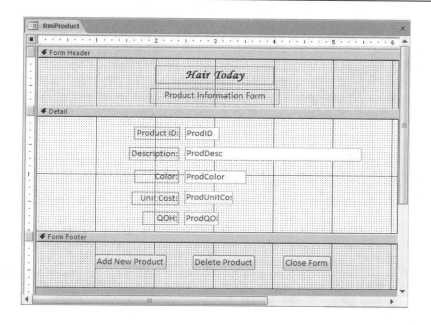

Figure T5.17 Product Information Form

Enter Sample Data
With these two forms now completed, it is time to enter some sample data.

Practice:
Open the customer form and enter the six records shown in Table T5.2 into your customer table.

Close the form when completed

CustID	CustFirstName	CustLastName	CustAddress	CustCity	CustState	CustZip
10001	Marco	Herrera	536 Mabel St	Tucson	AZ	85715-5630
10002	Alison	Henry	1320 Reed Ave	San Diego	CA	92109-5166
10003	Fiona	Campos	5086 Frink Ave	San Diego	CA	92117-1211
10004	Ryan	Evans	7400 Artesia Blvd	Buena Park	CA	90621-1867
10005	Adrianne	Smith	4051 Larwin Ave	Cypress	CA	90630-4124
10006	Susan	Stone	923 West Gary Dr	Chandler	AZ	85225-1438

Table T5.2 Sample Data for the Customer Table

Before you enter the data for the product table, notice that when you created the form, the ProdColor field was placed immediately after the ProdDesc field. The form is designed to match the way users will operate on a daily basis, not the loading of the initial data. Since the listing of the product information in Table T5.3 matches the order of the fields in the table layout, it is a little more cumbersome to enter this initial data via the form. This illustrates the importance of having a form layout match the way users will operate the form.

Practice:
Open the Product form and enter only the first two of the records shown in Table T5.3 into your product table.

Enter the remaining product data from Table T4.3 using either the form or the datasheet view of the table.
    Note: It is important to enter all of this data as it will be used later in the chapter.

Close the form (or table if you opened the table) when completed.

ProdID	ProdDesc	ProdUnit Cost	ProdQOH	ProdColor
5001	Barrette - Double Large Gem	$ 13.00	100	Amber
5002	Barrette - Gold Filigree Crystal Flower	$ 17.00	125	Amethyst
5003	Barrette - Gold Filigree Crystal Flower	$ 17.00	75	Ruby
5004	Barrette - Gold Filigree Crystal Flower	$ 17.00	80	Emerald
5005	Comb - Small	$ 5.00	80	Amber
5006	Comb - Small	$ 5.00	75	Tortoise
5007	Comb - Small	$ 5.00	90	Black
5008	Clip - Large Crystal Flower	$ 25.00	75	Multi
5009	Clip - Small Pansy	$ 15.00	130	Blue
5010	Clip - Small Pansy	$ 15.00	120	White
5011	Clip - Small Pansy	$ 15.00	95	Rose
5012	Pin - Austrian Crystal Mini Flower	$ 6.95	80	Green
5013	Pin - Austrian Crystal Mini Flower	$ 6.95	80	Rose
5014	Pin - Austrian Crystal Mini Flower	$ 6.95	80	Yellow
5015	Pin - Guppy Bobby Pins	$ 4.00	125	Tortoise
5016	Pin - Large Pearl and Crystal Silver French	$ 12.95	50	Pearl
5017	Pin - Tiger Eye Bobby Pins (set of 2)	$ 6.35	150	Blue
5018	Pin - Tiger Eye Bobby Pins (set of 2)	$ 6.35	125	Rose
5019	Scrunchy - Beaded Pony Elastic - Faux Pearl	$ 4.50	110	Pearl
5020	Scrunchy - Beaded Scrunchy	$ 3.75	175	Copper
5021	Scrunchy - Slinky Fabric Scrunchy	$ 5.00	100	Black
5022	Scrunchy - Slinky Fabric Scrunchy	$ 5.00	100	Red
5023	Scrunchy - Slinky Fabric Scrunchy	$ 5.00	90	Yellow
5024	Scrunchy - Slinky Fabric Scrunchy	$ 5.00	120	Blue

Table T5.3   Sample Data for the Product Table

In the next section you will create an Order Processing form which you will use to add orders and the associated line items to those orders. However, it will be helpful to have a few rows of sample data already entered into the Order and Line Item tables. Since you don't have a form made yet for those tables, you will need to enter the data directly into the tables.

> *Practice:*
>
> Open the Order table in datasheet view and enter the two orders shown in Table T5.4.
>
> Close that table.
>
> Open the Line Item table in datasheet view and enter the records shown in Table T5.5.
>
> Close that table.

OrderNumber	OrderDate	FKCustID
10001	1-Jul-07	10001
10002	2-Jul-07	10002

Table T5.4   Sample Data for the Order Table

FKOrderNumber	FKProductID	LIUnitPrice	LIQtyOrdered
10001	5002	$ 17.00	5
10001	5006	$ 5.00	1
10002	5001	$ 13.00	3

Table T5.5   Sample Data for the Line Item Table

Create a Form using a Main Form – SubForm Association

Now that you have the simple forms out of the way you can turn your attention to a more complicated form. When you have a database with several related tables you will often have a need to create a form that links several, if not all, of the tables together. Figure T5.18 shows an example of the Hair Today Order Processing Form based on the additional fields that we decided to store. What tables do you think are needed to create the Order Processing Form? Can you see fields from all the tables? Also notice that the form includes the calculated fields of extended price, subtotal, discount, tax and total. You are now going to learn how to build this form.

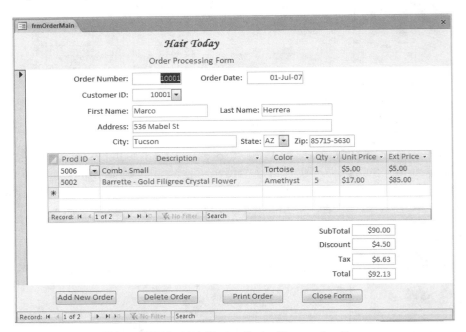

Figure T5.18 Hair Today Order Processing Form

The order processing form is made up of two parts: a *main form* and a *subform*. In Access, a **main form** has a one-to-many relationship with the subform. For Hair Today, the main form will contain information about an order while the **subform** will contain details about the products on that order (the LineItem table.) Since FKCustID is the only field with information about the customer in the Order table, we will want to include additional fields from the Customer table in the main form. On the subform, in addition to the fields from the LineItem table, additional fields from the Product table will be included.

The forms you have built so far in Tutorials 4 and 5 have all been based on tables. Because of the needs of the Hair Today system, those forms contained fields selected only from one table. It is possible to build a form containing fields from different tables. Additionally, forms in Access can also be based on queries. Queries provide an easy way to select the necessary fields from multiple tables and can utilize criteria and sorting options if desired.

For the Hair Today Order Processing form, the main form will be built by selecting fields from two tables – the Order and Customer tables. The subform will be built based on a query that will include fields from both the LineItem and Product tables. Building the Order Processing form involves several steps: 1) Build the main form, 2) Create the query that will be used to create the subform, 3) Create the subform and 4) Add the subform onto the main form and customize the complete Order Processing form by finalizing the layout, adding buttons, and adding calculated fields.

Step 1: Create the Order Form (the main form)

Practice:
Create a copy of the frmMaster form to be used as the Order Form. Save this form as frmOrderMain.

Include all the fields from the Order table on the form and all of the fields <u>except</u> the CustID field from the Customer Table (the CustID field is only needed once and it is already selected from the Order Table.)

Edit the form so that the completed from is similar to that shown in Figure T5.19.

The Form label should read "Order Processing Form."

Save and close the form when you are done.

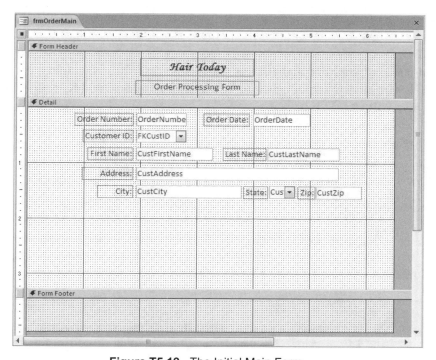

Figure T5.19   The Initial Main Form

Step 2: Create the Query that will be used for the SubForm

Practice:
Create a new query in design view (select the **Create Tab > Other Group > Query Design** option) to build the subform.

Add the Line Item and Product tables into the query grid.

Add the following fields into your query: FKOrderNumber, FKProductID, ProdDesc, ProdColor, LIQtyOrdered, and LIUnitPrice.

> While you could add the fields into the query in any order and then rearrange the fields later in the form, it is much easier to select the fields for the query in the order you wish them to be displayed on the form.

Now you are ready to learn how to add a calculated field to compute the Extended Price.

Creating a Calculated Field in a Query: A **calculated field** is used in a query to show the result of a formula. The formula is entered using the following general form:

Field Name for the Calculated Field:[table field] operator [table field] operator [table field]

* The field name appears first and will become the label for this new field.
  If you do not include a Field Name, Access will name the field for you. The default field name will be EXPR1.

* The colon separates the field name from the equation.

* In the equation, each table field must be enclosed inside of brackets.

* The standard mathematical operators (e.g. +, -, *, /) can be used along with parenthesis.

> An example of a formula for a calculated field to compute a student's average score is:
>
> Student Average:([Ex1]+[Ex2]+[Ex3]+[HW])/400

For Hair Today, the extended price calculated field should show the result of multiplying the LIQtyOrdered by the LIUnitPrice. You will place the calculated field in the empty cell next to the LIUnitPrice field. While the formula can be entered directly in the field row cell, the cell size makes it hard to see the complete formulas. Instead, use will learn to use the **Zoom** box to enter the formula. The **Zoom** box simply provides a large area in which can enter your formula.

Practice:
Select the field row cell to the right of LIUnitPrice and right click to open the **Shortcut Menu**.

Select **Zoom** to open the Zoom editing box.

Enter the formula: *Ext Price:[LIQtyOrdered]*[LIUnitPrice]*

Click OK to close the Zoom window

Run the query to ensure that it works.

Save the query as *qrySubForm*. The query grid should look similar to Figure T5.20.

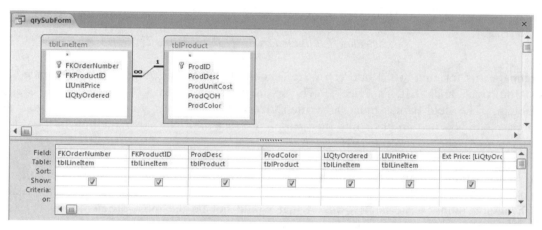

Figure T5.20   The Subform Query Grid

If desired the field properties of the calculated field can be changed by selecting **properties** from the shortcut menu. For example, you can change the **format** to currency so the result will display with the dollar sign and 2 decimal places. Always resave the query if you make any changes.

Practice:
Change the properties of this calculated field to have a *"currency"* **format** with 2 decimal places.

Save the query.

Potential Errors with the Calculated Field in a Query: If you have followed all of the naming suggestions in this tutorial the calculated field should have worked in the query. However, since there are many little steps that you have completed, it is possible that you have an error. A common problem that could result when you run your query is that you receive a message box similar to that shown in Figure T5.21.

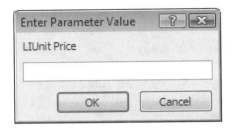

Figure T5.21 An example of potential problem with the calculated field

This message means that Access needs a data value (the parameter) to be supplied by you to compute your formula. This Parameter Value message box does not always mean that you have done something wrong resulting in an error, but in this case it does. Notice in the message box the words LIUnit Price. That is the field for which Access needs the value. The formula entered that caused this message is:

Ext Price: [LIQtyOrdered]*[LIUnit Price]

Compare this formula to the one you were asked to enter earlier. Notice the difference between "LIUnitPrice" and "LIUnit Price". The extra space between LIUnit and Price caused the problem. The field names must be written identically whenever you use them in your Access database. If you had an error like this, simply correct the field name spelling in the query and then the query should run correctly.

When would a parameter value be okay? Perhaps you wanted to write a query that would display only the customers in a specific state. You could write a separate query for each state, each having unique criteria. However, that would not be the most efficient way because you would end with 50 different queries. A better way is to create a parameter query where Access will ask the user to enter the state to use as the criteria when the query is run. You will learn how to write a parameter query later in this tutorial.

Step 3: Create the SubForm
In creating the subform, you will first build the form using the Form Wizard and then edit the form in both Design View and Datasheet View.

> **Practice:**
> Build the subform using the Form Wizard (refer back to Tutorial 4 if you need a refresher about the Form Wizard.) Make the following selections while working through the steps of the Form Wizard:
> - Base the form on the *qrySubform* query and add all of the fields **except** FKOrderNumber into the Selected Fields.
> - When prompted by the wizard, choose a *Datasheet* **layout** for the form and choose *None* for the **style**.
> - Enter *frmLineItemSubform* as the title for the Subform. Click **Finish** to complete the Wizard.

With the wizard completed, you are ready to edit the form.

Practice:

Open the form in Design View and edit the labels so that they are easier to read (use the labels in Figure T5.22 as a guide.)

In Design View:
- Remove the label from the Form Header Section.
- Drag the top of the Detail Section bar to the bottom of the Form Header bar to remove the space in that section.
- Drag the bottom of the Form Footer bar lower to add some space into the Form Footer section.

Switch to Datasheet View to size the subform as needed so that all the fields show. The width of the columns in the subform can be easily adjusted by sliding the column separator bars. Save the form.

The Datasheet View of your subform should appear similar to that shown in Figure T5.22.

Save and Close the form when you are finished.

Prod ID	Description	Color	Qty	Unit Price	Ext Price
5006	Comb - Small	Tortoise	1	$5.00	$5.00
5002	Barrette - Gold Filigree Crystal Flower	Amethyst	5	$17.00	$85.00
5001	Barrette - Double Large Gem	Amber	3	$13.00	$39.00

Figure T5.22   The Datasheet View of the Subform

Step 4: Add the SubForm onto the Main Form and Complete the Main Form

In this step you will first add the Subform onto the Main Form. This will establish a connection between the two forms. After this is done, the Main Form will contain the subform. At that point you will be ready to do any additional editing on the Main Form. In our example, one of the editing components will be to add a calculated field onto the form.

Practice:
Open *frmOrderMain*, created in step 1, in Design View.

Ensure that the **Control Wizards** tool is selected in the **Controls Group** on the **Form Design Tools Design Tab**.

Select the **Form Design Tools Design Tab > Controls Group > Subform/Subreport** icon [icon].

Click on the main form in the Detail Section, towards the left border below the City label to position the subform.

The Subform wizard will launch.

Choose the radio button to **Use An Existing Form** and select the *frmLineItemSubform*.   Click **Next**.

Choose the radio button for **Choose from a list** and Click **Next**.

Keep the name of the form as *frmLineItemSubform*. Click **Finish**.

When you are done the form should look similar to that shown in Figure T5.23.

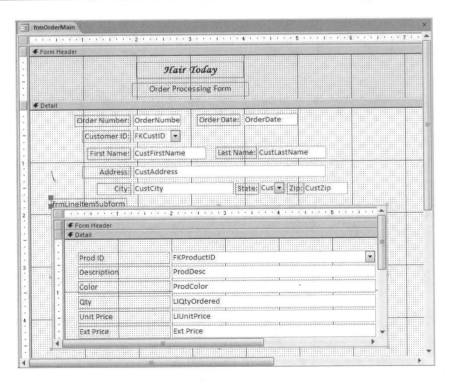

Figure T5.23 Initial Order Processing Form

Practice:
Switch to Form View to ensure that the form works.

If you need to make any sizing adjustments use the Design or Layout Views as appropriate.

Delete the label for the frmLineItemSubform.

The finished form will contain calculated fields and buttons. Use the design in Figure T5.17 as a guide for your final form design. You are now ready to learn how to create a calculated field on a form.

Creating a Calculated Field on a Form: A **calculated field** is added onto a form to show the result of formula. A textbox control will be placed onto the form to hold the calculated field. The formula is entered into the **control source** property of the textbox.   The **Control Source** property indicates the source of the data for the field. The source could be a field in a table or a formula. The general form of a textbox formula is:

= [form field] operator [form field] operator [form field]

* The formula begins with an equal sign.

* In the equation, each form field must be enclosed inside of brackets.

* The standard mathematical operators (e.g. +, -, *, /) can be used along with parenthesis.

An example of an entry for a calculated field is:

$=([Ex1]+[Ex2]+[Ex3]+[HW])/400$

For Hair Today, you will need to add 4 textboxes onto the main form to serve as the calculated fields for the subtotal, discount, tax and total. Since the formulas are cumulative (i.e. you need to know the subtotal before you can figure the tax) we will add them sequentially. There are quite a few details that need to be followed correctly in this section so take a deep breath before we begin!

Add Field 1 - The Subtotal Calculated Field: The subtotal is a slightly more complicated calculated field because it needs to get information from the subform, instead of only from the main form. This means that you will also need to add a calculated field onto the subform. The actual calculation of the subtotal will be done inside of the subform textbox and then the textbox on the main form will simply reference the textbox on the subform.

Practice:

Open the Main Form in design view.

Add the Calculated Field onto the Subform: In the subform (you should be working inside of the subform that is placed on the main form) perform the following tasks:

- In the **Form Footer** section of the subform, add a **textbox** control (from the Controls Group of the Form Design Tools Design Tab.)
  Note: If you don't have any area showing in the subform footer, drag the footer section separator down to create room in the footer.

- Right-click on that textbox and select **properties**.
- Select the **All Tab**.
- In the **control source** property, enter the correct formula to compute the subtotal.
  Note: Since the subtotal requires adding up the extended price for all of the line items on an order, this will require an **aggregate function**. An aggregate function will work by performing the calculating over a collection of rows of data. Aggregate functions include *Sum*, *Count*, and *Avg*. In our case, the formula that will sum together all of individual products ordered (these are represented on the Line Items) for one particular order..
  Assuming that you named the calculated field on the query Ext Price, the formula would be: *=Sum([Ext Price]).*

  Another option: If you didn't have the calculated field on the query, you could write the formula like this: =Sum([LIQtyOrdered]*[LIUnitPrice]).

- In the **name property** of the textbox enter *SFSubTot.* Note: When you view the form in Form View, this calculated field will not be displayed on the subform.

- Save your form so that you don't lose any of your work.

Add the Calculated Field onto the Main Form: In the main form do the following tasks:
- In the **Detail** section of the main form, below the subform, add a **textbox** control for the SubTotal.
- Enter *=frmLineItemSubform.Form!SFSubTot* in the **control source** property.
  Note: This assumes that you named your subform "frmLineItemSubform" and that you named the textbox "SFSubTot".
- In the **name property** of the subtotal textbox on the main form enter "*SubTot*".
- In the **format property** select *currency.*
- When you added the textbox onto the form, Access automatically created a label control to go with the textbox. In the **caption property** of the label control, enter "*SubTotal*".
- Save the form and switch to form view.

The subtotal for order 10001 should be $90.00. Navigate to order 10002. The subtotal should be $39.00.

Figure T5.24 visually summarizes key parts of the steps described above in the practice.

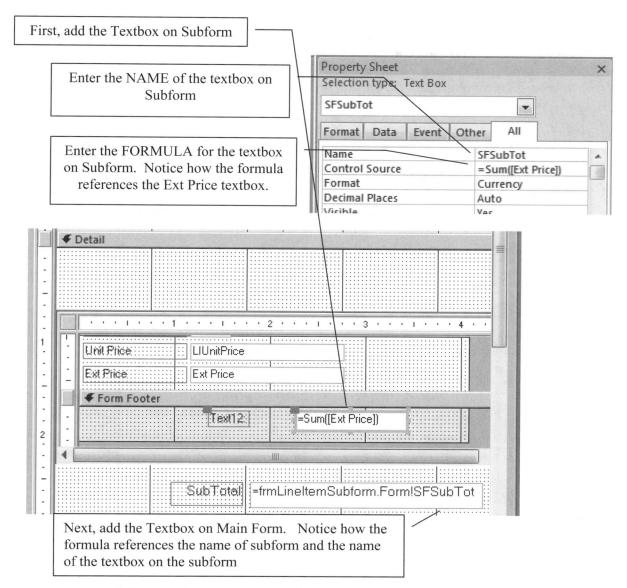

First, add the Textbox on Subform

Enter the NAME of the textbox on Subform

Enter the FORMULA for the textbox on Subform. Notice how the formula references the Ext Price textbox.

Property Sheet   ✕
Selection type: Text Box

SFSubTot   ▼

| Format | Data | Event | Other | All |

Name	SFSubTot
Control Source	=Sum([Ext Price])
Format	Currency
Decimal Places	Auto
Visible	Yes

⬧ Detail

⬧ Form Footer

Text12   =Sum([Ext Price])

SubTotal   =frmLineItemSubform.Form!SFSubTot

Next, add the Textbox on Main Form. Notice how the formula references the name of subform and the name of the textbox on the subform

Figure T5.24 Visual Overview of Key Tasks in Creating the Subtotal Calculated Field

Potential Errors with the Calculated Field in a Textbox: If you have followed all of the naming suggestions in this tutorial, the calculated field should have worked in the textbox. However, since it is possible that an error was made in either naming a field or entering the formula, the textbox formula may not work correctly.   The most common problem you may encounter is the **#Name?** error. This means that Access doesn't recognize the name of one of the variables in the formula. Verify that you have entered all form names, field names and textbox names correctly in the formula. Also ensure that brackets are used appropriately. A common mistake that you may have done is to have changed the name in the Caption Property of the label associated with the textbox, instead of actually changing the value of the Name Property of the textbox itself. If you have an error, verify each of the tasks in the previous Practice box to ensure that you have completed each task as specified.

Add Field 2 - The Discount Calculated Field: If a customer has purchased more than $75.00 worth of merchandise, they will receive a 5% discount of the subtotal amount. It will be necessary to use the **IIF function** in Access to accomplish this formula.

The general format of the IIF function is:

$$=IIf(condition,true,false)$$

* The IIF function in Access is truely spelled "IIf"; it is not a typographical error in this book.
* The Condition can be any logical test
* The True and False actions can be either text, numbers or formulas. As in Excel you can nest the IIF function.
* The IF statement in Access is really spelled "IIf".

The following two examples should help you understand how the statement functions:

=IIf([TotalPoints]>250,10,0)	This will put a value of 10 in the text box if the TotalPoints field on the form is greater than 250. If it is <=250 the textbox will contain a 0.
=IIf([TotalPoints]>250,[TotalPoints]*.03,0)	This will put a value of .03*TotalPoints in the text box if the TotalPoints field is greater than 250. If it is <=250 the textbox will contain a 0.

Add the Discount Calculated Field.

Practice:
In the **Detail** section of the main form, below the subtotal textbox, add a **textbox** control for the Discount.

Enter =IIf([SubTot]>75,[SubTot]*0.05,0) in the **control source property**.

In the **name property** of the textbox enter "*Disc*".

In the **format property** select *currency*.

In the **caption property** of the label control, enter "*Discount*".

Save the form and switch to form view.

The discount for order 10001 should be $4.50. Navigate to order 10002. The discount should be 0.

While it isn't required to save and switch to form view after you complete each textbox, doing so will enable you to identify any potential errors earlier. This will make it easier on you if you do have to find and correct a mistake. This is especially true in situations where the calculations build on each other. For example if you had not verified if the subtotal textbox worked correctly earlier, and now had an error with the discount textbox, fixing the problem would be harder because you would need to check both the subtotal and the discount to isolate the problem.

Add Field 3 - The Tax Calculated Field: The tax will be computed at 7.75% of the subtotal minus the discount. In the main form do the following:

Practice:

In the **Detail** Section of the main form, below the Discount Textbox, add a **textbox** control for the Tax.

Enter =([SubTot]-[Disc])*.0775 in the **control source property**.

In the **name property** of the textbox enter "*Tax*".

In the **format property** select *currency*.

In the **caption property** of the label control, enter "*Tax*".

Save the form and switch to form view.

The tax for order 10001 should be $6.63. Navigate to order 10002. The tax should be $3.02.

Add Field 4 - The Total Calculated Field: The total will add the subtotal and tax and subtract the discount. In the main form do the following:

Practice:

In the **Detail** Section of the main form, below the Tax Textbox, add a **textbox** control for the Total. The total will add the subtotal and tax and subtract the discount.

Use the skills you have learned to name the textbox, change the format to currency, and update the caption of the label.

Save the form and switch to form view.

Verify if your Total formula calculated the correct answers for orders 10001 and 10002. The total for order 10001 should be $92.13. Navigate to order 10002. The total should be $42.02.

Hang in there; you are almost done with the order form!

Create the Form Buttons: The last task is to add four buttons onto the Form Footer area of the Main Form.

Practice:
Use the Command Button tool to add four buttons to the footer of the main form with the following specifications:

      Add an Order (Record Operation category)
      Delete Order (Record Operation category)
      Print the Current Order (Record Operation category)
      Close the Form (Form Operations category)

Save the form when you are done. Your completed form should look similar to the form shown in Figure T5.18.

Wow! You have done a great job. Try out your new order processing form. In just a minute you will add the new orders that are shown in Table T5.6. As you add the order, pay attention to the way your database works. Notice that when you click the Add an Order button both the main form and the subform are cleared. When you add products onto the order in the subform they are being saved into the line item table.

Practice:
Open the Main Form in Form View.

Add the new orders that are shown in Table T5.6.

Close the form when you are finished.

OrderNumber	OrderDate	CustID	FKProductID	LIUnitPrice	LIQtyOrdered
10003	10-Jul-07	10001	5010	$ 15.00	2
			5016	$ 12.95	1
			5003	$ 17.00	2
10004	12-Jul-07	10006	5004	$ 17.00	1
10005	12-Jul-07	10002	5018	$ 6.35	2
			5020	$ 3.75	5
10006	14-Jul-07	10003	5017	$ 6.35	4
			5001	$ 13.00	3
			5006	$ 5.00	2
10007	15-Jul-07	10004	5022	$ 5.00	6
10008	15-Jul-07	10001	5010	$ 15.00	5

Table T5.6 Additional Data to enter in the Order Processing Form

Your form has many sophisticated features to help make the order processing task easier for the staff at Hair Today. However there are still a few tasks that have not yet been automated in the form. For example, currently you have to enter the unit price when you add a product onto an order. Additionally it would be best if your system checked the quantity on hand to ensure that there was enough of the product to fill the order, and then deducted the quantity ordered from the quantity on hand when it was ordered. These features require more sophisticated programming to occur within the database. You are starting to realize why database specialists are in such demand. We will revisit the skills to accomplish these tasks later in the tutorial.

Create Advanced Reports

Most database systems will have a set of predefined reports that can be run as desired by the users of the system. In Tutorial 4 you learned how to build a report and to customize that report by rearranging fields and labels and adding new controls. Recall that reports can be based on a table or a query.   In this section you will build two reports. First you will build a report that uses grouping and summary options. The second report will use a parameter query.

Report 1: Create a Report with Grouping and Summary Options

The first report is a Sales Report listing all orders, including the details of all items ordered. To accomplish this report the line item details will be grouped by the order number. Additionally calculated fields will be used on the report to show different totals. Building the report involves several steps: 1) Create the query that will be used to create the report, 2) Create the basic report using the report wizard, and 3) Customize that basic report by altering the layout.

Step 1: Create the Query that will be used by the Report

Practice:
Create a new "design view" query that includes all of the tables.

Include the following fields: OrderNumber, CustFirstName, CustLastName, OrderDate, FKProductID, ProdDesc, LIQtyOrdered, LIUnitPrice and an Extended Price (calculated field.)
    Refer back to the earlier part of this section if you need a review on how to add a calculated field to a query.

Run the Query.
    It should display one record for each row of the OrderLine table.

Save the query as *qryAllOrders* and close it.

Step 2: Create the Sales Report

Practice:

Create the Sales Report using the Report wizard.

Base the report on the query you just built.

Add all the fields into the "Select fields" **except** the FKProductID.

View the data by tblOrder.

Do not add any grouping levels.

Sort the report by ProdDesc in ascending order.

Click the **Summary Options** button.
- Click *Sum* under the Extended Price field. Ensure that the Detail and Summary option button is selected.
- Click OK to close the Summary Options window.

Click **Next**.

Choose a *Stepped* layout and *landscape* orientation.

Choose the *Office* style.

Enter *rptAllOrders* as the title.

The design view of your report should look similar to that shown in Figure T5.25.

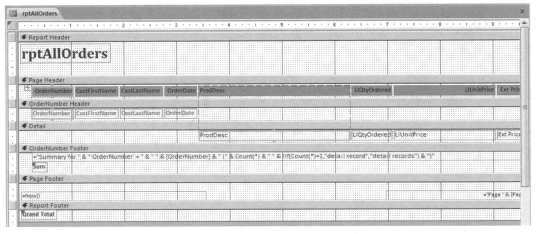

Figure T5.25 Initial Sales Report in Design View

Step 3: Customize the Report.

In this last step, you will use the design view to customize the report. The Design view of the completed report should look similar to that shown in Figure T5.26.

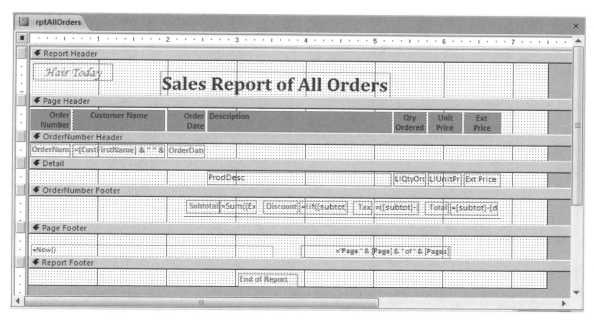

Figure T5.26 Design View of Modified Sales Report

Practice:
   Open the Report in Design View. Complete the following changes so the report will match Figure T5.26:
   a.   Select the **Report Design Tools Design Tab > Grouping & Totals Group > Group & Sorting** icon. The Group, Sort, and Total window will appear, similar to Figure T5.27.

Practice (continued):

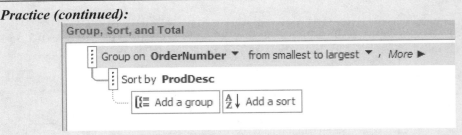

Figure T5.27 The Group, Sort, and Total Window

On the Group on OrderNumber line, click **More** to expand the window. Change *do not keep group together on one* page to *keep whole group together on one page.* Close the Group, Sort and Total window.

b. Edit the captions of the label controls as needed. Adjust the label size so that they fit better and are easy to read. The captions can be forced to break to a second line by entering the keystroke combination of Control + Enter at the point the text should wrap.

c. Delete the CustFirstName and CustLastName text boxes and labels.

d. Add a textbox control in the Order Number Header section to show the concatenated name. A **concatenated field** joins together separate fields. Usually concatenation is done to improve the readability of different fields. In this case it will remove the extra spaces between the first and last name. The **&** operator is used in the expression. Enter the formula *=[CustFirstName] & " " & [CustLastName]* in the **Control Source Property** of that textbox. Set the Fore Color and Font Weight properties to match those of the other text boxes.

e. In the OrderNumber Footer section, delete the label control that begins *='Summary for...'* Edit the label control with the word *Sum* to read "*Subtotal.*" Move that control closer to the control that actually shows the total.

f. Add textbox controls for the Discount, Tax and Total. Enter the correct formulas (this is done the same as entering formulas into textboxes on a form) into the **Control Source Property** of each control. Refer back to the earlier part of this section if you need a review on how to enter formulas into textboxes on a form. Set the **Format Property** to *currency.* Edit the label controls to have an appropriate caption and similar font color and formatting as the other labels. Move the controls to match the locations shown in Figure T5.25.

g. In the Report Footer section, delete the label control that contains *'Grand Total'* and the related textbox control with the total. Add a label control and change the caption to read "*End of Report.*"

h. Make any other adjustments needed to ensure your report looks nice and is consistent with the design of other objects in the system. This could include modifying labels, changing fonts, adding graphics, etc. Based on the adjustments you have made, your report probably no longer needs to be as wide as it currently is. Drag the sizing handles on the right side of your report to make it narrower. If the width of the report is now less than 8" you will be able to view the report in a Portrait orientation. Select the **Report Design Tools Page Setup Tab > Page Layout Group > Portrait** option. Save and View the Report. The completed report should appear similar to Figure T5.28.

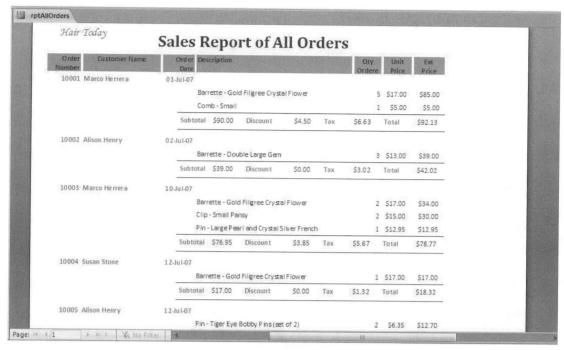

Figure T5.28 Print Preview View of Modified Report

Report 2: Create a Parameter Report

The second report will be used to show all the orders that have ordered a specific item. For example, you could find which customers have ordered the item "Pin - Austrian Crystal Mini Flower." Notice that the Product Description includes the type of product as well as a more detailed description. For example, Clip is used in both the Large Crystal Flower as well as the Small Pansy. To enable the query to find customers who have ordered any type of Clip, you will write the query to search for text that appears anywhere in the ProdDesc field. Additionally, since the content of the description also includes the color, the user can narrow down the selection based on the color of the item. A **Parameter Report** is a report that allows the user to enter the specific input, or criteria, at the time the report is run. Building the report involves several steps: 1) Create the query that will be used to create the report, 2) Create the basic report using the report wizard, and 3) Customize the basic report by altering the layout.

Step 1: Create the Query that will be used by the Report

This query will need to incorporate a calculated field. You have already learned how to put a calculated field into a query. In this case, you are going to learn a new formula that will combine the First and Last names together into one field. This is an example of a concatenated field. You used a concatenated field in the last report to display the customer name. Recall that a **concatenated field** is one in which several different text fields, and potentially other text constants, are combined together into one new field. The general form of using concatenation in a query is shown below along with several examples.

Field Name for the Concatenated Field:Piece1 & Piece2 & Piece3

* The field name appears first and will become the label for this new field.
    Recall that if you do not include a Field Name, Access will name the field for you.
    The default field name will be EXPR1.

* The colon separates the field name from the equation.

* In the equation, you can combine as many pieces as needed.
    - If the piece is a field from a table, it must be enclosed inside of brackets.
    - If the piece is hardcoded, or constant, text, it must be enclosed inside of quotation marks

Examining some examples:
Assume we have three database fields with the following contents:
    City = San Diego   State = CA   Zip = 92182

If we just use each field separately on a query, then when the results are returned, we end up with spaces or gaps between each field, based on the maximum length of the field.

The result of just including each field separately would be:

CITY	STATE	ZIP
San Diego	CA	92182

We can concatenate the fields so that they will appear next to each other when we run the query or generate a report. Several examples are illustrated below along with the results:
Note: In all cases we will name the new field "City, State Zip." It is acceptable to have spaces and punctuation inside of a field name for a calculated field.

Example	Result
City, State Zip: [City] & [State] & [Zip]	**City, State Zip** San DiegoCA92182

Note: The results put one field immediately after another because no spaces have been added

| City, State Zip: [City] & " " & [State] & " " & [Zip] | **City, State Zip**
San Diego CA 92182 |

Note: The results includes spaces between the fields

| City, State Zip: [City] & ", " & [State] & "   " & [Zip] | **City, State Zip**
San Diego, CA   92182 |

Note: The results includes a comma and space between City and State and 3 spaces between the State and Zip

In the examples shown above, the hardcoded values used were either spaces or punctuation. Those values could be any characters or numbers that you wish to use.

> ***Practice:***
> Create a new "design view" query that includes all of the tables.
>
> Include the following fields: OrderNumber, OrderDate, CustID, Customer Name: [custfirstname] & " " & [custlastname], FKProductID, ProdDesc, ProdColor and LIQtyOrdered.
>
> *Note: The Customer Name field is an example of a concatenated field.*

At this point we are ready to enter the criteria. If we were building this query to only find records that ordered a "Pin - Austrian Crystal Mini Flower" we would enter that value in the criteria cell for the ProdDesc field. In our case, remember that the query is going to be designed so that the user will enter the criteria, the product description, that they wish to use at the time the query is run. The way this is accomplished is to create a query parameter.

Creating a Query Parameter: A **query parameter** is a placeholder for the actual value that will be used in the query. The parameter is entered into the Criteria Row of the field inside of brackets. The text that you enter is what will be displayed in the Enter Parameter Value dialog box that is displayed when the query runs. The general form of a query parameter, along with some examples, is shown below.

[Text to Display in the Query Parameter Box]

* The query parameter is placed in the criteria row for the field which requires user input
* When the query is run, the query parameter box displays to the user. The value that the user enters is used as the criteria for the field
* The parameter text used is up to you but it must be enclosed inside of brackets.

Example:

To create a report where the user obtains a list of customers from a specific state, you would enter the following parameter into the Criteria Row of the State field:
[Enter the State]

When the query is run, the following parameter dialog box would display.

The user enters the State and clicks OK. The query displays the records that meet the criteria.

An Expanded example:

The parameter could be included as part of a larger expression. For example to broaden the search you may want the parameter to be surrounded by wildcard characters (e.g. "*" or "?") or you may want to the expression to include a comparison (e.g. >=[Enter the Beginning Date for the Report:].) Several variations of criteria for the state field will be shown, along with an explanation of the impact:

>=[Enter the State]

In this case you will get records from multiple states returned. The >= operator allows you to find all the records that have a value that equals, or comes later, in the alphabet. For example, if you entered CA, the states that would be returned include CA, but also CO, CT, DE, FL, etc.

>[Enter the State]

If CA was entered as the value by the user, then records where CA was the state would NOT be returned, but CO, CT, DE, FL, etc. records would be returned.

Like [Enter the State (or the first letter to find all states that begin with a certain letter):] &
""*

Recall in Tutorial 4 that you saw examples of using criteria that contained wildcards and the word "like" when we discussed validation rules. These can be applied to any situation that uses criteria. When like is used, together with the * wildcard character, the query allows the user to search for something that is similar to the query data specified. Recall that the * wildcard character represents any string of characters, up to the maximum length of the field.

If the user entered C, records that start with a C (which would be CA, CO or CT for our state field) would be returned. If the user entered CA, only records that started with CA would be returned. Since the state field is limited to 2 characters, this would effectively restrict the choice to CA.

Like "" & [Enter State (Leave blank to select all States):] & "*"*

In this example, we have combined the wildcard at the beginning and end, to allow for more flexibility.

If the user entered A, then any state that contains an A would be returned. If the user leaves the value blank, all the records would be returned.

You are now ready to enter the criteria into your query.

Practice:
Make the following changes in the design view of the query:

In the Criteria Row for the ProdDesc field enter the expression: *Like "*" & [Enter Product Description (Leave blank to select all products):] & "*"*

In the Criteria Row for the ProdColor field enter the expression: *Like "*" & [Enter Color choice (Leave blank to select all colors):] & "*"*

Save the query as *qryProductSelection*

Run the Query. You should see first see the Enter Parameter Value dialogue box for the Description and then next see the Enter Parameter Value dialogue box for the Color. The resulting query should display one record for each row of the OrderLine table that matches the parameter values you supplied. Run the query several times entering different combinations of criteria so that you can verify the query works as intended. Make any needed corrections. Save the query and close it.

Step 2: Create a product report using the wizard that is based on that query.

Practice:
Create the Product Report using the Report wizard. Base the report on the query you just built.

Add the fields in the following order into the "Select fields" :ProdDesc, ProdColor, FKProductID, OrderNumber, OrderDate, CustID, Customer Name, LIQtyOrdered. Adding them in this order minimizes the need to rearrange fields later in the design view of the report.

View the data by tblProduct.

Add a grouping level of ProdDesc.

Sort the report by CustID in ascending order.

Click the **Summary Options** button.
- Click *Sum* and *Avg* under the LIQtyOrdered field. Ensure that the Detail and Summary option button is selected.
- Click OK to close the Summary Options window.

Click **Next**.

Choose a *Stepped* layout and *landscape* orientation.

Choose the *Office* style.

Enter *rptProductSelection* as the title. Your report should look similar to Figure T5.29.

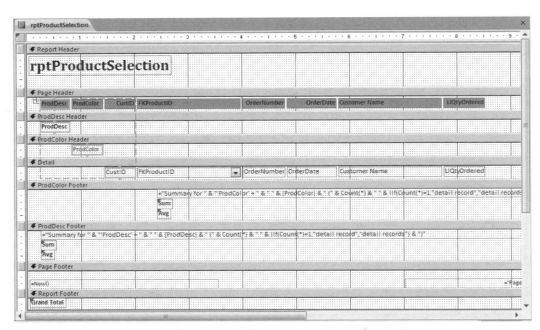

Figure T5.29 Design View of the Initial Product Sales Report

Step 3: Customize the basic report layout.

In this last step, you will use the Design View to edit the contents of several of the header and footer sections. Since this report has 4 different header sections (report, page, ProdDesc and ProdColor) along with 4 different footer sections, it will be important for you to pay attention to ensure you are working in the correct section. The Design view of your final report should look similar to that shown in Figure T5.30.

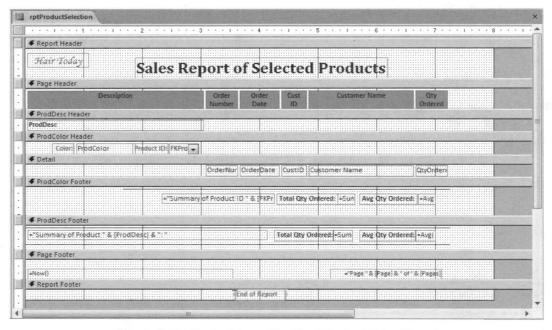

Figure T5.30 Design View of the Final Product Sales Report

Practice:

Open the Report in Design View. Complete the following changes so the report will match the design view shown in Figure T5.30:

  a. In the Report Header section, edit the label caption to read "*Sales Report of Selected Products*." Add a new label with the Hair Today title. Adjust the size and placement of the labels so that the basic report layout is similar to your other report.

  b. In the ProdColor Header section, delete the ProdColor field. From the Field List, add the ProdColor field back into the ProdColor Header section. Yes, that does sound ridiculous. However, it is necessary to do this to get the label for the ProdColor to be in the same section as the field.

  c. In the Detail section, delete the FKProductID field. Add the FKProductID field into the ProdColor Header Section.

  d. In the Page Header section adjust the caption, size and alignment of the labels as needed.

  e. In the Detail section, move the CustID textbox so that it appears to the right of Order Date. Adjust the alignment and size of the textboxes in the Detail section as needed.

  f. In the ProdColor Footer section, edit the label that begins with:

      ="Summary for " & "'ProdColor' = "

  so that it now reads:

      ="Summary of Product ID " & [FKProductID] & ": "

  Move the Sum and Avg labels and textboxes to match Figure T5.30. Edit the label captions. ***Note:*** The textboxes associated with Sum and Avg are located at the far right side of the report. You will need to scroll to the right to find the textboxes. It is possible that your textboxes were initially set to a very small size and may appear as either of the small lines shown in Figure T5.31. Those lines actually are the textboxes. Select one of the textboxes and use the sizing handles to make it wider.

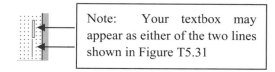

Note: Your textbox may appear as either of the two lines shown in Figure T5.31

Figure T5.31 Possible Textbox Markings for the Sum and Avg textboxes

Practice (continued):

  g. In the ProdDesc Footer section, edit the label text that begins with:

      ="Summary for " & "'ProdDesc' =

  So that it now reads:

      ="Summary of Product " & [ProdDesc] & ": "

  Move the Sum and Avg labels and textboxes to match Figure T5.30. These textboxes are also located at the far right side of the report. Edit the label captions.

  h. Select the **Report Design Tools Design Tab > Grouping & Totals Group > Group & Sorting** icon . On the Group on ProdDesc line, click **More** to expand the window. Change *do not keep group together on one* page to *keep whole group together on one page*. Close the Group, Sort and Total window.

Practice (continued):

i. In the Report Footer section, delete the label control that contains *'Grand Total'* and the related textbox control with the total. Add a label control and change the caption to read *"End of Report."*

j. Make any other adjustments needed to ensure your report looks nice and is consistent with the design of other objects in the system. This could include modifying labels, changing fonts, adding graphics, etc. Based on the adjustments you have made, your report probably no longer needs to be as wide as it currently is. Drag the sizing handles on the right side of your report to make it narrower. If the width of the report is now less than 8" you will be able to view the report in a Portrait orientation. Select the **Report Design Tools Page Setup Tab** > **Page Layout Group** > **Portrait** option.

k. Save and View the Report. The completed report should appear similar to Figure T5.32

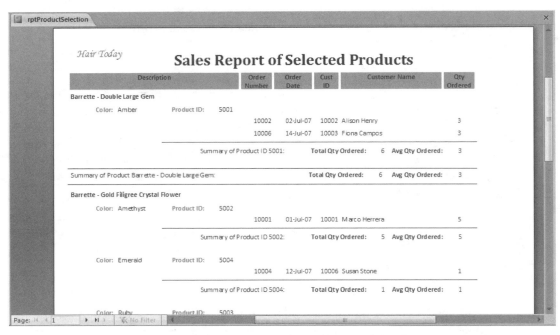

Figure T5.32 Print Preview View of Final Product Sales Report

Through these two reports you have had a chance to explore many different report features. While Hair Today would realistically need several other reports, you have learned many foundation skills which would help you easily create other reports. In Chapter 2 you learned about the three main types of reports: detail, summary and exception. How would you classify the two reports that you created? Since they both include details about the different orders, they would both be detail reports. Can you brainstorm any summary or exception reports that Hair Today might want? In the End of Tutorial Exercises you will have the opportunity to build summary and exception reports.

Customize the Navigation Pane

The **Navigation Pane** is used in Access 2007 to provide users with easy access to different database objects such as forms, reports, and tables. Each time you have created a new object it has appeared on the Navigation Pane. When you needed to open an object that was already built, you selected it from the Navigation Pane. But as you can see by looking at the Navigation Pane in your Hair Today system, it has become quite complicated.

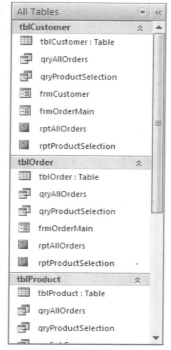

Figure T5.33 shows an example of the Hair Today Navigation Pane.

By selecting the drop-down arrow at the top of the Navigation Pane (where it currently reads All Tables) you can change the way that you view the objects. For example you can choose to view by Date Created or Object Type. You can also narrow the objects that display by applying a filter. That is certainly helpful for the database designer; however you need to find a way to make it easier for your users to work with the different objects that have been created, to essentially provide a menu of choices.

In the older versions of Access the Navigation Pane did not exist. Instead, developers created a switchboard to provide a menu of choices to the users. A **switchboard** is a special form in Access that allows users to more easily perform tasks in the database system. The switchboard acts as a menu, providing choices to the user. For example, a choice could be to open a form or open a report.

Figure T5.33 The Navigation Pane

Without a switchboard the users would have to navigate through the object listing in Access. They would also have to know the name of each objects and which ones they should use. If they are unfamiliar with the system they may accidentally delete or modify an object, which could cause severe problems in your system. What would happen, for example, if a user accidentally deleted your *frmLineItemSubform*? The Main Form – Subform association used to create the Order Processing capabilities would no longer work. In most cases you won't want your users to be able to see the design view you have been using to build the system. This will help prevent them from making mistakes.

While you still can create and use switchboards in Access 2007, the recommended method is to customize the Navigation Pane. Compared to using switchboards, the object can be more easily managed. Further, the Navigation Pane is always visible at the left of the Access window whereas switchboards could become hidden behind other objects.

The last task you will work on in this tutorial is to customize the Navigation Pane for Hair Today.

Practice:

1. Create a Custom Category

    *   On the Navigation Pane, right-click the menu bar at the top and select **Navigation Options**. The Navigation Options dialog box, as shown in Figure T5.34, will open.

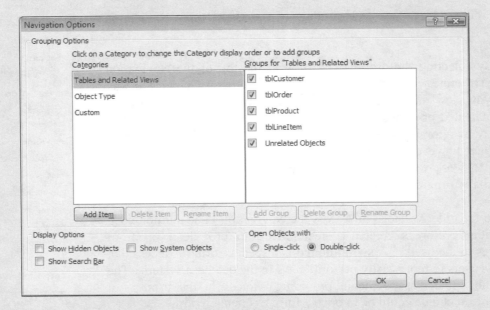

Figure T5.34 The Navigation Options Dialog Box

    *   Select **Add Item** below the Categories section.
    *   Enter *Hair Today Main Menu* as the name for the new category. Press Enter.

2. Create Custom Groups for the Hair Today Main Menu category.

    *   Select **Add Group** below the Groups for Hair Today Main Menu section.
    *   Enter *Customer Records* as the name for the new category. Press Enter.
    *   Repeat the above steps to add groups for *Product Records*, *Order Processing*, and *View Reports*.
    *   Select OK to close the Navigation Options dialog box.

3. Add objects to the Hair Today groups.

    *   Click the drop-down arrow at the top of the Navigation Pane and select the Hair Today Main Menu category. Your Navigation Pane should appear similar to that shown in Figure T5.35.

Practice (continued):

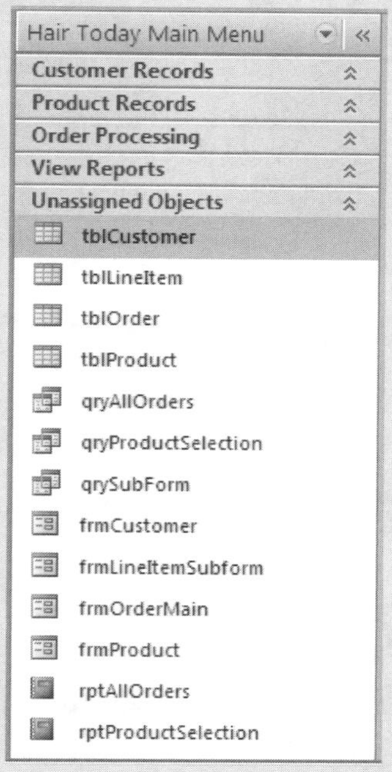

Figure T5.35 depicts the Navigation Pane with the following items:

```
Hair Today Main Menu          ▼  «
  Customer Records                ≈
  Product Records                 ≈
  Order Processing                ≈
  View Reports                    ≈
  Unassigned Objects              ≈
      tblCustomer
      tblLineItem
      tblOrder
      tblProduct
      qryAllOrders
      qryProductSelection
      qrySubForm
      frmCustomer
      frmLineItemSubform
      frmOrderMain
      frmProduct
      rptAllOrders
      rptProductSelection
```

Figure T5.35 The Initial View of the Hair Today Main Menu Navigation Pane

- Drag *frmCustomer* from the **Unassigned Objects** group into the **Customer Records** group.
- Drag *frmProduct* from the **Unassigned Objects** group into the **Product Records** group.
- Drag *frmOrderMain* from the **Unassigned Objects** group into the **Order Processing** group.
- Drag *rptAllOrders* form the **Unassigned Objects** group into the **View Reports** group.
- Drag *rptProductSelection* from the **Unassigned Objects** group into the **View Reports** group.

You have now assigned all of the objects that your users need to work with to the correct groups.

4. Hide the Categories and Groups that should not be visible to your users.

- On the Navigation Pane, right-click the menu bar at the top and select **Navigation Options**.
- Select *Hair Today Main Menu* in the Categories section.
- Clear the check box for *Unassigned Objects* in the Groups for "Hair Today Main Menu" section.   Click OK. The Hair Today Navigation Pane should appear similar to that shown in Figure T5.36.

Practice (continued):

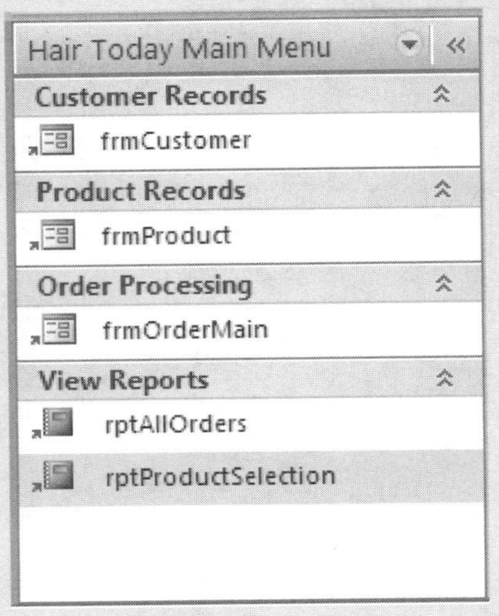

Figure T5.36 The Completed Hair Today Main Menu Navigation Pane

Notice that the drop-down arrow still shows next to Hair Today Main Menu in the Navigation Pane. If you click the arrow you will still see the predefined categories including Tables and Related Views, Object Type and Custom. Selecting any of those will still give your users access to the objects you do not want them to see. While you cannot remove those predefined categories, you can hide the groups inside of the categories.

- On the Navigation Pane, right-click the menu bar at the top and select **Navigation Options**.

- Select *Tables and Related Views* in the Categories section.
- Clear the check box for all of the groups in the Groups for "Tables and Related Views."
- Repeat these actions for the *Object Type* and *Custom* categories. Click OK when you have finished.

You have now customized the Navigation Pane to prevent your users from working with objects that they should not use, and to enable your users to perform their tasks more easily.

In this section you learned how to create queries with calculated fields. You then learned how to create a main form with a sub-form. Additionally, you learned how to create reports utilizing groupings and summary options as well as a parameter query. Finally you customized the navigation pane to link all the database components together.

LEARNING CHECK
Be sure you can *add a calculate field onto a query *create a mainform – subform *add calculated fields onto a form *build a report using groupings and summary options *create a parameter query *design a switchboard

WRAPPING IT UP

In this tutorial you learned how to build a more complete database system in Access. You began with designing the physical database tables. Then you built an Access database that had 4 related tables. After creating the tables you established the needed relationships. You built forms and reports based on multiple tables and set different properties to ensure data integrity. Finally, you linked different database objects together by customizing the Navigation Pane.

Study Questions Summary

1. How do you create the physical database model?
    - The process of converting the conceptual data model into the physical database model involves several steps.
    - Each entity is converted into a table
    - A primary key must be identified for each table
    - Relationships are represented through foreign keys
    - Determine if additional fields need to be stored in the tables
    - If calculated fields were identified during the conceptual design stage, you must determine if they will be stored in the tables

2. How do you establish relationships?
    - Referential integrity ensures consistency of data across the related tables
    - The lookup wizard provides a mechanism to provide users with a list of the allowable choices
    - The Relationships Window is used to set referential integrity constraints
    - Based on the business rules, decide whether Cascading Updates and Cascading Deletes will be allowed

3. How can you create a more complex database system in Access?
    - A Main form linked to a SubForm can be used to display a one-to-many relationship
    - Calculated fields can be added into queries or directly onto forms and reports
    - Textboxes are used on forms to hold the results of calculated fields
    - Form sections can be edited to alter the basic display
    - Parameter queries can be created to allow the user to enter the search criteria at run-time
    - Switchboard can open forms, reports and other switchboards

Key Terms

Page Number references are included in parentheses

Aggregate Function (422)	Concatenated field *in a Query* (431)	Physical Model (394)
Calculated field *in a Form* (421)	Control Source Property (421)	Query Parameter (433)
Calculated field in a Query (416)	IIF Function (424)	Referential Integrity (399)
Cascade Delete Related Records (400)	Lookup Wizard (401)	Row Source Property (402)
Cascade Update Related Fields (400)	Main form (414)	Subform (414)
Compound Key/Concatenated Key (395)	Navigation Pane (439)	Switchboard (439)
Concatenated field *in a Report* (430)	Parameter Report (431)	Zoom (416)

Multiple Choice Questions

1. You need to create a query that will find all International Business majors with at least a 3.2 GPA who are enrolled in the IDS 180 course. How many rows of criteria will you need in the Design grid?
   a. 1
   b. 2
   c. 3
   d. 4

2. In Access, which of the following can be used to restrict the data that is entered into a field?
   a. Size
   b. Validation Rule
   c. Validation Text
   d. A and B
   e. A, B, and C

3. To change a field to one where the user can select from a list of values, use the _____ data type.
   a. List Wizard
   b. Lookup Wizard
   c. Value Wizard
   d. Combo Wizard

4. Which of the following statements describes the effect of the relationship constraints, shown in the figure below, for the Student Registration database?

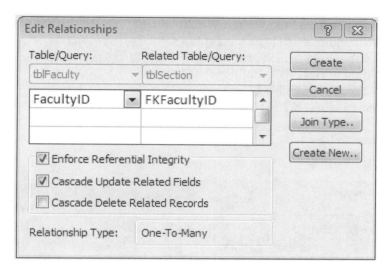

a. If you delete a Section, all the faculty associated with that section will be deleted.
b. You will be prevented from adding a faculty member unless they are teaching at least one section.
c. If you delete a Faculty member, all sections they teach will be deleted.
d. You will be prevented from adding a section until you assign a faculty member from the faculty table to teach that section.

5. What would be the correct formula to use in the control source of the unbound textbox shown below?

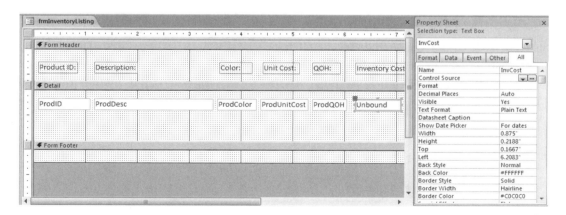

a. =[ProdQOH]*[ProdUnitCost]
b. =Sum([ProdUnitCost]*[ProdQOH])
c. =[ProdQOH *ProdUnitCost]
d. InvCost:[ProdQOH *ProdUnitCost]
e. =Sum([ProdUnitCost* ProdQOH])

6. A Bookkeeper Table has the following fields: Bookkeeper Number, Last Name, First Name, Hourly Rate and YTD Earnings. The bookkeeping company is required to withhold 18% of the YTD Earning for IRS purposes. In a query, what would be the correct formula to use in a calculated field to determine the Annual Withholdings?
    a. Annual Withholdings:[YTD Earnings]*0.18
    b. Annual Withholdings:YTD Earnings*0.18
    c. Annual Withholdings [YTD Earnings]*0.18
    d. Annual Withholdings:[YTD Earnings*0.18]
    e. Annual Withholdings=[YTD Earnings]*[.018]

7. Assume you have a client table and a trainer table that are joined by the trainer id field as shown in the figure below.

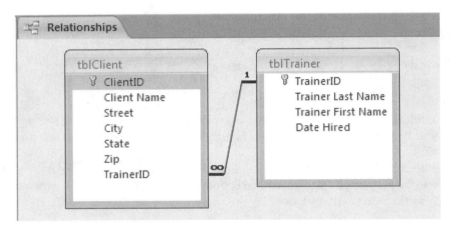

    Which of the following is a true statement about Access if only the "Enforce Referential Integrity" check box is marked on the Relationship Dialog Box?
    a. If you attempt to delete a Trainer who still has clients, you will be prevented from doing so.
    b. You will be prevented from adding a Client whose trainer number does not match an existing Trainer in the trainer table.
    c. You will be prevented from adding a Trainer unless that trainer has clients in the Client Table.
    d. A, B, and C are true
    e. Only A and B are true

Answers:
1. a   2. d   3. b   4. d   5. a   6. a   7. e

Review Questions

1. List and briefly explain the steps to converting an ERD into a physical model.
2. Convert the following Athletic Center ERD into a set of physical tables. Use the standard physical table notation illustrated in Tutorial 4.

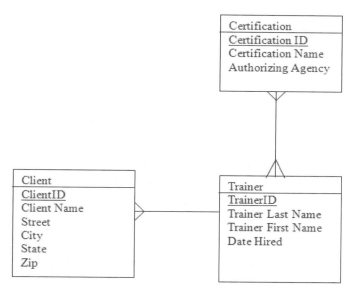

Hint: You should end up with 4 tables because the many-to-many relationship must be converted into two one-to-many relationships. Can you think of any attributes (besides the primary key) that could be stored in this intersection entity?

3. Define a concatenated primary key. Describe a situation when you would need to use one.
4. You need to create a table to store employee data. You need to decide which fields will be stored in the table and which will be calculated when needed. What would be your recommendation for the fields of "birthday" and "age"? Why?
5. Explain the 3 referential integrity decisions that need to be made in Access.
6. Explain the purpose of the Lookup Wizard.
7. Describe the relationship between a main form and subform.
8. What is a parameter value? Explain when it would be acceptable to have a parameter value dialogue box appear and when it would represent a problem to have a parameter value dialogue box appear.
9. Explain the difference between creating a calculated field on a query and on a report.
10. List and briefly explain the characteristics of a data warehouse.
11. Describe two examples of Data Mining.
12. Explain the differences between Knowledge Management and a Knowledge Management System.

Projects

1. Create an Exception Report for Hair today that will show all products that have fewer than 50 items in stock.

2. Create a new switchboard that contains the two report items currently on your Hair Today switchboard. Change the Hair Today switchboard to call this "submenu" instead of having the two reports on the main switchboard. Use Help to determine how to call a submenu.

3. Create a database for the ERD represented below. Add the three tables. Use the relationships window to create the relationships directly (do not use the Lookup Wizard.)

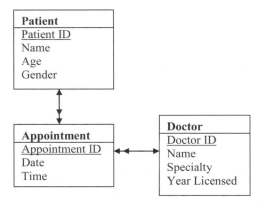

4. Build a database containing the physical tables you created in Review Problem 2 (the Athletic Center). For the four tables, determine appropriate field types and sizes based on analyzing a Fitness Center in your area. Implement lookup fields for all of the foreign keys. Restrict the State to a two digit field and have the user pick the state from a list of 50 state abbreviations. Create a form that will show the information about a trainer, including all of the certifications that the trainer has obtained.

TUTORIAL **6**

An Introduction to XHTML

PLANNING AHEAD

After reading Tutorial 6, you should be able to answer these questions in your own words

STUDY QUESTIONS

What is XHTML?

How do you create a Web Page using XHTML?

LEARNING PREVIEW

Students inevitably ask why it is important to spend time learning a markup language, such as HTML, when there are so many good software tools that will automatically generate the code that is used to create web pages. This is a fair question. Today, there are many software tools with graphical, or **WYSIWYG** (What You See Is What You Get), editors that enable just about anyone to efficiently create web pages. Unfortunately, the effectiveness of these applications is often lost on someone who lacks a fundamental understanding of HTML. In other words, working faster is not necessarily working smarter. This is similar to saying that a word processor can help a person be a better writer. The word processor isn't particularly useful if the person doesn't know much about grammar and punctuation, the syntax of a language. Web developers can also be more effective if they are familiar with the syntax and elements of their language. Minimally, a fundamental understanding of HTML and XHTML should give you the ability to edit and embellish your personal web pages on social networking sites such as Facebook and MySpace.

Another question that naturally follows the issue of studying markup languages is "why study XHTML when HTML is the primary language of the World Wide Web?" This too is a fair question. We are fairly certain that HTML will be the underlying markup language for many websites for some time. However, there are also newer, more robust markup languages that are evolving that are increasingly important to business and web communication. Many of these languages and applications are based on XML, the eXtensible Markup Language. One such application is XHTML, a reformulation of HTML in XML. By studying XHTML, we simultaneously gain exposure to both the concepts and syntax of HTML and XML.

This tutorial is explicitly designed to provide a broad understanding of XHTML. It covers everything from using your text editor to validating your XHTML documents. Ideally, this introduction to XHTML is also extensible. We hope that besides an understanding of markup languages, you can also understand how business is increasingly relying on markup languages, such as XML, to facilitate business processes and business communication.

VISUAL ORGANIZATION OF TUTORIAL

Study Question 1	Study Question 2
XHTML	Creating a Web Page with XHTML 1.0
• HTML or XML? • XHTML and HTML • Basic Structure of XHTML • Sample XHTML Elements	• Text Editors vs. Graphical Editors • Notepad vs. TextEdit • Creating a Web Page in XHTML • Validating your XHTML Code
Learning Check 1	Learning Check 2

XHTML

In Chapter 6, we learned that Web pages are typically created using a markup language called HTML. The popularity of the Web is largely attributable to HTML because it provides an easy, universal way to create web documents, independent of the hardware and software one uses. We also learned in Chapter 6 that the versatility of HTML influenced the development of web browsers and contributed to some of the challenges that confront web developers today.

In response to these challenges, the World Wide Web Consortium (W3C) created a set of specifications for HTML that are considered the official guidelines for developing web documents with HTML. The W3C specifications for HTML are being adopted, albeit slowly. Since the W3C is not empowered to enforce its own specifications, there is no mechanism for enforcing W3C rules. This means that many HTML elements and features that have been **deprecated**, or phased out, still exist on the Web today. Obviously, it is hard to predict when the deprecated HTML elements will no longer exist on the Web.

This is one of the reasons that web developers are turning to **XHTML**, the **eXtensible HyperText Markup Language**, to create web documents. XHTML is a reformulation of HTML in **XML**, the **eXtensible Markup Language**. With XHTML, web developers have the option of having their code interpreted, or parsed, by the web browser as either XML, or as HTML.

This duality of XHTML to be interpreted as either XML or HTML provides web developers considerable flexibility. It also provides an opportunity to efficiently satisfy two of the learning objectives of this textbook. First, students can use XHTML to become proficient with well-formed HTML and to create their own web pages using a markup language. Second, an understanding of XHTML offers students insight and familiarity with XML, the markup language that has become the primary language of machine-to-machine communications on the Web and the *lingua franca* of Web 2.0.   These objectives are the motivation of this tutorial, "An Introduction to XHTML"

HTML or XML?

In Chapter 6 you reviewed a simple web page created in HTML for BT's Rentals. In this tutorial, you will be able to create the same web page using XHTML 1.0. XHTML 1.0 is almost identical to HTML 4.01. XHTML 1.0 is also backward- and forward-compatible, which means web developers can choose how they want their XHTML 1.0 document to be interpreted, as either HTML, or as XML.

As we learned earlier, different web browsers do not always interpret HTML code the same way. As a result, a web page viewed through Internet Explorer may appear differently from the same web page viewed through Firefox or Safari. Using valid XHTML, we can reduce some of this variability because XHTML's syntax helps reduce some of the HTML parsing irregularities that browser developers have exploited since the early browser wars.

Today, all of the latest versions of the popular web browsers (Firefox, Internet Explorer, Chrome, Safari, and Opera) are capable of parsing web documents created in HTML or in XML. This capability, plus the similarity of XHTML 1.0 to HTML 4.01, makes XHTML 1.0 a good choice for gaining some familiarity with both HTML and XML simultaneously.

In order to appreciate XHTML, it is important to review how HTML is different from XML. Recall that XML is a subset of the more complex SGML specification that we discussed in Chapter 6 (Figure T6.1). XML was designed to allow users to define their own tags and to create their own document structure. HTML documents, however, are limited to the tags that are defined in the HTML specification. This makes XML, like SGML, a **meta-language** that can be used to create other markup languages, such as XHTML. Essentially, XHTML is a markup language that combines the strengths of both HTML and XML.

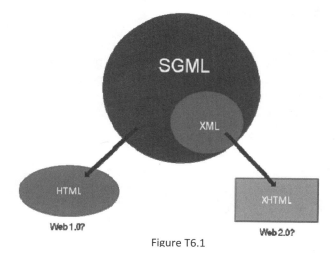

Figure T6.1

XHTML AND HTML

As we learned in Chapter 6, HTML and XHTML use words and symbols, called **elements**, to identify the structures, or pieces, of an electronic document. Titles, headings, tables and lists are just a few examples of the types of structures found in an XHTML document. XHTML and HTML elements are often referred to as "tags" but the tags are really the symbols that signal the beginning and ending of the markup element. The syntax of a typical **XHTML** (and HTML) **element** is shown in Figure T6.2.

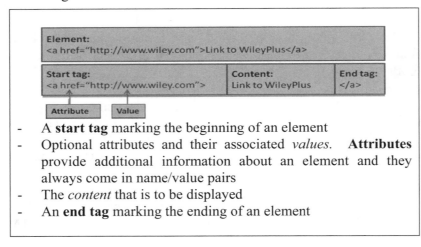

- A **start tag** marking the beginning of an element
- Optional attributes and their associated *values*. **Attributes** provide additional information about an element and they always come in name/value pairs
- The *content* that is to be displayed
- An **end tag** marking the ending of an element

Figure T6.2   – An XHTML

Element

Generally, the differences between XHTML and HTML are minor but the advantages of switching from HTML to XHTML appear to be significant, particularly as technology evolves. As example, more and more people are accessing Web content using non-traditional devices, such as cell phones and other devices that only support scaled-down versions of the web browser. This favors XHTML because valid, well-formed web pages are less dependent on the powerful browsers found on most desktop machines.

BASIC STRUCTURE OF XHTML

XHTML documents have the same basic structure and rely on the same structural elements as HTML documents. XHTML documents, however, are typically preceded by a <!DOCTYPE> declaration, or Document Type Definition (DTD) that appears in the first line of all XHTML code. Figure T6.3 below shows a generic <!DOCTYPE> declaration and the most common structural elements of an XHTML document.

```
<!DOCTYPE>
<html>
<head>
<title>Page Title</title>
</head>
<body>
<p>
CONTENT
</p>
</body>
</html>
```

Figure T6.3 – Basic Structure of HTML and XHTML documents

The **<!DOCTYPE>**, or **Document Type Definition (DTD)** refers to the syntax specifications associated with the XHTML code. The DTD of an XHTML document typically refers to one of three W3C specifications for XHTML 1.0: *Strict, Transitional and Frameset.* Web developers who want to prepare for the future should consider using the *Strict* DTD, the specification that disallows deprecated tags in the code.

At the end of this tutorial we discuss XHTML **validation**, the process of checking XHTML code against a DTD specification and report back problems. Valid XHTML ensures that a web page complies with an XHTML specification, and therefore, should display correctly on all browsers. Table T6.1 below provides the <!DOCTYPE> code for each DTD option. The More About IT section below provides additional details of the <!DOCTYPE> declaration.

Strict	<!DOCTYPE html PUBLIC "-//W3C//DTD XHTML 1.0 Strict//EN" "http://www.w3.org/TR/xhtml1/DTD/xhtml1-strict.dtd">
Transitional	<!DOCTYPE html PUBLIC "-//W3C//DTD XHTML 1.0 Transitional//EN" "http://www.w3.org/TR/xhtml1/DTD/xhtml1-transitional.dtd">
Frameset	<!DOCTYPE html PUBLIC "-//W3C//DTD XHTML 1.0 Frameset//EN" "http://www.w3.org/TR/xhtml1/DTD/xhtml1-frameset.dtd">

Table T6.1 – DTD code

> <u>More About IT</u>
> The <!DOCTYPE> declaration that appears in the first line of XHTML documents is not a specific XHTML element. Instead, it refers to the *Document Type Definition* (DTD), or specification, that is used to validate and display the XHTML code found in the document. XHTML validators use the <!DOCTYPE> to check the XHTML code against the DTD specification and report which, if any, parts of the code are non-compliant with the specification.

The presence of the <!DOCTYPE> declaration isn't the only thing that explicitly differentiates XHTML from HTML code. Because XHTML inherited the formality and consistency of XML's syntax, its differences from HTML are even more pronounced. Below are five additional traits of XHTML that suggest that XHTML is both more rigorous and robust than HTML.

1. XHTML is case-sensitive, HTML is not. All tags and attributes must be lowercase in XHTML.

Allowed in HTML, not in XHTML	Allowed in XHTML
\<BODY\> or \<Body\>	\<body\>

2. XHTML must be **well-formed**. This means that every XHTML element must have an end tag, or use the self-closing tag syntax. As you can see, HTML allows some end tags to be omitted.

Allowed in HTML, not in XHTML	Allowed in XHTML
\<p\> Some content goes here \<p\> 2nd paragraph \<br\> a break tag \<hr\> a horizontal rule	\<p\> Some content goes here\</p\> \<p /\> 2nd paragraph with self-closing tag \<br /\>a break tag with self-closing tag \<hr /\>a horizontal rule with self-closing tag

3. XHTML elements must be properly nested (Last-In, First-Out, LIFO, rule).

Allowed in HTML, not in XHTML	Allowed in XHTML
\<i\>\<b\> *Text that is italicized and in bold*\</i\>\</b\>	\<em\>\<strong\> *Text that is italicized and in bold*\</strong\> \</em\> Note: The \<i\> and \<b\> HTML elements have been changed to \<em\> and \<strong\> in XHTML

4. XHTML attributes must have a value. HTML allows some attributes to be processed without values.

5. All XHTML attribute values must be surrounded by double or single quotes. HTML generally allows quotes to be omitted if the value contains only alphanumeric characters.

The examples of XHTML code above are offered to help highlight some of the syntax differences between XHTML and HTML. If you understand these differences and incorporate the higher level standards of XHTML into your web development efforts, you will undoubtedly be rewarded with more efficient and less problematic code.

SAMPLE XHTML ELEMENTS

A comprehensive list of XHTML elements is too large to include in this Tutorial. For that reason, we offer a sample of the most common XHTML elements found on many web pages today in Table T6.2. Generally, these are the XHTML elements we used to create the BT's Rentals example that is provided at the end of the section. You can find many comprehensive XHTML and HTML references on the World Wide Web that list and describe the elements and their respective attributes that are used to create Web pages today. One popular XHTML reference, for example, can be found at *http://www.w3schools.com/tags/default.asp*.

Sample XHTML Tag Pairs (Note: only XHTML tag pairs are shown since not all XHTML tags are self-closing)	Description	Sample syntax with attribute(s) and value(s) (Note: XHTML attributes provide additional information about an XHTML command. XHTML tags that use an attribute must also have a value. XHTML values must be in quotations marks)
Core XHTML Tags		
<html> </html> <head></head> <title></title> <body></body>	These are the basic structural elements of an XHTML document.	
<h1></h1> <h2></h2> <h3></h3> <h4></h4> <h5></h5> <h6></h6>	Used to define XHTML headings. <h1> defines the largest heading and <h6> defines the smallest heading.	<h1>This is the largest heading</h1> <h6>This is the smallest heading</h6>
<p> </p>	Use to surround text that forms a paragraph. A blank line will be inserted after the text is concluded	
<hr> </hr>	Inserts a line across the page. (hr = Horizontal Rule)	<hr></hr>

 </br>	Inserts a line break (hard return) in your text and starts the text again on the next line	
Hyperlink Tags		
<a> </a>	Used to link to another resource or web page (a = Anchor)	<a href="http://www.sdsu.edu">Click here to learn more about SDSU.</a>
	Used to provide an email link	<a href="mailto:george.easton@sdsu.edu">Dr. Easton</a>
Image Tags		
<img> </img>	The image tag is used to display a picture on a web page.	<img src="ferrari.jpg" alt="Ferrari F430" title="My Dream Car"></img> The alt attribute is meant to be used as an alternative text if the image is not available, not as mouse-over text. To show a mouse-over text on images use the title attribute.

Table T6.2 – Sample of Common XHTML Elements

List Tags		
<ul> </ul>	Used to provide a particular type of list <ul> = An unordered (e.g. bulleted) list ------	<ul> <li>This is the 1st item in the list</li> <li>This is the 2nd item in the list</li> </ul> -------
<ol> </ol>	<ol> = an ordered (e.g. numbered) list XHTML lists have "list items" <li>	<ol> <li>This is the 1st item in the list</li> <li>This is the 2nd item in the list</li> </ol>
Table Tags		
<table> </table>	Used to create tables. Tables are made with rows and columns. The adjacent example is a table that consists of one table row <tr> and three columns of table data <td>	<table> <caption>My Example Table</caption> <tr> <td> Row 1, Column 1 </td> <td> Row 1, Column 2 </td> <td> Row 1, Column 3 </td> </tr> </table>

Table T6.2 (continued) – Sample of Common XHTML Elements

LEARNING CHECK

Be sure you can *describe the differences between XML and HTML * explain the relationship between XHTML and HTML * describe the use of the DOCTYPE declaration * list the five traits that make XHTML rigorous * describe the usage of the common XHTML elements introduced in this section

CREATING A WEB PAGE WITH XHTML 1.0

In this section you have the opportunity to create your first XHTML document. You will learn about using text editors to build your first XHTML web page. You will also learn how to validate your XHTML code.

TEXT EDITORS VS. GRAPHICAL EDITORS

In this section you have the opportunity to create an XHTML document "the old fashioned way." This means you will be using a **text editor** rather than a **graphical editor** or **WYSIWYG** (what you see is what you get) editor. You may recall from Chapter 6 that HTML documents have to be **device-independent** because web pages will undoubtedly be viewed on various types of devices (e.g., PCs, Macs, cell phones, etc) that use various operating systems and web browsers. To achieve device-independence, HTML, XHTML and XML files must be saved in a non-proprietary, universal file format. The most common, non-proprietary file format in use today is arguably the **text format** (which is also called the **text file type**). The *text* format is the default file format of email. *Text* files are a primary reason we can send an email message from one type of computer and operating system and be able to open and read that message on a different type of device that is controlled by a different operating system. The *text* file type is non-proprietary, unlike the ".docx" file type of Microsoft Word and the ".xlsx" format of Excel. Files saved in these proprietary formats typically require Word or Excel in order to open and use these files. Files saved in the *text* file type can be processed by a variety of devices and a number of different applications.

Microsoft Word and Excel, as well as many other "proprietary" applications, can be considered graphical or WYSIWYG editors because they are capable of automatically producing HTML code that will display a web page. Word and Excel, for example, both allow you to save a file as a web page using its "Save As …." option. You are probably familiar with numerous applications (e.g., PowerPoint) with similar "Save As" functionality. You may find it interesting to take a look at the HTML code produced by these applications. It is surprisingly verbose and therefore not recommended for serious web development efforts.

Professional web developers typically rely on more specialized web authoring tools with graphical editors for their craft. The list of such tools is long and diverse and includes applications such as Dreamweaver, ExpressionWeb, Homesite and SharePoint Designer. It should be mentioned that there are also web-based HTML editors and web design tools that many use for creating web pages and web sites. Often, these tools are template-driven which makes them relatively limited but easy to use. It also effectively eliminates the need for any knowledge of HTML or XHTML.

NOTEPAD AND TEXTEDIT

Since the earliest days of microcomputers, a *text editor* has been an embedded utility of the microcomputer operating system. For example, the Windows operating system typically comes with Notepad and Wordpad. Mac computers running an OS X operating system have the TextEdit editor for their use. Given that these utilities are already installed on our computers, and free, we have all of the necessary tools and a relatively painless way to become familiar with XHTML. Using a built-in text editor also gives us the opportunity to try out another feature of our computers.

The instructions for launching and saving XHTML files created Notepad are shown below in Figures T6.4a and T6.4b. If you are using a Mac computer and TextEdit, it is important to review the instructions provided in Figures T6.5a, T6.5b and T6.5c. TextEdit requires a simple change of the default file format before a document can be saved as a *text* file.

If You Use Notepad

Launch Notepad: Start→All Programs→Accessories→Notepad

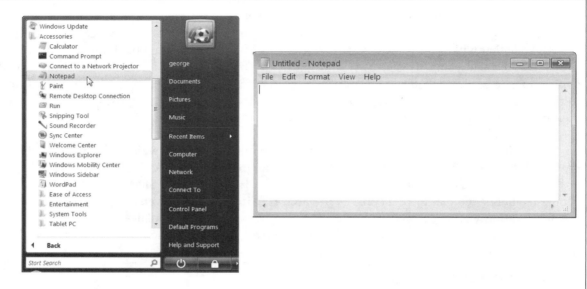

Figure T6.4a – Launching Notepad

Saving Your XHTML Document in Notepad

Remember that the file format of a XHTML document must be *text* and the filename extension must be either *.htm* or *.html*. Figure T6.4b below indicates that a Notepad file is being saved as a *text* document (.txt) with the filename "bts_rentals.html." Be sure to take note where your file is saved. In Figure T6.6, the file is being saved in a folder called "XHTML" that is within another folder called "textbook_files."

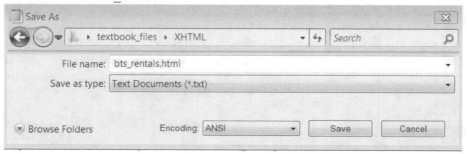

Figure T6.4b – Saving your XHTML file in Notepad

If You Use TextEdit

Launching TextEdit and Changing the File Format

If you are creating your XHTML web page with TextEdit, you must first change the default file format. TextEdit saves files in the *Rich Text Format* (rtf) by default. In order to create plain *text* files, you must switch the format. To do so, launch TextEdit, (Figure T6.5a) then use the TextEdit menu option Format→Make Plain Text. Your screen should then appear similar to Figure T6.5b (the ruler disappears). You are now ready to create an XHTML document.

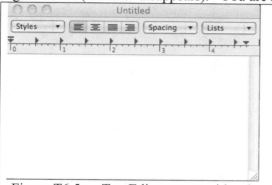

Figure T6.5a – TextEdit appears with ruler when files are saved as *.rtf*

Figure T6.5b TextEdit appears without ruler when files are saved as *text*.

Saving your XHTML File in TextEdit:

Remember that the file format of a XHTML document must be *text* and the filename extension must be either *.htm* or *.html*.

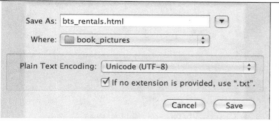

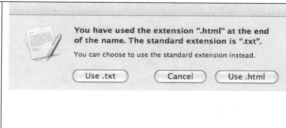

Editing an existing XHTML file in TextEdit

If you are trying to open an edit an existing HTML or XHTML file in TextEdit, you must check the box labeled "ignore rich text commands" before you open the file.

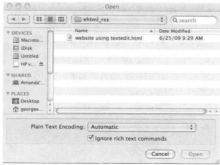

Figure T6.5c

CREATING A WEB PAGE IN XHTML

At this point, you could start entering XHTML code (coding). However, it is important not to forget the systems development concepts that you studied in Chapter 3. Web development efforts will undoubtedly be more successful if you do an analysis of the system requirements and have a good grasp of the objectives of the web site. Afterwards, you may want to sketch or prototype the layout and design of your web page before you actually start coding. The specific methodology and rigor of your web development efforts may vary but it important to remember that the better understanding you have of system and user requirements, the more likely the system will be successful.

Complete the following **Integrate IT** exercise to learn how to create a web page in XHTML.

Integrate IT

Review the BT's Rentals web page shown in Figure T6.6 below. This page was created and validated successfully as XHTML 1.0 – Strict. Using the sample XHTML elements provided earlier in the tutorial, and your knowledge of XHTML, can you duplicate this page using a *text editor?*

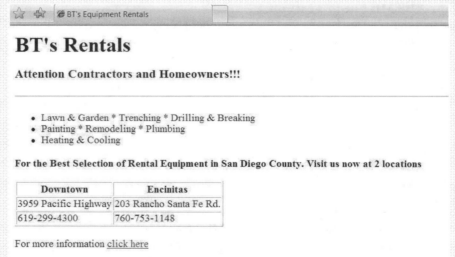

Figure T6.6 – BT's Rentals Web Page in XHTML

To make this exercise more efficient, the **HTML** code (not the XHTML code) for this web page is provided in Figure T6.7. Don't forget, the objective is to update and adjust the HTML code so it conforms to the XHTML 1.0 – Strict specification. This means the <!DOCTYPE> declaration will need to be inserted at the beginning of your code.

Integrate IT (continued)

```
<html>
<head>
<title>BT's Equipment Rentals</title>
</head>
<body>
<h1>BT's Rentals</h1>
<h3>Attention Contractors and Homeowners!!!</h3>
<hr>
<h3>
<ul>
<li>Lawn & Garden * Trenching * Drilling & Breaking</li>
<li>Painting * Remodeling * Plumbing</li>
<li>Heating & Cooling</li>
</ul>
</h3>
<h4>For the Best Selection of Rental Equipment in San Diego County.
Visit us now at 2 locations</h4>
<table border=1>
<tr>
<th>Downtown</th>
<th>Encinitas</th></tr>
<tr>
<td>3959 Pacific Highway</td>
<td>203 Rancho Santa Fe Rd.</td></tr>
<tr>
<td>619-299-4300</td>
<td>760-753-1148</td></tr>
</table>
<p>
For more information <a href="mailto:BThomas@BTsRental.com">click here</a>
</body>
</html>
```

(Note: if you want the ampersand to appear on your webpage (e.g. for Drilling & Breaking), enter **&** instead of only the & symbol. Example: Drilling & Breaking).

Figure T6.7 – HTML code for BT's Rentals page

After you have entered and edited the code, save the file with a descriptive filename and the .html extension. For example, you could use *yourname_rentals.html*. Don't forget, the filename must have an extension of .htm or .html.

Next view the page using your browser. This is easily accomplished, even without an Internet connection, since both the XHTML file and your web browser are both on your local machine. Once you navigate to the folder containing your XHTML file, simply double-click on the file containing your XHTML code and the web page should open in your browser.

When your code displays the page shown in Figure T6.6, you should consider extending the exercise by adding some additional code. For example:

- Edit the "BT's Rentals" heading so the web page reads "Your Name Rentals"
- Add one or two items to the unordered list
- Add another location to the table that currently displays the BT's two locations
- Add a picture to the page
- Add a hyperlink to the page

Recall that all of the XHTML code for these "updates" were provided in the coding samples in Figure T6.2. Save any of the updates that you made in your file.

Even though your web page appears in the browser, your XHTML code may not be valid. You will learn how to validate an XHTML web page in the next section.

VALIDATING YOUR XHTML CODE

As we discussed earlier, validating XHTML is a process of checking the code against a DTD specification and reporting any problems. A **validator** is a program designed to check for errors. **Valid XHTML** supposedly ensures that a web page complies with a particular XHTML specification, and therefore, should display correctly on all browsers. The process of validation for XHTML and XML code is relatively easy. Identifying and correcting validation errors is not as easy. If your code has errors when validating it is important to follow a systematic process to find and correct the errors. You should always start by fixing the first error and then revalidating. With code, such as XHTML, often one actual mistake will cause several errors to appear in the listing. For example, if you misspell or forget the </head> element, the validator will not accept your <body> element, even if it is spelled correctly. The reason is that a <body> element can't be found in a <head> section, and you never correctly closed the <head> section. As you work with the validator you will most likely have a chance to see how this plays out. The biggest thing to remember is not to panic if the validator comes back and tells you that you have many errors. Just be patient and fix items one at a time.

Complete the following **Integrate IT** exercise to learn how to validate the XHTML code you created for BTs rentals.

Integrate IT

Follow the numbered steps below to begin the validation process of the XHTML code you created for the BT's Rental page exercise. You will be using the web-based XHTML validator of the W3C organization for this example. The URL of this validator is http://validator.w3.org.

1. Use your web browser to access the W3C validator (http://validator.w3.org).
2. Click on the "Validate by Direct Input" tab to display the input form for your XHTML code.
3. Copy the XHTML code you created in Notepad (or TextEdit) and paste it into the direct input form.
4. Press the "Check" button.
5. Ideally, the validator will report that your code successfully validated, as shown in Figure T6.8. Note: You can ignore the 2 warnings that are provided. Those are generated because we used the Validate by Direct Input option.

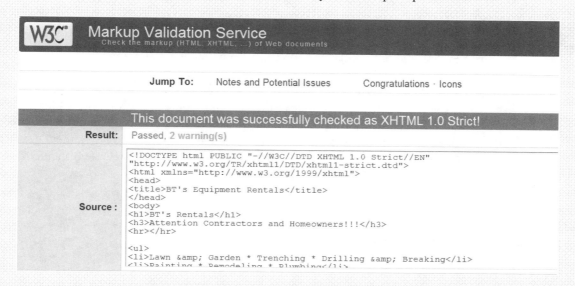

Figure T6.8 – Successful Validation of XHTML for BT's Rentals Web Page

6. Realistically, your code will probably not successfully validate the first time. That is because even though you were given most of the code to enter, many of us are not perfect typists and probably entered some mistakes when we were creating the XHTML file. If your code had errors, you will see a message similar to that shown in Figure T6.9. This result is caused just by having one mistake – misspelling the close tag for the head section.

Integrate IT (continued)

	Errors found while checking this document as XHTML 1.0 Strict!
Result:	5 Errors, 2 warning(s)

Source :	`<!DOCTYPE html PUBLIC "-//W3C//DTD XHTML 1.0 Strict//EN"`
	`"http://www.w3.org/TR/xhtml1/DTD/xhtml1-strict.dtd">`
	`<html xmlns="http://www.w3.org/1999/xhtml">`
	`<head>`
	`<title>BT's Equipment Rentals</title>`
	`</hed>`
	`<body>`
	`<h1>BT's Rentals</h1>`
	`<h3>Attention Contractors and Homeowners!!!</h3>`
	`<hr></hr>`
	
	`<ul>`
	`<li>Lawn &amp; Garden * Trenching * Drilling &amp; Breaking</li>`
	`<li>Painting * Remodeling * Plumbing</li>`
	`<li>Heating &amp; Cooling</li>`

Figure T6.9 – Unsuccessful Validation of XHTML for BT's Rentals Web Page

If the XHTML did not validate successfully complete the following steps:

7. Review the "Validation Output" section of the report. A subset of that section is shown in Figure T6.10. Notice that in this sample, you can see that the validator is telling you that you are trying to close an element "hed" which you did not open. Also notice, that you are getting an error message for the <body> element (even though it is written correctly), because you can't have a <body> element inside of a <head> section.

Validation Output: 5 Errors

❌ *Line 6, Column 6*: **end tag for element "hed" which is not open**

`</hed>`

The Validator found an end tag for the above element, but that element is not currently open. This is often caused by a leftover end tag from an element that was removed during editing, or by an implicitly closed element (if you have an error related to an element being used where it is not allowed, this is almost certainly the case). In the latter case this error will disappear as soon as you fix the original problem.

If this error occurred in a script section of your document, you should probably read this FAQ entry.

❌ *Line 7, Column 6*: **document type does not allow element "body" here**

`<body>`

The element named above was found in a context where it is not allowed. This could mean that you have incorrectly nested elements -- such as a "style" element in the "body" section instead of inside "head" -- or two elements that overlap (which is not allowed).

Figure T6.10 – Sample Error Listing for the Validation of BT's Rentals XHTML code

---

Integrate IT (continued)

Since your errors most likely will be different, it will be important for you to read the error messages specific to your XHTML code.

8. For each error message, find the corresponding code you pasted into the validator.
9. Fix the error(s) (this is easier said than done)
10. Revalidate
11. Repeat from step 7 until the XHTML successfully validates.
12. Copy and paste the validated code back into your text editor and save the file.

It should be noted that there is some disagreement over the value of validation for XHTML code. Some argue that validating XHTML is simply an exercise in frustration because the XHTML code behind most web pages is actually being interpreted by browsers as HTML. Web browsers, we know, are notoriously forgiving for HTML and will do everything possible to display a web page, syntax problems or not. However, if an XHTML web page contains syntax errors, and the code is being interpreted by the browser as XML, the attempt to display the page will abort.

It is interesting that many prominent companies today have web pages created in XHTML that do not successfully validate. As example, a recent validation check of Microsoft's home page at http://www.microsoft.com reported 291 validation errors (see Figure T6.11).

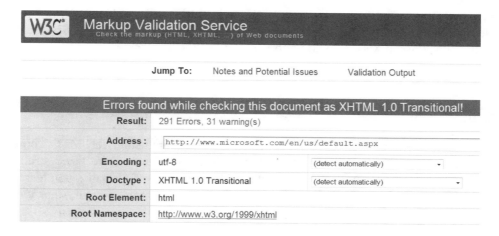

Figure T6.11 – XHTML Validation Results for Microsoft's Web Page

Microsoft obviously expects its web pages to display, rather than abort, when they are requested. This indicates that the XHTML code used to produce the web page was presented to the browser as HTML rather than XHTML. Microsoft is just one of many companies that do not yet fully comply with the W3C specifications for XHTML.

You can attempt to validate the XHTML code of websites yourself in the following **Integrate IT** exercise.

Integrate IT

Create a list in Excel of the URLs of a few of your favorite business or professional websites. One-by-one, attempt to validate the code behind each website using the http://validator.w3.org. You can use the "Validate by URI" tab for this exercise and simply paste the URL into the form. In an adjacent column in Excel, enter the validation results (for example, Successful; Failed – 300 errors). In the next column, indicate which XHTML DTD was used (Strict, Transitional). Save and print your Excel report. Bring your report to class and share the results.

While there may be disagreement regarding the value of *valid* XHTML, there is no disputing the educational value of the XHTML validation process. Adhering to the rigorous syntax of XHTML will undoubtedly help you become better web developers. Additionally, XHTML validation helps develop your debugging skills as it forces you to identify and correct the syntax errors of your code. Finally, while *invalid* XHTML may today be inconsequential, invalid XML is not. If there are errors in XML code, the browser or XML application parsing the code will abort the process. As you may recall, one of the primary objectives of covering XHTML in this text was this was to gain some understanding of XML. As a result, we strongly believe that learning to validate your XHTML code will be beneficial in the long run.

LEARNING CHECK
Be sure you can *discuss the differences between text editors and graphical editors * explain how to use either Notepad or TextEdit * describe how to create a web page using XHTML * describe the process to validate an XHTML web page

WRAPPING IT UP

In this Tutorial you learned the basics about creating a web page using XHTML. You learned to differentiate between HTML, XML and XHTML. You also learned the basic structure of an XHTML document, along with many of the basic XHTML elements. Finally, you learned how to use a text editor to create the web page and how to use a validator to ensure that your code is accurate.

An obvious omission in this Tutorial on XHTML is any discussion of Cascading Style Sheets (CSS). CSS is relevant to this material, but is currently beyond the scope of this course and book. If you desire to progress in your studies about creating web pages using XHTML it will be necessary for you to become familiar with CSS.

Study Questions Summary

1. What is XHTML?
    *   XHTML is a reformulation of HTML in XML.
    *   XHTML was developed to address the growing issues associated with the vagaries of HTML.
    *   The syntax of XHTML is considered more formal than HTML. For example, XHTML elements must be lowercase; HTML is not case sensitive.
    *   XHTML code is often *validated,* that is, checked for errors in syntax.

2. How do you create a web page in XHTML?
    *   Text editors and graphical editors are common tools for creating XHTML documents
    *   Notepad is a common text editor used on Windows' computers
    *   TextEdit is a common editor used on Mac computers
    *   Validators can be used to help ensure that your XHTML code is written correctly

Key Terms

Page Number references are included in parentheses

Deprecated (450)	Text format (456)	WYSIWYG (456)
Device-independent (456)	Text file type (456)	XHTML (450)
<!Doctype> declaration (453)	Text editor (456)	XHTML attribute (452)
End tag (452)	Valid XHTML (462)	XHTML element (452)
Graphical editor (456)	Validation (453)	XML (450)
Meta-language (451)	Validator (462)	
Start tag (452)	Well-formed XHTML (454)	

Multiple Choice Questions

1. XHTML is ___
    a. an application of SGML
    b. a meta-language
    c. an application of XML
    d. a reformulation of XML in HTML

2. What is the text editor that is an accessory of the Windows operating system
    a. Lindows   b. Text   c. Wordstar   d. Notepad

3. Which of the following is not one of the DTDs of XHTML 1.0?
    a. Strict
    b. Transitional
    c. Universal
    d. Frameset

4. TextEdit is associated with which of the following?
    a. Linux
    b. Windows
    c. Mac computers
    d. Microsoft

5. Which of the following XHTML elements is well-formed?
    a. <h1>This is a heading that is centered and large</h1>
    b. <img src="ferrari.jpg" alt="my next car">
    c. <a href=mailto:Easton@sdsu.edu</a>
    d. <ol>
       <li>1
       <li>2
       <li>3
       </ol>

6. Which of the following would not be considered a graphical editor?
    a. Excel
    b. PowerPoint
    c. Word
    d. Notepad

Answers:
1. c   2. d   3. c   4. c   5. a   6. d

Index

#Name? error, 423

<!DOCTYPE> declaration, 452

3rd Generation of mobile broadband (3G), 159

802.11a/b/g/n, 158

802.16, 159

Absolute cell reference, 251

Acceptance test, 100

Access controls, 230

Access privileges, 122

Accessibility standards, 181

Accessibility Standards, 182

Active cell, 241

Adware, 219

Aggregate function, 422

Aggregator, 190

Analysis phase, 88

AND function, 270

Application programmer, 15

Applications software, 12

Attribute, 124

Authentication, 230

Autofilter, 311

Average Function, 254

AverageIF function, 284

Bandwidth, 163

Best practices, 136

Binary number system, 151

Biometric identifiers, 231

Biometrics, 231

Bit, 117

Blog, 186

Bluetooth, 157, 160

Bot, 220

Botnet, 220

Broadband, 163

Business case, 80

Business intelligence systems, 134

business rule, 89

Byte, 117

Calculated attribute, 128

Calculated field in a query, 416

Calculated field on a form, 421

Caption, 375

Cascade Delete Related Records, 400

Cascade Update Related Fields, 400

Cascading Style Sheets (CSS), 184

Cell, 241

Cell reference, 243

Cell reference on a different worksheet, 322

Channel, 188

Chart

    Chart format, 278

    Chart Layout, 276

    Column chart, 274

    Data Range, 276

    Pie chart, 285

    Source Data, 276

Chief information officer (CIO), 17

Coaxial cable, 157

Column, 241

Command button, 378

Communications devices, 11

Compound condition, 270

Compound criteria, 381

Compound key, 395

Computer, 11

Computer aided design (CAD), 50

Computer aided manufacturing (CAM), 51

Computer center manager, 17

Computer center operator, 16

Concatenated field in a query, 431

Concatenated field in a report, 429

Concatenated key, 395

Conceptual data model, 123

Conditional formatting, 272

Constant, 243

Contextual tab, 241

Control, 31, 372

Control layout, 377

Control source property, 421

Cookies, 216

Cost-benefit analysis, 81
Count Function, 254
CountIF function, 281
Crackers, 217
Customer relationship management system (CRM), 46
Cyber crime, 215
Cyber security, 227
Data, 30, 34, 116
Data dictionary, 98
Data Flow Diagram (DFD), 94
Data isolation, 118
Data manipulation, 121
Data mart, 135
    Dependent data mart, 135
    Independent data mart, 135
Data mining, 135
Data modeling, 91
Data redundancy, 118
Data security analyst, 17
Data type, 351
Data Type
    Field Sizes for Number Data Types, 352
Data validation, 122, 289
    Drop-Down List, 290
    Type and Range Restriction, 291
Data warehouse, 134
Database, 117
Database administrator, 16
Database Management System, 121
Database management system (DBMS), 117
Database security, 122
Datasheet view, 353
Decision support system (DSS), 41
Decision table, 94
Decision tree, 94
Default value property, 371
Denial-of-Service (DoS), 222
Deprecated, 450
Design phase, 97
Design view, 353
Detailed report, 41
Device-independent, 456
Digital Native, 3
Distributed Denial-of-Service (DDoS), 222
Divisional structure, 38
Domain name, 152
Dotted decimal, 150
Drop-down filters, 311
E-Commerce, 193

Economic feasibility, 80
eDiscovery, 214
Electronic Data Interchange (EDI), 194
Electronic funds transfer (EFT), 50
Elements, 178
Encryption, 228
End-user development, 104
End-user liaison, 16
Enterprise resource planning system (ERP, 47
Enterprise wide system, 45
Entity, 124
Entity-relationship diagram (ERD, 124
Entity-relationship diagram (ERD), 92
Ethernet, 149
Exabyte, 205
Exception report, 41
Executive information system (EIS), 45
Executive support system (ESS), 45
Expert system (ES), 45
Explicit knowledge, 136
eXtensible Hypertext Markup Language (XHTML), 183
eXtensible Markup Language (XML), 178, 182, 450
External information, 35
Fact-finding techniques, 85
Feasibility analysis, 80
Federal Information Management Act of 2002, 210
Feedback, 31
Field, 117
Field list, 329
Field name, 350
Field properties, 367
File, 117
File management system, 118
Fill Handle, 255
Firewall, 232
Foreign key, 124
Form, 355
    Layout, 356
    Select fields, 356
    Style, 357
Format Cells Dialog Box, 256
Formula, 243
    Show Formulas, 246
Formula bar, 241
Formula View, 245
Function, 253

Functional structure, 38
Gantt chart, 79
Graham-Leach Bliley Act of 1999 (GLBA), 208
Graphical editor, 456
Group decision support system (GDSS), 44
Hackers, 217
Hardware, 11, 30
Health Insurance Portability and Accountability Act of 1996 (HIPAA), 209
Homeland Security Act of 2002, 210
Honeypot, 228
Hot spot, 158
HTML tags, 178
Hypertext, 175
Hypertext Markup Language (HTML), 172, 178
HyperText Transfer Protocol (HTTP), 175
Identifier, 125
Identity theft, 207
IF function, 267
IIF function, 424
Implementation phase, 100
Information, 34, 116
Information processing cycle, 12
Information security, 205
Information system, 13, 29
Information technology, 11
In-house development, 96
Input, 31
Input devices, 11
Instance, 124
Intellectual assets, 136
Internal information, 35
Internet, 146
Internet Service Provider (ISP), 164
IP address, 150
IPv6, 151
ISBLANK function, 269
Keyloggers, 219
Knowledge management (KM), 136
Knowledge Management System (KMS), 136
Knowledge worker, 13
Label (on a form), 376
Local Area Networks (LAN), 156
Logic modeling, 94
Logical functions, 267
Lookup wizard, 401
Main form, 414

Make or buy decision, 96
Malware, 216
Management information system (MIS), 41
Mashups, 191
Matrix structure, 38
Max Function, 254
Metadata, 119
Meta-language, 182, 451
Metropolitan Area Networks (MAN), 156
Microsoft Access, 347
Min Function, 254
Mixed cell reference, 251
MULTIPLE WORKSHEETS, 314
Name, 322
Named cell reference, 322
Navigation pane, 439
Near Field Communications (NFC), 160
Nested IF function, 318
Network engineer, 16
Network Service Provider (NSP), 164
Networks, 30
Newsreader, 190
Non-management employees, 37
Normalization, 124
Numeric data, 243
Object, 348
Object-oriented (OO) software development, 105
Office automation system (OAS), 40
Online analytical processing, 134
Online transaction processing system (OLTP), 133
Operational management, 37
Optical fiber, 157
OR function, 272
Order of Operations, 246
Organizational feasibility, 80
Organizational structure, 38
Output, 31
Output devices, 11
Outsource, 96, 106
Packaged software, 96
Packet switching, 148
Packets, 148
Page Setup Dialog Box, 258
Parameter report, 431
Passwords, 230
Patch Tuesday, 227
Payment Card Industry Data Security Standards (PCIDSS), 213

People, 30
Personal Area Networks (PAN), 157
Personally identifiable information (PII), 206
Pharming, 226
Phishing, 222
Phone phreak, 215
Physical database model, 123
Physical model, 394
Pivot table, 327
Planning phase, 88
Pretexting, 209
Primary key, 124
Print, 257
Procedures, 30
Process modeling, 94
Processing, 31
Product, 4
Program evaluation and review technique (PERT) chart, 79
Project development plan, 88
Project leader, 76
Project management, 78
Project management software, 79
Project manager, 17
Project plan, 78
Project scope, 79
Project team, 76
Protocol stack, 149
Protocols, 149
Prototyping, 89, 103
Quality assurance analyst, 16
Query, 359
    Select query, 359
Query by example, 360
Query By Example, 360
Query parameter, 433
Radio Frequency Identification (RFID), 160
Radio Frequency IDentification (RFID), 157
Range, 254
Rapid Application Development (RAD), 105
Really Simple Syndication (RSS), 187
Record, 117
Record navigation buttons, 358
Referential integrity, 399
Relational database model, 123
Relationship, 124
Relative cell reference, 249
Report, 362

Road apple, 218
Rootkit, 220
Row, 241
Row source property, 402
RSS Feed, 188
Sarbanes-Oxley Act of 2002 (SOX), 210
Schedule feasibility, 80
Scope, 323
Scope creep, 80
Search Engine Optimization (SEO), 196
Security Breach Notification Act (SB-1386), 210
Security patch, 227
Service, 7
Social engineering, 221
Software, 12, 30
Software developer, 15
Sorting data
    Sort Level, 307
Sorting Data, 306
    Criteria, 307
Spider, 197
Spreadsheet, 239
Spyware, 218
Standard Generalized Markup Language (SGML), 177
Statistical functions, 281
Steering committee, 76
Storage devices, 11
Strategic management, 37
Structured Query Language (SQL), 361
Subform, 414
Subtotal outline, 309
Subtotals, 308
Sum Function, 254
SumIF function, 285
Summary report, 41
Supply chain management system (SCM), 46
    Supply chain, 46
Support phase, 102
Switchboard, 439
System conversion, 101
System maintenance, 102
System proposal, 89
System requirements, 89
System software, 12
System test, 100
System unit, 11
Systems analyst, 15, 76

Systems development, 73
Systems development life cycle, 75
Table, 311, 348
Tabs and Groups, 241
Tacit knowledge, 136
Tactical management, 37
Team-based structures, 38
Technical feasibility, 80
Technical sales and marketing specialist, 16
Technical writer, 16
Telephone Records and Privacy Protection
    Act of 2006, 209
Tester, 16
Text data, 243
Text editor, 179, 456
Text file type, 456
Text format, 456
Top Level Domain (TLD), 154
Top-Level Domain (TLD), 152
Training, 101
Transaction, 40
Transaction processing system (TPS), 40
Transmission   Control   Protocol/Internet
    Protocol (TCP/IP), 149
Trojan horse, 218
Twisted pair, 157
Twitter, 186
Ultra-Wideband (UWB), 161
Uniform Resource Identifier (URI), 176
Uniform Resource Locator (URL), 176
Unit test, 100
User representatives, 76
Valid XHTML, 462
Validation, 453
Validation rule, 368
Validation text, 368
Validator, 462

Vice president of information technology,
    17
Virus, 216
VLookUp function, 292
Web 2.0, 184
Web developer, 15
Well-formed XHTML, 454
Wide Area Networks (WAN), 156
WiFi, 158
WiMax, 159
Wireless, 158
Wireless access point, 158
Workbook, 240
Worksheet, 240
    Active Worksheet, 240
    Worksheet Tab, 240
World Wide Web Consortium (W3C), 181
Worm, 217
Wrap Text, 280
WYSIWYG, 456
XHTML element, 452
    Body tag, 455
    End tag, 452
    Head tag, 455
    Heading tag, 455
    Horizontal rule tag, 455
    Hyperlink tag, 455
    Image tag, 455
    Line break tag, 455
    LIST TAG, 456
    Paragraph tag, 455
    Start tag, 452
    TABLE TAG, 456
    Title tag, 455
    XHTML attribute, 452
Zero-day attack, 228
Zombie, 220
Zoom, 416